The Essential Criticism of John Steinbeck's *Of Mice and Men*

Edited by Michael J. Meyer

The Scarecrow Press, Inc.
Lanham, Maryland • Toronto • Plymouth, UK
2009

4-2-10
ww
$55.00

SCARECROW PRESS, INC.

Published in the United States of America
by Scarecrow Press, Inc.
A wholly owned subsidiary of
The Rowman & Littlefield Publishing Group, Inc.
4501 Forbes Boulevard, Suite 200, Lanham, Maryland 20706
www.scarecrowpress.com

Estover Road
Plymouth PL6 7PY
United Kingdom

British Library Cataloguing in Publication Information Available

Library of Congress Cataloging-in-Publication Data

The essential criticism of John Steinbeck's Of mice and men / edited by Michael J.
  Meyer.
      p. cm.
  Includes bibliographical references and index.
  ISBN 978-0-8108-6733-8 (alk. paper) — ISBN 978-0-8108-6734-5 (e-book)
  1. Steinbeck, John, 1902–1968. Of mice and men. I. Meyer, Michael J., 1943–
PS3537.T3234O4 2009
813'.52—dc22   2008051372

∞ ™ The paper used in this publication meets the minimum requirements of American
National Standard for Information Sciences—Permanence of Paper for Printed Library
Materials, ANSI/NISO Z39.48-1992.
Manufactured in the United States of America.

For the eighth-grade classes at Grace Lutheran School, River Forest, Illinois, who each year remind me that reading *Of Mice and Men* is important because it touches the soul as well as the mind.

"We read to know we are not alone."—Anthony Hopkins as C. S. Lewis in *Shadowlands*, directed by Richard Attenborough (1993)

CONTENTS

CONTENTS

PART SIX

PART SEVEN

CONTENTS

PREFACE

The idea for *The Essential Criticism of John Steinbeck's* Of Mice and Men began over fifteen years ago. Originally considered for publication by Greenwood Press where a series of related volumes was in process in the late 1990s, the volume was never completed although many agreed that such a book was long overdue. The need became even more evident recently as several critical assessments went out of print, and the early reviews of the novel were largely unavailable or the cost to access them was excessive. Thus researchers and undergraduates who were seeking representative critical appraisals of a novel that has sold more than seven million copies in its lifetime and is on the reading lists of thousands of high school curriculums, often found themselves frustrated and unable to find the essays they wanted to read and cite. Noting the potential for a large reading public, Scarecrow Press wisely issued a contract, choosing not only to republish some of the early work but also to publish several studies that have not previously appeared in print.

While the present volume is unable to reproduce all of the significant criticism that has been published since *Of Mice and Men* appeared in 1937, it does include representative studies that address the major themes of the novel (the American Dream of land and property; loneliness/isolation; camaraderie/friendship; class-, gender-, race-, and age-centered prejudice; and a social critique that reflects the economic conflict between the haves and have nots in America); it also shows the progression of scholarship and reflects the depth of meaning that Steinbeck incorporated into the text.

Clearly, Steinbeck packed the pages of *Of Mice and Men* with significance, creating passages that still have impact enough to have lasted over seventy years and yet still retain the power to enthrall today's readers and to reflect twenty-first-century conditions that remain issues in the country that Steinbeck so valiantly tried to reform. The novel's creative use of language, including unique similes and metaphors; its employment of animal imagery; and its discussion of the diverse thematic elements listed above all seem fresh and new even on second and third readings. When these elements are combined in a concise dramatic form that reflects the author's experimental technique, it is no wonder that one individual at a 1989 conference held at the University of Alabama at Tuscaloosa exclaimed, "Why, them's my people!"

My people, indeed! The story of George and Lennie resonates to most readers for a variety of reasons. First of all, readers empathize with the characters' unlikely friendship and devotion to each other and identify keenly with the frustration George and Lennie experience over unrealized dreams and a denial of their hopes for independence and freedom. Moreover, such readers surely recognize present-day American problems in the shattered prospects of the bindlestiffs, problems that not only reflect the dilemma of racial and gender prejudice but also depict the divisiveness that occurs when perceived deficiencies based on age, wavering emotional stability, and lower mental ability are given prominence.

The critics represented here range from the earliest respondents to Steinbeck's novels (now considered classics) to the most recent analyses (by individuals who have impeccable credentials but perhaps less recognition). These are followed by four original essays written especially for this collection and offering unique assessments of the novel. I invite readers of this collection to savor the critics whose work is reproduced here, to consult the analysts whose essays are merely cited bibliographically due to space constraints, and to sample the new critical approaches offered within these pages. Once again you will discover the scope of Steinbeck's genius as a variety of critical opinions reopens a text that one early reviewer commended for "its compassion even more than [its] perfect sense of form," qualities that, for this writer at least, "mark off John Steinbeck, artist, so sharply from all the little verbal photographers who record tough talk and snarl in books which have power without pity."[1]

Note

1. Lewis Gannett, "Books and Things." *New York Herald Tribune*, 25 February 1937: 17.

ACKNOWLEDGMENTS

With grateful thanks to all who made this book a reality, including Stephen Ryan and Jayme Bartles at Scarecrow Press and the many students who typed or scanned manuscripts over the years. I am especially indebted to Linda Gibson for typing and to Shawn Koval for helping with the index. The illustrations were provided by a former student, Brenda Latzke Heinz, who now teaches art at Roosevelt Middle School in River Forest, Illinois.

EDITOR'S NOTE

In order to facilitate easy location of the quotes from *Of Mice and Men*, I have changed all references to the novel to a standard edition: *Of Mice and Men* (New York: Penguin Classics, 1993). Please consult this version for all quotes.

Part One

THE 1930s

wo years after the publication of *Of Mice and Men*, Harry Thornton Moore published *The Novels of John Steinbeck: A First Critical Study* (Chicago: Normandy House, 1939). According to Moore, Steinbeck's characters are quite realistic but are trapped in a web of circumstance that makes their fates inevitable. This initial reaction was to become a typical response from a critical majority that considered Steinbeck's work as an integral part of the American Naturalist movement, where human beings had little say so or ability to affect change in their lives. Moore also lamented the fact that the book depicted violence without tragedy, a trait that made its message melodramatic rather than eliciting pathos.

The early reviews indicated a much divided stream of criticism about Steinbeck's short novel, ranging from extravagant praise to dismissive critical assessment, indicating a dis-ease with the novel's slang and "questionable" vocabulary as well as its sentimentalism and its "predictable" if not obvious use of plot parallels. The positive reactions emphasize Steinbeck's compassion for the disenfranchised, his poetic and colorful use of language, and the accuracy of his recording of the speech of the common people.

Significant Study from the 1930s

Rascoe, Burton, "The Play Accentuates the Consummate Art of John Steinbeck." *English Journal* (March 1938): 205–16 [reprinted in E. W. Tedlock Jr. and

C. V. Wicker, (Albuquerque: University of New Mexico Press, 1957): 57–67 and also in Jill Karson, (San Diego: Greenhaven, 1996): 139–45].

This essay reviews the play version of the novel and comments on the compassion of Steinbeck for the misfits of life and for those who are handicapped by the imponderables of heredity and environment. Steinbeck's empathy for individuals who are warped physically and emotionally is foregrounded and is credited with evoking pity and wonder from his audience. Most importantly, Rascoe suggests that *Of Mice and Men*'s tragedy is Sophoclean in stature and that Steinbeck's Manichean tendencies indicate the author's concern with the problem of good versus evil and his effort to show the non-morality of Nature and the natural world.

CHAPTER ONE
BOOK REVIEWS

Charles A. Wagner. "Books." *New York Mirror,* 24 February 1937: 25.

Of the two selections for March made by the Book-of-the-Month Club, and just published, we like best the young American Steinbeck's novel, though the veteran Mister Wells, who shares the selection, has returned to the grand manner.

John Steinbeck's *Of Mice and Men* . . . is just about the closest thing to a little prose masterpiece in the social stir we've seen in years.

It is the story of two barley bucker pals who migrate from job to job along the grain belt. One is a towering giant with the strength of ten men but the mind of a child. The other hasn't the heart to get rid of him, for fear he will come to harm; to which, of course, he does.

But the cycle of friendship, even in tragedy remains unbroken. And, in the course of his swift-moving tale, Mr. Steinbeck gives us a holiday pagcantry of portraits in toil, in men's passions and repressions, in workers' dreams and devilments, told with a poet's eye to sounds and silences which makes his book a memorable thing indeed, and something at last to cheer about.

Lewis Gannett. "Books and Things."
New York Herald Tribune, 25 February 1937: 17.

"Guys like us, that work on ranches," George told Lennie, "are the loneliest guys in the world. They got no family. They don't belong no place. They make a little stake and then they go into town and blow it in, and the first thing you know they're poundin' their tail on some other ranch" (*OMM* 13–14).

"But not us," Lennie interrupted. (This is in John Steinbeck's story *Of Mice and Men* . . . which the Book-of-the-Month Club sends its members this month.) "We got a future. Some day gonna have a little house and a couple of acres an' a cow an' some pigs, an' live off the fatta the lan'- an' have rabbits! An' I get to tend the rabbits" (*OMM* 14).[1]

It was a sort of incantation with which George, a small, quick, bony-nosed man, soothed Lennie when that huge, shapeless halfwit grew restless. They had a dream, and Lennie lived for it, and George, who loved him, knew it could never come true.

"He's a nice fella," said Slim. "Guy don't need no sense to be a nice fella. Seems to me sometimes it jus' works the other way around. Take a real smart guy and he ain't hardly ever a nice fella" (*OMM* 40).

Danny and Big Joe Portagee and Jesus Maria Corcoran, citizens of *Tortilla Flat*, didn't have much sense either; nor did the farmers of *The Pastures of Heaven*. [Steinbeck's characters] talk tough, and [sometimes they have] no morals, but you ended [his] books loving them; and you will close this strange, tragic little idyll with a vast sense of compassion for big, dumb Lennie and for George, who knew Lennie would never get to tend those rabbits, and that if he did stroke their fur with his too strong hands he would kill them. And it is, perhaps, that compassion, even more than the perfect sense of form, which marks off John Steinbeck, artist, so sharply from all the little verbal photographers who record tough talk and snarl in books which have power without pity. The most significant things John Steinbeck has to say about his characters are never put into words; they are the overtones of which the reader is never wholly conscious—and that is art.

James Ross Oliver. "Book News and Views." *Monterey [CA] Peninsula Herald*, 25 February 1937: 5.

Book reviewing can be a joy at times, and it so happens that this is one of them. The cause for the good feeling at the moment is that we have just finished reading the one book we have encountered in some months which has impressed us with the extreme artistry of its composition. It happens less frequently than one might suppose.

As usual, this kind of a book can, and does, stir up all manner of argument, intellectual and violent. And John Steinbeck's *Of Mice and Men* . . . will be no exception. Of course, publishers and authors are quite willing to let the storm rage. Sales never suffer from it.

Of Mice and Men is a small book of only 185 pages, but it is big in its accomplishment. Again Steinbeck convinces us that his is the mission to bring to the reader the lives and minds of the lower class. It is that purpose that has brought upon him the condemnation of many; expressed doubts in no uncertain terms concerning the immorality of his writing. But considering the characters the author brings us, and considering again his thoroughness in doing this, no condemnation is just. If one will only glance through Steinbeck's pages, one will see that these things which they decry are not the author's—rather those of whom he writes. Pressing still further, and as a last plunge to get this thing off our chest, anyone who knows these people will agree that he is right in his work.

But enough of that.

Of Mice and Men is what it is because of its inherent simplicity. The plot is not great; nor are its characters great, but are both real and carried through to completion. It is a plot upon which the characterizations and story are laid as effectively as flesh upon bone.

Dramatically skillfully, Steinbeck takes us to as simple yet magnetic a climax as one could wish for. And the accomplishment which impressed us the most is that the author, in his faultless plot, has pegged or forewarned us of each development: some trifling event, some symbolic twist of character, goes before like a perfect prologue. The artistry of it we do not object to it in the least.

Once more John Steinbeck has presented us with a simple, realistic portrayal of simple, earthy men and women. They are the hardest characters to delineate.

***

F[anny] B[utcher]. "Books." *Chicago Daily Tribune*, 27 February 1937: 11.

The author of *Tortilla Flat* has written *Of Mice and Men* so simply, so movingly, so factually that only when its last page is finished does the reader realize what a remarkable literary feat John Steinbeck has performed.

The book tells the story of Lennie, a huge moron who has a passion to touch anything soft and goes into a panic if it is taken from him, and of George, who watches over Lennie with touching care. George, a little man with a quick mind, is the only person in the world (since Lennie's Aunt Clara's death) who can do anything with the giant moron. He can do everything with him, and does everything for him, including thinking. When the book opens, Lennie and George are about to start on a new job, after having had to flee for their lives from their last one. All they ask of life is to lay aside a little money and buy a farm and "live on the fatta the lan" where they can raise rabbits. They think they can. But the reader knows they can't—knows that fate is piling up something for them as one after another sinister shadow is cast.

Brutality and tenderness mingle in these strangely moving pages. Language that gentle ears would never hear seems as inevitable as Lennie's clumsy devotion to the puppy which he kills with his petting. The reader is fascinated by a certainty of approaching doom. It comes swiftly, inevitably, and the final moments of George's service to Lennie are high tragedy. One false word, and *Of Mice and Men* would have been melodrama, and bad melodrama at that. But the author never, after the first few pages, writes one false word.

Henry Seidel Canby. "Casuals of the Road."
Saturday Review 15 (27 February 1937): 7.

Mr. Steinbeck . . . has written a long short story which should please everybody. It should please everybody because it has every element of good story-telling, and it must be remembered that most of our successful novels of recent with any substance of art to them, succeeded by violating most of the canons of the storyteller's art in order to deemphasize ideology, the stream of consciousness, or behaviorism.

Of Mice and Men is the story of a defective. His weakness is soft things, strokable things. Upon them his fingers sooner or later close. He does "a bad thing," he kills them. But the principle in Lennie is nevertheless the principle of good. And defective though may be, it is his longing for living things that are lovable and to be taken care of—like rabbits—that makes articulate the longing of all the rough hands the ranch for something of their own, land, a house, animals, perhaps a wife, something different from their wandering from lousy bunks to gilt saloons, getting nowhere, owning nothing. Lennie's friend, who has got him out danger before, and Crooks, the nigger hostler, and Candy, the broken swamper, and even Slim, who is the just and capable man in the story, all feel it. And slowly the plan develops. "Everybody wants a little bit of land, not much. Jus' som'thin' that was his" (*OMM* 76).

This is the principle of good, even in the moron, Lennie. The principle of evil is, obscurely, in the conditions of life that keep these men bummers and vagabonds. But it focuses in the boss's vicious son, Curley, the ex-prizefighter, and on Curley's wife, a poor little prostitute infected by egoism because some one once told she could go into the pictures, and held here among these men by Curley all she can do is to wander about like some venereal germ looking salaciously for a victim. And she finds Lennie, trying not to do a bad thing.

The story is as simple as that, but superb in its understatements, its realisms which are used, not to illustrate behavior, but for character and situation. Indeed, there has been nothing quite so good of the kind in American writing since Anderson's early stories. It is a limited kind, but close to the heart of the whole fiction business. If you can create charac-ter—a fresh character, belonging to his soil and shaped by a fresh set of experiences; and if (choosing sentiment rather than the other offgivings of human nature—and sentiment is quite as real as its opposite), and if you can make that make its own story, you are to closer to the job of fiction than most writers come in our time.

"Steinbeck Touches the Sublime."
San Francisco Call, 27 February 1937: 6.

Through California's fertile valleys trudge loneliest guys in the world.

They are cattle-ranch hands, drifting job to job.

They got no fam'ly. They don't belong no place. . . . They ain't got nothing to look ahead to.

But George and Lennie HAVE something to look ahead to. They dream of saving a stake, of buying a few cheap acres in the hills, of having their own rooftree, of raising their own fruit and chickens and pigs and rabbits. Lennie is a simpleminded Hercules. George, wiser, watches over him, snatches Lennie from the disasters into which he blunders, keeps his dear dream alive.

The dream seems ready to come true when simple Lennie runs afoul of shrewd, bullying Curley, the boss's son, and Curley's man-chasing, painted, voluptuous, tantalizing wife. Then comes tragedy, stark, utter, smashing.

It IS tragedy. Pure classic, profoundly concerned with human weak-ness and suffering, hurtling from heights of pity to depths of agony. And all simple, direct, mincing no word, wasting not a single magnificent brush-stroke. Call it the finest published work of one of America's most gifted writers.

P. Ralph Thompson. "Of Mice and Men."
New York Times, 27 February 1937: 15.

The boys have whooped it up for John Steinbeck's new book, *Of Mice and Men* . . . so enthusiastically that there isn't much else left to say in the way of praise. It is a grand little book, for all its ultimate melodrama; and although this reader can't begin to string along with Harry Hansen, who calls it "the finest bit of prose fiction of this decade," he must admit that it is a long time since he laid eyes on anything as completely disarming.

Mr. Steinbeck's story is of two wandering farmhands, George and Lennie. George and Lennie are friends, sticking to each other in desperation and dreaming of the day when they won't have to bum around the country looking for work—of the remote day when they will have enough money to buy some sort of place of their own.

This probably sounds like sentimental truck, and in a way it is. But under Mr. Steinbeck's magic touch it is also strong, moving and very funny. Lennie is a grown-up baby, physically powerful and mentally weak, with a passion for soft, furry things. George is a tough and irritable codger, but he bears patiently with Lennie. . . .

. . . What happens when the two reach a ranch where they are to work is the story. Read it and see how aptly John Steinbeck turns a tale.

Joseph Henry Jackson. "Steinbeck's Art Finds Powerful Expression in *Of Mice and Men*." *San Francisco Chronicle*, 28 February 1937: Section D, 7.

Of Mice and Men, first of all, is not a "proletarian novel" in the sense in which the arm-wavers currently use the term. It does concern working men, yes, its setting is the road, the field and the bunkhouse. Its central figures—there are two of them—are workers who take what jobs they can get where they can get them, in the fruit, wrestling grain bags, running cultivators, skinning mules. But the author's first preoccupation is not with these men as symbols or even as units in the mass of beaten-down labor. As always, Steinbeck is interested in his characters as men as human beings who think and do and desire the many and serious things that men have always thought and done and longed for. Indeed it is the very commonplace desire of George and Lennie for their own little heaven-on-earth that gives Steinbeck his story. These two, like other men, had plans. And how their plans went astray (all right, "agley" if you insist. There will be a fine, grand misquoting of Burns before all the reviewers are done with this book.) How their plans, in fact, could never have come to fruition anyhow is Steinbeck's theme. It is a simple story, one that combines a curious dream-like quality with the swift streamlining of a good play. It is a story that will sweep you irresistibly with it, too; even though you may shudder more than once, you will not put it down.

You meet George and Lennie as they have made their way to a camping spot by a stream near the ranch where they have a job promised them for the next day.

George, small and shrewd, is the brains of the pair in much more than the usual sense. For Lennie, huge and strong and willing, hasn't good sense. He can't remember things. He will do anything George tells him but by himself he is lost. Sometimes George grows furious with Lennie for his stupidity, long as he has known him. Lennie repeats things he shouldn't because though he remembers what he has heard now and then he can never remember that he shouldn't blurt them out. Sometimes, too, Lennie gets into trouble. He never means to do anything bad, but he can't resist anything that feels soft to his enormous but sensitive fingers. When he pets a mouse he pets it hard and kills it. Up in the north George and Lennie had to clear out in a hurry because Lennie couldn't help himself—he had to feel the soft silk of a little girl's dress. Lennie had meant no more but the girl screamed, and they had to hide in a ditch all night. Sometimes George wished he could put Lennie in a cage with about a million mice and leave him there. But he couldn't. And he couldn't stay angry at Lennie. He had to take care of him anyway; somebody had to, that was sure. And besides, he and Lennie shared a dream.

That dream was a little ranch somewhere. Lennie liked to hear George tell about it, over and over again—"a big vegetable patch and chickens and a rabbit hutch [rabbits were soft and smooth and Lennie loved them]. "And when it rains in the winter we'll just say the hell with goin' to work, and we'll build up a fire in the stove and set around it an' listen to the rain on the roof" (*OMM* 14–15). There was nothing strange about their dream as you see. Men everywhere have had it. But so far George and Lennie had never been able to fulfill it.

As the story opens, however, they are still dreaming it. And when they come to the ranch and go to work there develops out of nowhere, by sheer luck, a chance that their dream may be realized. Another man has had that dream too. And he has the one thing George and Lennie have never been able to scrape together—a stake. A little more money, no more than George and Lennie can earn and save in a month or two, and they can buy the place they want. They even know the one, and how much it will take.

How that dream, so near fulfillment, was snatched away is the story, *Of Mice and Men*. You know what's coming; you can't help knowing. Steinbeck has done such a masterly job of story-telling that you feel the horror that is ahead even before it begins to grow. You see the fate that is going to overtake these men and their dream. You realize what's going to happen, what can't help happening. But—well, let me see you stop reading, that's all. And in spite of the grimness of the tale, let me hear you deny after you have finished it, that Steinbeck has written it beautifully as well as powerfully.

There is no question, of course, that there will be the usual chorus of recriminations. Here (so it will go) Steinbeck had the materials for a fine propaganda novel, a tale of the class struggle that might show how the working man is exploited, etc., etc., etc., and he didn't make use of his chance to strike a blow for freedom. He didn't unite with the Front. He didn't do this and he didn't do that. He might have done such-and-such and he should have done it thus-and-so. They've said it about Steinbeck before and they'll say it all again. And they'll make it sound plausible, too.

But I'm pretty sure that he won't care. I hope he won't. I hope he will go right on, sharpening his talent as he is doing, changing his subjects, his interests whenever he feels like it, writing about whatever is close to his heart at the moment he writes, doing books that are sensitive, beautifully written, imaginative works of art. That's plenty to expect of any writing man who cares as much for what he is doing as Steinbeck does. As for the books written to prove this or to demonstrate that, to put forward a thesis or to help the acceptance of an idea—let the ones who want to write them do so. Sometimes such books will be literature. Sometimes, if the writers of them happen to be artists, they will also be beautiful books. But more often you will find beauty in books that were written because their authors wanted to write them, just for their own sakes. So far, Steinbeck has stuck to that plan. And *Of Mice and Men* is the best evidence that it is the right way for him to write.

11

Fred T. Marsh. "John Steinbeck's Tale of Drifting Men." *New York Times Book Review* 86 (28 February 1937): 7.

John Steinbeck is no mere virtuoso in the art of story-telling; but he is one. Whether he writes about the amiable outcasts of *Tortilla Flat* or about the grim strikers of *In Dubious Battle*, he tells a story. *Of Mice and Men* is a thriller, a gripping tale running to novelette length that you will not set down until it is finished. It is more than that; but it is that.

George and Lennie belong to the floating army of drifting ranch hands. "Guys like us" George says, "are the loneliest guys in the world. They got no family. They don't belong no place. They come to a ranch and work up a stake and then they go inta town and blow their stake, and the first thing you know they're poundin' their tail on some other ranch. They ain't got nothing to look ahead to" (*OMM* 13–14).

The relationship between these two buddies of roads and ranches is a strange one and causes comment at the new ranch. George is small, dark, wiry, restless, keen-witted. Lennie is a huge, hulking man with an expressionless face, pale blue eyes and wide, sloping shoulders, walking heavily "dragging his feet a little, the way a bear drags his paws" (*OMM* 2). He is stupid, but well-meaning.

George and Lennie came from the same Southern town, and George has taken it on himself to take care of the big fellow. Sometimes he wishes he were free of him. He'd get ahead much faster, Lennie is always getting them into trouble—like the time he wanted to stroke the pretty red skirt of the girl on the last ranch and in his dumb strength tore it off her. They had to run away again to keep Lennie out of jail. The baby boy in the big man's body has baby urges—to stroke, pet and fondle animals, all soft or pretty things, and he kills or destroys them unaware of his strength. But when George is around he is all right, for he obeys George implicitly.

George is a keen thinking man. There is nothing in this knocking about. If only he and Lennie could get together $600 he knows of a little place with a few acres they could buy and settle down to work for themselves. If only Lennie can be kept out of trouble. And so he keeps drumming it into Lennie's head that he must be good and not do bad things. Then they can get a stake together and live on the fat of the land in a place of their own. They'll grow their own stuff, keep a few pigs and chickens and raise rabbits; Lennie can take charge of the rabbits and have all the pets he wants. The big fellow never grows tired of hearing this story just as a child likes to hear a tale told over and over again. And at the new ranch, the way things are shaping up, the dream seems to be on the point of coming true.

The tension increases and the apparently casual acts and conversation nevertheless fit together to create suspense in an atmosphere of impending doom. There are trouble makers in the bunkhouse. Curley, the boss's son, a little fellow handy with his fists, likes to take on big clumsy fellows, pick fights with them. He wins no matter how the fight comes out, because if he licks the big fellow every one says how game he is; and if he gets the worst of it every one turns on the big fellow for not taking [on] some one his own size. Then Curley's wife, a lush beauty, is always coming around where the men are, on the pretense of looking for Curley, giving all the men the eye and, because, being a town girl, she is bored on the ranch, bent on stirring up excitement. The other boys know how to keep out of trouble. But Lennie only knows what George tells him when George is right there on the spot. The girl spots Lennie as the only soft guy in the bunch. The climax comes, not as a shock, but as a dreaded inevitability. The theme is not, as the title would suggest, that the best laid plans *Of Mice and Men* gang aft agley. They do in this story as in others. But it is a play on the immemorial theme of what men live by besides bread alone. In sure, raucous, vulgar Americanism, Steinbeck has touched the quick in his little story.

Wilbur Needham. "John Steinbeck Does Dramatic Novel." *Los Angeles Times*, 28 February 1937: Part 3, 8.

Once more, John Steinbeck refuses to be neatly pigeonholed. He has qualities lamentably rare in modern novelists: imagination and a restless, inquiring mind. He will not sit down, like Thomas Wolfe, and contemplate his navel. He refuses to exploit one locality or any single idea or set of characters. That is the way novelists achieve fame and shelves of books all stamped with their trademarks; and Steinbeck cannot be accused of courting fame, for he chooses queer balconies.

Beyond that, the man is something more than original in creation. Those who seek originality are almost always experimenters; and the results they offer are—experiments, usually unsuccessful. Steinbeck, obviously, does experiment; but he has a discernment in approach, an uncanny touch in creation, that lift everything he writes out of ephemeral brackets of experimental work. That is because he always has his feet on the ground rooted in the earth and the things of earth—no matter what mountain peaks his level eyes look on. No two of [the author's] books had anything in common except John Steinbeck, who was outwardly different in each, inwardly no one but himself.

Now, *Of Mice and Men*. A little book, half the size of an ordinary novel (the gods be praised for that!) but containing more. In everything but its superficial form, the novel is a play. I was not surprised to learn that a second script is being rehearsed at a San Francisco theater now. It does not creak: and it will not, on the boards. There is fluid movement, here, and inevitability; never spoiled by theatrical mechanics—and yet, it is theater, as theater ought to be. With inner rhythms that move out into a prose that is Steinbeck's own.

George Milton and Lennie Small wander from one job to another on California ranches. They don't want to drift; but Lennie, a hulking fellow, is not quite bright, and he gets them both in trouble. Lennie likes to pet soft things, mice and rabbits and dresses and shining women's hair. The mice die, surprisingly, for Lennie is very gentle; or, he thinks he is. But his great paws have an unconscious power; and the mice die and the women scream. So they drift on to other parts, sometimes none too quickly.

Always before them is a dream of a little place of their own, where they can live on the "fatta the lan," and Lennie can "get to tend them rabbits." Always before them; and now, it seems about to turn real. Here the drama, ever close beside Steinbeck's strange inventiveness and native humor, begins to outpace it and to draw away.

Of the book's inner meaning, never obvious but never entirely obscured by unexpected laughter and the movement of the story, I will not speak. If you do not like inner meanings, you will certainly not find one here, and, if you do, you'll see more than one for yourself.

Louis Paul. "Prose Made of Wind and Soil and Weather." *New York Herald Tribune*, 28 February 1937: Books section, 5.

The weeds and the willows and the tall waving grain of California's sweet valleys, rabbits and mice and a woman's soft hair, the hot slanting sun and the hungry desire of a pair of floaters to own a handful of dirt are the materials out of which this lovely new novel by John Steinbeck is evoked. Purling water is purling water here, without overtones; a gracious sky is as beautiful as in any lyric poetry. The men are lads sent down to the ranch from Murray and Ready's in San Francisco: Lennie, like Nature itself, whose powerful fingers killed little animals before he knew it, and George, struggling to become human. *Of Mice and Men* is another of John Steinbeck's parables of earth, and no writer I know shapes the soil into truer patterns for us to understand.

[Steinbeck's earlier] works have been called dissimilar. Versatile, perhaps; in a day when success has the tendency to standardize, versatility in a novelist or any one else is thought of with some astonishment. The threads that run continuously through these stories by John Steinbeck are, under examination, more than perceptible. Not especially rare are those authors who think in terms of panaceas, whose lack of courage and vitality draws back from the monumental task of understanding; they are all for short cuts, for adopting some ready-made philosophy and rushing on from there, and what we get from these authors are drab second-hand discoveries, valueless intrinsically dull. Here, however, is an intelligence as explicit as any research scientists, an intelligence directed toward the understanding of the relationship between men and earth. In each successive book, this desire to explore the complex affinity is more apparent, until, with the publication of *Of Mice and Men*, it achieves such cumulative impact as to be undeniable.

Of Mice and Men is made of a theme which some lesser novelist might have called too insignificant to expound—two indigent members of the strange tribe of casual workers destroyed by the simple mystery of loyalty. But before they are destroyed there burns brilliantly between the covers of this little book the image of the fire inside the flesh of two human beings, whom fate has crushed before birth, human beings whose lives mean no more to Nature than robins caught up by hawks.

The story seems simple when accomplished by a superb craftsman: the desire and struggle of those who till the soil for others to own a tiny plot of the earth for themselves against this primitive hunger like the rising tide of a destructive river, is played the forces which make a naive aspiration impossible of attainment. "Sure, we'd have a little house an' a room to ourself. Little fat iron stove, an' in the winter we'd keep a fire goin' in it. It ain't enough land so we'd have to work too hard. Maybe six, seven hours a day. We wouldn't have to buck no barley eleven hours a day. An' when we put in a crop' why we'd be there to take the crop up. We'd know what come of our planting" (*OMM* 58). And while George dreams in the crummy ranch bunk-house, he knows that his words are lies; and the reader knows his words are the lies we use to escape our destinies. And the author knows. They are not ugly lies, you understand; merely the imagination evoking for the moment its little dream, an escape in to a fairyland where there is no barley to buck.

In the cities men go to "movies." There are little dumps on the Bowery where for 10 cents the disinherited may observe life aboard a yacht or in a penthouse, or cowboys riding the beautiful ranges of Arizona. In Arizona the cowboys ride fence, one leg propped over against the saddle horn, absorbed in a magazine of hair-raising adventure stories. Men in factories tiredly dream of grubbing for gold "out West," and office workers dance themselves all night into insensibility. Men take whisky into them and, with its drug, bump their heads against the stars in their rosy fancy. And serious observers, infuriated by a world which impels us frantically toward escape, babble in an impotent fashion of cures. Those who speak of books hunt down such observations and interpret them in terms of social significance.

But the poet who immortalizes the fleeting tragedy of two such men as George and Lennie is his own social force. That Lennie was an idiot, no less, and victim of a pathological disease, is entirely beyond the point. John Steinbeck does not know what makes men idiots and victims of disease; such knowledge comes slowly and painfully as does the cure for cancer. We sting the flesh of our economic body with patent medicines' wondering, let us say, if Lennie's tragedy might not be avoided if the government in Washington gave every crop floater and bindlestiff and lettuce picker and wheat sacker a little farm in Salinas Valley. Such nonsense invalidates the very spirit in which the author of such a work as *Of Mice and Men* is creating.

The verities we can live with are those thoughts born out of dreams which, in the end, distinguish us from the robins and the waving grain. Of such verities does John Steinbeck write, out of a warm and a rich knowledge. With the genuine artist's respect for his materials and love of his craft, he puts away cheap prejudice, the distortion which comes from anger; his thought is to tell the little truths he had discovered with his eyes and callused hands and intelligence, and if these truths do not touch your social conscience, nothing can. In *Of Mice and Men*, the truth is made into a moving and profoundly beautiful book full of singing prose and enchantment. If, standing upon some pinnacle of dry logic, we suspect that his creations of these ignorant American laborers are idealizations, that without the magic of his poetry they must remain sweat-soaked beasts of the fields, we but doubly assure ourselves of his essential humanity and pay his artistry the highest compliment we know.

Maxine Garrard. "*Of Mice and Men* by Steinbeck Powerful and Absorbing Novel." *Columbus [GA] Enquirer*, 1 March 1937: 2.

Of Mice and Men by John Steinbeck is a book so powerful it will make the reader's hair stand on end and curl a little in the bargain. Mr. Steinbeck is a contributor to *Esquire* and has been startling its readers since that magazine exploded upon the public a few years ago. His *Tortilla Flat* caused comment and *Of Mice and Men* will bring on even more talk. Weak-hearted readers and lovers of moonlight and romance should take a word of warning—this is not of the pleasant school of thought wherein things turn out fine in the end; they don't.

Serving his strong meat fresh and still warm from life's slaughter house, John Steinbeck shades nothing in presenting his terrifying tale; however, beneath the superficial horror of the story the reader senses a dream of breathless beauty shimmering through the lives of the two main characters. These vagabonds are men predestined to a stark, empty existence but between them flickers some unexplained devotion and future vision of the time when they will "live on the fatta the lan'." . . .

From the sordid lives of a cocky tramp and a balmy moron, John Steinbeck has written a drama of indescribable magic and heart-breaking futility. Even if you think you are tough and can "take it," this book will cause an emotional upheaval. It is strong, it is powerful and it is wonderful, but unless you can swallow raw stuff—lay off.

⟡

"Young Man's Dream." *Time* 28 (1 March 1937): 69.

George and Lennie were ranch hands. George was small, wiry tough, shrewd; Lennie was enormous, floppy-looking but Herculean, and a half-wit. George and Lennie were pals. Lennie was always getting them into trouble, losing them jobs, getting them run out of town because he liked to pet things—mice, little girls, rabbits. Not conscious of his blundering strength, Lennie was apt to kill what he petted. George kept him in line as well as he could by bawling him out, threatening to leave him, telling him a beautiful fairy story about how they would save enough money to buy a little farm, settle down in comfort, let Lennie take care of rabbits.

They had just had to leave one job in a hurry because Lennie's passion for petting things had been misunderstood by a frightened little girl. On the new ranch everything went all right at first. Lennie was a terrific worker, did beautifully as long as George was at hand to tell him what to do. It looked for a while as if they could really make their stake, buy their little farm, settle down to make their dream come true. But then things began to go wrong. The boss's son was an ugly customer, and he had just married a floozy who kept him at a white heat of suspicion. When he picked on Lennie, the big half-wit got so panicky that he seized his little tormentor's hand, crushed it nearly to bits. George managed to get them out of that scrape, but when Lennie accidentally broke the floozy's neck, there was only one thing George could do to remedy that. Knowing where Lennie was hiding, George got to him ahead of the posse, got trusting Lennie to turn his head while he shot him behind the ear.

To Americans whose eyes are still smarting from the unhappy ending of the Wall Street fairy tale of 1929, John Steinbeck's little dream story will not seem out of line with reality: they may even overlook the fact that it too is a fairy tale. An oxymoronic combination of the tough and tender, *Of Mice and Men* will appeal to sentimental cynics, cynical sentimentalists. Critic Christopher Morley found himself "purified" by this "masterpiece

18

. . . written in purest imagined compassion and truth." Readers less easily thrown off their trolley will prefer Hans Andersen.

P. Ralph Thomson. "Books of the Times."
New York Times, 2 March 1937: 19.

John Steinbeck's *Of Mice and Men* . . . is the most recently published of books mentioned here, and in bulk one of the smallest, yet it should not be overlooked by anyone interested in American fiction. In retrospect, the lovable half-wit Lennie seems even a more improbable character than at first reading it appeared to be. But improbable or not, he is memorable—a blend if such a thing can be imagined, of Paul Bunyan, Tiny Tim and Browning's sprawling Caliban. . . .

Harry Thornton Moore. "*Of Mice and Men.*"
New Republic 90 (3 March 1937): 118–19.

George and Lennie are two drifting ranch hands who dream, as rootless men do, of a piece of land of their own, where they will "belong." They have never been able to work up a stake because big, blundering, simple-witted Lennie keeps getting them into trouble. He can never remember things. He tenderly loves puppies and mice but always forgets about not squeezing them too hard, and kills them. Fabulously strong but very timid, he is quite docile in the hands of George, the pilot-fish of the pair. George feels that Lennie has been given into his keeping. He controls him by talking about the rabbit farm they will have one day, where Lennie may look after the rabbits if he is good—for George too is webbed in the dream. They come to work in the Salinas Valley, and it is there, among the people they meet at the ranch, that their story is worked out.

This story has that common denominator of most good imaginative writing, a shadow of the action that means something beyond the action. But the underlying theme (of the danger of dreaming) never clogs the primary story. The book is well contrived and effectively compressed, driving ahead with straight and rapid movement, as magnificently written as Steinbeck's other four California novels. He again shows a deep understanding of both place and people, and his presentation of the ranch and its daily life has the gleam of actuality. The people, human beings reduced to bareness of thought and speech and action, are on the side-tracks of the main line of western culture. They exist in a hard reality, but most of them are susceptible to dreams. Some of them are lost in compensatory dream-images of themselves, others are set afire by the wish-dream of George and Lennie. But in one way or another all the dreams and some of the people (both good and bad) are smashed: a spirit of doom prevails as strong as in Steinbeck's fellow Californian, Jeffers.

A writer deep in the ways of his own people feels (in many cases unconsciously) a racial compulsive: the actual and mythical experience of his people helps generate his material. But the final shaping of it depends upon the artist's own vision. In the present story, Lennie is cast up from the midst of us and we all know him. Baffled, unknowingly powerful, utterly will-less, he cannot move without a leader. And we also know many Georges, good-heartedly trying to help the Lennies of life muddle through; but all the while, despite their courage and good intentions, none too certain of themselves. John Steinbeck sees them as unable to prevent their charges (or often themselves) from steering into catastrophe. In book after book his protagonists, tragic or comic, are shattered; and it goes hardest with those who had the brightest dreams. It is disturbing to find these men of good will so consistently going down in spiritual defeat or meeting with a brutal death.

Heywood Broun. "It Seems to Me."
St. Paul [MN] Daily News, 4 March 1937: 8.

I'd like to come along with the large group of critics who have already recorded their enthusiasm for John Steinbeck's new novel, *Of Mice and Men*. This is a book written with compassion, celerity and an admirable sense of structure. It is that rare and much to be desired thing—a short novel. The telling takes no more than 31,000 words, and yet the narrative is fully rounded out and complete. For instance, in my opinion, *Of Mice and Men* is infinitely more important in the literary scheme of things than *Gone with the Wind*.

I am moved to great excitement about the emergence of Steinbeck because he so neatly splits the bracket between the old romanticists and the stern-faced boys and girls who have recently been treating the novel as if it were nothing more than a candid camera. Steinbeck knows his farm workers as well as anybody else. Lennie and George talk straight. No spurious literary phrase creeps into the mouth of either. Nevertheless many long stretches of their conversation are animated by true poetic content.

I think life is like that and that modern authors are beginning to find it out. Transcripts of talk may be as faithful as you please and still take on the cadence and color which make for beauty. Perhaps somewhat after the manner of Moliere's hero who discovered that he had been talking prose all his life, the common run-of-the-mine American may wake up to the fact that he uses a good deal of poetry in dealing with his daily concerns. That may be a shock to some, since along certain levels poetry means Eddie Guest and a rhyme scheme fit to break the ear with its persistent beat, like that of night club drums.

I do not know which native author should be selected as the spiritual ancestor of Steinbeck. Every writer has to have an ancestor forced upon him, whether or not he recognizes the old gentleman. Offhand it would seem to me that Ring Lardner might have suggested in part the manner and mode of John Steinbeck. To be sure, there is little similarity in subject matter and none at all in point of view save the quality of compassion for those who get pushed around.

I assume that at some period of his life Steinbeck read Upton Sinclair. Mr. Sinclair is a good model for young authors, since he can serve both as an inspiration and at the same time as a horrible example. I think that writers will be lucky if they can catch from Upton something of his terrific zeal about present problems in the workaday world, and yet if the younger men are exposed to his influence too long they may become infected with the flatness and bleakness of the Sinclair prose.

I'm aware that Upton Sinclair is a poet as well as a novelist. And his is a style which doesn't get in the way when he has a fast moving and deeply biting story to tell. It is smoother, of course, than the English of Dreiser, and yet never ornate. Fine writing and bad writing may be equally destructive in the matter of getting into the reader's eye when he is in close pursuit of the theme itself. Of course, I'm using "fine writing" in the worst sense of the phrase.

The proper time to admire the style of a man is when you have finished the last sentence on the last page of his story. So it was with *Of Mice and Men* as far as I was concerned. I had put the book down all stirred by the logical poignance of its conclusion. And it was only then that I suddenly realized that this man Steinbeck could write like a magician.

Until then I had been too much interested in what he had to say to pay very much attention to the manner in which he said it. Like a conjurer, a novelist should be able to take the rabbit out of the hat without letting his audience in on the way in which he did it. John Steinbeck seems to me right now to be the wonder man of current American letters.

Mark Van Doren. "Wrong Number." *Nation* 144 (6 March 1937): 275.

All but one of the persons in Mr. Steinbeck's extremely brief novel are subhuman if the range of the word human is understood to coincide with the range thus far established by fiction. Two of them are evil, one of them is dangerous without meaning to be, and all of them are ignorant—all of them, that is, except the one who shall be named hereafter. Far from knowing the grammar of conduct, they do not even know its orthography. No two of their thoughts are consecutive, nor for that matter do they think; it is rather that each of them follows some instinct as a bull follows the chain which runs through a hole in his nose, or as a crab moves toward its prey. The scene is a ranch in California, and the bunkhouse talk is terrific—God damn, Jesus Christ, what the hell, you crazy bastard, I gotta gut ache, and things like that. The dialect never varies, just as the story never runs uphill.

George and Lennie, the itinerant workers who come to the ranch one day with a dream of the little farm they will own as soon as they get the jack together, seem to think their new job will last at least that long; but the reader knows from the beginning that it will not last, for Lennie is a half-witted giant with a passion for petting mice—or rabbits, or pups, or girls—and for killing them when they don't like it. He is doomed in this book to kill Curley's wife; that is obvious; and then—. Lennie, you see, cannot help shaking small helpless creatures until their necks are broken just as George cannot relinquish his dream, and just as Curley cannot ever stop being a beast of jealousy. They are wound up to act that way, and the best they can do is run down: which is what happens when Mr. Steinbeck comes to his last mechanical page.

What, however, of the one exception. Ah, he is Slim the jerkline skinner, the tall man with the "God-like eyes" that get fastened on you so that you can't think of anything else for a while. "There was a gravity in his manner and a quiet so profound that all talk stopped when he spoke. . . . His hatchet face was ageless. He might have been thirty-five or fifty. His ear heard more than was said to him, and his slow speech had overtones not of thought, but of understanding beyond thought. His hands, large and lean, were as delicate in their action as those of a temple dancer" (*OMM* 33–34). He looks through people and beyond them—a feat never accomplished save in mechanical novels. And he understands—why he understands everything that Mr. Steinbeck understands. It is the merest accident of education that he talks like the rest. "Jesus, he's jes' like kid, ain't he," he says (*OMM* 43). If he had his creator's refinement of tongue he could write such sentences as this one which introduces Lennie: "His arms did not swing at his sides, but hung loosely and only moved because the heavy hands were pendula" (*OMM* 2). It wouldn't have done to write pendulums. That would have given the real sound and look of Lennie, and besides it is a real word.

Mr. Steinbeck, I take it, has not been interested in reality of any kind. His jerkline skinner (mule driver) is as hopelessly above the human range as Lennie or Candy or Curley's painted wife is below it. All is extreme here; everybody is a doll; and, if there is a kick in the story, it is given us from some source which we cannot see, as when a goose walks over our grave, or as when in the middle of the night the telephone rings sharply, and it is the wrong number. We shall remember it about that long.

S. W. "Current Literature." *Philadelphia Inquirer,* 6 March 1937: 14.

Most stories of those President Roosevelt calls the "underprivileged" sound a protestant note. It is as if the author had a graphophone record of remarks by Norman Thomas or Mr. John L. Lewis at his elbow. So fiction suffers; and argument is confused. Such things may not be said of the novels of John Steinbeck. On his record of six books he takes rank as the best interpreter of the semi-submerged in this country. Whether good or bad, unfortunate or self-stricken, he goes to the core of character with the precision of a surgeon whose diagnosis is given in terms of art. Tricky rhetoric he eschews. The manner of his expression is fine and true. In his newly published short novel, *Of Mice and Men*, [what] might seem vulgar is dignified, and at times transfigured, by a soul shining through. This is the story of George and Lennie, strange partners in grain-bucking on a California ranch. The story of George, small and active, and Lennie, the hulking giant with a child's mind and a passion for petting a mouse, a rabbit, a piece of velvet, anything soft. With affectionate strategy George stands between Lennie and disaster until Curley's wife, the foolish jade, invites him to stroke her hair. So there is one thing more for George to do in the most affecting passage of recent American fiction.

Eleanor Roosevelt. "My Day." *New York World Telegram*, 16 March 1937: 31.

I have just finished a little book called *Of Mice and Men* by John Steinbeck, which fellow columnist, Mr. Heywood Broun, reviewed in his column not long ago. My admiration for Mr. Broun leads me to want to look into anything he praises, and so I sent for the book to bring it away with me. It is beautifully written and a marvelous picture of the tragedy of loneliness.

I could see the two men, one comes across their likes in many places, not only in the West described in the book but in every part of the country. When I closed *Of Mice and Men*, I could not help but think how fortunate we are when we have real friends, people we can count on and turn to and who we know are always glad to see us when we are lonely.

Dorothea Brande Collins. "Reading at Random." *American Review* 9 (April 1937): 100–13.

As for *Of Mice and Men*—surely no more sentimental wallowing ever passed for a novel, or had such a welcome, as this sad tale of a huge half-wit and his cowboy protector! Mr. Steinbeck this time wrings the Tears of Things from a ten-gallon hat, and reviewers who cannot bear the mawkishness of a Milne, the crudity of a Coward, or the mysticism of a Morgan were able to take the sorrowful symmetries of a Steinbeck to their hearts and write their reviews with tears running down their cheeks. Who does not know by this time of Lennie, who loved to stroke soft furry things, but didn't know his own strength? Of Slim, with the "God-like eyes," knight sans peur et sans reproche of the bunkhouse? Of George, who loved Lennie well enough to shoot him? Of "Curley's wife," that wax-dummy girl who might have come straight out of the window of a chain dress-shop, so glossy, so hard, so brightly painted—and so far from ever having drawn a breath?

Mr. Steinbeck is "economical." He is, indeed. That is perhaps the secret of his charm. I feel sure that all those reviewers who cheered so hard for *Of Mice and Men* would, if they could have been caught while still sobbing over George and Lennie, have admitted that even critics are only boys at heart, for that is just the mood that Mr. Steinbeck's work induces. So perhaps again, they would admit that this secret of his success is that a certain simple type of reader feels, when he discovers that he has foreseen correctly any movement of a story, a kind of participation in the creative act of the author. Almost any critic would admit this if the book under consideration were one of the Tarzan books, or a book by Lloyd Douglas, or any one of a dozen "popular novelists" of the sort they affect to despise, but perhaps they have not noticed that the symmetry and expectedness (or if you prefer, read "economy") of Mr. Steinbeck's work put the average pulp writer to shame.

If Lennie kills a mouse by stroking it, you may be sure he will unintentionally kill something larger in the same way; when you hear of Curley's wife's soft hair, "like fur," you can begin to cooperate with the author by expectation of her end. When George learns that a poor old worthless smelly dog can be dispatched easily by a shot in the back of his head, you are unwarrantably guileless if you do not suspect the manner in which Lennie will meet his death. If an old man dreams of a home, peace, and security you may be sure that a home, peace, and security are what he will most agonizingly just miss. And so forth. You can call this sort of foreshadowing "economy" if it pleases you; but if "economy" is the word you choose you should abandon the word "obvious" hereafter and forever.

It may be some time before the current vogue for Steinbeck passes. Masculine sentimentality particularly when it masquerades as toughness, is a little longer in being seen through than the feminine or the inclusively human variety. Undoubtedly, there are plenty who would deny, even today that *The Sun Also Rises* and *What Price Glory?* are too hard to find the soft spots where the decay shows: the romantic overestimation of the role of friendship, the wax-figure women, bright, hard, treacherous, unreal—whether a Lady Brett, a French girl behind the lines or "Curley's wife," these are all essentially hateful women, women from whom it is a virtue to flee to masculine companionship. There was certainly a sort of stag-party hysteria and uproar about the approval we have been hearing for this padded short story about underdogs and animals, bunkhouses and bathos, which has seldom risen so high since "Wait for baby!" soared over the footlights. . . . Ah, I was forgetting Mr. Chips.

Edward Weeks. "The Bookshelf." *Atlantic* 159 (April 1937): 14, 16 at back of issue.

Since the death of Ring Lardner, an element once characteristic of American fiction has been conspicuous by its absence: laughter. The short stories and the novels of our younger writers are so often pervaded by a humorless intensity or by an irony and didacticism that leave the reader cold. Now from California comes a novelist with a better balance, a shrewder skill, a more native sense of reality. His name is John Steinbeck: he has five novels to his credit. Farsighted reviewers began to spot him three years ago; the reading public, slower with its recognition, will now hurry to make amends.

John Steinbeck must have footed his way through that California which is neither movies nor real estate. He knows the wanderers—the fruit pickers, the ranch hands, the hoboes; he knows this migratory race—its pride, its humor, its gullibility and futility. New Steinbeck readers might follow this programme: first, *Tortilla Flat*, light-hearted, wholly delightful; next, *In Dubious Battle*, which, partisan though it be, is quite our most vital story of an American strike; and so coming down to his *Of Mice and Men* . . . ?, a short tale of two harvest hands, the one a slow-witted elephant, the other a ferret. You feel the affection that binds Lennie and George together. You hear talk as natural as grass. You recognize in them a hunger which moves all men. There are moments when the tension and brevity of the story make it read like a theatrical script. I mean Slim's authority and Candy's dog mean more to me than the drama in the barn or at the pool. But, whatever be your favorite passages, here is indispensable proof of a vital and experienced story-teller.

"Dorothea Brande Doesn't Enjoy Steinbeck." *Charlotte [NC] News*, 6 June 1937: 9A.

In the same measure that John Steinbeck's *Of Mice and Men* gave pleasure to many readers, so it outraged the critical sensibilities of two reviewers—Mark van Doren and Dorothea Brande Collins. Professor van Doren was dreadfully put out by its profanity, which suggests that he is the Rip Van Winkle of our times. Mrs. Collins (the author of *Becoming a Writer*, which tells how to make your unconscious do the work) decided that the story was so obvious that it bowled over only critics who were boys at heart.

Commenting in the *American Review*, she says the secret of Steinbeck's success is "that a certain simple type of reader feels, when he has foreseen correctly any movement of a story, a kind of participation in the creative act of the author. . . . If Lennie kills a mouse by stroking it, you may be sure he will unintentionally kill something larger in the same way; when you hear of Curley's wife's soft hair 'like fur,' you can begin to co-operate with the author by expectation of her end."

Mrs. Collins evidently feels that in saying that the author meets the expectations of the readers she has dealt his story a body blow. As a matter of fact, she has merely expressed her dislike for a technique that is one of many employed by writers; her interests are intellectual. And her concern with the novel is chiefly as an exercise for the mind. This is a high form of artistic appreciation and expression, but by no means the only one. What counts in *Of Mice and Men* is that the author meets the expectations of his readers (women as well as the stag line) a bit more successfully than many other workers in his medium.

Harold Brighouse. "New Novels: Archers of the Long Bow." *Manchester Guardian*, 14 September 1937: 5.

In [Wallace Stegner's] *Remembering Laughter* the farm and the landscape are realized without sentimentality. Mr. Steinbeck, in *Of Mice and Men*, is both melodramatic and sentimental. Assume that there is love between a performing bear and its keeper; the bear hugs a woman to death and the keeper has to shoot it. For "bear" read Lennie, a giant of a man mentally defective, and for "keeper" read George. They came, partners, through the Californian woods to a farming ranch, and George's dream was to save wages till they could own land of their own. There is an incident, made significant, of the shooting of a sheepdog, stinking in useless old age, and insistence upon Lennie's passion for stroking mice and rabbits till his brutish affection killed them. So it was that he stroked the red hair, and she not unwilling, of the raffish wife of the rancher's son, and, stroking, killed her. It is a pitiful tragedy amongst people the brightest of whom is hardly more than half-witted, and the publisher is rhapsodical about it. Personally I think Mr. Steinbeck has done better work than this.

V. S. Pritchett. "New Novels." *New Statesman and Nation* [England] 14 (25 September 1937): 48–49.

Of Mice and Men is decidedly surprising and queer. It is the story of two casuals who run out of one job into the next. One is a huge half-wit with a grip like a vice and a brain like a pea. He has a sinister mania for touching things mice, puppies, velvet, girls' hair and sometimes he strokes too hard; the other is a dogged little chap who "travels around" with him and tries in vain to help the soft-headed, hard-handed fellow out of trouble. The feeble talk of cowboys, their pathetic hopes and affections, their childish preoccupations, are perfectly recorded. The American underdog has provided Mr. Steinbeck with some macabre material. The reader must not be put off the book by its awful jacket and its pointless illustrations.

"Of Mice and Men." London Mercury 36 (October 1937): 595.

Mr. Steinbeck's tale of two drifting cattle-ranch hands, Lennie, the "natural" and George, his devoted protector, is an extremely skilful variant of the tough tabloid. The companions have an escape-story of a place of their own with cows and rabbits where they will live "off the fatta of the lan'," which George tells Lennie on their long tramps from job to job. Lennie's daftness takes the form of killing small, soft things, including women. The final scene, in which George, preparing to shoot his friend to save him from being lynched, tells the little story for the last time, is a triumph of the sentimental macabre.

"Of Mice and Men." Times Literary Supplement [London], 2 October 1937: 714.

This is a moving story of two drifting cattle-ranch hands in California. George and Lennie are friends, owning nothing but what they pack from one job to the next. But they are optimists. The dream that buoys and binds them is of the bit of land they are going to buy—some day. The vision comes excitingly near, then vanishes.

The disaster is inherent in Lennie's nature. A phenomenal worker but a wantwit, he is pathetically incapable of looking after himself, or even of controlling his huge body. George, small, active, querulous, is incessantly watchful over his infantile friend and liability. They have been chased from their last job because Lennie innocently touched a girl's red dress. Now a promising fresh start offers on another ranch. But when the wanton wife of the owner's unpleasant son makes up to Lennie, he shakes her, not in anger but in fear of George's wrath, and finds he has killed her. He acts on George's standing instruction that in event of trouble he is to hide by the river. The lynchers go in pursuit. But George, with a stolen pistol, reaches Lennie first and deals quick death, the best that could come to his friend. It is a tremendous climax to a short tale of much power and beauty. Mr. Steinbeck has contributed a small masterpiece to the modern tough-tender school of American fiction.

Additional Reviews

Joseph Henry Jackson. "A Bookman's Notebook." *San Francisco Chronicle*, 6 February 1937: 13.

"Friendship." *Newsweek* 9 (27 February 1937): 38–39.

"A Tender, Touching Tale Admirably Told." *Chicago Tribune*, 27 February 1937: 11.

Walter Sidney. "Treacle from a Talent." *Brooklyn Eagle*, 28 February 1937: Section C, 17.

Harry Hansen. "Critic Hails John Steinbeck Story as Finest Bit of Fiction in Decade." *Pittsburgh Press*, March 1937: Society section, 14.

Sterling North. "Blessed Are the Meek Portrayed by John Steinbeck." *Chicago Daily News*, 3 March 1937: 31.

Somerset Maugham. "H .G. Wells and John Steinbeck." *Philadelphia Inquirer*, 6 March 1937: L4.

Russell Smith. "Steinbeck Humanizes Statistics." *Washington Post*, 7 March 1937: 8.

Joseph Henry Jackson. "John Steinbeck: A Portrait." *Saturday Review* 16 (25 September 1937): 11–12, 18.

James Newcomer. "Reappraisals IV: Steinbeck's *Mice and Men*." *Dallas News*, 14 August 1949: 32.

Note

1. This quote combines speeches by both Lennie and George. The critic mistakenly elides them.

Part Two
THE 1940s AND 1950s

axwell Geismar in *American Moderns, from Rebellion to Confor-
mity* (New York: Hill and Wang, 1958) was similarly dismissive of the novel, criticizing the lack of freewill demonstrated
by Steinbeck's protagonists—Lennie Small and George Milton. His
reflections suggested that the pair are more animal-like than human and
that the author's talent is questionable at best.

Albert Kazin's *On Native Grounds* (New York: Reynal and Hitchcock,
1942) continued the tendency of finding *Of Mice and Men* to be somewhat
inferior because of its popular appeal and the broad reading public it at-
tracted. Kazin concluded that the book's calculated sentimentality created
a far too general appeal for it to be considered a piece of "fine" literature.
Instead, it seemed designed for simplistic rather than mature readers.

E. W. Tedlock Jr. and C. V. Wicker's *Steinbeck and His Critics: A
Record of Twenty-five Years* appeared in 1957 (Albuquerque: University of
New Mexico Press) and called into question the assumptions of Steinbeck's
earlier critics, especially those who were critical of Steinbeck because they
felt his philosophy was not compatible with theirs; Tedlock and Wicker also
defended the author against charges of sentimentality and reprinted essays
that were to become classic commentaries on the Steinbeck canon.

The first full-fledged defense of Steinbeck's work both stylistically
and thematically had to wait until 1958 and the publication of Peter
Lisca's *The Wide World of John Steinbeck* (New Brunswick, NJ: Rutgers
University Press). Lisca's assessment of *Of Mice and Men* in particular
set the stage for future emphases by calling attention to what he labels

the previous myopic observations about the text and by discussing the author's employment of symbolic settings, his use of animal imagery, and his ability to design unique and creative figurative language to describe his characters and to further his plotline.

Other Significant Studies from the 1940s–1950s

Beach, Joseph Warren. "John Steinbeck: Journeyman Artist." In *American Fiction, 1920–1940*, 309–47. New York: Macmillan, 1941 [reprinted in Tedlock and Wicker, *Steinbeck and His Critics*, 80–81 and in Jill Karson (San Diego: Greenhaven Press, 1996), 90 ff].

This essay praises Steinbeck's skill as a storyteller and his versatility, objectivity, and diversification. Specifically calling attention to his depiction of human nature as fresh, direct and authentic (comparable to de Maupassant), Beach then goes on to single out *Of Mice and Men* for the beauty depicted in its tragic story line and the essential decency and pathos shown by George and Lennie.

Gibbs, Lincoln. "John Steinbeck, Moralist." *Antioch Review* 2 (June 1942): 172–84 [reprinted in Tedlock and Wicker, *Steinbeck and His Critics*, 92–103].

Gibbs praises Steinbeck for advocating social reform and confronting the vulgar and uncouth facts of life in concrete detail. Consequently, he posits that Steinbeck's readers will need tolerance (a good heart and strong stomach) to confront the author's realistic portraits. Labeling Steinbeck as a noncritical humanist, Gibbs praises him for penetrating the hearts of his most disrespectable characters like migrant laborers and underprivileged social classes, thus enabling readers to understand that often misrepresented "others" are not unlike themselves.

Burgum, Edwin Berry. "The Sensibility of John Steinbeck." *Science and Society* 10 (Spring 1946): 132–47 [reprinted in Tedlock and Wicker, *Steinbeck and His Critics*: 104–18].

In this article, Burgum explores John Steinbeck's attitude toward the poor, a class of people who had captured the attention of American novelists in the 1930s. Burgum found that Steinbeck presents a wide range of attitudes toward poor workers and vagabonds throughout his many novels. In the novel *Of Mice and Men*, Steinbeck creates characters that evoke complex sociological attitudes—some defined, some ambiguous—regarding the underprivileged. Burgum suggests that Steinbeck leaves the reader pondering at the end of the story, unclear about what attitude to take toward the moral dilemma surrounding Lennie and George.

Kennedy, John. "Life Affirmed and Dissolved." In *Fifty Years of The American Novel*, ed. Harold Gardiner, 217–36. New York: Scribner's, 1951 [reprinted in Tedlock and Wicker, *Steinbeck and His Critics*, 119–34].

This essay suggests that Steinbeck does not fit into categories of negativism so prevalent among other modern writers. While the author depicts human existence as unremitting conflict and a savage battle, he also emphasizes that life is worth living (baffling though it may be) by asserting the resiliency and tough durability of his characters.

Lisca, Peter. "Motif and Pattern in *Of Mice and Men*." *Modern Fiction Studies* 2 (Winter 1956): 228–34.

CHAPTER TWO

THE WIDE WORLD OF JOHN STEINBECK, CHAPTER 8

Peter Lisca

Although *Of Mice and Men* appeared almost exactly one year after *In Dubious Battle*, two years had elapsed since the strike novel had been completed. The delay this time, however, was not in publication. Covici-Friede received the completed manuscript in September of 1936, and *Of Mice and Men* was published in February of the following year. Steinbeck had hardly finished the final draft of *In Dubious Battle* when he wrote to his agents, "I'm doing a play now. I don't know what will come of it. If I can do it well enough, it will be a good play. I mean the theme is swell" (JS-MO, ca. February, 1935).

While this reference to "a play" probably indicates that *Of Mice and Men* was in progress two years before its publication, Steinbeck was doing so many other things during this time that attention to the new work must have been sporadic. . . . Despite these interruptions, however, *Of Mice and Men* was pretty well along by April [of 1936], when Steinbeck wrote he was working very hard on the new novel, and again that he had "struck a snag" in the new work (JS-MO, 4/15/36; 4/20/36). In May, . . . he underwent a baptism which many authors have undergone at some time or other. "Minor tragedy stalked," he wrote. "My setter pup, left alone one night, made confetti of about half of my manuscript book. Two months work to do over again. It sets me back. There was no other draft. I was pretty mad, but the poor little fellow may have been acting critically.

I didn't want to ruin a good dog for a manuscript I'm not sure is good at all. He only got an ordinary spanking" (JS-MO, 5/27/36). It was not until late in August Steinbeck finished the job of rewriting.[1]

Steinbeck's growing reputation and the publishers' promotion created an eager market for *Of Mice and Men* even before the book appeared. . . . On the eve of publication, he wrote: "I wish I could be personally elated about all the fuss but I can't. The book isn't that good. It's just one of these crazy streams starting. . . . But as for the unpredictable literary enthusiasms of this country—I have little faith in them" (JS-MO, 2/12/37). This opinion that "The book isn't that good" is repeated in an article which Steinbeck wrote for *Stage* just before *Of Mice and Men's* Broadway première, but after it had been performed directly from the book by the San Francisco labor-theater group; "The book *Of Mice and Men* was an experiment and, in what it set out to do, it was a failure."[2]

Since, in this article and elsewhere, Steinbeck is explicit about what the book "set out to do," it may be well to examine these intentions before undertaking a critical analysis of the work itself. Steinbeck's remarks on technique are particularly pertinent because *Of Mice and Men* was the first of four attempts (to date) in the play-novelette form, the beginnings of which can be seen in some chapters of *In Dubious Battle*.

As set forth in the *Stage* article, Steinbeck's intention was to write a play "in the physical technique of the novel." This technique was to offer certain advantages. First, "it would go a great way towards making the play easy to read [avoiding awkward and interrupting stage directions]". Second, "the novel's ability to describe scene and people in detail would not only make for a better visual picture to the reader, but would be of value to the director, stage designer, and actor . . ." Third, "it would be possible for the playwright by this method to set his tone much more powerfully. . . . And this tone is vastly important." While these advantages would accrue to the play, "the novel itself would be interfered with by such a method in only one way, and that is that it would be short." But several advantages for the novel would result. For one thing, "the necessity of sticking to the theme (in fact of knowing what the theme is), the brevity and necessity of holding an audience could influence the novel only for the better." In a play, "wandering, discussion, and essay are impossible." There is another advantage for the novel which can be "played," one related to Steinbeck's group-man theories: "For whatever reasons . . . the recent tendency of writers has been to deal in those themes and those scenes which are best understood and appreciated by groups of people." Some things (such as war, prize fights on the radio) "cannot be understood in solitude . . . the thing that is missing is the close, almost physical contact with other people."

So much for the technique. Concerning the book's theme, Steinbeck wrote his agents,

> I'm sorry that you do not find this new book as large in subject as it should be. I probably did not make my subjects and my symbols clear. The microcosm is rather difficult to handle, and apparently I did not represent insanity at all but the inarticulate and powerful yearning of all men. Well, if it isn't here it isn't there. (JS-MO, 9/1/36)

To Ben Abramson, he wrote a similar comment on the book's theme: ". . . it's a study of the dreams and pleasures of everyone in the world" (JS-BA, ca. September, 1936).

Such words as "microcosm," "of all men," and "everyone in the world" indicate that the problem he set himself in *Of Mice and Men* was similar to that he had solved in his previous novel, *In Dubious Battle*. But whereas in the earlier work the de-personalized protagonists were easily absorbed into a greater pattern because that pattern was physically present in the novel, in *Of Mice and Men* protagonists are projected against a very thin background and must suggest or create this larger pattern through their own particularity. To achieve this, Steinbeck makes use of language, action, and symbol as recurring motifs. All three of these motifs are presented in the opening scene, are contrapuntally developed through the story and come together again at the end.

The first symbol in the novel, and the primary one, is the little spot by the river where the story begins and ends. The book opens with a description of this place by the river, and we first see George and Lennie as they enter this place from the highway to an outside world. It is significant that they prefer spending the night here rather than going on to the bunkhouse at the ranch.

Steinbeck's novels and stories often contain groves, willow thickets by a river, and caves which figure prominently in the action. . . . For George and Lennie, as for other Steinbeck heroes, coming to a cave or thicket by the river symbolizes a retreat from the world to a primeval innocence. Sometimes, as in *The Grapes of Wrath*, this retreat is explicit overtones of a return to the womb and rebirth. In the opening scenes of *Of Mice and Men*, Lennie twice mentions the possibility of hiding out in a cave, and George impresses on him that he must return to this thicket by the river when there is trouble.

While the cave or the river thicket is a "safe place," it is physically impossible to remain there, and this symbol of primeval innocence becomes translated into terms possible in the real world. For George and Lennie, it becomes "a little house an' a couple of acres" (*OMM* 14). Out of this translation grows a second symbol, the rabbits, and this symbol serves several purposes. Through synecdoche, it comes to stand for the "safe place" itself, making a much more easily manipulated symbol than the "house an' a couple of acres." Also, through Lennie's love for the rabbits, Steinbeck is able not only to dramatize Lennie's desire for the "safe place," but to define the basis of that desire on a very low level of consciousness—the attraction to soft, warm fur, which is for Lennie the most important aspect of their plans.

The transference of symbolic value from the farm to the rabbits is important also because it makes possible the motif of action. This is introduced in the first scene by the dead mouse which Lennie is carrying in his pocket. . . . As George talks about Lennie's attraction to mice, it becomes evident that the symbolic rabbits will come to the same end—crushed by Lennie's simple blundering strength. Thus Lennie's killing of mice later and his killing of the puppy set up a pattern which the reader expects to be carried out again. George's story about Lennie and the girl with the red dress, which he tells twice, contributes to this expectancy of patterns, as do the shooting of Candy's dog, the crushing of Curley's hand, the frequent appearances of Curley's wife. All these incidents are patterns of the action motif and predict the fate of the rabbits and thus the fate of the dream of a "safe place."

The third motif, that of language, is also present in the opening scene. Lennie asks George, "Tell me—like you done before" (*OMM* 13), and George's voice became deeper. He repeated his words rhythmically, as though he had said them many times before." The element of ritual is stressed by the fact that even Lennie heard it often enough to remember its precise language: "*An' live off the fatta the lan'*. . . . An' have *rabbits*. Go on George! Tell about what we're gonna have in the garden and about the rabbits in the cages and about" (*OMM* 14). This ritual is performed often in the story, whenever Lennie feels insecure. And, of course, it is while Lennie is caught up in this dream vision that George shoots him, so that on one level the vision is accomplished—the dream never interrupted, the rabbits never crushed.

The highly patterned effect achieved by these incremental motifs of symbol, action, and language is the knife edge on which criticism of *Of Mice and Men* divides. For although Steinbeck's success in creating a pattern has been acknowledged, criticism has been divided as to the effect of this achievement. On one side, it is claimed that this strong patterning creates a sense of contrivance and mechanical action,[3] and, on the other, that the patterning actually gives a meaningful design to the story, a tone of classical fate.[4] What is obviously needed here is some objective critical tool for determining under what conditions a sense of inevitability (to use a neutral word) should be experienced as catharsis effected by a sense of fate. Such a tool cannot be forged within the limits of this study; but it is possible to examine the particular circumstances of *Of Mice and Men* more closely before passing judgment.

Although the three motifs of symbol, action, and language build up a strong pattern of inevitability, the movement is not unbroken. About midway in the novel (chapters 3 and 4), there is a countermovement which seems to threaten the pattern. Up to this point, the dream of "a house an' a couple of acres" seemed impossible to realization. Now it develops that George has an actual farm in mind (ten acres), knows the owners and why they want to sell it: "The ol' people that owns it is flat bust an' the ol' lady needs an operation." He even knows the price—"six hundred dollars" (*OMM* 59). Also, the old workman, Candy, is willing to buy a share in the dream with the three hundred dollars he has saved up. It appears that at the end of the month George and Lennie will have another hundred dollars and that quite possibly they "could swing her for that." In the following chapter this dream and its possibilities are further explored through Lennie's visit with Crooks, the power of the dream manifesting itself in Crooks's conversion from cynicism to optimism. But at the very height of his conversion, the mice symbol reappears in the form of Curley's wife, who threatens the dream by bringing with her the harsh realities of the outside world and by arousing Lennie's interests.

The function of Candy's and Crooks's interest and the sudden bringing of the dream within reasonable possibility is to interrupt, momentarily, the pattern of inevitability. But, and this is very important, Steinbeck handles the interruption so that it does not actually reverse the situation. Rather, it insinuates a possibility. Thus, though working against the pattern, this countermovement makes the pattern more credible by creating the necessary ingredient of free will. The story achieves power through a delicate balance of the protagonists' free will and the force of circumstance.

In addition to imposing a sense of inevitability, this strong patterning of events performs the important function of extending the story's range of meanings. This can best be understood by reference to Hemingway's "fourth dimension," which has been defined by Joseph Warren Beach as an "aesthetic factor" achieved by the protagonists' repeated participation in some traditional "ritual or strategy,"[5] and by Malcolm Cowley as "the almost continual per-formance of rites and ceremonies" suggesting recurrent patterns of human experience.[6] The incremental motifs of symbol, action, and language which inform *Of Mice and Men* have precisely these effects. The simple story of two migrant workers' dream of a safe retreat, a "clean well-lighted place," becomes itself a pattern or archetype which exists on three levels.

There is the obvious story level on a realistic plane, with its shocking climax. There is also the level of social protest, Steinbeck the reformer crying out against the exploitation of migrant workers. The third level is an allegorical one, its interpretation limited only by the ingenuity of the audience. It could be, as Carlos Baker suggests, "an allegory of Mind and Body."[7] Using the same kind of dichotomy, the story could also be about the dumb, clumsy, but strong mass of humanity and its shrewd manipulators. This would make the book a more abstract treatment of the two forces of *In Dubious Battle*—the mob and its leaders. The dichotomy could also be that of the unconscious and the conscious, the id and the ego, or any other forces or qualities which have the same structural relationship to each other that do Lennie and George. It is interesting in this connection that the name Leonard means "strong or brave as a lion," and that the name George means "husbandman."

The title itself, however, relates the whole story to still another level which is implicit in the context of Burns's poem.

But, Mousie, thou art no thy lane,
In proving foresight may be vain:
The best laid schemes o' mice and men
Gang aft a-gley
An' lea'e us nought but grief an' pain
For promis'd joy.

In the poem, Burns extends the mouse's experience to include that of mankind: in *Of Mice and Men*, Steinbeck extends the experience of two migrant workers to the human condition. "This is the way things are," both writers are saying. On this level, perhaps the most important, Steinbeck is dramatizing the non-teleological philosophy which had such a great part in shaping *In Dubious Battle* and which would be fully discussed in *Sea of Cortez*. This level of meaning is indicated by the title originally intended for the book—"Something That Happened."[8] In this light, the ending of the story is, like the ploughman's disrupting of the mouse's nest, neither tragic nor brutal, but simply a part of the pattern of events. . . . In addition to these meanings which grow out of the book's "pattern," there is what might be termed a subplot which defines George's concern with Lennie. It is easily perceived that George, the "husbandman," is necessary to Lennie; but it has not been pointed out that Lennie is just as necessary to George. Without an explanation of this latter relationship, any allegory posited on the pattern created in *Of Mice and Men* must remain incomplete. Repeatedly, George tells Lennie, "God, you're a lot of trouble. I could get along so easy and so nice if I didn't have you on my tail" (*OMM* 7). But this getting along so easy never means getting a farm of his own. With one important exception, George never mentions the dream except for Lennie's benefit. That his own "dream" is quite different from Lennie's is established early in the novel and often repeated:

God a'mighty, if I was alone I could live so easy. I could go get a job an' work, an' no trouble. No mess at all, and when the end of the month come I could take my fifty bucks and go into town and get whatever I want. Why, I could stay in a cat house all night. I could eat any place I want, hotel or anyplace, and order any damn thing I could think of. An' I could do all that every damn month. Get a gallon whiskey, or set in a pool room and play cards or shoot pool. (*OMM* 11)

Lennie has heard this from George so often that in the last scene, when he realizes that he has "done another bad thing," he asks, "Ain't you gonna give me hell? . . . Like, 'If I didn't have you I'd take my fifty bucks—'" (*OMM* 103).

Almost every character in the story asks George why he goes around with Lennie—the foreman, Curley, Slim, and Candy. Crooks, the lonely Negro, doesn't ask George, but he does speculate about it, and shrewdly—"a guy talkin' to another guy and it don't make no difference if he don't hear or understand. The thing is, they're talkin'. . ." (*OMM* 71). George's explanations vary from outright lies to a simple statement of "We travel together." It is only to Slim, the superior workman with "God-like eyes," that he tells a great part of the truth. Among several reasons, such as his feeling of responsibility for Lennie in return for the latter's unfailing loyalty, and their having grown up together, there is revealed another:

> He's dumb as hell, but he ain't crazy. An' I ain't so bright neither, or I wouldn't be buckin' barley for my fifty and found. If I was even a little bit smart, I'd have my own little place, an' I'd be bringin' in my own crops, 'stead of doin' all the work and not getting what comes up outa the ground. (*OMM* 39)

This statement, together with George's repeatedly expressed desire to take his fifty bucks to a cat house and his continual playing of solitaire, reveals that to some extent George needs Lennie as a rationalization for his failure. This is one of the reasons why, after the body of Curley's wife is discovered, George refuses Candy's offer of a partnership which would make the dream a reality and says to him, "I'll work my month an' I'll take my fifty bucks an' I'll stay all night in some lousy cat house. Or I'll set in some poolroom till ever'body goes home. An' then I'll come back an' work another month an' I'll have fifty bucks more" (*OMM* 95). The dream of the farm originates with Lennie, and it is only through Lennie, who also makes the dream impossible, that the dream has any meaning for George. An understanding of this dual relationship will do much to mitigate the frequent charge that Steinbeck's depiction of George's attachment is concocted of pure sentimentality. At the end of the novel, George's going off with Slim to "do the town" is more than an escape from grief. It is an ironic and symbolic twist to his dream.

The "real" meaning of the book is neither in the realistic action nor in the levels of allegory. Nor is it in some middle course. Rather, it is in the pattern which informs the story both on the realistic and the allegorical levels, a pattern which Steinbeck took pains to prevent from becoming either trite or mechanical.

But whether because of its realism, its allegory, or its pattern, *Of Mice and Men* was an immediate popular success. It appeared on the best-seller lists, was a Book-of-the-Month Club selection, and was sold to Hollywood. . . . Before leaving on a trip [to Europe], Steinbeck had been working on a dramatization of *Of Mice and Men*, and on his return to New York early in August (aboard another freighter) he stayed at George Kaufman's farm in Buck's County, Pennsylvania, and with some advice from Kaufman, who was to direct it, finished the final version of the play. *Of Mice and Men* opened on November 23, 1937, on the stage of the Music Box Theatre in New York and won great critical and popular acclaim. Upon completing the stage version, and not even waiting for the play to be produced, he went to Detroit, bought a car, and, after visiting Ben Abramson in Chicago, drove to Oklahoma. There he joined a group of migrant workers heading west, lived with them in their Hoovervilles, and worked with them when they got to California. He was already writing *The Grapes of Wrath*.

Notes

1. Harry Thornton Moore, *The Novels of John Steinbeck* (Chicago: Normandy House, 1939), 86. This source states that this incident did not occur "until after type had been set and proofs corrected," but this letter is explicit about there being "no other draft" and there being "two months work to do over again." Moore's contention is disproved also by Steinbeck's letter of February 12. Some twenty years later, Steinbeck repeated the story about the pup and added, "I don't know how close the first and second versions would prove to be" (John Steinbeck, "My Short Novels," *Wings* [October 1953], 6).

2. John Steinbeck, *Stage* (January 1938): 50–51. "The novel might benefit by the discipline, the terseness . . ." Although this article was published while *Of Mice and Men* was on Broadway, the editors inform us that it had been submitted earlier.

3. Mark Van Doren, "Wrong Number," *The Nation* 144 (6 March 1937), 275; also Joseph Wood Krutch, *American Drama Since 1918* (New York: Random House, 1939), 396.

4. Stark Young, "Drama Critics Circle Award," *The New Republic* 94 (4 May 1938): 396; also Frank O'Hara. *Today in American Drama* (Chicago: University of Chicago Press, 1939), 181.

5. Joseph Warren Beach, "How Do You Like It Now, Gentlemen?" *Sewanee Review* 59 (Spring 1951), 311–28.

6. Malcolm Cowley, "Introduction," *The Portable Hemingway* (New York: Viking, 1944).

7. Carlos Baker, "Steinbeck of California," *Delphian Quarterly* 23 (April 1940): 42.

8. Toni Jackson Ricketts (Antonia Seixas), "John Steinbeck and the Non-Teleological Bus," *What's Doing on the Monterey Peninsula* 1 (March 1947). Also available in *Steinbeck and His Critics*. Ed. E. W. Tedlock and C. V. Wicker (Albuquerque: University of New Mexico Press, 1957), 275–80.

Part Three
THE 1960s AND 1970s

S uggesting both the allegorical and realistic nature of the novel, Lisca's praise no doubt influenced the next major Steinbeck study, Warren French's *John Steinbeck* (New York: Twayne), a work that appeared in 1961 as part of the Twayne United States Author Series. French eventually issued a second edition of his critique in 1975, and then updated his ideas in a 1994 Twayne title, *John Steinbeck's Fiction Revisited*. According to French, *Of Mice and Men* marks the end of the first period in Steinbeck's career as in its publication, the author not only achieved fame but also discovered a solid method for creating objective structured story telling and an ability to convey his message in a convincing contemporary setting. In each of his books, French identifies the Arthurian elements in the novel and their relation to the American Dream (Camelot/Avalon). Indeed, the chapter entitled "End of a Dream" suggests the lack of success in attaining the American Dream and elicits a compassionate reader empathy with the failure of those individuals who continue to hope they can attain the impossible. French calls *Of Mice and Men* an indication of Steinbeck's developing expertise and evidence of his mastery of the craft of writing. Citing all the characters who lose their hopes for a better life in the novel (including not only George and Lennie but also Crooks, Candy, and Curley's wife), he concentrates on the demise of the Ameircan Dream. Oddly, French also categorizes the novel as a dark comedy in which survival and acceptance of one's lot in life are key themes.

F. W. Watt's *John Steinbeck* (New York: Grove, 1962) offered a more negative view of the novel, suggesting its main theme is slender and that the character relationships are artificial and unlikely. In contrast, Joseph Fontenrose's *John Steinbeck: An Introduction and Interpretation* (New York: Barnes & Noble, 1963), presented a brief six-page analysis and stressed man's longing for the land as well as asserting that the book offers a parable of the human condition—the inevitable futility of all human plans (see the Robert Burns poem "To a Mouse" that Steinbeck alludes to in the title). Fontenrose also noted the contrasting nature of the bindlestiff's dreams: lasting satisfaction (land ownership) with temporary pleasure (the whorehouse, drinking, card playing) and independence/the simple life with cooperation/group identity. Fontenrose praises Steinbeck's use of myth, science, and secular religion while rejecting prescriptive moralism. He concludes that Steinbeck's later works are much less deserving of praise, an attitude that continued to serve as the norm for future critics who found that Steinbeck's novels were sadly inconsistent in quality, especially as he began more experimentation in his work.

In direct contrast to Watt's 1962 dismissive analysis was William Goldhurst's groundbreaking study ("John Steinbeck's Parable of the Curse of Cain," *Western American Literature* 6 [1971]: 123–35), which drew a clear parallel between Steinbeck's story line and the Biblical myth of Cain and Abel and the question of whether we are indeed our brother's keeper. Goldhurst's essay was followed in 1973 by Richard Astro's discussion of the novel in *Steinbeck and Ricketts: The Shaping of a Novelist* (Corvallis: University of Oregon Press) which was broader based in its compliments, stressing the author's delicate handling of many fictional elements rather than concentrating on one element of thematic excellence.

Thematic Design in the Novels of John Steinbeck by Lester Jay Marks was the next full-length appraisal of the author's work (The Hague: Mouton, 1969) that identifies three thematic patterns that seem to reoccur consistently in Steinbeck's work. These include religiosity, group action, and non-teleological thinking, and his study seemed to bring fresh air to Steinbeck studies, invigorating and encouraging new approaches to the author's work.

In *Steinbeck: A Collection of Critical Essays* (Englewood Cliffs, NJ: Prentice-Hall, 1972), Robert Murray Davis seems to agree with earlier critics that much of what Steinbeck wrote after 1947 is negligible and indeed is stillborn, flawed in the strained quality of its prose; despite including essays that defend Steinbeck, Davis suggests that the author's work after this date is marginal at best.

Shortly thereafter, Howard Levant's book-length study, *The Novels of John Steinbeck*, was published by Missouri University Press in 1974. More a structural critique than a thematic analysis, Levant's critical assessment suggests that *Of Mice and Men*'s primary defect was that its simple plotline leads to a melodramatic rather than tragic ending, an observation that echoed Geismar's early reaction in the 1930s. Moreover, Levant suggests that *Mice* lacked a depth and breadth of insight. Calling Lennie a powerful semi-idiot, Levant sees his character as a reduction of humanity to its lowest common denominator, a perception which gels with the naturalist and fatalistic early readings of the novel. Levant also accuses Steinbeck of not fleshing out characters' traits and of relying on stereotypes; moreover, he blames the author for overworking such techniques as foreshadowing and for fostering a theme of unconventional morality that condones actions such as murder as "necessary evils." Such errors then resulted in an abrupt solution/ending to the plot. In conclusion, Levant finds the novel manipulative, and he laments the fact that Steinbeck's skill was directed toward such meaningless victims.

Other Significant Studies in the 1960s and 1970s

French, Warren. "End of a Dream." In *John Steinbeck*, chap. 7, 72–79. New York: Twayne, 1961.
Ganapathy, R. "Steinbeck's *Of Mice and Men*: A Study of Lyricism through Primitivism." *Literary Criterion* 5 (Winter 1962): 101–4.
    Ganapathy sees *Of Mice and Men* as reflecting influences by Wordsworth, romanticism, and the lyrical ballads and of espousing the theme of the noble savage and utilizing rhythmic colloquialisms as Wordsworth did.
Lisca, Peter. "Escape and Commitment: Two Poles of the Steinbeck Hero." In *Steinbeck: The Man and His Work*, ed. Richard Astro and Tetsumaro Hayashi, 75–88. Corvallis: University of Oregon Press, 1970.
Gray, James. *John Steinbeck*. Minneapolis: University of Minnesota Press, 1971. [University of Minnesota Pamphlets on American Writers No. 94]
Gurko, Leo. "*Of Mice and Men*: Steinbeck as Manichean." *U Windsor Review* [Canada] 8 (Spring 1973): 11–23 [reprinted in Jill Karson, *Readings on Of Mice and Men* (San Diego: Greenhaven, 1996): 59–69].

This essay portrays the novel as a dark parable equally matching goodness, God, light, and soul with evil, Satan, darkness, and body. George is depicted as mind and light while Lennie is body and darkness. Since they are opposing forces, their conflict is inevitable and will result in the death of one and the victory of the other

Dacus, Lee. "Lennie as Christian in *Of Mice and Men*." *Southwestern American Literature* 4 (1974): 87–91 [reprinted in Karson, *Readings on Of Mice and Men*, 80–85].

This article compares Lennie's dream of rabbits to a Christian's dream of heaven and portrays George as a Christ figure or "good shepherd" and Curley as satanic. Much of the analogies drawn are forced rather than probable].

Bellman, Samuel I. "Control and Freedom in Steinbeck's *Of Mice and Men*." *CEA Critic* 38 (November 1975): 25–27 [reprinted in Karson, *Readings on Of Mice and Men*].

This is a psychoanalytic study that views Lennie as George's id or subconscious and sees his influence as needing to be repressed. At times, according to this essay, Lennie is also a super-ego or conscience for George. Slim replaces Lennie as George's control mechanism.

Lisca, Peter. "*Of Mice and Men*." In *John Steinbeck: Nature and Myth*, 76–86. New York: Thomas Y. Crowell, 1978.

Beatty, Sandra. "Steinbeck's Play-Women: A Study of the Female Presence in *Of Mice and Men, Burning Bright, The Moon Is Down* and *Viva Zapata!*" In *Steinbeck's Women: Essays in Criticism*, ed. Tetsumaro Hayashi, 7–16. Muncie, IN: Ball State University, 1979.

Kiernan, Thomas. "Chapter Nineteen" in *The Intricate Music*, 211–22. Boston: Little Brown, 1979.

Jain, Sunita. "*Evil in Of Mice and Men*." In *Steinbeck's Concept of Man: A Critical Study of His Novels*. New Delhi, India: New Statesman Publishing, 1979 [reprinted in Harold Bloom, *John Steinbeck's* Of Mice and Men (Broomall, PA: Chelsea House, 1999), 47 ff].

CHAPTER THREE
JOHN STEINBECK'S PARABLE OF THE CURSE OF CAIN
William Goldhurst

ritical opinion on John Steinbeck's *Of Mice and Men* is surprisingly varied, miscellaneous, and contradictory. One critic calls the novella a dark comedy and says that it descends from myths of King Arthur. Other critics think of it as a tragedy, and at least one advances the idea that it has no mythic background at all. A few commentators feel very definitely that *Of Mice and Men* is political in its drift, that it illustrates "tensions created by the capitalistic system" or dramatizes "the role of the radical organizer attempting to lead the masses towards a workmen's utopia." Others contend that it has little or no political content but rather stresses sociological points such as our unenlightened treatment of old people and the mentally retarded. Several other critics have observed that Steinbeck's story emphasizes a simple thesis, variously identified as (1) each man kills the thing he loves, (2) our pleasures often oppose and thwart our schemes, and (3) the non-morality of Nature. Basic differences of opinion may be illustrated by the comments of two well-known literary historians who sum up their reactions to the story in almost antithetical terms: Joseph Warren Beach stressed "the tone of humanity and beauty with which Steinbeck invests his tragic episode . . . without the use of sentimental phrase or direct statement," while Alfred Kazin spoke of "the calculated sentimentality

"*Of Mice and Men*: John Steinbeck's Parable of the Curse of Cain" by William Goldhurst. Reprinted by permission of *Western American Literature*, English Department, Utah State University, where the essay originally appeared in Volume 6 (1971), 123–135.

of *Of Mice and Men*" which makes Steinbeck's fable "meretricious in its pathos, a moment's gulp."[1]

Perhaps this diversity reflects the sort of critical individualism which Steinbeck had in mind when he said that many critics fall under the heading of "special pleaders [who] use my work as a distorted echo chamber for their own ideas."[2] Two significant points do emerge, in any case, from a consideration of this body of critical comment. First, it affirms and reaffirms the inherent fertility of Steinbeck's novella; already *Of Mice and Men* has furnished two generations of readers with material for intellectual sustenance. Second, and perhaps this is a bit unforeseen, no one of the critics, as I see it, has penetrated to the essential meaning which luxuriates under the surface of Steinbeck's story. . . . I ought to say at the outset that my emphasis is on the religious sources of *Of Mice and Men* and its mythic-allegorical implications.

Of Mice and Men is a short novel in six scenes presented in description dialogue-action form that approximates stage drama in its effect (about this fact there is no critical disagreement). The time scheme runs from Thursday evening through Sunday evening—exactly three days in sequence, a matter of some importance, as we shall see presently. The setting is the Salinas Valley in California, and most of the characters are unskilled migratory workers who drift about the villages and ranches of that area picking up odd jobs or doing short-term fieldwork and then moving on to the next place of employment. Steinbeck focuses on two such laborers who dream of one day saving up enough money to buy a small farm of their own. One of these is George Milton, small of stature, clever, sensitive, and compassionate; the other is Lennie Small, who is oversized, mentally retarded, enormously strong, and prone to getting into serious trouble. Early in the story, the prospect of their ever realizing their dream seems remote, but as the action develops (they meet a crippled bunkhouse worker who wants to go in with them on the scheme, and who offers to chip in his life savings), the probability of fulfillment increases. If the three homeless migrants pool their salaries at the end of the current month, they can quit and move on to their farm, which, as Steinbeck emphasizes repeatedly, is a place of abundance and a refuge from the hardships of life.

Lennie manages to avoid disaster for exactly three days. He gets involved, innocently at first, with the flirtatious wife of Curley, the boss's violent son; and through a series of unfortunate circumstances he becomes frightened and unintentionally kills the girl. Curley organizes a posse to apprehend Lennie—with the idea either of locking him up in an asylum or, more likely, of killing him on the spot. George gets to Lennie first and out of sympathy for his companion shoots him in the head to spare him the pain of Curley's shotgun or the misery of incarceration.

The title of the story has a twofold application and significance. First, it refers to naturalistic details within the texture of the novella: Lennie likes to catch mice and stroke their fur with his fingers. This is a particularly important point for two reasons: it establishes Lennie's fatal weakness for stroking soft things and, since he invariably kills the mice he is petting, it foreshadows his deadly encounter with Curley's wife. Second, the title is, of course, a fragment from the poem by Robert Burns, which gives emphasis to the idea of the futility of human endeavor or the vanity of human wishes. "The best laid schemes o' mice and men / Gang aft a-gley / An' lea' us nought but grief an' pain / For promised joy." This notion is obviously of major importance in the novella, and it may be said to be Steinbeck's main theme on the surface level of action and development of character.

Other noteworthy characters and incidents in *Of Mice and Men* include Crooks, the Negro stablehand who lives in the harness room. Here on one occasion he briefly entertains Lennie and Candy, the bunkhouse worker who wants to be a part of the dream farm. Crooks tells them they will never attain it; he says he has known many workers who wanted land of their own, but he has never heard of anyone who has actually realized this ambition. Then there is Carlson, the blunt and unfeeling ranch hand who insists on shooting Candy's aged sheep dog, which, having outlived its usefulness, has become an annoyance to the men who occupy the bunkhouse. This is a significant episode which anticipates George's mercy killing of Lennie at the conclusion. ("I ought to of shot that dog myself," says Candy later. "I shouldn't ought to of let no stranger shoot my dog" [*OMM* 61]). Steinbeck is also at some pains to establish an important aspect of the ranch workers' existence: their off-hours recreation, which consists of gambling, drinking, and visiting the local brothel. Upon such indulgences, which they find impossible to resist, these men squander their wages and thereby remain perpetually penniless, tied to a monotonous pattern of work, transitory pleasure, homelessness, and dependence upon job bosses for the basic needs of existence.

Of Mice and Men was published early in 1937 and was a Book-of-the-Month Club selection and one of the year's top best-sellers. . . . If my own high school experience was at all typical, spontaneous parodies of Lennie's speech and behavior were a common feature of adolescent get-togethers in the 1940s. But from that time to the present *Of Mice and Men* has been a favorite topic for serious discussion in college literature classes; and a sensitive television production in the late 1960s revealed new subtleties and power in the little tale which, critical controversy or no, has now assumed the status of an American classic.

Viewed in the light of its mythic and allegorical implications, *Of Mice and Men* is a story about the nature of man's fate in a fallen world, with particular emphasis upon the question: Is man destined to live alone, a solitary wanderer on the face of the earth, or is it the fate of man to care for man, to go his way in companionship with another? This is the same theme that occurs in the Old Testament, as early as chapter 4 of Genesis, immediately following the Creation and Expulsion. In effect, the question Steinbeck poses is the same question Cain poses to the Lord: "Am I my brother's keeper?" From its position in the scriptural version of human history, we may assume with the compilers of the early books of the Bible that it is the primary question concerning man as he is, after he has lost the innocence and non-being of Eden. It is the same question that Steinbeck chose as the theme of his later book *East of Eden* (1952), in which the Cain and Abel story is reenacted in a contemporary setting and where, for emphasis, Steinbeck has his main characters read the biblical story aloud and comment on it, climaxing the discussion with [Steinbeck's assertion that] "this is the best-known story in the world because it is everybody's story. I think it is the symbol story of the human soul." As an early Steinbeck variation on this symbolic story of the human soul, the implications of the Cain and Abel drama are everywhere apparent in the fable of George and Lennie and provide its mythic vehicle.

Contrary to the confident assertion in *EOE*, however, most people know the Cain and Abel story only in general outline. The details of the drama need to be filled in, particularly for the purpose of seeing how they apply to Steinbeck's novella. Cain was a farmer and Adam and Eve's firstborn son. His offerings of agricultural produce to the Lord failed to find favor, whereas the livestock offered by Cain's brother, Abel, was well received. Angry, jealous, and rejected, Cain killed Abel when they were working in the field, and when the Lord inquired of Cain, Where is your brother? Cain replied: "I know not: Am I my brother's keeper?" For his crime of homicide, the Lord banished Cain from his company and from the company of his parents and set upon him a particular curse, the essence of which was that Cain was to become homeless—a wanderer and an agricultural worker who would never possess or enjoy the fruits of his labor. Cain was afraid that other men would hear of his crime and try to kill him, but the Lord marked him in a certain way so as to preserve him from the wrath of others. Thus Cain left home and went to the land of Nod, which, the story tells us, lies east of Eden.

The drama of Cain finds its most relevant application in *Of Mice and Men* in the relationship between Lennie and George, and in the other characters' reactions to their association. In the first of his six scenes, Steinbeck establishes the two ideas that will be developed throughout. The first of these is the affectionate symbiosis of the two protagonists, their brotherly mutual concern and faithful companionship. Steinbeck stresses the beauty, joy, security, and comfort these two derive from the relationship:

> "If them other guys gets in jail they can rot for all anybody gives a damn. But not us."
>   Lennie broke in, "But not us! An' why? Because . . . because I got you to look after me and you got me to look after you, and that's why." He laughed delightedly. (*OMM* 14)

The second idea, which is given equal emphasis, is the fact that this sort of camaraderie is rare, different, almost unique in the world George and Lennie inhabit; other men, in contrast to these two, are solitary souls without friends or companions. As George says in scene 1:

> Guys like us, that work on ranches, are the loneliest guys in the world. They got no family. They don't belong no place. They come to a ranch an' work up a stake and then they go into town and blow their stakes, and the first thing you know they're poundin' their tail on some other ranch. (*OMM* 13)

The alternative to the George-Lennie companionship is Aloneness, made more dreadful by the addition of an economic futility that Steinbeck augments and reinforces in later sections. The migratory ranch worker, in other words, is the fulfillment of the Lord's curse on Cain: "When thou tillest the ground, it shall not henceforth yield unto thee her strength; a fugitive and vagabond shalt thou be in the earth" [Genesis 4:12]. Steinbeck's treatment of the theme is entirely free from a sense of contrivance; all the details in *Of Mice and Men* seem natural in the context and organically related to the whole; but note that in addition to presenting Lennie and George as men who till the ground and derive no benefits from their labor, he also manages to have them "on the run" when they are introduced in the first scene—this no doubt to have his main characters correspond as closely as possible to the biblical passage: "a fugitive and a vagabond shalt thou be . . ."

To the calamity of homelessness and economic futility, Steinbeck later adds the psychological soul corruption that is the consequence of solitary existence. In scene 3, George tells Slim, the mule driver on the ranch:

> "I seen the guys that go around on the ranches alone. That ain't no good. They don't have no fun. After a long time they get mean."
>
> "Yeah, they get mean," Slim agreed. "They get so they don't want to talk to nobody." (*OMM* 41)

Again, in scene 4, the Negro stable buck Crooks tells Lennie: "A guy needs somebody—to be near him. . . . A guy goes nuts if he ain't got nobody. Don't make no difference who the guy is, long's he's with you. I tell ya, I tell ya a guy gets too lonely and he gets sick." (*OMM* 72)

This is Steinbeck's portrait of Cain in the modern world, or Man Alone, whose fate is so severe that he may feel compelled to echo the words of Cain to the Lord: "My punishment is more than I can bear" [Genesis 4:13]. In *Of Mice and Men* Steinbeck gives us the case history of two simple mortals who try to escape the homelessness, economic futility, and psychological soul corruption which Scripture embodies in the curse of Cain.

If, in scene 1, Lennie and George affirm their fraternity openly and without embarrassment, in scene 2 George is more hesitant. "He's my . . . cousin," he tells the ranch boss. "I told his old lady I'd take care of him" (*OMM* 22). This is no betrayal on George's part, but a cover-up required by the circumstances. For the boss is highly suspicious of the Lennie-George fellowship. "You takin' his pay away from him?" he asks George. "I never seen one guy take so much trouble for another guy" (*OMM* 22). A short time later Curley also sounds the note of suspicion, extending it by a particularly nasty innuendo: when George says, "We travel together," Curley replies, "Oh, so it's that way" (*OMM* 25). Steinbeck is implying here the general response of most men toward seeing two individuals who buddy around together in a friendless world where isolation is the order of the day: there must be exploitation involved, either financial or sexual. At the same time Steinbeck is developing the allegorical level of his story by suggesting that the attitude of Cain ("I know not: Am I my brother's keeper?") has become universal.[3] Even the sympathetic and understanding Slim expresses some wonder at the Lennie-George fraternity. "Ain't many guys travel around together," Slim says in scene 2. "I don't know why. Maybe ever'body in the whole damned world is scared of each other" (*OMM* 35). This too, as Steinbeck interprets the biblical story, is a part of Cain's curse: distrust. Later on, in order to give the theme of Aloneness another dimension, Steinbeck stresses the solitude of Crooks and Curley's wife, both of whom express a craving for company and "someone to talk to."

Notwithstanding the fact that they are obviously swimming against the current, Lennie and George continue to reaffirm their solidarity all along, right up to and including the last moments of Lennie's life in scene 6. Here a big rabbit, which Lennie in his disturbed state of mind has hallucinated, tells the half-wit fugitive that George is sick of him and is going to go away and leave him. "He won't!" Lennie cries. "He won't do nothing like that. I know George. Me an' him travels together" (*OMM* 102).

Actually Steinbeck's novella advances and develops, ebbs and flows, around the basic image of the Lennie-George relationship. Almost all the characters react to it in one way or another as the successive scenes unfold. In scenes 1, 2, and 3, despite the discouraging opinions of outsiders, the companionship remains intact and unthreatened. Midway into scene 3 the partnership undergoes augmentation when Candy is admitted into the scheme to buy the little farm. Late in scene 4, Crooks offers himself as another candidate for the fellowship of soul brothers and dreamers. This is the high point of optimism as regards the main theme of the story; this is the moment when a possible reversal of the curse of Cain seems most likely, as Steinbeck suggests that the answer to the Lord's question might be, "Yes, I am my brother's keeper." If we arrive at this point with any comprehension of the author's purposes, we find ourselves brought up short by the idea: What if this George-Lennie-Candy-Crooks fraternity were to become universal?

But later in the same scene, the entrance of Curley's wife signals the turning point as the prospects for the idea of brotherhood-as-a-reality begin to fade and darken. As throughout the story she represents a force that destroys men and at the same time invites men to destroy her, as she will finally in scene 5 offer herself as a temptation which Lennie cannot resist, so, in scene 4, Curley's wife sows the seeds that eventually disrupt the fellowship. Entering into the discussion in Crooks's room in the stable, she insults Crooks, Candy, and Lennie, laughs at their dream farm, and threatens to invent the kind of accusation that will get Crooks lynched.[4] Crooks, reminded of his position of impotence in a white man's society, immediately withdraws his offer to participate in the George-Lennie-Candy farming enterprise. But Crooks's withdrawal, while extremely effective as social criticism, is much more. It represents an answer to the question Steinbeck is considering all along: Is man meant to make his way alone or accompanied? Obviously this is one occasion, among many others in the story, when Steinbeck suggests the answer. Crooks's hope for fraternal living is short-lived. At the conclusion of the scene, he sinks back into his Aloneness.

From this point on, even though the dream of fellowship on the farm remains active, the real prospects for its fulfillment decline drastically. In scene 5, after George and Candy discover the lifeless body of Curley's wife, they both face the realization that the little farm is now unattainable and the partnership dissolved. Actually, the plan was doomed to failure from the beginning; for fraternal living cannot long survive in a world dominated by the Aloneness, homelessness, and economic futility which Steinbeck presents as the modern counterpart of Cain's curse. Immediately following his discovery of Curley's wife's body, George delivers a speech that dwells on the worst possible aftermath of Lennie's misdeed; and this is not the wrath of Curley or the immolation of Lennie or the loss of the farm, but the prospect of George's becoming a Man Alone, homeless, like all the others and a victim as well of economic futility: "I'll work my month an' I'll take my fifty bucks and I'll stay all night in some lousy cat house. Or I'll set in some poolroom til ever'body goes home. An' then I'll come back an' work another month an' I'll have fifty bucks more" (*OMM* 95). This speech represents the true climax of the novella, for it answers the question that is Steinbeck's main interest throughout. Now we know the outcome of the Lennie-George experiment in fellowship, as we know the Aloneness of man's essential nature. In subtle ways, of course, Steinbeck has been hinting at this conclusion all along, as, for example, in the seven references spaced throughout scenes 2 and 3 to George's playing solitaire in the bunkhouse. For that matter, the answer is implied in the very first line of the story when the author establishes his setting "a few miles south of Soledad . . ." (*OMM* 1), Soledad being at one and the same time a town in central California and the Spanish word for solitude, or aloneness.

But there are still other suggested meanings inherent in the dream farm and the failure of the dream. The plan is doomed not only because human fellowship cannot survive in the post-Cain world, but also because the image of the farm, as conceived by George and Lennie and Candy, is overly idealized, the probability being that life, even if they obtained the farm, would not consist of the comfort, plenty, and inter-personal harmony they envision. The fruits and vegetables in abundance, the livestock and domestic animals, and the community of people involved ("Ain't gonna be no more trouble. Nobody gonna hurt nobody nor steal from 'em")—these are impractical expectations. George and Lennie, who were to some extent inspired by questions growing out of the story of Cain in chapter 4 of Genesis, want to retreat to chapter 2 and live in Eden! Of all ambitions in a fallen world, this is possibly the most unattainable; for paradise is lost, as the name of Steinbeck's hero, George Milton, suggests. And though there will always be men like Candy, who represents sweet hope, the view of Crooks, who represents black despair, is probably a more accurate appraisal of the human condition: "Nobody never gets to heaven, and nobody gets no land. It's just in their head. They're all the time talkin' about it, but it's jus' in their head" (*OMM* 74). Obviously in this context Crooks's comment about nobody ever getting land refers not to literal ownership but to the dream of contentment entertained by the simple workmen who come and go on the ranch.

To pursue the Milton parallel a step further, we perceive immediately that Steinbeck has no intention of justifying the ways of God to man. On the contrary, if anything, *Of Mice and Men* implies a critique of Hebrew-Christian morality, particularly in the area of the concept of punishment for sin. This opens up still another dimension of meaning in our interpretation of Steinbeck's novella. If George and Lennie fail to attain their dream farm (for reasons already explored), and the dream farm is a metaphor or image for heaven (as suggested by Crooks's speech in scene 4), then the failure to achieve the dream farm is most likely associated with the question of man's failure to attain heaven. Steinbeck's consideration of this last-named theme is not hard to find.

Along this particular line of thought, Lennie represents one essential aspect of man—the animal appetites, the craving to touch and feel, the impulse toward immediate gratification of sensual desires.[5] George is the element of Reason which tries to control the appetites or, better still, to elevate them to a higher and more sublime level. As Lennie's hallucinatory rabbit advises him near the conclusion: "Christ knows George done ever'thing he could to jack you outa the sewer, but it don't do no good" (*OMM* 102). Steinbeck suggests throughout that the appetites and Reason coexist to compose the nature of man ("Me an' him travels together" [*OMM* 25]). He goes on to suggest that the effort to refine man into something rare, saintly, and inhuman is another unattainable ambition. Even when Reason (George) manages to communicate to the appetites (Lennie) its urgent message ("You crazy son-of-a-bitch. You keep me in hot water all the time . . . I never get no peace" [*OMM* 11]), the appetites are incapable of satisfying Reason's demands. This submerged thesis is suggested when Aunt Clara—like the big rabbit a product of Lennie's disturbed imagination—scolds Lennie in scene 6:

> "I tol' you an' tol' you. I tol' you. 'Min' George because he's such a nice fella an' good to you.' But you don't never take no care. You do bad things."
> And Lennie answered her, "I tried, Aunt Clara, ma'am. I tried and tried. I couldn' help it." (*OMM* 101)[6]

The animal appetites, even though well attended and well intentioned, cannot be completely suppressed or controlled. Thus, the best man can hope for is a kind of insecure balance of power between these two elements—which is, in fact, what most of the ranch hands accomplish, indulging their craving for sensual pleasure in a legal and commonplace manner each payday. Failing this, man must suppress absolutely the appetites that refuse to be controlled, as George does in the symbolic killing of Lennie at the conclusion of the novella. Possibly this is a veiled reference to the drastic mutilation of man's nature required by the Hebrew-Christian ethic. At the same time, the theological implications of *Of Mice and Men* project the very highest regard for the noble experiment in fraternal living practiced by George and

Lennie; and possibly the time scheme of their stay on the ranch—from Friday to Sunday—is a veiled reference to the sacrifice of Christ. He too tried to reverse the irreversible tide of Cain's curse by serving as the ultimate example of human brotherhood.

At this point, without, I hope, undue emphasis, we might attempt to answer some specific objections which have been raised by critics of *Of Mice and Men.* The faults most often cited are the pessimism of Steinbeck's conclusion, which seems to some readers excessive; and the author's attempt to impose a tragic tone upon a story which lacks characters of tragic stature.[7] Both of these censures might be accepted as valid, or at least understood as reasonable, if we read the novella *on the surface level of action and character development.* But a reading which takes into account the mythical-allegorical significance of these actions and characters not only nullifies the objections but opens up new areas of awareness. For example, although Lennie and George are humble people without the status of traditional tragic characters, their dream is very much like the dream of Plato for an ideal Republic. And their experiment in fellowship is not at all different from the experiment attempted by King Arthur. And at the same time it is reminiscent of at least one aspect of Christ's ministry. These are remote parallels to *Of Mice and Men*, yet they are legitimate and lend some measure of substance, nobility, and human significance to Steinbeck's novella. Its pessimism is not superimposed upon a slight story, as charged, but has been there from the opening line, if we know how to read it. Furthermore, the pessimism is not inspired by commercialism or false theatrics but by the Hebrew Testament. ("And Cain said unto the Lord, 'My punishment is greater than I can bear.'")

But let us tie up our loose ends, not with reference to critics but with a brief summary of our discoveries during this investigation. *Of Mice and Men* is a realistic story with lifelike characters and a regional setting, presented in a style highly reminiscent of stage drama. Steinbeck's technique also includes verbal ambiguity in place names and character names, double entendre in certain key passages of dialogue, and a mythical-allegorical drift that invites the reader into areas of philosophical and theological inquiry. Sources for the novella are obviously Steinbeck's own experience as a laborer in California; but on the allegorical level, *Of Mice and Men* reflects the early chapters of the Book of Genesis and the questions that grow out of the incidents therein depicted. These consist primarily of the consideration of man as a creature alone or as a brother and companion to others. In addition, Steinbeck's story suggests the futility of the all-too-human attempt to recapture Eden, as well as a symbolic schema that defines human psychology. Steinbeck also implies a critique of the Hebrew-Christian ethic, to the effect that the absolute suppression of the animal appetites misrepresents the reality of human experience.

Finally, we should say that Steinbeck's emphasis, on both the allegorical and realistic levels, is on the nobility of his characters' attempt to live fraternally. Even though the experiment is doomed to failure, Steinbeck's characters, like the best men of every age, dedicate themselves to pursuing the elusive grail of fellowship.

Notes

1. Frederic I. Carpenter, along with several others, calls *Of Mice and Men* a tragedy. See "John Steinbeck: American Dreamer," in *Steinbeck and His Critics*, ed. E. W. Tedlock Jr. and C. V. Wicker (Albuquerque: University of New Mexico Press, 1957), 76 (referred to hereinafter as Tedlock and Wicker). Warren French calls *Of Mice and Men* a "dark comedy" in *John Steinbeck* (New Haven, CT: College and University Press, 1961), 76. French also pushes the thesis of the novella's descent from Arthurian legend (73). Joseph Fontenrose says, "*Of Mice and Men* has a recognizable mythical pattern," in *John Steinbeck: An Introduction and Interpretation* (New York: Barnes and Noble, 1963), 59. The political theories of *Of Mice and Men* are quoted from Edwin Berry Burgum and Stanley Edgar Hymen, 109 and 159, respectively, in Tedlock and Wicker. Sociological points are stressed by French in *John Steinbeck*, 77. Freeman Champney says *Of Mice and Men* is "little other" than the theme of "every man [sic] kills the thing he loves" (in Tedlock and Wicker, 140). The "pleasures often oppose and thwart our schemes" thesis is in Fontenrose, *An Introduction and Interpretation*, 57. "The non-morality of Nature" is the interpretation of Burton Rascoe, in Tedlock and Wicker, 65. The quotations from Beach and Kazin, respectively, are in Tedlock and Wicker, 90, and *On Native Grounds* (New York: Doubleday, 1956), 109–19.

2. The quotation is in Tedlock and Wicker, 307.

3. One of Steinbeck's critics unconsciously confirms this discouraging thesis when he says, "Steinbeck represents George as being closely attached to Lennie. But George's feeling is not convincing because it is not that of most men in real life" (Woodburn O. Ross in Tedlock and Wicker, 175). To Mr. Ross we might reply, with John Steinbeck, *tant pis*! This is the same outlook that provides the context for the *tragedy* of George and Lennie!

4. First appearance suggests that Steinbeck might be guilty of antifeminist sentiment by his use of the Hemingwayesque "Men without Women" theme: "Everything was fine with us boys until that trouble-making female came along," etc. Curley's wife, however, is represented as the victim of the same impulses as the men in the story; she too is impelled out of loneliness to seek company, and she too is the victim of a dream: "Coulda been in the movies, and had nice clothes," etc. With this emphasis Steinbeck includes Curley's wife in the problems and striving of all men who inherit the curse of Cain. In any case, though she does in fact have trouble-making propensities, she is no worse in this respect than her husband and overall is unquestionably a more sympathetic character than Curley.

5. Obviously Steinbeck faced a problem in his portrait of Lennie as a sympathetic though dangerous moron who has great difficulty in keeping his hands off women. (Compare William Faulkner's treatment of Benjy in *The Sound and the Fury*.) The author's entire emphasis would have been thrown off balance if Lennie had attacked Curley's wife (or the girl in Weed) in some gross and lascivious manner. Clearly, if he were prone to this sort of behavior, George would not be traveling with him in the first place. Lennie must be as he is—powerful and potentially dangerous, but essentially childlike and innocent—for other reasons as well. His condition lends emphasis to the basic idea of general aloneness of men; if Lennie were normally intelligent, he would most likely be busy pursuing his own interests. Finally, the basic innocence of Lennie's sensual impulses reinforces Steinbeck's critique of Hebrew-Christian-morality theme by making the point that there is nothing evil, per se, in man's natural sensuality.

6. All quotations from *Of Mice and Men* are taken from *Of Mice and Men* (New York: Penguin Classics, 1993).

7. See Fontenrose, *An Introduction and Interpretation*, 60; and Edward Wagenknecht, *Cavalcade of the American Novel* (New York: Henry Holt, 1958), 496.

CHAPTER FOUR

OF GEORGE AND LENNIE AND CURLEY'S WIFE: SWEET VIOLENCE IN STEINBECK'S EDEN

Mark Spilka

Nearly everyone in the world has appetites and impulses, trigger emotions, islands of selfishness, lusts just beneath the surface. And most people either hold such things in check or indulge in them secretly. Cathy knew not only these impulses in others but how to use them for her own gain. It is quite possible that she did not believe in any other tendencies in humans, for while she was preternaturally alert in some directions she was completely blind in others. Cathy learned when she was very young that sexuality with all its attendant yearnings and pains, jealousies and taboos, is the most disturbing impulse humans have.

My cpigraph is from Steinbeck's postwar novel *East of Eden*, published in 1952. It concerns a woman called Cathy Ames who deserts her husband and newborn twins to become the successful proprietor of a California whorehouse. In his diaries for the composition of the novel, Steinbeck calls this woman a "monster" and says he will prove to his readers that such monsters actually exist. His choice of her as the archetypal mother of a California family, his peculiarly Miltonic view of her as an exploiter of men's lusts, and his awareness of the exploitability of such feelings—this complex of psychological tendencies in the later Steinbeck has much to do, I think, with the force behind his early

Mark Spilka, "Of George and Lennie and Curley's Wife: Sweet Violence in Steinbeck's Eden." *Modern Fiction Studies* 20:2 (1974), 169–179. © Purdue Research Foundation. Reprinted with permission of the Johns Hopkins University Press.

social fiction. I want to examine one of his early social tales, *Of Mice and Men*, with that possibility in mind.

A minor classic of proletarian conflict, *Of Mice and Men* was written in 1937, first as a novel, then as a play. Both versions proved enormously popular and established Steinbeck as a leading writer of the decade. The play won the Drama Critics' Circle Award, and the film produced from it in 1941 was widely applauded. A recent television version testifies to the dramatic power of the basic story.

Certainly the novel's dramatic force has much to do with its continuing appeal. Steinbeck conceived it as a potential play, with each chapter arranged as a scene and the action confined to a secluded grove, a bunkhouse, and a barn. In the play itself each chapter does in fact become a scene; the dialogue is transferred almost verbatim, and the action—except for a few strategic alterations—remains unchanged. Plainly Steinbeck was able to convert the novel with comparative ease.

It may have helped that a paper-chewing dog destroyed his original manuscript. Thanks to that fateful interference he rewrote the tale completely, proceeding now at a high pitch of masterful control. The opening scene epitomizes the new compactness, the new surcharge of meaning, which sets the book off from all his previous work, and which testifies—as we shall see—not only to its dramatic but to its psychological power.

The sycamore grove by the Salinas River, so lovingly described in the opening lines, is more than scene setting: it is an attempt to evoke the sense of freedom in nature which, for a moment only, the protagonists will enjoy. By a path worn hard by boys and hobos two migrant laborers appear. The first man is mouselike: "small and quick, dark of face, with restless eyes and sharp, strong features. Every part of him was defined: small strong hands, slender arms, a thin and bony nose" (*OMM* 2). He is the planner from the poem by Robert Burns: as with other mice and men, his best arrangements will often go astray. A bus driver has just tricked him and his friends into getting out four miles from the ranch where jobs await them. Now he decides to stay in the small grove near the river because he "like[s] it here." There will be work tomorrow, but tonight he can "lay right here and look up" at the sky through the sycamore leaves; he can dream and plan with his friend of the farm they will never own.

The nearest town is Soledad, which means "lovely place" in Spanish; the town where they last worked, digging a cesspool, was Weed. Their friendship is thus quickly placed as a creative defense against rank loneliness; it will be reinforced, thematically, by the hostility and guardedness of bunkhouse life, and by the apparent advance of their dream toward realization. But the secluded grove, the site of natural freedom, provides the only substantiation their dream will ever receive; and when our mouselike planner tells his friend to return there in case of trouble, we sense that the dream will end where it essentially begins, in this substantiating site.

The second man to appear is "opposite" to the first: "a huge man, shapeless of face, with large, pale eyes, with wide, sloping shoulders" and loose-hanging arms; he walks heavily, "dragging his feet a little, the way a bear drags his paws" (*OMM* 2). This bearlike man becomes equine when they reach the grove: flinging himself down, he drinks from the pool there, "snorting into the water like a horse" (*OMM* 3). Then again like a bear, he dips his whole head under, "hat and all," sits up so the hat drips down his back, and "dabble[s] his big paw in the water" (*OMM* 3).

These animal actions and his childish speech place him for us quickly as an idiot. What the first man plans for, the second already has. Like other Steinbeck idiots—Tuleracito in *The Pastures of Heaven* (1932), Johnny Bear in *The Long Valley* (1938)—he participates in natural life freely, has access to its powers, and his attraction for Steinbeck is his freedom to use those powers without blame or censure. More nearly animal than human, more nearly child than man, he eludes responsibility for his actions. Again like the natural artist Tularecito and the uncanny mimic Johnny Bear, he is extraordinarily gifted; he has superhuman strength which inevitably threatens a society whose rules he cannot comprehend. He is thus the perfect denizen of the secluded grove where, for a moment, natural freedom reigns; the perfect victim, too, for an intruding social world which will eventually deny that freedom.

In his pocket the idiot carries an actual mouse, dead from too much handling. Later he kills a puppy with playful buffeting. A child fondling "lesser" creatures, he is Steinbeck's example of senseless killing in nature. He is also part of an ascending hierarchy of power. His name is Lennie Small, by which Steinbeck means subhuman, animal, childlike, without power to judge or master social fate. His friend's name, George Milton, puts him by literary allusion near the godhead, above subhuman creatures, able to judge whether they should live or die. The title and epilogue of *In Dubious Battle* (1936) were also drawn from Milton, whose grand judgmental abstractions take humble proletarian forms in Steinbeck's world. Thus, in a later set-up scene (which may have been inspired also by Steinbeck's paper-chewing dog), old Candy, the lowly bunkhouse sweeper, says that he should have shot his own decrepit dog—should not have let a stranger do it for him. George too will decide that he must shoot Lennie, like a mad rather than decrepit dog, for the unplanned murder of another man's wife; that he cannot allow strangers to destroy him.

Both shootings have been sanctioned by the jerkline skinner, Slim, "prince of the ranch," who moves "with a majesty achieved only by royalty" and looks with "calm, God-like eyes" upon his bunkhouse world. Since his word is "law" for the migrant farmhands, and since Milton, a rational farmhand, can recognize and accept such godlike laws, he must choose to shoot his friend. By *East of Eden* Steinbeck would conclude that it is choice which separates men from animals, a belief which supports one critic's view of George's decision as "mature." But it is not his "ordinariness" which George will accept in destroying Lennie and the comforting dream they share, as this critic holds: it is his *humanness*, his responsibility for actions which the animal Lennie, for all his vital strength, cannot comprehend.

And yet George will be diminished—made "ordinary"—by his choice. As many critics insist, he uses Lennie selfishly, draws from him a sense of power, of superiority, which he sorely needs. If he is sensitive to Lennie's feelings—cares for and about him in demonstrable ways—he also "lords" it over him almost vengefully. The opening scene indicates nicely how much petty satisfaction he takes in giving Lennie orders and complaining about the burden of thinking for him. But more than this: the scene creates a causal expectation—that one way or another Lennie will always feed this satisfaction, will always do, in effect, what George desires—which means that George himself invites the troubles ahead, makes things go astray, uses Lennie to provoke and settle his own quarrel with a hostile world.

This is evident enough when he tells Lennie not to talk, to leave job negotiations to him so as not to expose his idiocy before his strength has been displayed. Inevitably bosses are annoyed when Lennie fails to speak for himself; suspicions are aroused, and future troubles more or less ensured. This is exactly what George desires, first with the boss of the Soledad ranch, then with two extensions of the boss's power—his son

Curley and Curley's straying wife. George resents these people so much, and pins such frightening taboos on them, that Lennie is bound to panic when he meets them, to clutch with his tremendous strength—like a child caught with some forbidden object—and so punish people George openly dislikes. In a very real sense, then, George lordfully creates the troubles for which Lennie will himself be blamed and punished—though he only obeys his master's vengeful voice.

This is to move from social into psychological conflict: but Steinbeck, in taking a boss's son and his wife as sources of privileged pressure on migrant farmhands, has moved there before us. He has chosen aggressive sexuality as the force, in migrant life, which undermines the friendship dream. This variation on the Garden of Eden theme is, to say the least, peculiar. There is something painfully adolescent about the notion of a cooperative farm run by bachelor George and idiot Lennie, with the probable help of a maimed old man and a defiant black cripple. The grouping is not unlike the Arthurian circle around Danny in *Tortilla Flat* (1935): four good-hearted lads sticking together against the world, who can drop work and go into town whenever they want to see "a carnival or a circus . . . or a ball game." Their self-employment seems more like freedom from adult supervision than from harsh conditions; and their friendship seems more like an escape from the coarseness of adult sexuality than from bunkhouse loneliness. Even their knightly pledge to help each other seems oddly youthful. That Steinbeck read the Arthurian legends at an early age, and that he also worked on ranches during boyhood summers, may be relevant here: for the world of friendship he imagines is a boy's world, a retreat from the masculine grossness and insecurity of the bunkhouse, from whorehouse visits and combative marriages like Curley's, which in his youth he must have found disturbing. George Milton shows enough insecurity and disgust about sex, and enough hostility toward women, to make these speculations about Steinbeck's choices worth pursuing. . . .

In *Of Mice and Men*, Lennie first pets Curley's wife, then breaks her neck, without any awareness that she provokes both reactions. His conscious desires are simple: to stroke something furry, and to stop the furry thing from yelling so George won't be mad at him. But George has predicted this episode, has called Curley's wife a rattrap, a bitch, a piece of jailbait; and he has roundly expressed disgust at Curley's glove full of

Vaseline, which softens the hand that strokes his wife's genitals. Lennie has obligingly crushed that hand for George, and now he obligingly breaks the rattrap for him, that snare for mice and men which catches both in its furry toils.

In the play Steinbeck goes out of his way to make it clear that George's hostility to Curley's wife prefigures Lennie's. In a scene not in the novel, he arranges an exchange in the Negro Crooks's room in which George's arm is raised in anger against this woman: he is about to strike her for threatening the friendship dream, for trying to "mess up what we're gonna do." Then Curley's father arrives, the girl retreats from the room, and George lowers his hand as the scene closes.

As such manipulations imply, Steinbeck projects his own hostilities through George and Lennie. He has himself given this woman no other name but "Curley's wife," as if she had no personal identity for him. He has presented her, in the novel, as vain, provocative, vicious (she threatens Crooks with lynching, for instance, when he tries to defy her), and only incidentally lonely. Now in the play—perhaps in response to the criticisms of friends—he reverses her portrait. She is no longer vicious (her lynching threat has been written out of the script), and she is not even provocative: she is just a lonely woman whose attempts at friendliness are misunderstood. Thus she makes her first entrance with a line transferred from a later scene in the novel: "I'm just lookin' for somebody to talk to," she says, in case we might think otherwise. In her final scene, moreover, in a sympathy speech written expressly for the play, she joins Lennie in the lost world of childhood:

> Curley's Wife: My ol' man was a sign-painter when he worked. He used o get drunk an' paint crazy pitchers an' waste paint. One night when I was a little kid, him an' my ol' lady had an awful fight. They was always fightin'. In the middle of the night he come into my room, and he says, "I can't stand this no more. Let's you an' me go away." I guess he was drunk. *(Her voice takes on a curious wondering tenderness.)* I remember in the night—walkin' down the road, and the trees was black. I was pretty sleepy. He picked me up, an' he carried me on his back. He says, "We gonna live together. We gonna live together because you're my own little girl, an' not no stranger. No arguin' and fightin'," he says, "because you're my little daughter." *(Her voice becomes soft.)* He says, "Why you'll bake little cakes for me, and I'll paint pretty pitchers all over the wall."

(Sadly) In the morning they caught us . . . an' they put him away. *(Pause)*
I wish we'd a' went (*OMM*, play version).

Here Steinbeck overcompensates, creates a new imbalance to correct
an old one. His sentimentality is the obverse side of his hostility. We see
this in the novel when it breaks through in another form, as a mystic moment of redemption for Curley's wife. Thus, as she lies dead in the barn,
"the meanness and the plannings and the discontent and the ache for attention" disappear from her face; she becomes sweet and young, and her
rouged cheeks and reddened lips make her seem alive and sleeping lightly
"under a half-covering of hay." At which point sound and movement stop,
and, "as sometimes happens," a moment settles and hovers and remains
"for much, much more than a moment." Then time wakens and moves
sluggishly on. Horses stamp in the barn, their halter chains clink, and
outside, men's voices become "louder and clearer."

Restored to natural innocence through death, Curley's wife is connected—for a timeless moment—with the farm dream. Then men's voices
and stamping horses indicate the sexual restlessness she provokes in adult
life. Only when sexually quiescent—as in death or childhood—can she
win this author's heart. . . .

Herein lies his strength and weakness in *Of Mice and Men*: for the
passage from stroking rabbits to stroking genitals is both profoundly and
ridiculously conceived. As literary zanies like Max Schulman and Steve
Allen have been quick to see, Lennie's oft-repeated line, "Tell about
the rabbits, George," comes perilously close to self-parody. Lifted only
slightly out of context, it reduces the friendship farm to a bad sexual joke.
As a sentimental alternative to the emptiness, divisiveness, and gross
sexuality of bunkhouse life, it seems fair game for satire. But Steinbeck
is never that simple. He is fascinated not by Lennie's innocent pleasures
but by the low threshold which his innocent rages cross whenever he is
thwarted. Consider Lennie's reaction when George imagines that striped
cats may threaten his beloved rabbits: "You jus' let 'em try to get the rabbits," he says, breathing hard. "I'll break their God damn necks. I'll . . . I'll
smash 'em with a stick."

This frightening capacity for violence is what Lennie brings into the
unsuspecting bunkhouse world: he carries within him, intact from childhood, that low threshold between rage and pleasure which we all carry

within us into adulthood. But by adulthood we have all learned to take precautions which an idiot never learns to take. The force and readiness of our feelings continue: but through diversions and disguises, through civilized controls, we raise the threshold of reactions. This is the only real difference, emotionally, between Lennie and ourselves.

A great deal of Steinbeck's power as a writer comes, then, from his ability to bring into ordinary scenes of social conflict the psychological forcefulness of infantile reactions: his creation of Lennie in *Of Mice and Men* is a brilliant instance of that ability—so brilliant, in fact, that the social conflict in this compact tale tends to dissolve into the dramatic urgencies of Lennie's "fate." In his next novel, *The Grapes of Wrath* (1939), Steinbeck would find a situation commensurate with his own low threshold for idiot rage. The epic scope of the Okies' tribulations, of their forced migration from their farms and later exploitation in California, contains and absorbs his immense capacity for anger. It is no accident that this novel begins with the return of a blameless murderer, Tom Joad, imprisoned for an almost pointless crime involving sexual rivalry (when a jealous friend knifes him at a dance, Tom smashes him with a nearby shovel); nor that the problem for Tom, for the rest of the novel, is how to control his easy rages (once he leaves the state he violates parole; any brush with police will return him to prison); nor that the novel ends with his commission of another blameless but now socially significant murder (when a strikebreaker kills ex-preacher Casy, now a Christ-like labor leader, Tom smashes him with his own club). Nor is it an accident that the erotic potential of sensual innocence is diffused, in the novel's closing scene, by an act of social compassion. With Lennie's pathetic fate in mind, the meaning of Rose of Sharon's mysterious smile as she breastfeeds a starving middle-aged man is not hard to fathom: she has found in the adult world what Lennie has never been able to find—an adequate way to satisfy inchoate longings, a way to nurture helpless creatures, perform useful tasks, indulge innocent pleasures, without arousing self-destructive anger. Steinbeck has called *Of Mice and Men* "a study of the dreams and pleasures of everyone in the world" and has said that Lennie especially represents "the inarticulate and powerful yearning of all men," their "earth longings" for land of their own, for innocent-pleasure farms. In a profoundly psychological way he was right about the pleasures, though strangely neglectful of the rages which, in his world at least, accompany them. Tom Joad's confident smile, his flaunting of homicide to a truck driver as *The Grapes of Wrath* begins, and Rose of Sharon's mysterious satisfaction as it closes, suggest that fuller accommodation of universal urges which gives his greatest novel much of its extraordinary power.

Of Mice and Men helped him to release that power by making murder seem as natural and innocent as love. He had been trying his hand at blameless murders in stories like "Flight," where a young Indian reaches manhood through a killing, then flees to his own death in the wilderness; or like "The Murder," where a husband kills his foreign wife's lover and then beats her into admiring submission. There are natural killings too in *The Red Pony*, where the little boy, Jody, cuts up the bird he has stoned and hides the pieces out of deference to adults: "He didn't care about the bird, or its life, but he knew what older people would say if they had seen him kill it; he was ashamed because of their potential opinion." Jody is too small to push these primitive sentiments very far; but Lennie, a more sizable child, is better able to amplify their meaning. After killing Curley's wife, he flees to the grove near the Salinas River, as George has told him to. Back in his own element, he moves "as silently as a creeping bear," drinks like a wary animal, and thinks of living in caves if George doesn't want him any more. Then out of his head come two figures: his aunt Clara and (seven years before Mary Chase's *Harvey*) a giant rabbit. These figments of adult opinion bring all of George's petty righteousness to bear against him, shame him unmercifully, and threaten him with the only thing that matters: the loss of his beloved bunnies. Then out of the brush, like a third figment of Miltonic pettiness, comes George himself, as if to punish him once more for "being bad." But for Lennie as for Jody, badness is a matter of opinions and taboos, not of consequences and responsibilities. He doesn't care about Curley's wife, who exists for him now only as another lifeless animal. Nor does Steinbeck care about her except as she arrives at natural innocence; but he does care about that, and through Lennie, who possesses it in abundance, he is able to affirm his belief in the causeless, blameless animality of murder. Of course, he also believes in the responsibility of those who grasp the consequences of animal passion, and it is one of several paradoxes on which this novel ends that George comes humbly now to accept responsibility for such passions, comes not to punish Lennie, then, but to put him mercifully away, to let him die in full enjoyment of their common dream. So he asks him to face the Gabilan Mountains, which in *East of Eden* are said to resemble the inviting lap of a beloved mother; and, like a bedtime story or a prayer before execution—or better still, like both—together they recite the familiar tale of the friendship farm.

What makes this ending scary and painful and perplexing is the weight given to all that Lennie represents: if contradictory values are affirmed—blameless animality, responsible humanity, innocent longing, grim awareness—it is Lennie's peculiar mixture of human dreams and animal passions which matters most. George's newfound maturity is paradoxically a triumph: without Lennie he seems more like a horseless rider than a responsible adult. "The two together were one glorious individual," says Steinbeck of the boy Jody and his imagined pony, Black Demon, the best roping team at the rodeo. Without such demonic vitality, by which any kind of meaningful life proceeds, George is indeed friendless and alone. With it, needless to say, he is prone to destructive rages. On the horns of that adolescent dilemma—that inability to take us beyond the perplexities of sexual rage—Steinbeck hangs his readers. Impales them, rather, since the rich tensions of this poignant perplex, however unresolved, are honestly and powerfully presented. . . .

Steinbeck himself liked simple stories well enough to write straight allegories like *The Pearl* (1947). But chiefly he liked the puzzling kind. In *Tortilla Flat*, an otherwise comic novel, he shows, for instance, how Danny tires of the chivalric life and reverts to the "sweet violence" of outlawry. "Sweet violence" means something more here than the joys of boyish rebellion: it means delight in pulling the house down on one's own and other people's heads, which is what Danny does when the friendship dream proves insubstantial, and he pays with his life—and later, with his friends' help, with his house—for the pleasure of destroying it. Lennie too pays with his life for the pleasure of destructive rages; but he serves in this respect as an extension of his friend's desires: he is George Milton's idiot Samson, his blind avenger for the distastefulness of aggressive sexuality. Which may be why their friendship seems impossible from the first, why the pathos of their dream, and of its inevitable defeat, seems less important than the turbulence it rouses. Once more, "sweet violence" is the force which moves these characters, and which moves us to contemplate their puzzling fate.

By *East of Eden* Steinbeck would learn that rages generally follow from rejected love, that parental coldness or aloofness breeds violence in youthful hearts; and he would come also to accept sexuality as a vulnerable condition, a blind helplessness by which men and women may be "tricked and trapped and enslaved and tortured," but without which they would not be human. Oddly, he would create in Cathy Ames a monstrous projection of his old hostility toward women as exploiters of the sex impulse; and he would impose on her his own preternatural alertness to its selfish uses and his own fear of being absorbed and blinded by it in his youth. But by accepting sex now as a human need, he would redeem his Lennies and Dannys from outlawry and animality, and he would finally repair the ravages of sweet violence. *Of Mice and Men* remains his most compelling tribute to the force behind those ravages, "the most disturbing impulse humans have," as it moves a selfish master and his dancing bear to idiot rages. And once more it must be said to move us, too. For however contradictory it seems, our sympathy for these characters, indeed their love for each other, is founded more deeply in the humanness of that impulse that in its humanitarian disguises.

CHAPTER FIVE

THE NOVELS OF JOHN STEINBECK, EXCERPT FROM CHAPTER 5

Howard Levant

John Steinbeck's only published excursion into literary theory is an effort to justify the form of the play-novelette–a term he invented. Also, in the span of thirteen of the middle years of his career, Steinbeck published three play-novelettes. These facts suggest that for Steinbeck the play-novelette is an important novelistic form. It is therefore appropriate to consider the theory and the practice of the form as well as its implications in the larger frame of Steinbeck's development of a simplified novelistic structure in longer fiction after about 1940.

Steinbeck presented the theory in an oddly titled article, ". . . the novel might benefit by the discipline, the terseness . . . ," in the January 1938 issue of *Stage*.[1] Steinbeck's view is that a play-novelette is a pure dramatic structure—in the theatrical, not in the Jamesian, sense. He argues that if a novelist can simplify narrative and characterization by ordering a novel as if it were a play, the result must be an immediately powerful communication of theme and an enormous intensification of all the other novelistic values. He adds that *Of Mice and Men*, one of his efforts in the genre, is a failure as a play-novelette.

One can praise Steinbeck's intention to vitalize the novel through a new form, but without doubt his theory is absurd.[2] (It should be added that Steinbeck's practice does little to redeem the theory.) Foremost, a

Reprinted from *The Novels of John Steinbeck* by Howard Levant, by permission of the University of Missouri Press. Copyright © 1974 by the Curators of the University of Missouri.

novel is not a play, and terms do not make it so. Consider a key passage in Steinbeck's argument:

> For some years the novel has increasingly taken on the attributes of the drama. . . . To read an objective novel is to see a little play in your mind. All right, why not make it so you can see it on a stage? This experiment, then, is really only a conclusion towards which the novel has been unconsciously heading for some time.[3]

The argument is serious, as the tone suggests. But the logic is unconvincing because the analogy is false. To know that Henry James and his literary heirs succeeded in making the novel a direct rendering of experience does not mean that a novelist can remove every vestige of form and, in that sense, "make it so you can see it on a stage." Steinbeck takes the issue beyond the limits of analogy in an effort to sharpen a point; he confuses what a novel and a play are and can do; in short, he loads the argument in his favor.

The logical trick is not worth consideration, as Steinbeck seems to know, since he uses a second argument that is based on a quite different theory: The best way to reach an audience is by a direct effect. He asserts that the trouble with the novel as a form is that it is made for the individual "alone under a reading lamp," whereas a play depends on a group response:

> Now if it is true, and I believe it is, that the preoccupation of the modern novelist lies in these themes which are most poignantly understood by a group, that novelist limits the possibility of being understood by making it impossible for groups to be exposed to this work.[4]

Again the logic is unconvincing because the analogy is false. The argument rests only on Steinbeck's feeling that the group responds to a literary effect with more emotional validity than any individual can generate. Even if a measure of emotion could be devised, and if the private reading of drama were outlawed, the fact remains that a play is not a novel. Finally, the analogy is qualified by the direction of much modern writing, including the novel, into private or subjective content and form.

The *Stage* article is an aberration of logic and of literary history, but it is more illuminating to consider how deeply the aberration is rooted in Steinbeck's practice.[5]

Much of the longer fiction is organized around some abstraction, a technical device or an intellectual point of view that operates as a "universal," giving a spurious dramatic structure to panoramic materials. Steinbeck can overcome this tendency by accident (as in *Tortilla Flat*) or by exorcising a part of his skill that is dangerous to cultivate (as in *The Grapes of Wrath*—but only in part). The excellent work and the aberrant work are both characteristic. Dates of publication alone prevent critical simplicity: *Of Mice and Men* and the *Stage* article were published between *In Dubious Battle* and *The Grapes of Wrath*. It is quite probable, as Moore and Lisca suggest, that the beginning of the play-novelette form can be seen in the more objectively rendered chapters of *In Dubious Battle*.[6] The factual and probable evidence indicates that the play-novelette form, aberration as it may be, nevertheless is rooted deeply in some of the best of Steinbeck's previous work. Further, the evidence suggests why Steinbeck engages in so patently absurd a confusion of form over a period of thirteen years. He tries to achieve a harmony between structure and materials in every novel, but the effort is a constant struggle, open in part to accident. Now, the play-novelette form is eminently a way to *formulate* a harmony—to remove accident and struggle by a formula. To a novelist like Steinbeck, afflicted with artistic ambition but limited in structural insight, the attraction of the play-novelette form is obvious. Its theory may rest on false analogy, may be only a gimmick, or may indicate Steinbeck's lack of judgment with a terrifying clarity. But we must keep in mind that the theory and the practice of the play-novelette, in Steinbeck's hands, is a continuation of his constant effort to achieve a harmony between structure and materials. To do less is to limit criticism to a club.

These various matters can be understood more deeply and perhaps more clearly through analysis of *Of Mice and Men*. Despite Steinbeck's disclaimer in *Stage*, *Of Mice and Men* is certainly a play-novelette according to Steinbeck's own theory. Biographical information supports this view. Steinbeck reported to his agents, at the beginning of his work in February 1935, "I'm doing a play now," and Harry Thornton Moore records several illuminating contemporary facts:

> After *Of Mice and Men* was published and the suggestion was made that it be prepared for the stage, Steinbeck said it could be produced directly from the book, as the earliest moving pictures had been produced. It was

staged in almost exactly this way in the spring of 1937 by a labor-theater group in San Francisco, and, although the venture was not a failure, it plainly demonstrated to Steinbeck that the story needed to be adapted to dramatic form. . . . But, when Steinbeck transferred the story into final dramatic form for the New York stage, he took 85% of his lines bodily form the novel. A few incidents needed juggling, one or two minor new ones were introduced, and some (such as Lennie's imaginary speech with his Aunt Clara at the end of the novel) were omitted.[7]

It would seem that the novel was intended to function as a play, and Steinbeck did not alter the novel in any essential way during the tinkering in preparation for the New York stage production. Aesthetic considerations support the biographical information, as in Moore's observation: "Structurally, the novel was from the first a play: it is divided into six parts, each part a scene—the reader may observe that the action never moves away from a central point in each of these units."[8] And clearly the novel does "play": Characters make entrances and exits; plainly indicated parallels and oppositions that are characteristic of the drama exist in quantity and function as they should; suspense is maintained; characters are kept uncomplicated and "active" in the manner of stage characterization; since there is little internal or implicit development, events depend on what is said or done in full view; the locale is restricted mainly to one place; the span of time is brief; the central theme is stated and restated—the good life is impossible because humanity is flawed—and in itself is deeply poignant, as Steinbeck had defined a play-novelette theme. In short, I do not see how *Of Mice and Men* could meet more completely the specifications of a play-novelette as Steinbeck listed them. If critics have been displeased with *Of Mice and Men*, as Steinbeck was, the trouble cannot lie in the application of the theory but in the assumption that inspired the theory. I shall explore this point in detail.

As a dramatic structure, *Of Mice and Men* is focused on Lennie and occurs within the context of the bunkhouse and the ranch. Within these confines, Steinbeck develops theme and countertheme by exploring the chances for the good life against the flawed human material that Lennie symbolizes most completely and the code of rough justice that most people accept. Even this initial, limited statement points to the central difficulty in the novel. The "well-made" dramatic form that Steinbeck defined in *Stage* and did construct in *Of Mice and Men* is conducive to abstraction because it is limited to visible action. Lennie is limited in much the same way. As a huge, powerful, semi-idiot who kills when he is frightened or simply when he is thoughtless, Lennie is a reduction of humanity to the lowest common denominator. It may be possible to construct a parable out of so limited a structure and materials, but it is impossible to handle complex human motives and relationships within those limits. *Of Mice and Men* is successful to the extent that it remains a parable, but the enveloping action is more complex than the parable form can encompass.

Lennie is the most fully realized character, yet he is presented necessarily as a personification, an exaggerated, allegorized instance of the division between mind and body; the sketch that is Lennie is incapable of conveying personality. The other characters are personified types rather than realized persons. Though less pathetic than Lennie, they do not have his moral impact. In short, every structural devise except personification is sacrificed to highlight Lennie's moral helplessness. The sacrifice is much too great. It thins out the parable. The stripped language furthers this effect of extreme thinness. For example, Lennie's one friend, George, is not a realized man but a quality that complements Lennie's childlike innocence. George fills out Lennie's pattern to complete a whole man. He is a good man, motivated to protect Lennie because he realizes that Lennie is the reverse image of his own human nature. George is a representation of humanity that (unlike Lennie) is aware of evil. An extended abstract passage (pages 38-43) makes this clear.`

Everything in the development of the novel is designed to contribute to a simplification of character and event.

The opening scene of the green pool in the Salinas River promises serenity, but later the pool is the background for Lennie's violent death. George's initial hope that Lennie can hide his flawed humanity by seeming to be conventional is shattered in the end. Lennie's flaw grows into a potential for evil, and every evil is ascribed to him after his unwitting murder of Curley's wife. The objective image of the good life in the future, "a little house and a couple of acres an' a cow and some pigs," is opposed sharply to the present sordid reality of the bunkhouse and the ranch (*OMM* 14). Minor characters remain little more than opposed types, identifiable by allegorical tags. Curley is the unsure husband, opposed to and fearful of his sluttish, unnamed wife. Slim is a minor god in his perfect mastery of his work. His serenity is contrasted sharply with Curley's hysterical inability to please or to control his wife, and it contrasts as easily with the wife's constant, obvious discontent. Candy and Crooks are similar types, men without love. Both are abused by Curley, his wife, and the working crew. (Lennie might fall into this category of defenselessness if he were aware enough to realize the situation; but he is not.) These sharp oppositions and typed personae restrict the development of the novel. The merely subordinate characters, such as Carlson and Whit, who only begin or fill out a few scenes, are strictly nonhuman, since they remain abstract instruments within a design.

The climax of that design is simplified in its turn, since it serves only to manipulate Lennie into a moral situation beyond his understanding. The climax is doubled, a pairing of opposites. In its first half, when Curley's wife attempts to seduce Lennie as a way to demonstrate her hatred of Curley, Lennie is content (in his nice innocence) to stroke her soft hair; but he is too violent, and he snaps her neck in a panic miscalculation as he tries to force her to be quiet. In the second half, George shoots Lennie to prevent a worse death at the hands of others. The melodramatic quality of these events will be considered at a later point. Here, it is more important to observe, in the design, that the climax pairs an exploration of the ambiguity of love in the rigid contrast between the different motives that activate Curley's wife and George. Curley's wife wants to use Lennie to show her hatred for Curley. George shoots Lennie out of a real affection for him. The attempted seduction balances the knowing murder; both are disastrous expressions of love. Lennie is the unknowing center of the design in both halves of this climax. Steinbeck's control is all too evident. There is not much sense of dramatic illumination because the quality of the paired climax is that of a mechanical problem of joining two parallels. Lennie's necessary passivity enforces the quality of a mechanical design. He is only the man to who things happen. Being so limited, he is incapable of providing that sudden widening insight which alone justifies an artist's extreme dependence on a rigid design. Therefore, in general, *Of Mice and Men* remains a simple anecdote.

It would be a mistake to conclude that the limited scope of the materials is the only or the effective cause of the simplification. Writers frequently begin their work with anecdotal materials. Most often, however, they expand the reference of such materials through a knowing exercise of their medium.[9] It is Steinbeck's inability to exercise his medium or, perhaps more fundamentally, to select a proper medium, which ensures the limited reference, the lack of a widening insight.

In his discussion of the play-novelette form in *Stage*, Steinbeck dismisses the objection that allegory is an overly limited form,[10] but the objection is serious. *Of Mice and Men* is not merely a brief novel. It is limited in what its structure can make of its materials. Moreover, Steinbeck hoped to achieve precisely that limitation—the *Stage* essay leaves no doubt of this—although, it is true, he felt that form would ensure a concentration, a focus, of the materials. Instead, there is a deliberate thinning of materials that are thin (or theatrical) to begin with.

In fact, Steinbeck uses every possible device to thin out the effect of the materials. Foreshadowing is overworked. Lennie's murder of Curley's wife is the catastrophe that George has been dreading from the start. It is precisely the fate that a fluffy animal like Curley's wife should meet at the hands of Lennie, who has already killed mice and a puppy with his overpowering tenderness (*OMM* 8, 84–85). When Curley's wife makes clear her intention to seduce the first available man and the course of events abandons Lennie to her, the result is inevitable. But that inevitability does not have tragic qualities. The result is merely arranged, the characters merely inarticulate, and the action develops without illumination. Lennie can hardly distinguish between a dead pup and the dead woman: "Lennie went back and looked at the dead girl. The puppy lay close to her. Lennie picked it up. 'I'll throw him away,' he said. 'It's bad enough like it is'" (*OMM* 92).

The relative meaninglessness of his victims substitutes pathos for tragedy. Curley's rather shadowy wife underlines the substitution: She is characterless, nameless, and constantly discontent, so her death inspires none of the sympathy one might feel for a kind or a serene woman. Others respond to her death wholly in light of Lennie's predicament—from George's loving concern to Curley's blistering need for revenge—not his character. Everything that is excellent in the novel tends to relate, intensely if narrowly, to that emphasis. Within these limits, much that Steinbeck does is done excellently. The essential question is whether the treatment of the materials is intense enough to justify their evident manipulation, their narrowed pathos.

The novel communicates most intensely a theme of unconventional morality. Lennie does commit murder, but he remains guiltless because he is not responsible for what he does.[11] Yet the morality is only a statement of the pathos of Lennie's situation, not an exploration of guilt and innocence. A development through parallels and juxtapositions does little to expand the stated theme. Carlson parallels Lennie's violence on a conventional level when he insists on killing Candy's ancient, smelly dog. Carlson's reasoning is that the group has a right to wrong the individual. Lennie is incapable of any logic, even of this twisted sort, and he is never cruel by choice; that potential moral complexity is neglected in the design to permit the brutal simplicity of the group's response to Carlson's argument and to Lennie's crime. Carlson's crime is approved by the group: He abuses power to invade another man's desire for affection, reduced to a worthless dog. Lennie's crime is an accident in an attempt to express affection; murder is too serious for the group to ignore, so Lennie is hunted down. We are intended to notice the irony that Carlson's crime inverts Lennie's. That simple, paralleled irony substitutes for a possible, intense, necessarily complex, and ambiguous development of the materials. The rendered development, not the materials themselves, produces this simply mechanical irony.

Certainly the theme of unconventional morality offers tragic possibilities in a dimension beyond the anecdotal or the sketch of a character or event. From that viewpoint, the oppositions can expand into tragic awareness, at least potentially. They can even be listed as follows. Lennie is good in his intentions, but evil in fact. The group is good in wanting to punish a murderer, but evil in misunderstanding that Lennie is guiltless. Counterwise, George, Candy, and Slim are endowed with understanding by their roles as the friend, the man without hope, and the god, but they are powerless against the group. Curley's wife is knowingly evil in exploiting Lennie's powerful body and weak mind. Curley is evil in exploiting all opportunities to prove his manhood. These two are pathetic in their human limitations, not tragic. George enacts an unconventional morality less by accident than any of the others. He feels strongly that, in being compelled to look after Lennie, he has given up the good times he might have had, but he knows the sacrifice is better, that he and Lennie represent an idealized variety of group-man. Slim's early, sympathetic insight makes this explicit:

> "You guys travel around together?" [Slim's] tone was friendly. It invited confidence without demanding it. "Sure," said George. "We kinda look after each other." He indicated Lennie with his thumb. "He ain't bright.

Hell of a good worker, though. Hell of a nice fella, but he ain't bright. I've knew him for a long time." Slim looked through George and beyond him. "Ain't many guys travel around together," he mused. "I don't know why. Maybe ever'body in the whole damn world is scared of each other." "It's a lot nicer to go around with a guy you know," said George. (*OMM* 34–35)

This important passage centers the theme of unconventional morality. It celebrates a relationship "the whole damn world" is incapable of imagining, given the ugly context of ranch life and sordid good times, and it locates the good life in friendship, not in the material image of the little farm. This passage is the heart of the novel.

But a novel cannot be structured solely on the basis of a theme, even a fundamental theme. Too much else must be simplified. Worse, the unconventional morality located in friendship produces Lennie's death, not only because Steinbeck can see no other way to conclude. Lennie dies necessarily because friendship can go no further than it does go, and nothing can be made of the dreamlike ideal of little farm. The extreme simplification is that Steinbeck can do nothing with Lennie after he has been exhibited. These limitations derive from the simplification required by the play-novelette form. Steinbeck appears to be aware that formal limitations need some widening, since he imbeds Lennie's happiest and most intense consciousness of the good life of friends in an ironic context:

George said, "Guys like us got no fambly. They make a little stake an' then they blow it in. They ain't got nobody in the worl' that gives a hoot in hell about 'em—"
"*But not us*," Lennie cried happily. "Tell about us now."
George was quiet for a moment. "But not us," he said.
"Because—"
"Because I got you an'—"
"An' I got you. We got each other, that's what, that gives a hoot in hell about us," Lennie cried in triumph. (*OMM* 104)[12]

The passage extends friendship beyond its boundary; it celebrates a species of marriage, minus the sexual element, between Lennie and George. But the content of the passage is qualified heavily by its position; George shoots Lennie after retelling the story about the little farm that always quiets Lennie. As further irony, precisely the responsibilities of a perfect friendship require George to shoot Lennie. The mob that would hang Lennie for murder is in the background throughout the scene. The situation is moving, but the effect is local. The ironies relate only to Lennie's pathetic situation; they do not aid an understanding of Lennie or account (beyond plot) for his death. Too, the scene is melodramatic; it puts aside the large problems of justifying the event in order to jerk our tears over the event itself.

To say that Steinbeck avoids the problems of structure by milking individual scenes is not to say that *Of Mice and Men* is a total failure. As mature work, it is not a depot for the basic flaws in Steinbeck's earliest work. Many of the scenes are excellently constructed and convincing in themselves. Considerable attention is given to establishing minor details. For example, George shoots Lennie with the Luger that Carlson used to kill Candy's old dog. The defenseless man is linked by the weapon with the defenseless dog in the group's web of created power. George does his killing as a kind of ritual. If the police or the mob had taken Lennie, the death would have been a meaningless expression of group force, the exaction of an eye for an eye rather than an expression of love. The background of language is the workingman dialect that Steinbeck perfected in *In Dubious Battle*, realized here to express a brutally realistic world that negates idealism and exaggerates the sadistic and the ugly. Its perfection is enhanced by a factual context—the dependence of the men on their shifting jobs, the explicit misery of their homelessness, and the exposure of their social and economic weaknesses. The more sensitive men dream of escape into some kind of gentleness. The thread of possible realization of that dream tends to hold the novel in a focus. The opposite pole of man's imperfect moral nature motivates Curley's wife and Carlson. Steinbeck's fine web of circumstance reaches from the ideal possibility to the brutal fact.

Of Mice and Men is strongest in precisely this plot sense, in a sequence and linkage of events controlled by ironic contrast and juxtaposition. The result is limited to the rendering of a surface, yet the necessarily external devices of plot are used with artistic care and skillful tact.

Just after George, Lennie, and Candy agree to realize the dream of the little farm by pooling their savings and earnings, Curley appears, searching for his wife. Frustrated, Curley punches Lennie without mercy until (on George's order) Lennie grabs and crushes Curley's hand. This violent event suggests that Curley's sadistic vision of the world will not be shut out by the idealized vision of cooperative friends. More closely, the ugly inversion of "the good, clean fight" serves to contrast Lennie's innocence with his surprise and helplessness before evil. The other men in the bunkhouse are unconcerned; violence is an ordinary element in their lives. The incident enacts and announces the implicitly universal moral imperfection of humanity—an insight that broadens and becomes more overt in the following scenes. When Curley has to go to town to have a doctor care for his crushed hand, the men take the chance to go into town for a spree. Crooks, Candy, and Lennie—the Negro, the old man, and the idiot—are left on the ranch with Curley's wife. The circumstances provide her with an opportunity to seduce Lennie; she hates Curley, and the Hollywood ideal of the seductive movie queen is her only standard of love. Crooks cannot protect Lennie because his black skin leaves him open to sexual blackmail; Candy's feeble efforts are useless; and Lennie does not understand what is happening. The ultimate irony in this tangle of violence is that none of the characters is evil or intends to do evil. . . . In her need as in her amoral unawareness of good and evil, Curley's wife is not unlike Lennie, just as the various moral defects of other people conspire by chance to leave Lennie alone and defenseless with Curley's wife. Yet "love" has different meanings for Lennie and for Curley's wife; the clash of meanings ensures their deaths.

The death of Curley's wife switches the narrative focus to George and to the device of the split hero. Steinbeck is fond of this device of a divided (not duplicated) hero, usually two men of opposite nature, one distinctly secondary to the other but both sharing the center of the novel. For a few suggestive, not inclusive, examples: Henry Morgan, Jim Nolan, and Aaron Trask are coldly thoughtful, knowing men, either selfish or idealistic in what they do; Coeur de Gris, Mac, and Caleb Trask are relatively warmer men, possibly as knowing as their opposites, but usually more subject to their emotions. Jim Casy and Tom Joad extend and complicate the pattern as they become suggestive types of Christ and Saint Paul, the human god and the coldly realistic organizer, but they do not break the pattern. There are obvious narrative virtues of clarity in a device that is recognizable as well as flexible. The secondary hero is subordinate in Steinbeck's fiction—except in *Of Mice and Men*. There, Lennie's murder propels George into a sudden prominence that has not structural basis.

Is the novel concerned with Lennie's innocence or George's guilt? The formal requirements of a play-novelette mandate a structural refocus. Steinbeck needs a high point to bring down the curtain. With Lennie dead, Steinbeck must use and emphasize George's guilt. The close is formulated—the results of a hasty switch—not structured from preceding events, so it produces an inconclusive ending in view of what has happened previously. And the ideal of the farm vanishes with Lennie's death, when George tells Candy the plan is off.

Here the difficulty is with a structure that requires a climax which cannot be achieved once Lennie, the center of the novel, is removed; but Lennie must be killed off when his existence raises problems of characterization more complex than the play-novelette form can express. Materials and structure pull against each other and finally collapse into an oversimplified conclusion that removes rather than faces the central theme.

The abrupt "solution" rests on melodrama, on sudden, purely plot devices of focus and refocus. Such overt manipulation indicates that in its practice the play-novelette is not a new form. Steinbeck's experience, his mature technical skill do not finally disguise his wish to return to his earliest fictional efforts to realize complex human behavior by way of an extreme simplification of structure and materials. His deliberate avoidance of an organic structure and his consequent dependence on a formula, on the exercise of technique within an artistic vacuum, exhausts the significance of the play-novelette theory. His practice, as in *Of Mice and Men*, does not lead to serious efforts and to a real achievement in the art of the novel. Rather, it leads to manipulations designed to effect a simplification of structure and materials. So much skill, directed toward so little, is disturbing. But the skill is absolutely there.

Notes

1. John Steinbeck, ". . . the novel might benefit by the discipline, the terseness . . . ," *Stage* 15 (January 1938): 50–51. Excerpts from this work are quoted by permission of McIntosh and Otis, Inc.

2. Antonia Seixas was Steinbeck's secretary for a time, and the wife of Steinbeck's close friend, Edward Ricketts; she speaks with authority from within the circle. Consequently, her opinion—published in March 1947—that *Of Mice and Men* is a great novel primarily on philosophic grounds is a fascinating echo of

Steinbeck's low view of the actual novel and his high view of the abstract theory of the form presented in the *Stage* article.

3. Steinbeck, *Stage*, 51.

4. E. W. Tedlock Jr., and C. V. Wicker, eds., *Steinbeck and His Critics: A Record of Twenty-Five Years* (Albuquerque: University of New Mexico Press, 1957). The abbreviation is embarrassing. Tedlock and Wicker omit the *Stage* article from an otherwise important collection of Steinbeck's observation on his craft.

5. Harry Thornton Moore, *The Novels of John Steinbeck* (Chicago: Normandie House, 1939), 48–49; Peter Lisca, *The Wide World of John Steinbeck* (New Brunswick: Rutgers University Press, 1958), 132–33.

6. John Steinbeck, *Of Mice and Men* (New York: Penguin, 1993). Hereafter cited as *OMM*.

7. Moore, *Novels*, 49; Lisca, *Wide World*, 130.

8. Moore, *Novels*, 48.

9. Mark Schorer, "Technique as Discovery," *Hudson Review* 1 (Spring 1948), 67–87. I am much indebted to Schorer's argument.

10. Steinbeck, *Stage*, 51.

11. This paradox is the "moral" of the poem by Robert Burns which supplies the title of the novel; the title indicates Steinbeck's own concentration on a thematic development, not on characters or events as important in themselves. Further: A "moral" does tend to be simple.

12. This is a repetition of an earlier passage in a less sinister context (13–14). Compare the close of *In Dubious Battle*.

CHAPTER SIX

STEINBECK'S *OF MICE AND MEN* (NOVEL) (1937)
John F. Slater

[*Editor's note: Portions of this article have been omitted as the content does not directly apply to* Of Mice and Men.]

I. Background

The publication of *Of Mice and Men* in January of 1937 opened an impressive new horizon in the course of Steinbeck's literary development and brought about significant alterations, not entirely welcome, in his personal situation. Especially during his early years as a writer, Steinbeck had shown restless attraction to imagery that focused on the activity of learning. When he wrote, in *Tortilla Flat*, "the waves gently practiced at striking and hissed a little," he seemed to amplify his private concern with the laborious reiterations needed to establish the wavelength of a distinctive voice. In *Of Mice and Men*, Steinbeck continued to learn through practice. True to the scientific attitude he adopted toward the procedures of his craft, he viewed the novel as a kind of laboratory, a theater of operations where he could master innovative dramatic skills. . . . The "experiment," he said, was an attempt to make "a play that can be read or a novel that can be played."[1] What he achieved was a union of competing genres that reflects simultaneously his respect for formal order

Previously published in *A Study Guide to Steinbeck*, ed. Tetsumaro Hayashi, 129–48. Lanham, MD: Scarecrow Press, 1974. Reprinted with permission.

and his suspicion of it, his need for design without the expense of yielding to any one orthodoxy. The surfacing at this time of Steinbeck's overt interest in dramatic modes indicates another, related conflict as well. His emergence as a public figure was threatening to impinge on his role as artist. *Of Mice and Men* was an immediate popular and critical success. The novel, with the play and movie adaptation that followed, brought financial security and engendered lasting respect among critics who have treated few other of Steinbeck's works as kindly with the passage of time. But even during the two-year period when he was working on *Of Mice and Men*, Steinbeck was already troubled by the prospect of wide recognition and acceptance: "I am scared of popularity. It has ruined everyone I know."[2] Steinbeck welcomed a moderately sized audience and subscribed to "the recent tendency of writers . . . to deal in those themes and those scenes which are best understood and appreciated by groups of people."[3] An unbridled reception, however, could be as harmful as a formless novel, and consequently Steinbeck declared his intention of "holding an audience," necessarily imagined as a finite one if the book were to become a play, and of creating intimate, "almost physical contact"[4] with his readers. For Steinbeck, the readership equivalent to a packed house was a few tens of thousands, and he addressed himself to them, not to the millions who eventually materialized in the wake of *The Grapes of Wrath*.

Prefatory comments that link *Of Mice and Men* to the decade that produced it must issue a precautionary note. To the extent that the book is a documentary account as well as an artistic *tour de force*, it touches on Steinbeck's private history more than the contemporary public history of his country. Despite the continuation of the era's great event, the Depression, Steinbeck was relatively unencumbered, at least by 1936, in the management of his family affairs. On the other hand, he had become reflective and inward-looking about the direction his career increasingly promised to take. Correspondingly, *Of Mice and Men*, unlike the two novels that embraced it, is not about the alignment of massive economic forces. Certainly the story is interested in how modular groups of people, even two men together, formulate effective myths of social cohesion; but the emphasis is on individual performance or its failure, not monolithic external factors. In *Of Mice and Men*, Steinbeck is steadfastly sympathetic toward men less fortunate than himself. On this occasion, however, the overwhelming power that leads to the prosperity of those who harness it while maiming countless unenfranchised victims is represented, not by titanic accumulations of economic might but by the supremacy of Steinbeck's own verbal and imaginative faculties. The twentieth-century subculture in which Lennie and George find themselves is no doubt a diminished source of romantic fantasy or its fulfillment, but Steinbeck goes out of his way to indicate that the realization of what dreams they can salvage is economically well within their grasp. Lennie, by virtue of his psycho-physical abnormality, and George, by virtue of his fatally dependent, self-defeating temperament, represent regrettable limitations of personal talent more than the defects of a nation divided into warring factions. Their world is a hard one, inhospitable to pastoral visions drawn from the American past, but it does not deny a place to people like Slim, ordained by special accomplishments, any more than the demanding world of American literature withheld acclamation from the novel *Of Mice and Men* and its author.

II. Synopsis

[Editor's note: This section of text merely repeats the plot line of Of Mice and Men.*]*

III. Critical Explication

[See editor's note.]

In terms of literary criticism, Leslie Fiedler's controversial book *Love and Death in the American Novel* ushered in the revolution of the 1960s. The controversy centered on Fiedler's thesis that the American novel is distinguished by an archetypal sequence of close relationships between "male pairs," such as Huck Finn and Jim, that border on what Fiedler now calls, with some reservations, the "homoerotic." Fiedler's contention helps place *Of Mice and Men* in an important historical tradition, although no one would quarrel with Burton Rascoe's early assessment that "the relationship between George and Lennie is a paradigm of all the nonphysical, nonsexual (let us use the so tritely inadequate and now almost meaningless word 'spiritual' to help out in indicating the meaning) emotions, concerns, and aspirations in the world."[9] But Fiedler provided another kind of access, as well, to the reader who sought to base his admiration of Steinbeck on the solidest possible ground. Fiedler impatiently rejected the strictures of New Criticism and reasserted the right, even of academic critics, to share the motivations of general readers who view factors other than artistic performance—factors such as the light a given novel might shed on cultural continuities—as valid if not indeed essential dimension of reading activity.

. . . *Of Mice and Men* is relevant to current concerns, including the concern of students to be subjective, even sentimental, free from fear of recrimination while reserving the right to be tough-minded about immutable realities when occasion requires. A generation of students that introduced the word "scenario" to the lexicon of political activism can appreciate Steinbeck's abiding interest in the wellsprings of social drama. Furthermore, powerful sympathy has revived for the downtrodden protagonists Steinbeck chronicled. Like George and Lennie, many young people profess to "give a damn," and their experience often vindicates the use of the slogan. Thoreau's vision of a life uncluttered by academic sophistication has won new adherents—and has its counterpart in Lennie and George's dream of a farm of their own. Salinas remains the scene of economic and social friction, and even Soledad has lent its name to the headlines. *Of Mice and Men* proves no exception to the renewed timeliness of Steinbeck's work. . . .

Throughout Steinbeck, rhetorical arrangements, however liberated compared with ordinary ones, complement the victimization of characters by uncontrollable, even unrecognizable imperatives latent in nature and in manmade systems like the rudimentary verbal ones the characters themselves put together. Thus when the reader of *Of Mice and Men* submits to the exciting flow of unfolding events, he also perceives himself in the presence of an architectural scheme analogous to the rise-and-fall trajectory of classical drama. This recognition of the novel's structural integrity reveals that, even as they manipulate one another, Steinbeck's characters are as subservient to the dictates of his master plan as to the urgencies of natural impulse.

To implement the economy of an "experiment" in dramatic form, Steinbeck communicated the parallels he sensed between natural and rhetorical forces by focusing on a specific image in *Of Mice and Men*, the image of a "trap." Most obviously, he used the slang word for "mouth," "trap," to suggest that even apparently casual utterances can hem men in. . . .

An explicit "trap" reference occurs in *Of Mice and Men* when Curley's wife says to Crooks, "Listen, Nigger. . . . You know what I can do to you if you open your trap?" (*OMM* 80). The reference seems insignificant in isolation, but in the context of George's warning Lennie that Curley's wife is "a rat-trap if I ever seen one" (*OMM* 32), it elevates sensitivity to the trap of racial discrimination that imprisons Crooks. Given the title of the novel, George's comment about a "rat-trap" also brings to mind Burns' couplet, "The best laid schemes o' mice an' men / Gang aft a-gley," and its implication that destiny, chance, is a trap set for men, mice, and perhaps rats too. *Of Mice and Men* is as much concerned with references to "chance," often in connection with games, as it is with traps. George's "rat-trap" comment also shows how rhetorical and natural threats coincide in *Of Mice and Men*. Women, and by extension human sexuality, are a biological trap for Steinbeck's characters. The Salinas bordellos trap men's money and sap their will power. Steinbeck perhaps intended an oblique disparagement of Lennie's Aunt Clara when he bestowed the name Clara on the more expensive of the town's two madams. References to Curley's "glove fulla vaseline" (*OMM* 27) disagreeably symbolize the entrapment of husband and wife in mutual sexual exploitation. These references supplement Candy's loss of his hand, prepare the ground for the crushing of Curley's hand and, again by extension, show the meaning of Crooks's crippled spine. Crooks's infirmity is emblematic of his handicapped racial status, a brand of impotence cruelly thrust home by what Curley's wife says to him.

Thus far, we have noticed historical factors that have influenced the reception of *Of Mice and Men*, . . . [but] the history of critical reactions to the book also deserves attention. The conclusions that critics have drawn about *Of Mice and Men* can best be summarized by quoting one of Steinbeck's astutest readers, Peter Lisca, who accepts the lead of Antonia Seixas in his finding that "the simple story of two migrant workers' dream of a safe retreat, a 'clean well-lighted place,' becomes itself a pattern or archetype which exists on three levels."

"There is the obvious story level on a realistic plane, with its shocking climax. There is also the level of social protest, Steinbeck the reformer crying out against the exploitation of migrant workers. The third level is an allegorical one, its interpretation limited only by the ingenuity of the audience."[22] Referring to Burns' poem, Lisca goes on to identify a final, fourth level:

In the poem, Burns extends the mouse's experience to include that of mankind; in *Of Mice and Men*, Steinbeck extends the experience of two migrant workers to the human condition. "This is the way things are," both writers are saying. On this level, perhaps the most important, Steinbeck is dramatizing the non-teleological philosophy which had such a great part in shaping *In Dubious Battle* and which would be fully discussed in *Sea of Cortez*.[23]

Lisca's comments are definitive, and his chapter on *Of Mice and Men* in *The Wide World of John Steinbeck* is the indispensable point of departure for any survey of the novel's critics.

The current explication has sought to show that the "inevitableness" Lisca notices in *Of Mice and Men* is the effect of the novel's rhetorical components, not just of the superficial course of events. Lennie's actions repeat themselves with a regularity that soon becomes predictable, and Steinbeck similarly marshals his artistic resources to produce a cyclical, rather than linear dramatic action. In addition to the recurrent elements already discussed at some length, the reader will probably have recognized several others in the novel itself. Apparently minor details often serve to buttress the novel's taut, interlocking arrangement. When George tells Lennie, "You ain't gonna put nothing over on me" (*OMM* 8), his language forecasts the boss's parting shot in the following section. The color red repeatedly signifies feminine allure. A great, mysterious fish, at home in the natural surroundings of the novel's opening, ironically anticipates the desperate human "fish," Curley and his wife, that Lennie maims and kills. Larger rhetorical units form patterns, too. The end of the novel recapitulates almost verbatim the description at the beginning, although by the end Steinbeck has progressively educated his audience about the symbolism of incidental detail. The unassailable dispassion with which a water bird swallows a snake throws in starkest contrast George's agonized resignation to Lennie's death. Less overtly, the series of references to the characters' literary tastes draws attention to the much greater capability and complexity of Steinbeck's own. Even the mechanical procedure of noting the length of the novel's six sections illuminates Steinbeck's self-conscious artistry. The initial sections expand at a measured tempo into the spacious central episodes; then follows the compression and acceleration that leads to the denouement.

In closing, it is worthwhile reemphasizing an issue raised in the introduction: in every way, *Of Mice and Men* reflects Steinbeck's exceptional concern for the implications of his craft at the time he wrote the novel. The novel arbitrates between an urgent need for freedom and a no less importunate need for control, personal needs that appertain more to the universal history of artists than to the passing history of the mid-1930s. Steinbeck's characters are equally engrossed in the private dilemmas and decisions common to untutored creativity in every age. George has the faculty of creating dream worlds that seem real as long as he can improvise an audience. With Lennie's death, he falls from grace. Recognizing that his audience, like his fable, has been ephemeral, the captive of circumstances, he accommodates himself to a more mundane version of reality than the one he has made in his mind. The importance for any story teller of a suitable audience is a principal theme of the novel. Crooks cannot read without a companion; George cannot sustain his story without Lennie. In this respect, the end of *Of Mice and Men* seems purposefully equivocal. George has located a new audience in Slim, a man whose consummate elan and professional composure is the clearest surrogate for the finesse Steinbeck's literary proficiency represents. Vicariously, George is compensated for Lennie's loss by participating in the special amalgam of stylistic ingenuity and compassionate sensibility, the blend of pragmatism and idealism, that Steinbeck displays at his very best. Unlike the ending of *Tortilla Flat* when, after the death of Danny, "no two walked together,"[24] George is not alone. But unlike the ending, too, of the opening section of *Of Mice and Men*, when "a coyote yammered, and a dog answered from the other side of the stream," Lennie has gone "acrost the river," but the final question, "Now what the hell ya suppose is eatin' them two guys?" (*OMM* 107) remains unanswered. Steinbeck had won an audience, but its understanding was not necessarily proportionate to its size. . . .

Notes

[*Editor's note: Portions of this article have been omitted as the content does not directly apply to* Of Mice and Men. *Thus, several notes have also been omitted.*]

   1. As quoted in Lewis Gannett, "John Steinbeck's Way of Writing," in *Steinbeck and His Critics: A Record of Twenty-five Years*, Ed. E. W. Tedlock Jr. and C. V. Wicker (Albuquerque: The University of New Mexico Press, 1957), 30.
   2. Gannett, "John Steinbeck's Way," 28.

3. As quoted in Peter Lisca, "*Of Mice and Men*," in *The Wide World of John Steinbeck* (New Brunswick, NJ: Rutgers University Press, 1958), 133.

4. Lisca, *Wide World*, 133.

9. Burton Rascoe, "John Steinbeck," in Tedlock and Wicker, *Steinbeck and His Critics*, 61.

22. Lisca, *Wide World*, 138–39.

23. Lisca, *Wide World*, 139–40.

24. John Steinbeck, *Tortilla Flat*, 1935 (New York: Viking, 1963), 179.

Part Four
THE 1980s

Paul McCarthy's 1980 study, *John Steinbeck* (New York: Frederick Ungar), concentrates on dreams and the importance of sharing and cooperation in attaining them. Calling *Mice* one of the best short novels of the decade, McCarthy emphasizes Steinbeck's use of the Greek unities—time, place, and character—as he employed simple and dramatic action and eliminated the superfluous and complex. McCarthy also discusses the symbolism of Steinbeck's settings and praises the variety and depth of his characterization, directly contradicting earlier commentaries that found these elements lacking in the novel. Definitely disagreeing with detractors, McCarthy stresses that Steinbeck's excellence is reflected in his ability to draw credible characters.

Peter Lisca's second book on Steinbeck, *Nature and Myth* (New York: Crowell, 1978), linked the novel with Steinbeck's previous work *In Dubious Battle* (1936) and drew attention to its similarly paired characters, Mac and Jim. Once again defending the novel against charges of sentimentality, altruism, and middlebrow appeal, Lisca incorporates a Jungian and religious analysis into his second reading. Relying on Goldhurst's 1961 essay, Lisca extends the Cain and Abel parallels and calls attention to the complex imagery and the circular plot structure as evidence of Steinbeck's artistry. In addition, he develops a reading of the theme of loneliness and the need for companionship and loyal camaraderie.

John Timmerman's 1986 study entitled *John Steinbeck: the Aesthetics of the Road Taken* (Norman: University of Oklahoma Press, 1986) also pairs *Mice* with *In Dubious Battle* and praises the crafted structure as an indication of its stature as one of the most compressed and unified works in Steinbeck's canon. Specifically, he mentions the novel's meticulous framing and foreshadowing and the richness of Steinbeck's themes of friendship and the fragile nature of all human dreams. In addition, Timmerman asserts that although the theme of loneliness may appear to be dark and depressing, the inevitable doom is countered by the potential for human glory and its ability to seek a hopeful future as mankind strives for seemingly unattainable desires.

Louis Owens's 1985 analysis, *John Steinbeck's Re-Vision of America* (Athens: University of Georgia Press), is the first study of the author that does not utilize a chronological approach to assess the Steinbeck canon. Instead Owens uses physical locations as an organizing principle and divides his comments into three sections: "The Mountains," "The Valleys," and "The Sea." Placing *Of Mice and Men* in the second category, he entitles his chapter on *Mice* "The Dream of Commitment." In his discussion of the novel, Owens stresses Steinbeck's use of the Eden myth and the lush valleys of middle California that grow much of the nation's produce. Concentrating on George and Lennie's isolation and their social position as outcasts, Owens then goes on to reiterate many of the previous observations about *Mice*, including the Cain myth, animalism and Jungian psychology, making it clear that the characters' descent into the valley (read despair and death) is countered at the end of the novel by two men (Slim and George) walking off together, an ending which suggested a strong note of hope and affirmed Steinbeck's belief that the commitment of mankind to other humans has not perished.

Other Significant Studies from the 1980s

McCarthy, Paul. "Conflicts and Searches in the 1930s." In *John Steinbeck*, chap. 3, 57–64. New York: Frederick Ungar, 1980.

Owens, Louis. "*Of Mice and Men*: The Dream of Commitment." In *John Steinbeck's Re-Vision of America*, 100–106. Athens: University of Georgia Press, 1985.

Wyatt, David. "Steinbeck's Lost Gardens." In *The Fall into Eden: Landscape and Imagination in California*, 124–57. Cambridge: Cambridge University Press, 1986.

Fensch, Thomas, ed. *Conversations with John Steinbeck.* Jackson: University of Mississippi Press, 1988.

CHAPTER SEVEN
A GAME OF CARDS IN STEINBECK'S
OF MICE AND MEN
Michael W. Shurgot

Midway through section two of *Of Mice and Men*, after George and Lennie have met Candy, the boss, and his son Curley, Steinbeck describes George walking to the table in the bunkhouse and shuffling some of the playing cards lying there. Often during the rest of section two and throughout section three, Steinbeck pictures George playing solitaire with these cards. Although George's card-playing may seem just a means of passing time during his and Lennie's first night on the ranch, the frequency of George's card games and Steinbeck's careful juxtaposition of them with the prophetic events of sections two and three indicate that the game of cards is the central symbol of the entire novel.

George's card games are generally symbolic in three ways. Lester Jay Marks writes that Steinbeck's novel is "disciplined by his non-teleological methods of observing 'phenomena.' He is concerned not with the *why* but with *Of Mice and Men* the *what* and *how* of the individual's illusions."[1] Steinbeck's original title, "Something That Happened," is, according to Marks, an unsentimental comment upon the "tragic reversal of fortunes" that George and Lennie experience (59). A non-teleological world is one of chance, of reversals of fortune beyond man's comprehension or his power to control. And a game of cards is an exact symbol of this kind of world. In card games there is no pattern to the cards' random appearance; their sequence is solely a matter of chance. Analogically, although George

Previously published in *Steinbeck Quarterly* 25, nos. 1–2 (Winter–Spring 1982): 38–43. Used by permission of Archives and Special Collections, Ball State University Libraries.

tries to control Lennie's activities and movements on the ranch, he cannot prevent Lennie's tragic meeting with Curley's wife in the barn.

Further, George's card game is solitaire. From the opening dialogue between George and Lennie, to the novel's final, terrifying moments, Steinbeck's characters talk about the isolation, rootlessness, and alienation of their lives. Steinbeck introduces the theme of isolation shortly after George and Lennie arrive at the clearing in part one. George laments,

> Guys like us, that work on ranches, are the loneliest guys in the world. They got no family. They don't belong no place. They come to a ranch an' work up a stake and then they go inta town and blow their stake, and the first thing you know they're poundin' their tail on some other ranch. They ain't got nothing to look ahead to. (*OMM* 13–14)[2]

George's sense of the loneliness and rootlessness of ranchhands is echoed several times in the novel. In section two, Slim observes, "Ain't many guys travel around together. . . . I don't know why. Maybe ever'body in the whole damn world is scared of each other" (*OMM* 38). Early in section three, Slim elaborates on the uniqueness of George's relationship with Lennie:

> Funny how you an' him string along together. . . . I hardly never seen two guys travel together. You know how the hands are, they just come in and get their bunk and work a month, and then they quit and go out alone. Never seem to give a damn about nobody. It jus' seems kinda funny a cuckoo like him and a smart guy little guy like you travelin' together. (*OMM* 39)

George tells Slim he "ain't got no people," and insists that, although Lennie is a "God damn nuisance most of the time," nonetheless traveling with him is preferable to the loneliness and misery of most ranchhands' lives: "I seen the guys that go around on the ranches alone. That ain't no good. They don't have no fun. After a long time they get mean. They get wantin' to fight all the time" (*OMM* 41).[3] Later, after George has told Candy about his and Lennie's dream of owning their own place, Candy, obviously enthralled at being included in their plans, says that he would leave his share of the place to them ". . . 'cause I ain't got no relatives nor nothing" (*OMM* 59).

On the ranch itself, the most hopelessly alienated characters besides Candy are Crooks and Curley's wife. Crooks, the crippled black stable buck, although serving an important function, is nonetheless isolated in a world of physically powerful white men. Because he is disfigured, and thus less mobile than the ranchhands, he is ironically more permanent than they, but he is barred from their quarters and sleeps in a "long box filled with straw" (*OMM* 66), a symbolic coffin. Echoing George's remarks about the psychological effects of constant loneliness, Crooks complains bitterly to Lennie, "A guy goes nuts if he ain't got nobody" (*OMM* 72). [Curley's wife] insists that at one time she "could of went with shows," and that "a guy tol' me he could put me in pictures" (*OMM* 78). But instead, she now spends Saturday nights "talkin' to a bunch of bindlestiffs—a nigger an' a dumdum and a lousy ol' sheep—an' likin' it because they ain't nobody else" (*OMM* 78).[4] Although the circumstances of their lives on the ranch are quite different, Crooks and Curley's wife are similarly isolated within and segregated from the white, predominately masculine world of the novel. Fortune has been kind to neither Crooks nor Curley's wife, and their lives emphasize the pervasive isolation (and occasionally despair) that haunts Steinbeck's characters.

Besides symbolizing the lonely, disjointed lives of the ranchhands and the alienation of Crooks and Curley's wife, George's games of solitaire are symbolic in a third way. George tries, quite naturally, to "win" his games of solitaire, and when considered along with several of his remarks to Lennie, such efforts at victory became quite ironic.[5] Early in section one, after pleading with Lennie not to "do no bad things like you done in Weed," George describes, as he does frequently in the novel, what he could do if he were alone: "God, you're a lot of trouble," said George. "I could get along so easy and so nice if I didn't have you on my tail. I could live so easy and maybe have a girl" (*OMM* 7).

Twice more in part one, George repeats this sentiment. The first time, Lennie's innocent wish for some ketchup precipitates one of George's most violent explosions against him in the novel. George angrily recounts their narrow escape from Weed—"You crazy son-of-a-bitch. You keep me in hot water all the time"—(*OMM* 11) and brutally claims, "I wisht I could put you in a cage with about a million mice an' let you have fun" (*OMM* 12). Moments later, after Lennie pathetically insists that had they any ketchup George could have all of it, George says, "When I think of the swell time I could have without you, I go nuts. I never get no peace" (*OMM* 12). Just after returning to the clearing in part six, Lennie says, "George gonna wish he was alone an' not have me botherin' him" (*OMM* 100). Shortly after Lennie's remark, George is alone, and as lonely as the other ranchhands he describes earlier in part one. Although he certainly wants and needs Lennie to fulfill their dream together, George's frequent wish to be alone, to be free of the burden of minding Lennie, is ironically forecast in his frequent resorts to solitaire in the first half of the novel.

Steinbeck enhances the general symbolism of George's games of solitaire by carefully interweaving them into the narrative of sections two and three. George first plays with the cards during his conversation with Candy about Curley and his wife. Candy explains that Curley is a fighter and has become "cockier'n ever since he got married" (*OMM* 27). George remarks that Curley had better "watch out for Lennie," walks to the table and picks up the cards, and fumbles with them continually as Candy describes Curley's "glove . . . fulla vaseline" (*OMM* 27) and his wife:

"Wait'll you see Curley's wife."
    George cut the cards again and put out a solitaire lay, slowly and deliberately. "Purty?" he asked casually. (*OMM* 28)

Steinbeck's careful positioning of Candy's description of Curley's wife and George's first hand of solitaire juxtaposes the immediate cause of the failure of George and Lennie's dream and the ultimate consequence of that failure for George: his solitude. A similar juxtaposition occurs moments later. Candy says to George, "Well, you look her mister. You see if she ain't a tart" (*OMM* 28). Steinbeck writes: "George laid down his cards thoughtfully, turned his piles of three. He built four clubs on his ace pile. . . . George stared at his solitaire lay, and then he flounced the cards together and turned around to Lennie" (*OMM* 28–29).

George warns Lennie about Curley, whom he correctly perceives as a threat to their plans, and repeats his instructions to him about returning to the pool in the river should trouble occur. Curley's wife enters immediately, and Lennie's twice-repeated "She's purty" elicits George's fierce warning to him about her being "jail bait" and his insistence that he and Lennie must stay at the ranch until they make their stake: "'We gotta keep it till we get a stake. We can't help it, Lennie. We'll get out jus' as soon as we can. I don't like it no better than you do.' He went back to the table and set out a new solitaire hand" (*OMM* 33).

George's card games precede and follow the appearance of Curley's wife and Lennie's reactions to her, thus symbolically framing their first meeting in a realm of chance. Further, when Slim enters he sits down at the table across from George. While Slim plays with the cards, he talks to Carlson about his dog's pups and Candy's old dog. This conversation foreshadows Lennie's death; and the sense of his and the dog's similar fates is suggested by the hand of cards that George and Slim, with ironic nonchalance, manipulate during this scene. Section two closes with Slim about a pup, thus initiating the chain of events that leads to Lennie's presence in the barn when Curley's wife tempts him the following Sunday.

Section three opens with George's confiding in Slim about Lennie's troubles in Weed. Twice during their dialogue Steinbeck describes George playing solitaire: "'Course he ain't mean. But he gets in trouble alla time because he's so God damn dumb. Like what happened in Weed—.' He stopped, stopped in the middle of turning over a card (*OMM* 41) and "Slim's eyes were level and unwinking. He nodded very slowly. 'So what happens?' George carefully built his line of solitaire cards" (*OMM* 42). Steinbeck's careful interweaving of George's hand of solitaire with his narrative of Lennie's seizure of the girl in Weed is his most effective apposition in the novel. Lennie's actions in Weed clearly presage his killing Curley's wife, and George will be alone after he shoots Lennie.

Steinbeck employs this card symbolism variously in the rest of section three. Just before Carlson shoots Candy's dog, George and Whit start a game of euchre (*OMM* 49), but when Whit mentions Curley's wife, he drops his cards and George immediately lays out another hand of solitaire (*OMM* 51). After Carlson and Lennie return to the bunkhouse and Curley inquires about his wife and Slim, Lennie joins George at the table: "He got up from his bunk and sat down at the table, across from George. Almost automatically George shuffled the cards and laid out his solitaire hand. He used a deliberate, thoughtful, [sic] slowness" (*OMM* 55).

George's "automatically" laying out his solitaire hand as he sits across from Lennie is acutely ironic and prophetic, for George will be as solitary as the rest of the ranchhands after Lennie's death. A moment later, as George "look[s] carefully at the solitaire hand," he mentions that Andy Cushman is "in San Quentin right now on account of a tart" (*OMM*

56). As an anonymous tart was responsible for Andy Cushman's fate, so Curley's wife, whom Candy describes as a "tart" in section two, will be responsible for Lennie's. Even as he and Lennie talk, George's conversation obliquely foreshadows the novel's climatic scene and ironically reinforces the symbolism of his game of solitaire.

Lennie's repetitive questioning about their "little place" abruptly changes the mood in the bunkhouse. "George's hands stopped working with the cards. His voice was growing warmer" (*OMM* 57). Significantly, George abandons the cards while describing their dream, as if its fulfillment were within their own control, beyond chance. Indeed, Candy's unexpected offer of his $300 suddenly convinces George that his and Lennie's long quest may finally be successful. "They all sat still, all bemused, by the beauty of the thing, each mind was popped into the future when this lovely thing should come about" (*OMM* 60). But their illusion is quickly shattered. It is sheer chance, like the unexpected appearance of a card, and brutal irony that Lennie is still smiling "with delight at the memory of the ranch" (*OMM* 62) when the enraged Curley, after being repulsed by Slim, enters the bunkhouse spoiling for a fight and misinterprets Lennie's smile. In the ensuing battle between Lennie and Curley, Steinbeck vividly and prophetically describes the terrible strength that will destroy the dream and insulate George: "The next minute Curley was flopping like a fish on a line, and his closed fist was lost in Lennie's big hand" (*OMM* 63). Steinbeck uses the same image to describe the death of Curley's wife: "'Don't you go yellin',' he said, and he shook her; and her body flopped like a fish" (*OMM* 91).

In the final moments of section three, Steinbeck's disciplined nonteleological vision is clearly evident; chance rules in the bunkhouse as later it will in the barn. The genius of Steinbeck's narrative *Of Mice and Men* lies in the consistency of this vision, and, in George's card games, Steinbeck provides an exact symbol of the unpredictable, often merciless world in which his characters vainly strive to maintain their dignity and fulfill their dreams.

Notes

1. Lester Jay Marks, *Thematic Design in the Novels of John Steinbeck* (The Hague: Mouton, 1971), 59. Peter Lisca, in *John Steinbeck: Nature and Myth*

(New York: Thomas Y. Crowell, 1978), explains that in a non-teleological point of view "the author assumes that there is no final cause or ultimate purpose in the universe" (78). The narrator of Hardy's "HP" summarizes precisely the non-teleological viewpoint in lines appropriate to Steinbeck's novel:

> How arrives it joy lies slain,
> And why unblooms the best hope ever sown?
> —Crass Casualty obstructs the sun and rain,
> And dicing Time for gladness casts a moan. . . .
> These purblind Doomsters had as readily strown
> Blisses about my pilgrimage as pain. (ll. 9–14)

2. John Steinbeck, *Of Mice and Men*, modern critical edition (New York: Penguin, 1993). All textual references are to this edition.

3. Two apparently minor incidents in the novel support George's and Slim's descriptions of ranchhands' lives. Candy tells George about Whitey, a former employee, who "just quit, the way a guy will. Says it was the food. Just wanted to move" (*OMM* 19). Candy also tells George about the Christmas party during which Smitty, a skinner, "took after [Crooks]" (*OMM* 20).

4. Even Curley goes into town on Saturday night, presumably to "Susy's place," thus leaving his wife alone on the ranch.

5. Peter Lisca, "Motif and Patterns in *Of Mice and Men*," *Modern Fiction Studies* 2 (Winter 1956–1957): 228–34, claims that George's playing solitaire "reveals that to some extent George needs Lennie as a rationalization for his failure" (234). This may be so, but certainly the symbolism of George's card games is far more extensive than Lisca allows.

CHAPTER EIGHT
JOHN STEINBECK'S FICTION:
THE AESTHETICS OF THE ROAD TAKEN:
"OF MICE AND MEN" (CHAPTER 4)
John Timmerman

F ortunately, few people have been deterred from serious consideration of *Of Mice and Men* by Maxwell Geismar's surprising judgment: "How thin *Of Mice and Men* is after all, how full of easy
sensations it appears upon a little reflection." Lamenting the thinness of
the characters, Geismar declare that "Lennie . . . seems rather more like a
digestional disturbance than a social problem."

"*Of Mice and Men* is a tribute to Steinbeck's narrative power, to the
brilliance with which he clothes such mechanical literary types, to the
intensity which somehow gives breath to these poor scarecrows. We see
here the dominance of the creative fire over common sense, so that we are
held by such apparitions as these characters who, when removed from the
framework of the play, crumble under the weight of their own improb-
ability."

Those are a few of his kinder judgments, but regardless of such
early reactions, readers have found themselves very much intrigued by
Steinbeck's scarecrows. The popular reception of Steinbeck's work had, in
fact, grown to the point where he would mutter that fame was "a pain in
the ass," partly, of course, because of the demands on time that he would
rather give to writing. By the same token, one cannot measure aesthetic
excellence by popular reception, but there are excellences in the work itself
that account for its enduring appeal.

Portions reprinted from *John Steinbeck's Fiction: The Aesthetics of the Road Taken*, by John
Timmerman. © 1986 by the University of Oklahoma Press. Used by permission.

. . . Although while he was writing *In Dubious Battle*, Steinbeck concentrated on conveying action through dialogue and providing clear character portraits that in novelistic form contain a forceful sense of concentrated action, the novel itself was too unwieldy for successful adaptation to the stage. It is curious that while more films have been made of Steinbeck's work than of the work of any other modern novelist, no film has been made of *In Dubious Battle*—curious because the *movements between* the concentrated actions and the tight sequence of the novel, while difficult for the narrower confines of the stage, lend themselves very nicely to cinematic art. *Of Mice and Men*, however, was written with deliberate staging design; in fact, over 80 percent of the lines went directly into the play. Joseph Fontenrose comments on the artistic technique of the work. Each of the six chapters is confined to one scene and opens with a description of the scene; there follows dialogue with entrance and exit of characters. Every descriptive or narrative remark can be considered a stage direction (of the Shavian kind at any rate). The chapters can easily be converted, as they stand, into acts or scenes; and this is nearly what was done when *Of Mice and Men* was published and produced as a play in November 1937. The dialogue was altered very little, and the conversion of description and narrative required more changes in form than in content. As drama or novel, *Of Mice and Men* is economical, tightly knit, carefully constructed.

The effect is clear in the novel. *Of Mice and Men* is one of Steinbeck's most compressed and unified works. Nonetheless, it achieves an artistic richness of structure and theme that ranks it among the best of his works. Three items in particular distinguish the novel: the framing and foreshadowing through structure, the development of Lennie's character and the theme of friendship, and the nature of human dreams.

The novel opens with the objective specificity of locale that would mark stage directions, or perhaps cinema. Like a long pan of the camera, the opening scene traces the Salinas River where it "drops in close to the hillside bank and runs deep and green" near Soledad. Following the flow of the river, the scene narrows and becomes more specific in detail, moving from the broad expanse of the "golden foot-hill slopes" of the Gabilan Mountains to the very small setting of "the sandy bank under the trees," where we find details as minute as "a lizard makes a great skittering" and "the split-wedge tracks of deer" (*OMM* 1). The narrowing vision provides a smooth and gentle transition to the two bindlestiffs hunkered by a fire in the evening of the day. The light, too, narrows and focuses, from the broad, golden flanks of the Gabilans to the evening duskiness and the shade "that climbed up the hills toward the top" (*OMM* 2).

The expertly framed opening is precisely echoed and inverted at the close of the novel, where the same two bindlestiffs stand by "the deep green pool of the Salinas River" (*OMM* 99) in the evening of the day. Once again shade pushes the sunlight "up the slopes of the Gabilan Mountains, and the hill-tops were rosy in the sun" (*OMM* 99). We find the same, familiarly routine skitterings of birds and animals by the sandy bank, only now a small something has happened. The original title of the novel, "Something That Happened," is precisely the point here; a small thing occurs, however momentous and tragic in the lives of Lennie and George, that goes virtually unnoticed in the ways of the world. Antonia Seixas comments in her article "John Steinbeck and the Non-Teleological Bus" that "the hardest task a writer can set himself is to tell the story of 'something that happened' without explaining 'why'—and make it convincing and moving."[1] Again, as if viewing the scene through a movie camera, we observe the "what" without the explanatory "why." While Lennie stares into the sun-washed mountains, George recreates the dream as he levels the Luger at the base of Lennie's skull.

The mountains that frame the story, as they frame the little thing that happened in the lives of George and Lennie, always carry large significance for Steinbeck. In *The Grapes of Wrath*, crossing the mountains represents the entrance into the promised land for the Okies. In *East of Eden*, Steinbeck provides two mountain ranges, one dark and one light, which symbolically frame the struggle between good and evil in the valley between those ranges. In *The Red Pony*, as in *To a God Unknown*, the mountains represent mystery; in the former work old Gitano goes to the mountains on Easter to die; in the latter Joseph Wayne witnesses strange, ancient rituals. In *Of Mice and Men* also, the darkening mountains represent the mystery of death, carefully sustained in the minor imagery of the heron seizing and eating the little water snakes.

In between the two scenes of the mountains on those two evenings, and in the serene willow grove that, as Peter Lisca points out, symbolizes "a retreat from the world to a primeval innocence," we have the quiet drama of George and Lennie's dream unfolding and unraveling. But this dream is doomed, and Steinbeck provides ample foreshadowing in the novel, most notably in Candy's dog. According to Carlson, Candy's dog has to die because he is a cripple, out of sorts with the normal routine of society, something in the way. With careful detail, Carlson describes how he would shoot the dog so that it would not feel any pain: "'The way I'd shoot him, he wouldn't feel nothing. I'd put the gun right there.' He pointed with his toe. 'Right back of the head. He wouldn't even quiver'" (*OMM* 45). Candy's huge regret is that he didn't do so himself. It would have been kinder to have the dog die by a familiar and loved hand than to have a stranger drag him to his death. The same feeling motivates George as he leads the social cripple Lennie to his dream world. For Steinbeck, this act constitutes a rare heroism. Years later he wrote in a letter to Annie Laurie Williams:

> M & M may seem to be unrelieved tragedy, but it is not. A careful read-ing will show that while the audience knows, against its hopes, that the dream will not come true, the protagonist must, during the play, become convinced that it will come true. Everyone in the world has a dream he knows can't come off but he spends his life hoping it may. This is at once the sadness, the greatness and the triumph of our species. And this belief on stage must go from skepticism to possibility to probability before it is nipped off by whatever the modern word for fate is. And in hopelessness—George is able to rise to greatness—to kill his friend to save him. George is a hero and only heroes are worth writing about.[2]

Lennie is not the only dreamer in the novel, however, and each of the other dreamers also seems afflicted with the loneliness of non-attainment. Most notable is the woman known only as "Curley's wife," a mere thing possessed by her flamboyant husband. From the start, George recognizes the incipient danger posed by Curley's wife, a recognition that proves prophetically true: "She's gonna make a mess. They's gonna be a bad mess about her. She's a jail bait all set on the trigger" (*OMM* 51). But Curley's wife is also caught in a hopeless little valley of small dreams. She dreamed of being an actress, of sweeping Hollywood, but when Curley came along he simply represented escape, and that was better than nothing. When Lennie shares his dream in response to her candor, she exclaims: "You're nuts. . . . But you're a kinda nice fella. Jus' like a big baby. But a person can see kinda what you mean" (*OMM* 90). Similarly, Crooks, the stable hand and another small outcast, has his dream, one of companionship to assuage the terrible, haunting lonliness: "Books ain't no good. A guy needs somebody to be near him. . . . A guy goes nuts if he ain't got nobody" (*OMM* 72). And Candy too, another social outcast, is captivated by the dream: "Sure they all want it. Everybody wants a little bit of land, not much. Jus' som'thin' that was his. Som'thin' he could live on and there couldn't nobody throw him off of it. I never had none" (*OMM* 76).

But through his careful foreshadowing, Steinbeck suggests that each dream is doomed. Curley, the flamboyant fighter, stands ever ready to goad someone into a fight, particularly those larger than he, and who is larger on the ranch than Lennie? The dead mouse that Lennie strokes prefigures the dead girl's hair and the impossible dream of rabbits. And George knows these things; he senses the inevitable end. Early in the novel he tells Lennie to remember good hiding places, even as he tells him once more of the dream farm and the "fatta the lan."

What keeps these little social outcasts going? What motivates them when all dreams seem doomed? In a sense, the large-scale battle of *In Dubious Battle* is played out here in a small, quiet, but equally tragic scene, as if George and Lennie are the Everymen in a microcosmic universe. They are drawn together by the human need born of loneliness. George's words to Lennie, which form a dark refrain in the book, might have occurred equally well in *In Dubious Battle* or *The Grapes of Wrath*: "Guys like us, that work on ranches, are the loneliest guys in the world. They got no family. They don't belong no place. They come to a ranch an' work up a stake and then they go into town and blow their stake, and the first thing you know they're poundin' their tail on some other ranch. They ain't got nothing to look ahead to" (*OMM* 13–14).

Even though the dream seems inevitably doomed, that is also at once man's glory—that he can dream and that others participate in the dream. Finally, this sets Lennie apart from the animal that he is imaged as being. At first the novel seems to set forth one more reductionistic pattern of imagery so familiar to Steinbeck's work. Lennie seems little more than an animal in human form: "Behind him walked his opposite, a huge man, shapeless of face, with large, pale eyes, and wide, sloping shoulders; and he walked heavily, dragging his feet a little, the way a bear drags his paws" (*OMM* 2). Lennie bends to the water and drinks "with long gulps, snorting into the water like a horse" (*OMM* 3). After drinking, he "dabbled his big paw in the water and wiggled his fingers so the water arose in little splashes" (*OMM* 3). But as Tularecito [in *The Pastures of Heaven*] rises above the animal by virtue of his creative gift, Lennie also rises above the animal in several ways. He is, for example, marked by kindness, a trait that at once sets him above Curley. Lennie is sensitive to the small and the forlorn, and it is no accident that Crooks and Curley's wife confide freely in him. But he does lack the rational acuity to survive in this society; killing Curley's wife is not qualitatively different for Lennie from killing the mouse. As Howard Levant points out, "The relative meaningless of his victims substitutes pathos for tragedy." Clearly Lennie is not a tragic figure, for he has nothing of the required nobility about him. But, in a sense, the deeper tragedy lies in his pathos; there is no place for a Lennie in society. Yet in the novel there is a kind of subtle reversal of animal imagery that makes animals of those who establish society's norms that disallow the survival of a Lennie. In the story of Tularecito, Miss Martin is closer to the animal in her fanatical insistence that Tularecito be whipped. In *Of Mice and Men*, Curley is closer to the animal in his predatory desire to fight. Oppression of any life is the animalistic trait, the struggle for survival that kills off or hides away the weaker members. For Steinbeck, on the other hand, that human life, which might be observable upon first glance as animalistic, often carries a warm dignity. While Lennie is a social misfit, it may be because society itself is ill.

Although *Of Mice and Men* quickly became one of Steinbeck's most popular works, it met with a great deal of puzzlement. Readers may have expected another angry *In Dubious Battle* from him and got instead this sad little drama of something that happened, something so small it escapes common attention. George walks away at the end, just one more bindlestiff. Yet part of Steinbeck's success here lies in investing those small, barely noticeable lives with both pathos and dignity. If, as Carlson points out, there is a right way to kill a cripple, one still wonders why the cripple has to be killed.

But Steinbeck himself was dissatisfied with the novel, largely on aesthetic grounds. With the failed effort to block *In Dubious Battle* for the stage, he wanted very much to succeed with this effort. Steinbeck referred to the book as an experiment "designed to teach me to write for the theatre" (*LIL* 132), and he often spoke of it in pejorative terms such as a "simple little thing," or "the Mice book." Whatever his attitude, the dramatic adaptation, like the novel, was a commercial success, opening at the Music Box Theatre in New York on November 23, 1937, and running for 207 performances.

Steinbeck at this time, however, was back home in California, well into the background work for his greatest achievement, *The Grapes of Wrath*.

Notes

1. Antonia Seixas. "John Steinbeck and the Non-Teleological Bus," in *Steinbeck and His Critics*. Ed. E. W. Tedlock, Jr. and C. V. Wicker (Albuquerque: University of New Mexico Press, 1958), 277.

2. Elaine Stenbeck and Robert Wallsten, eds., *Steinbeck: A Life in Letters* (New York: Viking Press, 1975), 562–63. Subsequent citations are given parenthetically in the text as *LIL* followed by the page number.

THE 1990s

The appearance of *"Of Mice and Men": A Kinship of Powerlessness* (New York: Twayne) by Charlotte Cook Hadella in 1995 marked the first critical book length study that concentrated solely on *Of Mice and Men*. As such, it devotes eighty-two pages to a wide variety of issues, including historical content, importance of the work in Steinbeck's career, a survey of the novel's critical reception and an exploration of its experimental structure and the layers of complexity the author discovered in the symbols and myths that lay beneath its surface. Hadella's final chapter also discusses the stage and screen adaptations of the novel and is designed to help readers to see the changes that were made in each different production of Steinbeck's novella.

The 1990s also brought a number of studies of Steinbeck's supposed "misogynistic" portrait of Curley's wife while still other critics began to examine the "supposed" homosexual innuendos that had caused numerous objections by conservative readers and that accounted for the fact that the novel had become a frequent target for advocates of censorship and book-banning. Along with its questionable language (the use of the n word and swear words) and its frequent sexual innuendo (the "cat" house, Curley's wife's reputation as a promiscuous flirt or "rat trap"), the implied sexual relationship between Lennie and George had been consistently cited by those who objected to the fact that the novel addressed far too many issues that had previously been taboo for writers. Specifically, such critics cited the implications of improper sexual bonding that had been suggested by the suspicion of both Curley and the Boss that Lennie and George's travel together implied they were more than just friends. Several studies (see the chapters by Irr and Person) now found it comfortable to directly confront this "gay" issue. Certainly, these essays are helpful in seeing why, despite its sentimental appeal, Steinbeck's novel ranks fourth on the Most Challenged Books of The Twentieth Century list and sixth on the list of Most Frequently Challenged Books of the 1990s. As the 1990s drew to a close, the days of seeing the novel as merely about loneliness or about prejudice gave way to more complex readings, readings that acknowledge that the novel offers far more than an examination of the American dream, a look at the demise of the Jeffersonian land ethic, or a study of the moral dilemmas of "I" versus "we" ethics. While over sixty years had passed since its publication, the slim novella still had much more to offer than anyone in the thirties had imagined when it was first appeared.

Other Significant Studies from the 1990s

Benson, Jackson J., ed. *The Short Novels of John Steinbeck*. Durham: Duke University Press, 1990.

Chadha, Raini. *Social Realism in the Novels of John Steinbeck*. New Delhi: Harmon, 1990.

Fensch, Thomas. "Reflections of Doc: The Persona of Ed Ricketts in *Of Mice and Men*." In *John Steinbeck, The Years Of Greatness, 1936–1939*, ed. Tetsumaro Hayashi, 106–10. Tuscaloosa: University of Alabama Press, 1993.

Hadella, Charlotte. "The Dialogic Tension of Curley's Wife." In *John Steinbeck: The Years of Greatness, 1936–1939*, ed. Tetsumaro Hayashi, 64–76. Tuscaloosa: University of Alabama Press, 1993.

Hayashi, Tetsumaro, ed. *John Steinbeck: The Years of Greatness, 1936–1939*. Tuscaloosa: University of Alabama Press, 1993.

Morsberger, Robert. "Tell Again, George." In *Steinbeck: The Years of Greatness*, ed. Tetsumaro Hayashi, 111–31. Tuscaloosa: University of Alabama Press, 1993.

Scarseth, Thomas. "A Teachable Good Book: *Of Mice and Men*." In *Censored Books: Critical Viewpoints*, ed. Nicholas J. Karolides, Lee Burress, and John M. Kean, 388–94. Lanham, MD: Scarecrow Press, 1993.

French, Warren. "*Of Mice and Men*." In *John Steinbeck's Fiction Revisited*, 72–74. New York: Twayne, 1994.

Railsback, Brian. *Parallel Expeditions: Charles Darwin and the Art of John Steinbeck.* Moscow: University of Idaho Press, 1995.

Atell, Kevin. "*Of Mice and Men.*" In *Novels for Students*, ed. Diane Telgen. Vol. 1. Detroit: Gale Research, 1997.

Johnson, Claudia Durst. *Understanding "Of Mice and Men," "The Red Pony" and "The Pearl": A Student Casebook to Issues, Sources and Historical Documents.* Westport, CT: Greenwood Press, 1997.

　　See especially chapter 1: "The Triumph of Our Species: A Literary Analysis," 15–19; chapter 3: "Land Ownership"; chapter 4: "The Vagrant Farmworker: Homeless in Paradise"; and chapter 5: "Losers of the American Dream."

Lisca, Peter. "Motif and Pattern in *Of Mice and Men.*" *Fiction Studies* (Winter 1956–57): 228–34. Reprinted in *Novels for Students*, ed. Diane Telgen. Vol. 1. Detroit: Gale Research, 1997.

Telgen, Diane, ed. *Novels for Students.* Vol. 1. Detroit: Gale Research, 1997.

CHAPTER NINE

A HISTORICAL INTRODUCTION TO
OF MICE AND MEN
Anne Loftis

S teinbeck wrote *Of Mice and Men* midway through the 1930s, the most creative decade of his career. During this time he was becoming increasingly concerned about current social and economic problems in California, and he published three successive novels about farm workers, each distinctive in tone and conception.

Of Mice and Men was a deliberate change from his previous book, *In Dubious Battle* (1936), an imaginative interpretation of a contemporary farm strike and a study of the movement and action of crowds. In the new project, he set out to work within a narrow framework, concentrating on a small number of characters in carefully detailed settings, telling his story as economically and dramatically as possible. He explained that he was teaching himself to write for the theater, and, in fact, he soon did translate the novel into a play.

The subject was less controversial than that of his previous book. He was writing about people who were isolated in the society of their time, who belonged to a group that was fast disappearing from the American scene. Only a short time before, thousands of itinerant single men had roamed the Western states following the harvests. Their labor was essential to the success of the bonanza grain-growing enterprises that had been started in the second half of the nineteenth century and had proliferated

Anne Loftis, "A Historical Introduction to *Of Mice and Men*," in *The Short Novels of John Steinbeck*, by Jackson J. Benson, Ed., pp. 39–47. Copyright, 1990, Duke University Press. All rights reserved. Used by permission of the publisher.

so rapidly that by the year 1900 some 125,000 threshers were migrating along a "belt" that extended from the Brazos Bottoms in Texas north to Saskatchewan and Manitoba, and from Minnesota west to the state of Washington. Many of them traveled by rail, arriving in the fields in empty boxcars that were later used to transport the grain.

In the early years, they were paid an average wage of $2.50 to $3 a day plus board and room. The "room" was frequently a tent: living conditions were spartan. But wages rose at the time of the First World War when the price of wheat was high, partly through the action of the Industrial Workers of the World, which established an eight-hundred-mile picket line across the Great Plains states.

In California, where grain was the chief farm commodity in the 1870s and 1880s before the advent of irrigated agriculture, some of the early harvesters were disappointed miners returning from the goldfields. In the social and occupational hierarchy, they were on a level considerably below the mule drivers, who, like Steinbeck's character Slim, were valued for their skill in handling as many as twenty animals "with a single line" and who were generally employed permanently on the ranches.

Steinbeck's recognition of the status of the mule driver epitomizes his re-creation of a working culture that was undergoing a historic change even as he wrote about it. In 1938, the year after *Of Mice and Men* was published, about half the nation's grain was harvested by mechanical combines that enabled five men to do the work that had been done formerly by 350. The single farm workers who traveled from job to job by train, or like George and Lennie by bus, were disappearing. They were being replaced by whole families migrating in cars, like the people in Steinbeck's next novel, *The Grapes of Wrath*.

The physical background for *Of Mice and Men* came from Steinbeck's own early years in a California agricultural valley. His native city of Salinas, eighty miles south of San Francisco, is the seat of Monterey County. . . .

More important in planting the germ of the novel was an experience he had during a period when he dropped out of college. He entered Stanford in 1919, already ambitious to become a writer and determined to follow his own particular interests in the curriculum. Experiencing some difficulty with courses and grades the following year, he decided to break away, shed his identity as a university student, and make his way for a while as a workingman. "I was a bindlestiff myself for quite a spell," he told reporters some years later. "I worked in the same country that the story is laid in."[1]

Tall and husky, he was hired as a laborer on a ranch near Chualar, a short distance—in miles—from the prosperous neighborhood in Salinas where he was born, and, for a time, he became a part of this very different world. The fact that he was promoted to straw boss suggests that he got on well with his fellow workers.[2] He had a talent for being inconspicuous: they probably learned very little about him while he was gathering impressions of them.

After he returned to the campus, he published a story in the *Stanford Spectator* about a runaway girl who takes shelter during a storm in the bunkhouse of some Filipino farm workers. She marries the crew leader, who alternately showers her with presents and beats her. Eventually she leaves him.[3] Although the prose is vigorous, this sketch, full of bizarre details that strain the reader's credulity, is an amateur's experiment.

It is instructive to compare this apprentice effort with Steinbeck's achievement as a mature artist a dozen years later. *Of Mice and Men* is a work of symmetry and balance in which the action moves with a compelling momentum toward an inevitable conclusion. The social history which he had learned firsthand is woven seamlessly into the fabric of the story.

In the first scene by the river, he introduces the mute evidence of the past: the ash pile left by previous campers and the tree limb overhanging the water, worn smooth by tramps who have come there over the years to jungle up. Linking the past with the present, George and Lennie make their entrance in the tradition of bindlestiffs, carrying blankets on their backs. The story then moves into the opening dialogue, justly famous in American literature, through which we come to know and believe in the touching partnership of the moronic giant and his gruff protector.

The next scene at the ranch opens with a description of the empty bunkhouse with its tiers of beds, each with an apple box nailed to the wall to hold the meager possessions of men who travel light. The place is not particularly clean. Flies dart through the motes of dust stirred up by the push broom of Candy, the old swamper; a can of bug powder suggests lice or bedbugs in the mattress ticking.

The characters who come in one by one create the social dimensions of the place. This rough lodging in which nothing has been provided beyond the bare necessities is governed by the harsh code of the men who live there for a week, a month, or a year. It is a society intolerant of weakness or difference. Old Candy, helpless to stop the shooting of his dog, knows that he too will be banished when he is no longer useful. Crooks, the black stable hand, is excluded except on Christmas when the boss brings in a gallon of whiskey for the entire crew. The rest of the year Crooks plays horseshoes outside with the others, but when they come indoors to sleep, he goes off alone to his bed in the harness room of the barn.

Women are not welcome in the male enclave. Curley's wife, wandering around the ranch in a wistful quest for some kind of human contact, is stereotyped by the men, whose experience of women comes from "old Suzy" and her girls in town. Curley's wife (in the novel she has no other name) goes along with the typecasting by playing the vamp, inflaming her jealous husband, who, as the son of the boss, is as powerful as he is vicious. It is on this explosive situation that the plot turns. Lennie, sensing trouble too complicated for a simple mind to unravel, begs to leave after George tells him that Curley's wife is "poison" and "jail bait."

Steinbeck had a different view of her, as he explained in a letter to the actress who played the role in the Broadway production of the play. Curley's wife acts seductively because she "knows instinctively that if she is to be noticed at all, it will be because someone finds her sexually attractive." But her pose is deceptive. "Her moral training was most rigid." She was a virgin until her marriage and had had no sexual experience outside her unfulfilling union with Curley. She had grown up "in an atmosphere of fighting and suspicion" and had "learned to be hard to cover her fright." But she is fundamentally "a nice, kind girl" who has "a natural trustfulness. . . . If anyone—a man or a woman—ever gave her a break—treated her like a person—she would be a slave to that person."[4]

Steinbeck captured this aspect of her character in her final scene with Lennie. In the presence of this childlike man, she drops her defenses and expresses her real feelings. Her rambling monologue of blighted hopes and tawdry fantasies is, in effect, a last confession.

Steinbeck has prepared his readers for the shocking climax of the novel through his portrait of Lennie. He might have created a caricature in the mental defective who crushes soft creatures in his powerful hands. He had worked with a real-life Lennie, he told reporters, when he was writing the stage version of Of Mice and Men. "He didn't kill a girl. He killed a ranch foreman. Got sore because the boss had fired his pal and stuck a pitchfork right through his stomach."[5] The fictional Lennie is passive and nonviolent. Would he be capable of a murderous rage if George was threatened? Perhaps. It is through his connection with his intelligent partner that he becomes believable. In the opening scene, Steinbeck establishes the dynamics of their relationship, in which George's exasperated bossing of Lennie appears as a form of protectiveness that masks their mutual dependence.

Loneliness is a recurrent theme in the novel, articulated in George's speech that begins:

> "Guys like us, that work on the ranches, are the loneliest guys in the world. They got no family. They don't belong noplace."
> "But not us," Lennie replies. "And why. Because . . . because I got you to look after me, and you got me to look after you, and that's why." (*OMM* 13)

Their plan to find a place of their own, which Candy and Crooks, outcasts on the ranch, are hungry to share, is straight out of the American Dream. They have set down the details in a kind of litany which George recites while Lennie chimes in with the chorus. They repeat the comforting words from time to time like an incantation to ward off trouble and rekindle hope. In the last scene—a final irony in a work compounded of ironies—George, in order to calm Lennie, utters the familiar refrain, which becomes an epitaph for his friend.

Before he found the apt title from Robert Burns's poem, Steinbeck called his work in progress "Something That Happened." While he was at work on the book, he sent revealing bulletins to his literary agent and his friends. Describing a state of mind familiar to writers, he commented in February 1936, "I have to start and am scared to death as usual—miserable, sick feeling of inadequacy. I'll love it once I get down to work."[6]

It was as he predicted. In a postcard to the same friend, he reported that "after two months of fooling around my new work is really going and that makes me very happy—kind of excitement like that you get near a dynamo from breathing oxygen." He explained, "I'm not interested in the method as such but I am interested in having a vehicle exactly adequate to the theme."[7]

On April 4: ". . . my new work is moving swiftly now."[8]

Eleven days later: "Pages are flying."[9]

Toward the end of May, he reported a setback. His setter pup had "made confetti" of half of the manuscript. "Two months work to do over again. . . . There was no other draft." He tried to be philosophical. The pup may have been "acting critically. I didn't want to ruin a good dog for a ms. I'm not sure is good at all."[10] He finished the work during the summer.

Almost immediately after sending the manuscript to his publishers, he set out on a research trip around California in preparation for writing a series of newspaper articles on newly arriving Dust Bowl migrants and the employers who were making life difficult for them. While starting in a direction that led eventually to *The Grapes of Wrath*, he could not ignore the book he had just completed. He reported that there was a mixed reaction to the manuscript. (He didn't say *whose* reaction.) His publisher, Pascal Covici, liked it.[11]

Steinbeck said that he was not expecting a large sale, and he was surprised that *Of Mice and Men* was chosen as a Book-of-the-Month Club selection and that 117,000 copies were sold in advance of the official publication date, February 25, 1937. The reviews were enthusiastic. "The boys have whooped it up for John Steinbeck's new book," Ralph Thompson wrote in the *New York Times*.[12] The novel was praised by, among others, Christopher Morley, Carl Van Vechten, Lewis Gannett, Harry Hansen, Heywood Broun, and Eleanor Roosevelt. Henry Seidel Canby wrote in the *Saturday Review of Literature* that "there has been nothing quite so good of the kind in American writing since Sherwood Anderson's early stories."[13]

In early April, it was on the best-seller list in six cities across the country, and it continued to be among the top ten best sellers in fiction into the fall. Steinbeck, who said that he would never learn to conceive of money in larger quantities than two dollars, was surprised by the large checks he received from his agents. He was not by any means an unknown writer. *Tortilla Flat* (1935) had been a popular success, and *In Dubious Battle* and some of his short stories had been praised by critics. But he was now treated as a celebrity, something he had always feared. As he and his wife Carol passed through New York en route to Europe, his appearance in his publisher's office was considered newsworthy in literary circles.

On his return, he worked with playwright George F. Kaufman, who was going to direct the stage version of *Of Mice and Men*. Kaufman wrote Steinbeck that the novel "drops almost naturally into play form," but he had a couple of suggestions for changes. He thought that Curley's wife "should be drawn more fully: she is the motivating force of the whole thing and should loom larger." He told Steinbeck: "Preserve the marvelous tenderness of the book. *And*—if you could feel it in your heart to include a *little* more humor, it would be extremely valuable, both for its lightening effect and the heightening of the subsequent tragedy by comparison."[14]

Steinbeck seems to have ignored the latter idea, but he considerably enlarged the role of Curley's wife, who is presented in the play as a person with strongly articulated feelings about her past history and family relationships. Another change was his decision to end the play with George's speech to Lennie just before he pulls the trigger, an improvement over the anticlimactic group scene in the novel.

Of Mice and Men opened at the Music Box Theatre in New York on November 23, 1937, with Wallace Ford as George and Broderick Crawford as Lennie. Claire Luce appeared as Curley's wife. Will Geer, who was prominent in many plays in the 1930s, took the part of Slim. The reviews were ecstatic, and the play drew enthusiastic audiences during a season in which *Tobacco Road*, *Golden Boy*, *Stage Door*, and *You Can't Take It with You* were among the offerings on Broadway. It ran for 207 performances and won the New York Drama Critics' Circle Award in competition with Thornton's Wilder's *Our Town*.

The film version of *Of Mice and Men*, written by Eugene Solow from the novel and the play, is considered by Joseph R. Millichap to be the most faithful screen adaptation of any of Steinbeck's works.[15] It was a labor of love on the part of the director, Lewis Milestone, who consulted with Steinbeck and visited ranches in the Salinas Valley in his company. Although he shot most of the outdoor sequences in southern California, the landscape has an authentic look. He commissioned Aaron Copeland to compose the background music, and he took pains with the casting. He hired Burgess Meredith to play George, Lon Chaney, Jr., was Lennie, and Betty Field played Curley's wife, called Mae. Charles Bickford appeared as Slim. Milestone brought Leigh Whipper from the Broadway cast to repeat his performance as Crooks.

The movie, released in 1939, was not a box-office success. Never as famous as John Ford's *The Grapes of Wrath*, it deserves more recognition than it has received. An excellent television version *Of Mice and Men* based on Milestone's film was brought out in 1981, featuring Robert Blake, Randy Quaid, Pat Hingle, and Lew Ayers. In 1970, an opera by Carlisle Floyd, who wrote both the music and libretto, had its premiere in Seattle. The composer changed the story slightly (he eliminated Crooks, the black stable buck, and created a chorus of ranch hands), but he was faithful to Steinbeck's theme. One critic, obviously no lover of the original work, thought that the new form was an improvement: "The operatic conventions impose a frame that makes Steinbeck's basic sentimentality infinitely more acceptable."[16]

Warren French has suggested that readers who spoke of *Of Mice and Men* as sentimental should "think of it as an expression of Steinbeck's outrageous compassion for the victims of chaotic forces."[17] Criticism of the novel became noticeable at the end of the 1930s when there was an evaluation of Steinbeck's total literary achievement up to that point. On the one hand, he was praised for his versatility, and on the other, denounced for trying to do too much, for mixing romance and realism,[18] for "weakness in characterization" and "puerile symbolism."[19] The most damaging assessment, one that would be echoed by later critics, was Edmund Wilson's statement that Steinbeck's preoccupation with biology led him "to present life in animal terms," to deal "almost always in his fiction . . . either with lower animals or with human beings so rudimentary that they are almost on the animal level." Wilson found a prime example of his point in the character Lennie.[20] (More recently Jackson Benson has given a different interpretation of Steinbeck's concern with biology. According to this view, science and nature provided a philosophical framework for Steinbeck's writing, his conviction that meaning and stability came from a sense of connection with the natural universe.[21] This thesis supports Peter Lisca's emphasis on the importance in *Of Mice and Men* of the camp by the river, "a retreat from the world to a private innocence," and of George and Lennie's dream of the farm, "a safe place," as a symbol of happiness.)[22]

Wilson summarized the novel as "a compact little drama, contrived with almost too much cleverness, and a parable which criticized humanity from a nonpolitical point of view."[23] During the 1940s and 1950s Steinbeck's fiction, in particular the three farm-worker novels on which his reputation was largely based, was criticized on ideological grounds. His work had been popular when it appeared because it expressed the values of the Depression decade: a passion for social justice and concern for the common man. Yet, fittingly for a man of independent judgment, he was attacked by both radicals and conservatives. Left-wing critics complained of his nonconformity to the doctrines with which he was identified by the growers' groups whose actions he had exposed in *In Dubious Battle* and *The Grapes of Wrath.*

It is interesting that *Of Mice and Men*, which represents a break in the sequence of Steinbeck's "problem" novels, took on some political coloration from his other writings and from his ongoing connection with the controversies of the 1930s. In the summer of 1937, the Theatre Union of San Francisco, which supported maritime workers in their fight for unionization, gave what was probably the first stage performance of the work, creating their own script from the novel. Two years later, Steinbeck gave permission to some Stanford students to give a benefit reading from the book to raise money to help the migrants. In the 1970s, scenes from the play were presented to the supporters of Cesar Chavez's United Farm Workers' Union.

Yet the continuing popularity of *Of Mice and Men*, both as a drama and in its original novel form, indicates the degree to which it has transcended its historical context. As a work of literature, it has attained the status of a modern classic. A staple of the middle-school curriculum in England and the United States, it has been translated into a dozen foreign languages. The arguments of the critics will go on, no doubt, but we have come to acknowledge that Steinbeck's "little book"[24] has a quality that defies analysis. It touches our deepest feelings and enlarges our understanding of the human condition. As a tragedy, with the power to arouse pity and terror implicit in that art form, it has drawn readers for half a century and, it seems safe to predict, will reach new generations in the century to come.

Notes

1. "Mice, Men and Mr. Steinbeck," *New York Times*, 5 December 1937, quoted in Jackon J. Benson, *The True Adventures of John Steinbeck, Writer* (New York: Viking, 1984), 364.

2. Steinbeck's college roommate, Carlton Sheffield, gives an account of Steinbeck's experience on the ranch in his introduction to *Letters to Elizabeth: A Selec-*

tion of Letters from John Steinbeck to Elizabeth Otis, ed. Floran Shasky and Susan F. Riggs (San Francisco: Book Club of California, 1978).

3. John E. Steinback [sic], "Fingers of a Cloud: A Satire on College Protervity," *Stanford Spectator*, February 1924.

4. John Steinbeck to Claire Luce, 1938, from *Steinbeck: A Life in Letters*, ed. Elaine Steinbeck and Robert Wallsten (New York: Viking Press, 1975), 154–55.

5. "Mice, Men and Mr. Steinbeck." Jackson Benson suggests that Steinbeck may have been putting on a "wild west" act for reporters.

6. Letter to Louis Paul, February 1936, in *Life in Letters*, 120.

7. Postcard to Louis Paul, undated in *Life in Letters*, 123–24.

8. Letter to Elizabeth Otis, Stanford University Library, Department of Special Collections.

9. Letter to Elizabeth Otis, 15 April 1936, Stanford University Library, Department of Special Collections.

10. Letter to Elizabeth Otis, 27 May 1936, Stanford University Library, Department of Special Collections.

11. Letter to George Albee, 1936, in *Life in Letters*, 132.

12. 27 February 1937 review.

13. 27 February 1937 review.

14. Quoted in *Life in Letters*, 136.

15. Joseph R. Millichap, *Steinbeck and Film* (New York: Ungar, 1983), 13.

16. Frank S. Warnke in *Opera News Review*, 14 March 1970.

17. Warren French, *John Steinbeck* (New York: Twayne, 1961), 74.

18. James D. Hart, *The Oxford Companion to American Literature* (New York: Oxford University Press, 1941), 722–23.

19. Margaret Marshall, quoted in Peter Lisca, *The Wide World of John Steinbeck* (New York: Rutgers University Press, 1958), 5.

20. Edmund Wilson, *The Boys in the Back Room: Notes on California Novelists* (San Francisco: Colt Press, 1941), 41–43.

21. Jackson J. Benson, "Hemingway the Hunter and Steinbeck the Farmer," *Michigan Quarterly Review* 24, no. 3 (Summer 1985): 452–53.

22. Lisca, *Wide World*, 134–36.

23. Wilson, *The Boys in The Back Room.*

24. So described by Steinbeck in a letter to George and Anne, 11 January 1937, in *Life in Letters*, 133–34.

CHAPTER TEN
MANHOOD BESET:
MISOGYNY IN *OF MICE AND MEN*
Jean Emery

Of Mice and Men is not, as most critics would have us believe, a poignant, sentimental drama of an impossible friendship and an unattainable dream. Rather, the story actually demonstrates the achievement of a dream—that of a homogeneous male fraternity not just to repress, but to eliminate women and femininity. *Of Mice and Men* depicts the rescue of men from women, "a melodrama of beset manhood," to use the words of Nina Baym (70).

Textual evidence suggests that John Steinbeck, as chronicler of America's social inequities, intended *Of Mice and Men* as a critique of our society's most fundamental injustice. George and Lennie represent the duality of masculinity and femininity, their partnership a kind of marriage. Ultimately, George's need and desire to confirm his membership in the powerful and dominant male community drives him to kill his partner as a sacrificial rite of initiation. Bolstered by smaller, less dramatic, but nonetheless significant sacrifices, the text illustrates the insidious presence of this practice in our culture at large. That for more than 50 years literary critics have read the text purely as an exposé of a failed *economic* dream corroborates a basic blindness to this issue and complicity in preserving the patriarchy.

George and Lennie as a couple display the stereotypical attributes of husband and wife. Lennie's refrain, "I got you to look after me, and you got me to look after you," solemnizes a kind of marriage vow between

Previously published in *San Jose Studies* 15, no. 1 (Winter 1992): 33–41. Used by permission of the Martha Heasley Cox Center for Steinbeck Studies.

them (14). "We got a future," George says in reply. The glue that binds George and Lennie is the dream of a house and a couple of acres where they can "live off the fatta the lan'" (14). George, the masculine creator of this dream, gives it voice and grounds it in the realm of possibility. But it is "feminine" Lennie who nurtures it and keeps it alive with his boundless obsession for hearing George tell it "like you done before" (13).

As in many traditional marriages, this is not a partnership of equals but one of lord and vassal, owner and owned. George as the patriarch makes the decisions, controls the finances, decides where they'll work and live, dictates the conditions of the relationship ("no rabbits" is the threat employed), even regulates when Lennie can and cannot speak. Yet George wants power without the burden of responsibility. "God, you're a lot of trouble," he says more than once to Lennie. "I could get along so easy and so nice if I didn't have you on my tail" (7).

George's droning retelling of the dream is done primarily for Lennie's benefit. George's own dream is really something quite different: "If I was alone I could live so easy. I could go get a job an' work, an' no trouble. No mess at all, and when the end of the month come I could take my fifty bucks and go into town and get whatever I want" (11). The latent message, of course, is that life would be better without the complications of a relationship of a dependent "other."

Relationships in this story center on the issue of power: who will have it and who will not. Obsessed with his ability to control Lennie's behavior (just as Curley is driven to regulate his wife's), George admonishes Lennie for carrying dead mice in his pocket, for directly responding to a question from the Boss, for bringing a pup into the bunkhouse. Such power frightens and, at the same time, thrills George. "Made me seem God damn smart alongside him," George tells Slim. "Why he'd do any damn thing I tol' him. If I tol' him to walk over a cliff, over he'd go" (40). George then recounts the time Lennie nearly drowned demonstrating exactly such obedience.

Peter Lisca suggests that George needs Lennie as a rationalization for his own failure (141). But George's failure is not just his inability to establish his own autonomy. It is also his struggle to assure himself of his own masculinity and reject the disturbing influence of such feminine traits as gentleness, compassion, submissiveness, and weakness. Lennie's size and strength, a constant reminder of George's own physical puniness, presents a constant threat to George's vulnerable masculinity, clearly displayed in Lennie's effortless emasculation of Curley when Lennie crushes the bully's hand.

Demonstrations of masculinity suffuse the text. The ranch George and Lennie come to work—a stronghold of physical effort, rationality, and orderliness—reeks with maleness. The bunkhouse, utilitarian and void of decoration except for "those Western magazines ranch men love to read and scoff at and secretly believe" (23), exemplifies the heroic male struggle to control nature, other men, and, inevitably, women.

Women as Intruders

Woman and, correspondingly, feminine traits are intruders and threats to this world, "entrappers" and "domesticators" in Baym's words, woman as temptress thwarting man in his journey of self-discovery and definition (73).

In the novel some of the central female figures are the whores, who use their sexual powers to seduce men, robbing them of their financial stake. Women are poison, George tells us, "jailbait on a trigger" (51). George and Lennie's dream, one all the men subscribe to in some measure, is, not surprisingly, devoid of women. The female taint precipitates the pathetic destruction of Lennie and, invariably, the ruination of every man's dream.

Curley's wife, the evil, disloyal seductress, personifies the "fallen" woman. She flaunts her sexuality (her only effective weapon in this arena), dressing like a bordello whore—heavy makeup, painted fingernails, red ostrich feathers on her slippers. She triggers the story's tragic events and George foresees this. "Been any trouble since she got here?" he asks (51).

Curley's wife (the only woman appearing in the story aside from the spectral Aunt Clara), is, in fact, so antagonistic to this environment that she remains nameless. She's called "tease," "tramp," "tart," "rat-trap," "jailbait," "bitch," "Curley's wife"—identities always contingent upon her relationship to men. By refusing to speak her name, these men attempt to rob her of her power over them, just as a superstitious and primitive native might refuse to invoke the name of a feared spirit.

George's reaction to her is particularly intriguing, since his vehemence seems vastly out of proportion to her possible influence on his life. "I seen 'em poison before, but I never seen no piece of jail bait worse than her" (32). George clearly doesn't trust or even like women; to him they are liars and manipulators like the girl in Weed who cries rape when Lennie clutches at her dress. Curley's wife threatens the same action when Crooks and Candy try to throw her out of Crooks's room.

The essential conflict of the story—the strength of the bond between George and Lennie—hinges upon this desire for a world without the con- taminating female. Lennie, despite his size, possesses characteristics tra- ditionally identified as feminine; and his continued habitation of the male sphere eventually becomes intolerable for everyone, including George.

Stereotypically feminine, docile and submissive, dependent and lack- ing in self-assertiveness, Lennie obeys George like a good woman. "Baf- fled, unknowingly powerful, utterly will-less, he can not move without a leader," observes Harry Thornton Moore (50). Lennie is a pleaser, seeking approval, desiring love. We first see him mimicking George's behavior, a conscious ploy to endear himself to his protector. Lennie loves soft, sensual objects: mice, puppies, silky curls. He possesses maternal cravings, revealed in his affection for small animals. And playing into long-held prejudices against women's intelligence, Steinbeck makes Lennie a half-wit.

Lennie's superhuman strength does not contradict this interpretation of him as a feminine figure, but rather confirms it. Throughout history, taboos surrounding virginity, menstruation, and sexual intercourse have expressed men's dread of female sexuality. Images such as *vagina dentata* exemplify men's inordinate fear of submitting to a force that is unseen, uncontrollable, and menacing to their essential nature—"a generalized dread of women," in Freud's assessment: "The man is afraid of being weakened by the woman, infected with her femininity and of then show- ing himself incapable" (198–99).

George displays mistrust, disgust, and barely disguised rage on the topic of women. He seems particularly to resent the shackles of his prom- ise to Aunt Clara to care for Lennie (a vow, notably, given to a woman).

Of Mice and Men's solution to this strangling bind is the rescue of men by men from the grip of women. Freud, of course, vigorously promoted the significance of a boy's separation from his mother in achieving his sense of masculinity. Here the struggle manifests itself in the creation of what anthropologists call "men's house institutions." These cultural centers of male ritual and values ensure male solidarity and the overall segregation of the sexes within the tribal group. Any breach of house norms meets with severe censure and even social ostracism.

Sexual segregation is *de rigueur* on the ranch. "You ain't wanted here," Candy hisses at Curley's wife when she invades Crooks's room (79). Curley's wife and Lennie are excluded from the male rituals of card games, trips to town, and horseshoe tournaments. But then, so too are Crooks and Candy, despite their possession of the correct biological anatomy.

Crooks is ostracized because of race, a nonconformity to the norms of the tribal group. Candy's case is more complicated. His strength and usefulness are on the wane. He has been crippled; hence he is less of a man. More importantly, however, he fails to uphold the standards of desired male behavior. Just as his muscle has withered, Candy's emotional state has grown soft and sentimental. Male power demands a code of behavior that asserts control over property and possessions, whether they be wife or dog. Sentiment and attachment—dare one mention love—is of no consequence. Candy's dog is too old and feeble for work and has a "bad stink" to boot. But Candy cannot bring himself to perform his manly duty of ridding himself of this no-longer-useful appendage. Carlson, rational, cold-hearted, eminently practical, the antithesis of femininity, takes on the job himself, in the process sealing Candy's expulsion from the male community.

Lesson for George

The lesson is not lost on George. When the crisis comes and Lennie is no longer "manageable," George, like a rancher suddenly confronted with a pet dog that has taken to killing sheep, follows Carlson's example, right down to shooting Lennie in the very spot Carlson marked on the dog's head. George's killing of Lennie is, in effect, his sacrificial rite of initiation into the male enclave.

By his action, George chooses virility over compassion, masculinity over femininity. Stoic, calm, and nearly emotionless, George's behavior, unlike Candy's, is manly. His lie about the actual events of Lennie's death, which on the surface suggests deep-felt emotion, actually serves to enhance his own male stature: diminutive George wrestling the giant, bone-crushing brute, Lennie, for a loaded Luger—and winning, getting off a clean shot to the back of the neck like a skilled marksman—a narrative straight out of a Western pulp magazine. Slim's proposal to go into town for a drink validates George's membership in the clubhouse. "Ya hadda, George. I swear you hadda" (107).

By murdering Lennie, George rids himself of the very thing that sets himself apart from other men. Without Lennie, he is no longer a curiosity, a man of questionable masculinity because he travels with another. The demise of Lennie is also the demise of the dream. George thus establishes his solidarity with the other men for whom the dream will remain just talk.

Lennie's death need not necessarily mean the end of the dream, however. After all, Candy is still eager to pursue it. But partnership with Candy requires a different kind of relationship than the one George had with Lennie; and unwilling to reestablish a new hierarchy of dominator and dominated, one where George is not so obviously superior, he quickly abandons the dream.

What really stands in the way of the dream, however, is George's inability to accept the implied responsibility of the dream: shared contact with another—equal—human being. As Louis Owens writes, "It is Lennie's need for contact with other living beings, a craving the men of this world deny, that brings about his destruction" (104). George, of course, is the instrument of this destruction and the ultimate judge of its validity. The inherent message of the text is that a partnership based on mutual caring and respect is doomed and the model of marrying masculine with feminine is by nature destructive and tragic. Ironically, while the masculine world despises female dependence and submissiveness, membership in the male community in fact rejects the possibility of true independence and autonomy.

The melodrama of beset manhood neatly rescues the men on this Salinas Valley ranch from the entrappers and domesticators. By story's end, all vestiges of femininity have been eliminated—Lennie, Curley's wife, Candy's dog, Lennie's mice and rabbits, even the deer that bound silently across the path through the willows to the pool; a path, it should be noted, "beaten hard by boys" and men.

Despite the prevailing belief that this story portrays the pathos of the quest for the American dream, the foregoing evidence suggests that *Of Mice and Men* is a Steinbeckian condemnation of the American male's inability to accommodate diversity and nonconformity, a terse commentary on misplaced values.

Carlson and Slim epitomize this conflict between domination and compassion. Warren French notes that Carlson is insensitive and brutal; Slim, kindly and perceptive (78). There is no sentiment in Carlson, an eminently practical, albeit destructive man. Curley's wife and Lennie, like Candy's dog, are to Carlson useless, intrusive, and annoying. A man of action, Carlson does not let emotional weakness keep him from doing what a man's got to do. His having the last word in the story—"Now what the hell ya suppose is eating them two guys?" (107)—attests to the weight given the text's masculine message.

Slim's Characterization

The characterization of Slim, however, suggests some slight hope for reconciliation between male and female components and saves the text from a completely cynical misogyny. Slim is androgynous, what Carolyn Heilbrun defines as "a condition under which the characteristics of the sexes, and the human impulses expressed by men and women, are not rigidly assigned" (x). Kindly, perceptive, compassionate, tender, intuitive, Slim is described in feminine terms. Even his hands are lean, delicate and as graceful as a temple dancer. "His ear heard more than was said to him, and his slow speech had overtones of thought, but of understanding beyond thought" (34).Yet his feminine traits are coupled with images of virility. "His authority was so great that his word was taken on any subject, be it politics or love" (33). He is "the prince of the ranch, capable of driving ten, sixteen, even twenty mules with a single line to the leader" (33). Physically strong, powerful and in control, the others take their cue from Slim, who combines the finest attributes of male and female.

When he finds George and Lennie beside the pool, Slim perceptively recognizes George's internal struggle. He soothes George as a woman might; and yet, unlike a woman, he instructs George as to what he must do next, what "story" he must tell. The two leave together, as George and Lennie first arrived, a couple. *This* partnership may be different. Slim, the only character to integrate the masculine and feminine attributes of his own nature, may well influence the man who has so forcefully denied this integration.

Steinbeck's sympathy clearly lies with the feminine. Lennie tugs at a reader's heart in the same way that a child or defenseless animal might.

So, too, his portrayal of Curley's wife in death softens earlier, vituperous images of her: "And the meanness and the plannings and the discontent and the ache for attention were all gone from her face. She was very pretty and simple, and her face was sweet and young" (92).

But most revealing of Steinbeck's attitude toward the material is a simple image he creates in the opening pages, one that becomes a metaphor for the text. Shortly before we meet George and Lennie, "a big carp rose to the surface of the pool, gulped air and then sank mysteriously into the dark water again, leaving widening rings on the water" (10). If Steinbeck had intended our sympathy to lie with the status quo, the fish that rises to the surface would have been something other than a carp—a rainbow trout or a cut-throat perhaps, game fish known as strong, wiley fighters. Instead Steinbeck gives us the carp, a sucker fish, an invader that eventually takes over a pond or stream, muddying the waters and irrevocably altering the environment it penetrates. Smaller, weaker, and less aggressive species are quickly subsumed. Diversity cannot be accommodated once the carp arrives. Over time, all except the carp disappear. The pond is no longer a very interesting or "wild" place. It is ruined.

"Violence without tragedy; that is the weakness of this book," writes Moore (50). "Sentimental," say others, dismissing the work as minor. The dictionary tells us sentimental means "influenced more by emotion than reason; acting from feeling rather than from practical and utilitarian motives." In short, feminine.

Steinbeck's carp, the men of the Salinas Valley, eliminate diversity and complexity out of a fear for their own survival. They huddle like a school of fish in their bunkhouse, confidence in their own self-definition residing in the absence of contrasting existences. They reign homogeneous, unvarying, sterile—big fish in ever-dwindling ponds.

Works Cited

Baym, Nina. "Melodramas of Beset Manhood: How Theories of American Fiction Exclude Women Authors." In *The New Feminist Criticism*, ed. Elaine Showalter, 65–79. New York: Pantheon Books, 1985.

French, Warren. *John Steinbeck*. New York: Twayne, 1961.

Freud, Sigmund. "The Taboo of Virginity." In the *Standard Edition*, ed. James Strachey, 191–208. London: Hogarth Press, 1961.

Heilbrun, Carolyn G. *Toward a Recognition of Androgyny.* New York: W. W. Norton, 1964.

Lisca, Peter. *The Wide World of John Steinbeck.* New Brunswick, NJ: Rutgers University Press, 1958.

Moore, Harry Thornton. *The Novels of John Steinbeck.* Chicago: Normandie House, 1939.

Owens, Louis. *John Steinbeck's Re-vision of America.* Athens: University of Georgia Press, 1985.

Steinbeck, John. *Of Mice and Men.* New York: Penguin Classics, 1993.

———. *Cannery Row.* New York: Penguin, 1937.

CHAPTER ELEVEN

STEINBECK'S *OF MICE AND MEN* (1937)
Charlotte Hadella

[*Editor's note: Portions of this article have been omitted when the content does not directly apply to* Of Mice and Men.]

I. Background

By 1937, the year that *Of Mice and Men* was published and also produced as a Broadway play, Steinbeck had survived the poverty of his writing apprenticeship and achieved commercial success with *Tortilla Flat* (1935). . . . With the popular and critical success of *Of Mice and Men* and the enormous reaction to *The Grapes of Wrath* just two years later, Steinbeck never again had to worry about making his living as a writer.

Curiously, what did concern the writer while he was composing *Of Mice and Men* was that financial security and public attention would make him unfit for his craft. . . . After *Mice* was chosen by the Book-of-the-Month Club, Steinbeck informed Otis that the news was both gratifying and frightening. He claims, "I shall never learn to conceive of money in larger quantities than two dollars. More than that has no conceptual meaning to me" (*LIL* 134). Perhaps the subject matter of the novel, which took him back to his earlier, more frugal years of working on the Spreckles

Previously published in *A New Study Guide to Steinbeck's Major Works with Critical Explications*, ed. Tetsumaro Hayashi, 139–63. Lanham, MD: Scarecrow Press, 1993. Reprinted with permission.

Sugar Company ranches, intensified Steinbeck's uneasiness with financial security. As his biographer, Jackson J. Benson, observes, the composition of *Of Mice and Men* "was certainly an exercise in humility. For an author who lived through the lives of his characters, [Steinbeck] was reminding himself on the gut level what it was to have nothing, truly, and very little hope for anything."[2] Details of the writer's financial struggles in the early years of his marriage to Carol Henning underscore the authenticity of Steinbeck's interest in marginally subsistent characters whose fiscal futures are always uncertain.[3]

Artistic uncertainty also plagued Steinbeck during the 1930s. Though there were times while he was composing *Mice* that he judged the work to be going very well, he did not allow himself to assume success (*LIL* 123–24). Steinbeck insisted that *Of Mice and Men* was different from anything else that he had ever written. He referred to the book as an experiment, "a tricky little thing designed to teach me to write for the theater" (*LIL* 132). The relative ease with which the novel was transformed into a playscript testifies to the validity of Steinbeck's plan; but since the form was experimental, Steinbeck maintained a note of modest skepticism whenever he commented on the project. In fact, when the earliest version of the manuscript was partially devoured by his dog, Steinbeck wrote to Otis that although he was "pretty mad," he only gave the dog "an ordinary spanking." Maintaining that "the poor little fellow may have been acting critically," Steinbeck writes, "I didn't want to ruin a good dog for a ms. I'm not sure it is good at all" (*LIL* 124). Thus, in spite of previous accomplishments, Steinbeck's distrust of publishers and critics tempered his enthusiasm for the book.

With *Of Mice and Men* Steinbeck was breaking new ground philosophically as well as formally, a circumstance which may also have contributed to his reticence concerning its critical reception. By 1936, he had become very interested in non-teleological thinking. Benson explains that in *In Dubious Battle* the author wanted to present a conflict without taking sides. In Steinbeck's non-teleological fictions, he attempted to create situations with "no cause and effect, no problem and solution, no heroes or villains."[4] Working within this philosophical framework, which might best be described as "is" thinking, Steinbeck originally titled George and Lennie's story "Something That Happened."[5] Happily, the novel proved to be a successful marriage of form and philosophy. With the dramatic structure focusing upon the characters' dialogue and action, Steinbeck achieved a narrative intensity in the story which is largely untainted by authorial voice. Ironically, the "little book" (*LIL* 129) which received such a tentative evaluation from its author would not only find an immediate audience, but would be recognized decades later as a minor American classic.

II. Plot Synopsis

[*Editor's note: This section of text merely repeats the plot line of* Of Mice and Men.]

III. Critical Explication

The frugal text of Steinbeck's little book has inspired a wealth of critical commentary. Moreover, a number of interpretive strategies have been applied to *Of Mice and Men*, producing varied readings of the text over the last few decades. Though this discussion will highlight what has already been said about *Of Mice and Men*, the primary aim is to offer a fresh analysis by subjecting the novel to various critical probes.[7] The eclectic nature of this study suggests that productive examination of Steinbeck's work can follow any one or several critical approaches: a New Historical consideration which notes the interconnections between the work of literature and the culture of its period; interpretive strategies such as structuralist or psychoanalytic readings which assume that the text is integrally whole; and discourse analysis which views the text as open and self-conflicted.

New Historical

Certainly each of Steinbeck's stories about California farm workers includes realistic details which were gleaned from the writer's own experiences as an agricultural laborer and his journalistic investigations of farm labor conditions. The description of the land and the river, the names of real California towns like Soledad and Weed, the language of the men in the bunkhouse, the details of everyday life such as the horseshoe matches and the trips to town on payday, all contribute to the realistic impression of *Of Mice and Men*. Nevertheless, Steinbeck mined his sources for convincing detail, but he was primarily interested in constructing power-ful metaphors. For example, in reference to *In Dubious Battle*, Steinbeck wrote, "I have used a small strike in an orchard valley as the symbol of man's eternal, bitter warfare with himself."[8]

Though *In Dubious Battle* has most often been discussed as a work of realism, recent critics have noted that Steinbeck virtually ignored the important roles played by women and minorities in the California work-ers' strikes in the 1930s.[9] Likewise, Steinbeck did not attempt to draw a realistic picture of the lives of racial minorities in *Of Mice and Men*. Just before George and Lennie first enter the grove by the Salinas River, the author sets the stage with this description: "In front of the low horizontal limb of a giant sycamore there is an ash pile made by many fires; the limb is worn smooth by men who have sat on it" (2). Judging by the characters depicted in the novel, we might assume that all (or most) of the men who have sat on that sycamore limb have been white men. Crooks, the stable buck, is the sole representative of a racial minority in the story. Yet, when Steinbeck worked on the Spreckles Sugar Ranches during the 1920s (while he was on and off as a student at Stanford), most of the workers were foreign nationals: Japanese, Mexican, or Filipino. Benson identifies Spreckles Ranch Number 2, just south of Soledad on the west side of the Salinas River, as the ranch where George and Lennie hire on.[10] Of course, Steinbeck also worked alongside migrant laborers of Anglo-Saxon stock—workers like George, Lennie, Slim, Carlson, and Candy; but it is unlikely that every hired hand in the bunkhouse during haying season would be Caucasian. In fact, in a very early piece, "Fingers of Cloud," published in a Stanford literary magazine, Steinbeck tells the story of a retarded teenage girl who wanders away from home and finds refuge in the bunkhouse of a Filipino work gang.[11]

Other historical and biographical details might lead us to question Steinbeck's choice of a cast of Anglo characters for his play-novelette. Cletus E. Daniel, in *Bitter Harvest: A History of California Farmwork-ers, 1870–1941*, states that Mexicans had become the mainstays of the agricultural labor force in California by the mid-1920s as growers took advantage of the liberalized federal immigration policy toward Mexico and as the flow of illegal immigration from Mexico steadily increased.[12] Furthermore, Steinbeck's choice of the "land dream" as a central motif in the story may have even been inspired by his trip to Mexico in 1935 during which he witnessed the struggle of masses of poor people longing to own a piece of land. Also during this trip, the Steinbecks had observed poor, illiterate workers attending concerts and theatrical productions. Benson believes that this experience prompted Steinbeck to consider writing a play instead of a novel because his work was not reaching the people he was writing about. In keeping with this original intention, Steinbeck read his novel-as-play to the Green Street Theater Union, a group which presented works with a socialist-worker philosophy. The Union opened its new theater in North Beach, California, on May 21, 1937, with Steinbeck's *Of Mice and Men*—six months before George Kaufman produced it on Broadway.[13]

Given the multi-racial configuration of the California farm labor force in the 1920s and 1930s, along with the possible Mexican influence on the form and theme of Steinbeck's novel, we must conclude that Steinbeck was not attempting to render an accurate socio-historical picture in *Of Mice and Men*. However, the subsistence-level economy, the tensions between workers and owner, and the social marginality of the migrant laborers in *Of Mice and Men* ring true to the historical details of the actual setting. Most importantly, the American Dream theme of owning a piece of land, becoming self-sufficient, and realizing a sense of place, was a realistic facet of the American psyche. By 1936, the year that Steinbeck was writing *Mice*, the technological revolution in agribusiness was threatening what little job security itinerant workers had. Anne Loftis reports that mechanical combines enabling five men to do the work of 350 men were responsible for half the nation's grain harvest in 1938.[14] Cletus E. Daniel writes that

> [b]y the twentieth century, employment in California's large-scale agriculture had come to mean irregular work, constant movement, low wages, squalid working and living conditions, social isolation, emotional deprivation, and individual powerlessness so profound as to make occupational advancement a virtual impossibility.[15]

He goes on to stress that

> whatever the differences of race, national origin, language, and psychology that existed among farmworkers in California from 1870 to 1930, working for wages in industrialized agriculture normally conferred mem-

bership in an unhappy fraternity whose cohering force was a kinship of powerlessness.[16]

Daniel's phrase "kinship of powerlessness" aptly describes the brother-hood of George, Lennie, and Candy as they plan for their escape from the ranch to the dream farm. Thus it seems that in spite of Steinbeck's failure to render "truthfully" the racial identities of his California farm-workers, he does create an accurate social milieu in *Of Mice and Men*. Loftis contends that the "social history which [Steinbeck] had learned firsthand is woven seamlessly into the fabric of the story."[17] The rapid decline in family farming and the impersonal profile of the burgeoning agribusiness in California at the turn of the century contributed to the decline of small communities and the rise of economic class distinctions. Family farming as a way of life be-came even more difficult as a result of the Great Depression. Hence, when *Of Mice and Men* appeared in 1937, many Americans could identify with the powerlessness and social marginality of Steinbeck's characters.

Finally, it would seem that though America has experienced un-countable cultural and economic changes since the publication of *Of Mice and Men*, the isolation of individuals in our modern society still persists. In fact, the social problems of unemployment, underemployment, and homelessness, problems of which Steinbeck was acutely aware, plague this country even as we enter the final decade of the twentieth century. Pic-ture, if you will, the disheveled transient standing on the street corner of any large American city today with his dirty cardboard sign which reads, WILL WORK FOR FOOD. Would he not be captivated by George and Lennie's dream? Perhaps he, too, dreams of "a vegetable patch and a rabbit hutch and chickens. And when it rains in the winter, [he could] say the hell with goin' to work, and . . . build up a fire in the stove and set around it an' listen to the rain comin' down on the roof . . ." (14–15). But even if the details of the dream vary, the fact that some people have little else but dreams to sustain them has not changed.

The selection of subject and theme for *Of Mice and Men* reveals Stein-beck's understanding of basic human needs, and the author's social con-sciousness has appealed to a wide audience for five decades. However, to appreciate Steinbeck's achievement as a storyteller, we must go beyond the socio-historical fabric of his novella and give some attention to its struc-ture, its psychological framework, and the complexity of its discourse.

CHARLOTTE HADELLA

Symbol, Myth, and Theme: Structuralist Interpretations

The allusive title *Of Mice and Men* signals from the outset of the story that mice symbols will appear and that the schemes of men will go astray.[18] Before the central characters delineate those plans specifically, however, Steinbeck physically associates George with mice by describing him as "small and quick, dark of face, with restless eyes and sharp, strong features" (2). Lennie's connection with mice is more obvious: he carries a mouse in his pocket because he loves to pet soft, furry things. Consequently, Lennie associates mice with the dream of owning a farm and keeping rabbits which, unlike the mice, will be able to survive his petting them.

Of Mice and Men is a tightly structured work which unfolds as a series of scenes, each of which develops naturally from the preceding dialogue or action. In *The Wide World of John Steinbeck*, Peter Lisca analyzes recurring motifs of language, action, and symbol in *Mice*. Discussing the sense of inevitability in the novel, Lisca notes that for Lennie, the rabbits, and by extension all soft, furry things, represent the dream of owning the farm, a dream that has Edenic overtones.[19] Louis Owens, in *John Steinbeck's Re-Vision of America*, expands upon Lisca's discussion of the Eden myth in *Of Mice and Men* to show that "[t]here are no Edens in Steinbeck's writing, only illusions of Eden."[20] Steinbeck indicates the inevitable failure of the land dream by introducing a dead mouse into the opening scene of the story to show that Lennie destroys soft, furry things—as his later killing of the puppy indicates. In this symbolic system, Curley's wife is simply another nice-to-touch object that is doomed for destruction when Lennie pets her. Her death is just the "something" that was bound to happen to insure the shattering of George and Lennie's plans for escaping from their transitory existence as migrant workers.[21]

To reinforce the notion of illusive dreams, Steinbeck also has the girl recount her fantasy of escaping the lonely, restricted life of the ranch. When Candy, Crooks, and Lennie shun her company on Saturday night, she tells them contemptuously, "I could of went with the shows. Not jus' one, neither. An' a guy tol' me he could put me in pitchers . . ." (78). Curley and most of the hired men have gone into town to carouse at the saloons and whorehouses. Just "the weak ones" (77) have been left behind, and Curley's wife seeks the only companionship available to her. The next day she describes her dream again in a conversation with Lennie in the barn just before he accidentally breaks her neck. Here she tells her story "in a passion of communication, as though she hurried before her listener could be taken away" (88). With this narrative commentary Steinbeck emphasizes that being able to share one's dream with a sympathetic audience—the companionship implied by such an action—is as important as realizing the dream.

Following this same line of thought, Owens argues convincingly that loneliness is the central theme of *Of Mice and Men* and that the novel is not as pessimistic as some critics have insisted. If we accept the non-teleological premise of the story, we understand that human beings are flawed and that their hopes of regaining Eden are illusory. In Steinbeck's novel, the characters' commitment to the dream and to each other, however, is not flawed. Owens explains:

> The dream of George and Lennie represents a desire to defy the curse of Cain and fallen man—to break the pattern of wandering and loneliness imposed on the outcasts and to return to the perfect garden. George and Lennie achieve all of this dream that is possible in the real world: they are their brother's keeper.[22]

Similarly, William Goldhurst offers an allegorical reading of *Mice* as Steinbeck's parable of the curse of Cain.[23] The question "Am I my brother's keeper?" permeates the story as other characters are affected by the commitment between George and Lennie. Curley is suspicious of it, Slim admires it, and Candy and Crooks briefly participate in the brotherhood by looking after Lennie when George is not around. Although all of the plans for buying the farm are shattered when Lennie dies, Steinbeck still leaves the reader with an image of two men together as George and Slim walk away from the grove by the river where the story had begun.

The Unconscious

In addition to analyzing the patterns of symbol and myth in *Of Mice and Men*, we might also employ psychoanalytic strategies to interpret the action of the novel and to understand the major characters. Because Steinbeck uses animal imagery on several occasions to describe Lennie, critics often speak of Lennie as a symbol of humankind's animal nature. When Lennie drinks from the pool in the grove, he "dabble[s] his big paw in the water" (3); when he returns to the river at the end of the novel, "Lennie appear[s] out of the brush, and he [comes] as silently as a creeping bear moves" (100). Obviously, Lennie often functions on the level of the unconscious. His violent responses to fear illustrate that strong, destructive forces loom just beneath the surface of his consciousness. Even hypothetical threats, such as cats eating the rabbits on the imaginary farm, move Lennie to violent outbursts: "You jus' let 'em try to get the rabbits," he tells George. "I'll break their God damn necks. I'll . . . I'll smash 'em with a stick" (58). It is also clear that George tries to exert a conscious control over Lennie. George tells Lennie when to speak and to whom; he makes Lennie promise to return to the grove by the river if there is any trouble on the ranch. But, as evidenced by the earlier incident in Weed and the fracas in the bunkhouse during which Lennie crushes Curley's hand, George's control of his partner's powerfully destructive physical strength is actually quite tenuous.

In this interpretive frame, we might say that Lennie acts as an extension of George, a powerful id to George's ego. Mark Spilka develops this kind of Freudian reading of the novel, though he does not use the terms id and ego to describe the relationship between the two characters.[24] Clearly, Lennie, without thinking about what he is doing, seems to be carrying out George's wishes when he severely injures Curley in the bunkhouse fight. Earlier in the story, George had expressed his hatred for Curley, declaring, "I'm scared I'm gonna tangle with that bastard myself" (37). George also instantly detests Curley's wife and honors her with such invectives as "bitch" and "jail bait" (32). Though Lennie responds to the girl sensually and thinks that she is "purty," that stroking her hair is "nice" (32, 91), he becomes the instrument of her destruction.

This analysis of characters and events gives a reasonable account of the partnership between the two central characters; it even suggests that George needs Lennie as much as Lennie needs George. However, it does not satisfactorily explain why George so vehemently despises Curley's wife or why he kills his partner at the end of the novel. We may come to terms with these issues by recognizing the antagonistic forces within George's psyche, forces which may be interpreted as Jungian archetypes. We know from Carol Henning, Steinbeck's first wife, that Steinbeck's friendship with the Jungian psychologist Joseph Campbell in the early 1930s had a discernible effect on the writer's intellectual development. The two men met frequently at Ed Ricketts's laboratory in Monterey where they discussed ideas and books.[25] Recognizing Steinbeck's familiarity with Jung's work, critics have noted the psychoanalytic influences in *To a God Unknown*, *In Dubious Battle*, and in several stories in *The Long Valley*. Likewise, Jung's ideas about the ego and the unconscious self are useful in interpreting *Of Mice and Men*. In Jungian terms, we may see Lennie as George's "shadow self" and Curley's wife as his "anima," archetypes which invade the personal unconscious of one's ego personality.[26]

Jung describes both the shadow and the anima or animus as projections which "change the world into the replica of one's unknown face."[27] The shadow is always of the same sex as the subject and may even be recognized as the subject's evil nature. But the contra-sexual figure—the animus of a woman, and the anima of a man—represents the face of "absolute evil" and is usually not recognized by the subject as part of his or her own psyche.[28] One face of a man's anima is the seductress, a projection which embodies the negative, unconscious, and unlived aspects of the psyche to which a man responds with fear. At the same time that the anima arouses libidinal drives within the psyche, a patriarchal consciousness strives to repress the feminine force.[29]

Curley's wife represents a mysterious and autonomous force which stimulates George's sexual consciousness, challenges his manhood, inspires self-doubt, and taunts him for his meanness. At various times throughout the story, George gives conscious expression to these feelings. For instance, he admits that it is mean of him to lose his temper over Lennie's wanting ketchup with his beans (12); and he tells Slim about the tricks that he played on Lennie when they were youngsters (40). Also, George seems reluctant to express himself sexually, and when Whit tries to interest him in visiting Suzy's place on Saturday night, he insists that if he does go to the whorehouse, it will only be to buy whiskey. The overt sexuality of Curley's wife is an inversion of George's puritanical nature, and, as George's anima, she sparks an intensely negative reaction from him. She also serves as a conscious reminder of his longing to "live so easy and maybe have a girl" (7), the dream that he represses because of his association with Lennie.

The shadow, on the other hand, is a lower level of personality than the ego. Jung explains that the shadow self is a projection of the ego's dark characteristics, inferiorities of an emotional, obsessive, or possessive quality. Jung writes: "On this lower level with its uncontrolled or scarcely controlled emotions one behaves more or less like a primitive, who is not only the passive victim of his affects but also singularly incapable of moral judgment."[30] We see Lennie at once as a primitive entity who responds instinctively to various stimuli and is incapable of moral judgment. Yet, it just so happens that Lennie manages to harm the people towards whom George harbors animosity. At times, George even expresses an extreme dislike of Lennie. He complains that because of Lennie he can't keep a job, or "[g]et a gallon of whiskey, or set in a pool room and play cards or shoot pool" (11). Ultimately, Lennie brings about the circumstances which allow George to rid himself of the illusive land dream and the responsibility of taking care of his mentally deficient partner.

If we look closely at the text, we see that in the opening scene Steinbeck subliminally defines Lennie as George's shadow. But first the author draws our attention to the river, a symbol of the Jungian collective unconscious. Then as Lennie follows George into the sycamore grove, Steinbeck underscores the fact that they are dressed exactly alike; they walk single file down the path, "and even in the open one stayed behind the other. . . . The first man stopped short in the clearing, and the follower nearly ran over him" (2–3). After both of them have had a drink of water from the pool, George

> replaced his hat, pushed himself back from the river, drew up his knees and embraced them. Lennie, who had been watching, imitated George exactly. He pushed himself back, drew up his knees, embraced them, looked over to George to see whether he had it just right. He pulled his hat down a little more over his eyes, the way George's hat was. (3–4)

The shadow motif is unmistakable in this scene which serves as our introduction to the main characters.

That Lennie has survived as long as he has testifies to George's conscious commitment to his care. George, however, has a violently aggressive nature. Both fearing and repressing the primitive impulses in himself, he projects them onto Lennie. The dream farm represents a haven in which George's aggressive nature (represented by Lennie) can be repressed. George devises the plan to escape from the real world of migrant life—bunkhouses, rough men, whiskey, and whorehouses—because he is disturbed by the qualities in himself that such a life brings to the surface. Unconsciously, he projects these disturbing qualities onto his shadow self and feels the need to control that self by isolating it in the safe haven of the Edenic dream farm. Meanwhile, George inadvertently directs Lennie towards disaster by staying at the ranch even after the trouble with Curley, and by making Lennie afraid of Curley's wife. Though George realizes that Lennie will eventually do something so terrible that he will have to be incarcerated or destroyed, he does not take him away from the ranch because of an unconscious desire to rid himself of his shadow. Not until Lennie's death is George really free to join the community of men represented by Slim. As the only character in the novel who understands that George did not kill Lennie in self-defense, Slim expresses his approval of George's actions. Then he offers to buy George a drink, and together they walk away from the river grove where Lennie has died.

This Jungian interpretation of *Of Mice and Men* highlights the conflict of personalities and priorities in the story. It hints that there is more to the characterization of Curley's wife than has previously been assessed, and it suggests that the novel does not simply relate the story of disillusioned dreamers. By focusing on the conflicting forces in George's life, we discover that the text itself may be ambiguous and self-conflicted.

Discourse Analysis

Several times in the novel, George expresses the desire to change his life. Sometimes he imagines himself free of the responsibility of looking after Lennie: he could keep a job and not always have to be on the move; maybe he could have a girl, or he could go into town with the guys whenever he wanted to; he could shoot pool, drink whiskey, and so on. At other times, he talks about buying a little farm where he could raise a garden, and Lennie could tend rabbits. These "dreams" have several elements in common: each represents a change from the status quo and each holds forth some form of freedom for George. Nevertheless, the two scenarios are mutually exclusive.

In a sense, George's dreams compete throughout the text for actualization and verbalization; and though they are voiced by the same character each time, they are spoken in different "voices." The narrative expletive attached to George's speech about life without Lennie is, "George exploded"

(11). His description of living "so easy" comes out in anger; the words spew forth in an unrehearsed explosion. In contrast, when George tells Lennie about the dream farm, his voice "became deeper. He repeated his words rhythmically as though he had said them many times before" (13). The signal is clear: we are not experiencing George's "voice" as we had been in the present-tense situation of the story, and the words of his speech may not even be his own. Eventually, we learn that George's partnership with Lennie and the notion of living in a place where he can keep Lennie safe from the real world are the results of a promise made to Lennie's Aunt Clara. The plan reflects the illusion of the American Dream and the mythic innocence of pre-lapsarian Eden.

This close examination of the narrative syntax in the passages related to the competing dreams reveals that Steinbeck consciously creates dialogic tension in the text. To explain this dialogic tension, or double-voicedness, in *Of Mice and Men*, I am borrowing from Mikhail Bakhtin's theory of discourse as dialogue between a speaker and a listener, about a hero or subject.[31] In verbal and written utterances, the subject becomes an active agent, interacting with the speaker "to shape language and determine form," and the subject (or hero) often becomes the dominant influence.[32] Dialogic tension exists in all discourse because words, the elements of the dialogue, are loaded with various social nuances which influence each other and perhaps even change as a result of the association. According to Bakhtin, "Each word tastes of the context and contexts in which it has lived its socially charged life; all words and forms are populated by intentions. Contextual overtones . . . are inevitable in the word."[33]

The contextual overtones of the dream-farm passages in *Of Mice and Men* are twofold: mythical and communal. Sometimes the description of the land dream is delivered as if it were a religious incantation, as when George deepens his voice and speaks rhythmically. Sometimes the story is related as a dialogue or as a chorus of two or more speakers who combine their "speech acts" (Bakhtin's term) to create a composite image. This happens when Lennie interrupts George's recitation and is coaxed into completing the story himself (14). Later, in the bunkhouse, after George has agreed to a partnership with Candy, Steinbeck notes that "each mind was popped into the future when this lovely thing would come about" (60). With their minds on the future, Lennie, George, and Candy discuss their plan, each one adding a specific detail to the description of life on the farm. Lennie, of course, mentions feeding the rabbits; Candy asks if there will be a stove; and George imagines taking a holiday and going to a carnival, a circus, or a ball game (60–61).

Notice that both Lennie's and Candy's comments deal with specific details of farm life. On the other hand, George's contribution to this idyllic picture focuses on activities which would take him away from the farm, not on the farm itself. Though his comments are in keeping with the spirit of camaraderie which flows through the conversation, the narrative shift to non-farm activities is a subtle clue that George's version of the future does not coincide with his partners'. What George seems to be doing in this speech is reconciling the mythic vision with the more personal vision of how he would live his life if he did not have to look after Lennie. Though George gives lip service to the dream-farm myth, it is possible that he is not really committed to it. After all, the primary reason for acquiring the farm is to remove Lennie from the everyday working world in which he cannot seem to stay out of trouble. While Lennie's presence necessitates keeping the dream alive, his uncontrollable strength and outbursts of violence virtually assure that the dream will not come true.

By introducing both of George's dreams in the opening scene of the story, and by emphasizing the differences in the way they are "voiced," Steinbeck highlights the dialectical nature of the narrative. From scene to scene, as George appears to be working conscientiously toward achieving the land dream, he is actually moving closer and closer to the competing dream which is not a dream at all, but a rather realistic description of the bunkhouse life which might be possible for George if he did not have to worry about Lennie.

Through the dialogical structure of the text, Steinbeck maintains narrative tension without imposing moral judgments. George is neither unreasonable nor unrealistic when he imagines himself unencumbered by his promise to Lennie's Aunt Clara. Any moral judgments which might influence our interpretation of the final scene must come from outside of the text. Lennie's death, of course, leads to the inevitable resolution of the narrative tension, but Steinbeck offers few syntactical clues to help the reader decide exactly what motivates George to kill Lennie. As George calmly tells Lennie about the farm, he hesitates to raise the pistol even after he hears the footsteps of Curley and the other men. Steinbeck prolongs the inevitable resolution of the crisis with this comment: "The voices came close now. George raised the gun and listened to the voices" (106). Though Steinbeck lets the reader decide which George speaks through the pistol—the one who creates the world of protected innocence or the one who expresses a desire for freedom—he makes one thing very clear: George's pulling the trigger is a reaction to the voices of cruelty from which neither he nor Lennie can escape any longer.

Notes

[*Editor's note: Portions of this article have been omitted, including notes 1 and 6. Those notes are reprinted here for easy reference:*

Note 1: John Steinbeck, Steinbeck: A Life in Letters, *ed. Elaine Steinbeck and Robert Wallsten (New York: Viking Press, 1975). Subsequent references to the letters are from this edition and are cited in the text as LIL with page number.*

Note 6: John Steinbeck, Of Mice and Men/Cannery Row *(New York: Penguin, 1993). Subsequent references to the novel are from this edition and page numbers are cited parenthetically in the text.*]

2. Jackson J. Benson, *The True Adventures of John Steinbeck, Writer* (New York: Viking, 1984), 326.

3. Benson, *True Adventures*, 163–413.

4. Benson, *True Adventures*, 327.

5. Louis Owens, *John Steinbeck's Re-Vision of America* (Athens: University of Georgia Press, 1985), 103.

7. For the structure of this critical explication, I credit Eugene K. Garber, "'My Kinsman, Major Molineux': Some Interpretive and Critical Probes," in *Literature in the Classroom*, ed. Ben F. Nelms, 83–104 (Urbana, IL: NCTE, 1988).

8. Benson, *True Adventures*, 304.

9. Benson refers to the Mexicans and the Mexican-Americans involved in the 1933 cotton strike (304). Also, Louis Owens discusses the role played by women and minorities in the strikes in "'Putting Down the Thing': Irony of *In Dubious Battle*," a paper delivered at The Third International Steinbeck Congress in Honolulu, Hawaii, on May 30, 1990.

10. Benson, *True Adventures*, 39.

11. Benson, *True Adventures*, 61.

12. Cletus E. Daniel, *Bitter Harvest: A History of California Farmworkers, 1870–1941* (Berkeley: University of California Press, 1982), 67.

13. Benson, *True Adventures*, 326, 351.

14. Anne Loftis, "A Historical Introduction to *Of Mice and Men*," in *The Short Novels of John Steinbeck*, ed. Jackson J. Benson (Durham, NC: Duke University Press, 1990), 39.

15. Daniel, *Bitter Harvest*, 64.

16. Daniel, *Bitter Harvest*, 64.

17. Loftis, "Historical Introduction," 41.

18. The allusion is to Robert Burns's poem, "To a Mouse."

19. Peter Lisca, *The Wide World of John Steinbeck* (New Brunswick, NJ: Rutgers University Press, 1958; reprint, New York: Gordian Press, 1981), 136 (page references are to the reprint edition).

20. Owens, *John Steinbeck's Re-Vision*, 101.

21. Lisca, *Wide World*, 136–38.

22. Owens, *John Steinbeck's Re-Vision*, 102.

23. William Goldhurst, "*Of Mice and Men*: John Steinbeck's Parable of the Curse of Cain," in Benson, *Short Novels*, 48–59.

24. Mark Spilka, "Of George and Lennie and Curley's Wife: Sweet Violence in Steinbeck's Eden," in Benson, *Short Novels*, 59–70.

25. Benson, *True Adventures*, 223–25.

26. Carl G. Jung, "Aion: Phenomenology of the Self," in *The Portable Jung*, ed. Joseph Campbell, 139–62 (New York: Penguin, 1976).

27. Jung, "Aion," 147.

28. Jung, "Aion," 148.

29. Bettina L. Knapp, *Women in Twentieth-Century Literature: A Jungian View* (University Park: Pennsylvania State University Press, 1987), 164–65.

30. Jung, "Aion," 146.

31. Mikhail Bakhtin, *The Dialogic Imagination: Four Essays*, ed. Michael Holquist, trans. Caryl Emerson and Michael Holquist (Austin: University of Texas Press, 1981), 314–15.

32. Charles I. Schuster, "Mikhail Bakhtin as Rhetorical Theorist," *College English* 47 (October 1985), 595.

33. Bakhtin, *Dialogic Imagination*, 293.

CHAPTER TWELVE
OF MICE AND MEN: STEINBECK'S SPECULATIONS IN MANHOOD
Leland S. Person Jr.

U ntil Jean Emery's recent essay, Mark Spilka's 1974 *Modern Fiction Studies* article represented the most thorough analysis of gender questions in *Of Mice and Men*. Spilka emphasizes George Milton's flight from adult sexuality and his use of Lennie Small to rid his world of the sexual "trap" embodied in Curley and his wife (64). Spilka works with traditional gender categories, invoking a normative heterosexuality, for example, as the ground from which George imagines a "boy's world" of friendship, predicated on a "retreat" from "masculine grossness" and "from whorehouse visits and combative marriages like Curley's" (63).

Emery unaccountably ignores Spilka in her provocative feminist reading of *Of Mice and Men*, which she derives from Nina Baym's classic essay on "beset manhood," but she too assumes that masculine identity is constructed out of misogyny and a desire of eliminate "all vestiges of femininity" (40). Lennie is George's "wife," she claims, because he is "stereotypically feminine, docile and submissive, dependent and lacking in self-assertiveness," and he "obeys George like a good woman" (35). Unlike Spilka and Emery, who defuse male relationships in the novel by infantilizing or heterosexualizing them, I want to examine *Of Mice and Men* within a pluralized discourse of masculinity—as a novel about men's relationships to other men. My reading will be "homosexual" in the sense that Robert K. Martin uses the term for male friendships in Melville's sea

Previously published in *The Steinbeck Newsletter* 8, nos. 1–2 (1995): 1–4. Used by permission of the Martha Heasley Cox Center for Steinbeck Studies.

novels—for intimate same sex relationships that do not necessarily involve genital sexuality (13).

Like Melville's novels, *Of Mice and Men* destabilizes conventional constructs of masculinity (patriarchal, heterosexual, and phallocentric) in order to explore alternative and subversive masculinities—indeed, a utopian dream founded on male bonding and a sublimated homosexual domesticity. *Of Mice and Men* resembles *Moby Dick* in particular in marking out an imaginative space where male-to-male relationships can flourish. The novel opens at a "deep pool" in the Salinas River to which both ranch boys and tramps have beaten hard paths (1), and it is tempting to hear echoes of the "twenty-eighth bather" section of Whitman's "Song of Myself" and of the sperm-squeezing scene in *Moby-Dick* each scene suggesting the potential fluidity of male identity and male-to-male relationships. Martin notes two erotic forces in Melville's fiction: a "democratic eros" expressed "in male friendship and . . . the celebration of a generalized seminal power not directed toward control and production; and a hierarchical eros expressed in social forms of male power" (4). Whereas heterosexuality remains deeply rooted in subject-object power relationships, men who enter into homosexual relationships abdicate their roles in an "economy of power" over women and other men (Martin 14). Male friendships, such as the one between Ishmael and Queequeg, have the potential to subvert the economic, political, and sexual hierarchies that the normative heterosexual economy supports and to install cooperation rather than competition as the founding principle of male relationships.

Of Mice and Men positions its male characters between similar male sexual economies. The ranch economy is patriarchal and capitalistic—heterosexual and homosocial. The hierarchy descends from the boss through his son Curley to the jerkline skinner, Slim, and then to the workers. This fragile economy is homosocial in precisely the ways Eve Sedgwick describes in *Between Men*, because it depends upon the repression and sublimation of sexual desire, enabling men to get along and produce work. "Guys like us, that work on ranches, are the loneliest guys in the world," George tells Lennie. "They got no family. They don't belong to no place. They come to a ranch an' work up a stake and then they go inta town and blow their stake, and the first thing you know they're poundin' their tail on some other ranch" (13). Trapped within a vicious cycle of hard work, low wages, and wasteful expenditure, "guys" who work the ranches are perpetually exploited and then, like Curley's dog, put out to a "pasture" they cannot own. Instead of saving for the future, the men spend their wages and their sexual selves in town at "old Suzy's place," where they can get a "flop" or "have a couple of shots" (51). Heterosexual desire is carefully policed, in other words, relegated to the margins and incorporated into the capitalistic economy that governs the normative world of the ranch.

Curley's wife emphasizes the fragility of this economy because she crosses the carefully drawn lines between the ranch house and the bunk house, the owners and workers, and she exaggerates the fault lines between homosocial and heterosexual desires. A kind of outlaw virgin, Curley's wife is a "jail bait all set on the trigger," in George's terms. "Ranch with a bunch on it ain't no place for a girl, specially like her" (51), precisely because she threatens the homosocial working relationship between men. Instead of cooperating with one another, the men compete with each other—often violently, like Cain and Abel (see Goldhurst and Lisca), as Curley's compulsive effort to thwart his wife's relations with the men clearly show. Or as she herself puts it, "You're all scared of each other. . . . Ever' one of you's scared the rest is goin' to get something on you" (77). Her appearance in the bunk house, her suggestive comment that "Nobody can't blame a person for lookin'" (31), her open invitation of the male gaze as she throws her body forward (31)—her actions require immediate interdiction and especially the proscription of Lennie's desire. "Listen to me, you crazy bastard," George tells Lennie. "Don't you even take a look at that bitch" (32). Lennie's libido, or desire, seems largely narcissistic—expressed in petting behavior that seems more masturbatory than object-oriented. Indeed, Lennie's preference for mice that he can keep in his pocket and pet with his thumb as he walks along (5) pointedly suggests the masturbatory quality of his desire. Proscribing Lennie's attraction to Curley's wife enables the translation of Lennie's desire to vengeful violence—Curley's symbolic castration through the gloved hand he keeps "soft for his wife" (30). In contrast to Ishmael's, Lennie's "squeeze of the hand" perverts the sort of homo-subjective bond that Melville realizes in *Moby-Dick*, converting desublimated desire into triangulated heterosexual and homosocial competition—dominant-subordinated mastery.

In contrast, the "little house" dream that George and Lennie regularly invoke features democratic cooperation and communalism—an all-male version of the matriachy that Warren Motley has detected in Ma Joad's role in *The Grapes of Wrath*. The two men collaborate dialogically to rehearse a mutual fantasy that subverts the conventionally entrepreneurial "ranch" ideal predicted on owner-worker and subject-object relationships. In effect, the two men share a single subjectivity in the act of collaboration. "You got it by heart," George tells Lennie. "You can do it yourself" (14). But Lennie prefers to supplement George's rhythmic narrative with interpolations of his own—melting his desire into George's in a verbal analogy to Ishmael's mergence of body and mind with other men's in the big tub of sperm. "Someday," George begins, "we're gonna get the jack together and we're gonna have a little house and a couple of acres an' a cow and some pigs and—." "*An' live off the fatta the lan'*," Lennie shouts. "An' have *rabbits*. Go on George! Tell about what we're gonna have in the garden and about the rabbits in the cages and about the rain in the winter and the stove" (14).

Let me emphasize that what I am calling the homosexual dream is not genitally sexual. Indeed, it depends upon the sublimation of sexual energy in shared labor and homemaking. "We'd have a little house an' a room to ourself," George says. "An' when we put in a crop, why we'd be there to take the crop up. We'd know what come of our planting" (58). Lennie's sexuality, furthermore, is pointedly sublimated in stroking and petting—fantasmatically invested in tending rabbits, traditional symbols of unrestrained sexuality.

Not only does the homosexual dream dissolve competitive relationships, but it attracts and encourages other men to enter imaginatively into an all-male fantasy. Much like Melville, who discovered in the Ishmael-Queequeg bond a "radical potential for social reorganization, based on principles of equality, affection, and respect for the other" (Martin 94), Steinbeck explores alternative economic and social structures through the interdependent bond between George and Lennie. Not unlike Ishmael's reverie in "the Squeeze of the Hand," when George and Lennie share the dream with Candy, "They all sat still, all bemused by the beauty of the thing, each mind was popped into the future when this lovely thing should come about" (66). The stoop-shouldered, one-handed Candy volunteers to invest his $350 stake for the chance to "cook and tend the chickens and hoe the garden some" (59)—his proposal reflecting the diversification of gender roles on which such a male utopia would be founded. "An' it'd be our own, an' nobody could can us," George says. "If we don't like a guy we can say 'Get the hell out,' and by God he's got to do it. An' if a fren' come along, why we'd have an extra bunk, an' we'd say, 'Why don't you spen' the night?' and by God he would" (58). George and Lennie's homo-topic dream even dissolves racial barriers, as the crippled stable buck Crooks offers to "work for nothing—just his keep"—if he can be allowed to join them (76). "A guy needs somebody—to be near him," Crooks says. "Don't make no difference who the guy is, long's he's with you" (72–73).

George and Lennie's relationship obviously represents the emotional and thematic center of *Of Mice and Men*—microcosmically embodying the possibilities and the limitations of the world outside. Allegorical examples of partial manhood, the two men are opposites (2)—"two parts of a single being," with Lennie representing "the Freudian id" and George "its controlling ego" (Lisca 79). In the gendered terms that concern me here, however, it is more useful to look back to Plato's *Symposium* than to Freud. In Aristophanes' famous parable, the sexes were originally three: man, woman, and the union of the two (30). Zeus cut man in two, however, leaving him "always looking for his other half" (32), and Aristophanes imagines a plurality of potential pairings—homosexual as well as heterosexual. They who are "of the male," he says, "and while they are young, being slices of the original man, they hang about men and embrace them, and they are themselves the best of boys and youths because they have the most manly nature" (32). Linking the greatest manliness with same-sex bonding, Aristophanes constructs a utopic masculine identity—a super Manhood of sorts that *Of Mice and Men* intertextually explores.

I want to focus on the execution that ends the novel—and violently destroys the possibility of intra-psychic union that Plato describes—because the ending bears so heavily on what I am calling Steinbeck's speculations in manhood. Positing the Lennie-George relationship in terms of investment and exchange helps show how personal relationships exemplify large male-to-male economies—how the violent end of their relationship represents death of the homosexual dream and, by default, the recovery of the patriarchal, capitalistic economy that the dream challenged.

Steinbeck carefully stages the murders in chapters 5 and 6 to emphasize the trade offs necessary in this complex sexual economy. When Lennie kills the puppy—in effect by loving it too much—he reasons that George will no longer let him tend the rabbits at their little place (85–86).

One experience cancels the other. Similarly, as he shifts his attention to Curley's wife, he understands the "economic" consequences of his actions. "If George sees me talkin' to you," he tells her, "he'll give me hell" (87), and even as she talks to him in a "passion of communication," Lennie strokes the dead puppy and thinks of his rabbits—exchanging heterosexual desire for autoerotic fantasy and the homosexual utopia that promotes such innocent pleasure. The crisis comes, of course, when Lennie crosses the line between narcissistic and object-oriented, homosocial and heterosexual, desire. Lennie likes all soft things equally—a puppy, a mouse, a piece of velvet, a woman's hair—but petting Curley's wife subjects him to the same police action he had suffered in Weed when he grabbed the girl in the red dress. He kills Curley's wife so that George won't find out that he has "messed up" again, because "messing up" jeopardizes the homosexual dream he shares with George.

That dream remains imperiled throughout the novel—questioned repeatedly by the other men. Slim, for example, tells George that "It jus' seems kinda funny how a cuckoo like him and a smart little guy like you travelin' together" (39). Although Emery considers Slim an androgynous character who integrates masculine and feminine attributes (41), she exaggerates Slim's femininity. Despite having hands "as delicate in their action as those of a temple dancer" (34), Slim illustrates the successful masculinization of a male character along lines of classic manhood: "he moved with a majesty only achieved by royalty and master craftsmen"; he was "capable of killing a fly on the wheeler's butt with a bull whip without touching the mule"; there was a "gravity in his manner and a quiet so profound that all talk stopped when he spoke"; his "authority was so great that his word was taken on any subject, be it politics or love" (33). If Lennie reflects a regressive, narcissistic stage of undistributed desire, Slim suggests the inscription of a stereotypically masculine self-image that writes over any potential androgyny. Slim's crucial part at the very end of the novel—consoling and leading George away from Lennie's dead body—reinforces the message that killing Lennie has meant killing and repressing the homosexual dream and the male bond.

George, like Slim, will eventually offer another example of successful repression. Earlier in the novel, in the bunkhouse, Slim had "fastened" his "calm, God-like eyes" on George while he described his relationship to Lennie. Under the gaze and sign of the patriarch, George adopts a "tone of confession" (40), guiltily recalling the jokes he played on Lennie and, most importantly, the incident in Weed—the girl who cried rape when Lennie touched her red dress (45–46)—both of these memories suggesting the dangers of unregulated sexuality. This tête-a-tête also foreshadows the final scene when Slim helps George compose himself, as well as compose the story of why he finally shot Lennie. Both scenes position George, as Sedgwick might say, "between men"—triangulating and mediating his desire between competing discourses of manhood.

The collective police action that closes the novel is designed to restore order to this male economy. Such vigilantism executes a final solution to the problem of destabilized manhood by eliminating the homosexual dream—and the homosexual dreamer. Not by accident does George position Lennie on his knees, tell him to stare vacantly "across the river" and imagine their little house, and then shoot him in the head. Despite the subtle references to Nazism in the images of the Luger and the behind-the-head execution, it would be going too far to compare George to the "fascist male" that Klaus Theweleit has anatomized in *Male Fantasies*, but executing Lennie does suggest a similar desire to purge the male self of an "other" manhood that threatens traditional masculine integrity. George is careful, therefore, to show the other men that he wasn't "in on" the murder of Curley's wife, and he tells Lennie just before he shoots him that he wants a life with "no mess"—alone and living "easy," taking his fifty bucks at the end of the month and going to a "cat house" (104)—in other words, the traditional masculine life of the ranch and the other "guys."

Where some critics see hope at the end of the novel—in the form of a new partnership between Slim and George (Emery 40; Owens 105)—I see the recuperation of traditional masculinity and George's re-incorporation into the normative heterosexual and homosocial economy of the ranch. "Now what the hell ya suppose is eatin' them two guys?" (107)—Carlson's concluding rhetorical question—may be answered later for George and Slim via some return of the repressed, but immediately, it seems to me, this new pairing simply confirms George's place within a traditional patriarchal economy. "Me an' you'll go in an' get a drink," Slim says (107), and he leads George up toward the highway—away from the liminal space of the homosexual dream and into town, presumably to old Suzy's place, where "It's a hell of a lot of fun" and a guy doesn't even have to "want to flop" (52). Unlike the fantasmatic bond between Lennie and George, this male bonding occurs within a framework of carefully invested heterosexual desire in which the homosocial and the heterosexual conspire to repress the homosexual fantasies George and Lennie once shared. In effect, the "squeeze of the hand" becomes a squeeze of the trigger that blows away the utopian homosexual dream.

Works Cited

Benson, Jackson J., ed. *The Short Novels of John Steinbeck: Critical Essays with a Checklist to Steinbeck Criticism*. Durham: Duke University Press, 1990.

Emery, Jean. "Manhood Beset: Misogyny in *Of Mice and Men*." *San Jose Studies* 18 (Winter 1992): 33–42.

Goldhurst, William. "*Of Mice and Men*: John Steinbeck's Parable of the Curse of Cain." In Benson, *Short Novels*, 48–59.

Lisca, Peter. *John Steinbeck: Nature and Myth*. New York: Thomas Crowell, 1978.

Martin, Robert K. *Hero, Captain, and Stranger: Male Friendship, Social Critique, and Literacy Form in the Sea Novels of Herman Melville*. Chapel Hill: University of North Carolina Press, 1986.

Motley, Warren. "From Patriarchy to Matriarchy: Ma Joad's Role in *Grapes of Wrath*." *American Literature* 54 (1982): 397–412.

Owens, Louis. *John Steinbeck's Re-Vision of America*. Athens: University of Georgia Press, 1985.

Plato. *Symposium*. Trans. Benjamin Jowett. Indianapolis: Bobbs-Merrill, 1956.

Sedgwick, Eve Kosofsky. *Between Men: English Literature and Male Homosocial Desire*. New York: Columbia University Press, 1985.

Spilka, Mark. "Of George and Lennie and Curley's Wife: Sweet Violence in Steinbeck's Eden." In Benson, *Short Novels*, 59–70.

Steinbeck, John. *Of Mice and Men* (1937). New York: Penguin, 1993.

Theweleit, Klaus. *Male Fantasies* (1978). Trans. Erica Carter and Chris Turner. 2 vols. Minneapolis: University of Minnesota Press, 1989.

CHAPTER THIRTEEN
QUEER BORDERS:
FIGURES FROM THE 1930s FOR
U.S.-CANADIAN RELATIONS
Caren Irr

"Canada as a separate but dominated country," wrote Margaret Atwood during the free trade debates of the late 1980s,
"has done about as well under the United States as women
worldwide have done under men. About the only position they have ever
adopted toward us, country to country, has been the missionary position,
and we were not on top. I guess that is why the national wisdom vis-à-vis
them has so often taken the form of lying still, keeping your mouth shut
and pretending you like it."[1] Like many opponents to the Canada-U.S.
Free Trade Agreement (the predecessor to the North American Free
Trade Agreement [NAFTA]), Atwood expressed her disapproval of the
treaty by implicitly comparing its effects to rape. Above all, this depiction
of international power relations involved figuring the United States as a
man and Canada as a woman. Of course, in Atwood's passage, the metaphor suggests that Canada's status as female victim will not be rectified
until she acts up, opens her mouth, and tells the truth. The assumption
is that Canadians, like women, have something to say as a group about
efforts to subsume them under a larger, putatively generic category.

Strangely, though, during the free trade debates, this gendered metaphor was also used by the treaty's proponents; pro–free trade economists
wrote pieces with titles such as *Canada at the U.S.-Mexico Free-Trade
Dance: Wallflower or Partner?* and "The Draft Agreement: Cohabitation

Previously published in *American Quarterly* 49, no. 3 (1997): 504–30. Reprinted by
permission.

Worth A Try."[2] These pieces also figure a feminine Canada, but they suggest that courtship and marriage—or at least "fruitful and mutually invigorating intercourse"—are the most desirable outcomes of a relationship between masculine and feminine entities. The assumption for these writers is that having a voice is less important than having a home inside the walls of Fortress America. Despite their alternative goals, though, the economists share with Atwood and generations of Canadian intellectuals before her, the premise that Canada is a smaller, gentler, weaker body bound by contract and affection to an invasive, domineering, and often inconsiderate partner; for persons across the ideological spectrum, the gendered metaphor expresses an important power differential between the United States and Canada.

Even while noting the expressiveness of this metaphor, though, we should recall a few situations in which it also operates as a limit. For instance, several pieces in the semiotext(e) collection *canadas* draw attention to the fractures and stresses that disrupt the association between gender and nation. Susanne de Lotbinière-Harwood's meditations on "quadrophenia"—the dissonance produced by hearing English, French, masculine and feminine voices simultaneously—show that the United States : Canada :: man : woman metaphor can also be retooled to describe conflicts within Canada, such as the long-standing dispute over the status of Francophone culture; for Lotbinière-Harwood, English Canada is to Québec as man is to woman. Similarly, Marie Ann Hart Baker's piece "Gotta Be on Top: Why the Missionary Position Fails to Excite Me" recycles Atwood's metaphor as a description of relations between white and Native writers; for Baker, white women's efforts to appropriate Native stories can also be read as efforts to enforce the top-bottom hierarchy of the missionary position.[3] This chain, in which a "feminine" Canada becomes "masculine" when the points of reference shift, suggests that the gendered metaphor for national power differentials may have lost some of its descriptive power through proliferation. Because the male-female metaphor is so commonly used to describe relations of unequal power, it may well be that it does not describe any link on the chain precisely. If this is the case, it will be to our advantage to locate descriptive metaphors for U.S.-Canadian relations that not only articulate features of this relationship but also locate that relationship in an extensive and complex field of power and disempowerment.

One suggestion offered in *canadas* is that we "see Canada not so much as effeminate, but as a kind of 'queer' country." Especially in relation to a hegemonic U.S. popular culture, Canadians are put in queer positions, Thomas Haig argues; passing, ironizing, and outing are strategies as familiar to Canadians in the United States as to queers. This is the thesis that I would like to explore in this essay—although with the crucial proviso that we will be examining relations between nations rather than intervening in what Haig calls "the incessant (and often tedious) question of Canadian national identity."[4] By shifting the metaphor for U.S.-Canadian relations from a gendered to a queer one, I hope also to suggest that the multinational narrative in which we situate this relationship might be rethought. If the gendered metaphor encourages us to imagine U.S.-Canadian relations as a monogamous courtship leading to marriage or break-up, a queer metaphor might draw attention to the wider field of global relations in which the U.S.-Canadian encounter is an important, but not necessarily an exclusive, alliance.

Now, to shift attention from the gendered metaphor for U.S.-Canadian relations it will be useful to move away, for a while, from the historical situation which it most accurately describes. That is, in so far as it does articulate an important relationship, the Atwood metaphor is most appropriate for the period of U.S.-Canadian relations that began after the 1939–1945 war and came, some have argued, to a close in the 1960s. It was during this period that the United States' export of cultural materials most closely approximated a campaign of cultural imperialism, a campaign designed to be particularly overwhelming to a nearby neighbor that had only recently begun to foster a sense of national culture.[5] By contrast, before the war—before the homogenizing institution of alliance—the dynamics of U.S.-Canadian relations were less completely marked by U.S. dominance. There was considerably more uncertainty in the relationship, and a somewhat wider array of figures for North American relations was available. In particular, I want to turn to the 1930s, a decade during which ways of conceiving national identity and international relations arose that were later foreclosed. During the 1930s, certain counter-narratives to the dominant gender ideology were imagined—counter-narratives that stressed the utopian side of relations among men.

I will not be arguing that this interest in male-male relations arose because the language of sexual liberation extended to homosexual men during the 1930s—usually, it did not. Instead, male-male relations became a site of particular interest because one of the most powerful ideological effects of the Great Depression was the reformulation of gendered economic roles. When basic manufacturing industries slashed wages and laid off record numbers of workers during the 1930s, the white-male working class lost much of the ground that it had gained during the prosperity of the 1920s. Arguably, this group was the most brutally affected by the depression; many of the jobs traditionally held by women in domestic and service sectors remained available—although these, of course, paid little and offered little security.[6] Also, racial discrimination and low farm prices of the 1920s meant that most minorities and agricultural workers had already begun experiencing the reduced living standard associated with a depression well before the stock market crash of 1929.[7] The result was that in many white families, the responsibility for "providing" shifted during the depression from the male wage earner to the female or was dispersed among the family members; in many cases, the depression led white working-class men to experience an erosion of the kind of self-reliance crucial to the ideology of manhood. This is one reason why the most famous image from the 1930s, Dorothea Lange's photograph of a pea picking family, represents the crisis so well: not only does it forcefully depict the burden of responsibility thrust upon the mother, but also, its composition dramatically recalls the absent father. In Lange's Madonna with children, Joseph is not hovering nearby but, presumably, wandering far afield. This figure of the man without family, a man unable to support himself—this figure of the down-and-out white male drifter—was for many observers the most woeful symbol of the 1930s.

Certainly, many writers used the white male transient as a signal of social protest during the 1930s. He appears in films such as *Sullivan's Travels* and a number of novels from the period; Nelson Algren's *Somebody in Boots*, Edward Dahlberg's *Bottom Dogs*, John Dos Passos's *U.S.A.*, Henry Roth's *Call It Sleep*, and Nathanael West's *A Cool Million* come to mind. In Canadian literary magazines, this figure was so common that when asked to comment on the stories appearing in a new radical periodical, the established novelist Morley Callaghan remarked, "If this keeps on it will appear that either all the young writers of the country are out of work, or that they all feel a little frustrated, a little cynical, or even defeated, and that living in this country doesn't leave one with a strong feeling."[8] This remark reveals the way that the transient figure was most commonly used; rootless and alone, he signified defeat or even despair to many readers. Often appearing on the margins of stories about local communities in crisis, he was a reminder of the crisis being played out at the national level. Also, as Callaghan's comment reminds us, it was not uncommon during the 1930s for writers to identify themselves as spokespersons for the nation. Certainly, Callaghan and many of his Canadian peers understood even their more ephemeral periodical writing as articulations of a national condition.

In this context, it is not surprising that the appearance in the late 1930s of two novels concerned with transient white men would provoke not only discussion of social issues relating to unemployment but also generalizations about national culture. These two texts, John Steinbeck's *Of Mice and Men* (1936) and Irene Baird's *Waste Heritage* (1939), both push beyond the stereotype of the lonely drifter to pair men who support one another in an aggressive, uncomfortable social world.[9] Each text offers a brief glimpse of an all-male utopia, though in each case this projection is foreclosed by the contradictions of the culture at large. Furthermore, both texts seem to have been written with a national context in mind, and their generic projects and reception illustrate much about U.S.-Canadian relations before 1945. Finally, I will argue that reading these texts together helps us locate pieces of a counter-narrative of North American cultural relations that may be of use today.

Imagining Communities of Men during the 1930s

In both Steinbeck's short best seller and Baird's longer and relatively obscure documentary novel, the focus of attention is the male couple. *Of Mice and Men* centers on the relationship between Lenny, a physically large and mentally small innocent, and George, his physically small, but caring and intelligent companion. From the first scene, Steinbeck foregrounds the interdependence of these two characters by outfitting them in similar apparel, while insisting that their physical qualities make each the other's "opposite" (*OMM* 2). However, by the end of the novel, the fixity of this opposition has dissolved somewhat; there, Lenny's major character trait—his death grip on the objects he loves—is adopted by George. In an act of love, George kills Lenny in order to preserve his innocence.

This pattern of entangled binaries also occurs in *Waste Heritage*. This novel revolves around the small, smart Matt and the large, humble Eddy. In Baird's novel, however, the opposition between the two central characters does not turn on violence versus nonviolence as it does in *Of Mice and Men*, since both Matt and Eddy have violent tempers. The result is that, in Baird's novel, the two male characters are less securely opposite. Here Matt constantly struggles to maintain control of himself and his desire to control Eddy is partly an externalization of this struggle. So, when, in the final pages, Matt loses control and indirectly kills his buddy, the dissolution of the opposition between controller and controllee reads as a failure, rather than the bittersweet moral triumph we find in Steinbeck's conclusion.

Despite this shift in the central relationship, though, in both novels, the male couple produces similar effects on other characters. "'I never seen one guy take so much trouble for another guy,'" the boss says suspiciously in *Of Mice and Men* (22); and "'I heard there was plenty of that kind of thing down there among you boys,'" a prostitute leers at one point in *Waste Heritage* (138). Of course, here the phrase "that kind of thing" implies that the two men might be lovers. Both novels raise the possibility that the impregnable, obscurely sentimental relationship between the central characters could be considered in sexual terms. The relationship is close and emotional enough to disrupt the conventional patterns of male friendship during this period, and this makes it anxiety-producing. Very little of this anxiety is confronted directly in either text; instead, the relationship is recoded into other, fairly weak, explanations—explanations which, in the end, produce as much anxiety as the original relationship. As the above citations reveal, the potentially queer bond is only articulated as a nervous joke, while the ties of political or class-based solidarity which are also implied attain even less credibility. Especially in *Waste Heritage*, solidarity is imagined as a requirement imposed from above, as it were, and the emotional, psychological or sentimental aspects of the relationship are regularly contrasted to this political imperative. In both novels, the essence of solidarity—taking "trouble for another guy"—is a sign of perversion or idiotic compliance with authority. In the end, the only explanation for the male couple's bond that the novels can openly support is transparently inappropriate: George pretends for a while that he and Lenny are cousins, and Matt somewhat more plausibly accepts Eddy as a kind of little brother.

But, in both novels, this screen of family relations is eventually dropped, and the only remaining link between characters is the excessively significant and mysteriously affective relationship between men.

Of course, such puzzling relationships are not unprecedented in modern literature in English. Readers of D. H. Lawrence, Wyndham Lewis, Herman Melville, Walt Whitman, Oscar Wilde, and even Horatio Alger will find them familiar, and, in recent years, a number of critics have suggested that the male couple represents to these authors the last authentic intimacy available in a culture that vigorously commodifies heterosexual love.[10] That is, in these writings, the male couple often reconstitutes the domestic ideology in which the family is posited as safe haven from the commercial world. The intimations of illicit or so-called non-productive sexuality in these writings thus might indicate a kind of resistance to the fetishization of production in monopoly capitalism.

This recent scholarship implicitly revises Leslie Fiedler's influential thesis on the interracial male couple in *Love and Death in the American Novel* (1961).[11] Fiedler argued that couples such as Natty Bumppo and his Indian companions, Ishmael and Queequeg, and Huck and Jim represent American authors' collective fantasy of escaping from a repressive, orderly, female-dominated civilization; he tied this fantasy to infantalizing representations of women and the absence of a tradition of what he viewed as the proper topic of the novel—the heterosexual seduction narrative. However, where Fiedler saw the male couple as a figure for utopian escape from civilization, today, in light of queer studies, we might see the male couple as a fractious subculture of "civilization" that is produced in, and shares qualities with, that civilization.[12] In the wake of poststructuralist theories of textuality as contextuality, this kind of residual excess seems more likely than escape, especially once we recognize that excess can still provide sites at which the problematic of the wider field of culture is exposed.

Certainly, it is as a sign of a difficult excess that the male couple seems to function for Baird and Steinbeck. In *Of Mice and Men* and *Waste Heritage*, the indigence of the male couple exposes crises in the social fabric, but this anxious bond between characters does not promise a utopia outside the confines of culture. Instead, the relationship is a sign of excess that links these novels to the major site of social critique during the 1930s. Both Baird and Steinbeck read the male couple through the lens of Depression-era radicalism; in particular, the opposition both novels make between the central characters' size and intelligence can be traced to contemporaneous radical representations of the ways that class marks the body. As cartoons from this period in the Communist magazine *New Masses* demonstrate, 1930s leftists habitually represented the working class with a hyper-muscular male body and the bankers, capitalists or other representatives of the bourgeoisie with a puny one. Although the positions were occasionally reversed so that the capitalist was the larger figure, in leftist cartoons, as in the drawings of small children, the size of a figure almost always indicated its social power. This symbolist habit was perpetuated by many New Deal artists working officially in the social realist vein, such as the sculptors of Post Office friezes.[13] While realistically representing musculature and work habits, pneumatic male bodies were also used symbolically to represent relations among classes and class fractions. Frequently, for social realist painters, sculptors, and muralists, as for Steinbeck and Baird, the thesis proposed visually was that proper relationships among men had been "perverted" and would only be righted when the sleeping giant awoke.

These depictions were not "outside" of contemporaneous discourses on sexuality that read homosocial/sexual relations as a perversion of natural (because biologically based) power relations; in fact, the radicals' representations often fit fairly seamlessly with modernist homophobia. During the 1930s, prominent Communist theorists, such as *New Masses* editor Mike Gold used the male couple as a figure for everything they disapproved of, from the careless sadism of a teacher to the decadence of a fading cultural aristocracy.[14] It is important to note, though, that the 1930s left was not simply mirroring the values of the period; it was also acting on and reformulating the ideological scene. Gold's homophobia—although powerful and long-standing—did not dominate the entire left movement. For some of his contemporaries, such as novelist Tess Slesinger, the male couple also functioned as a sign of intellectuals' corrupt dependence on the wealthy classes, but that relationship was of interest precisely because it also provided an occasion for the transformation of the risky seduction/pedagogical narrative into something more egalitarian. In *The Unpossessed*, Slesinger's roman à clef about left-wing intellectuals, it is the dynamics of a male couple's relationship that rouse the group to a climactic crisis in consciousness. Since this doubled reference to the same-sex couple—as site of critique and sign of possibility—recurs in other left-wing fiction of the period, such as Fielding Burke's *Call Home the Heart* and Nathanael West's *A Cool Million*, we may conclude that it was not a fluke particular to Slesinger's work.[15] In fact, it is not altogether surprising that an era that took Whitman as its culture-hero would make use of the male couple in this doubled fashion. Although the 1930s left did often employ an official discourse that suggested "natural" relations among men were non-sexual, it also based much of its literary practice on writings that represented the more or less openly physical form of camaraderie and solidarity among men as a conflicted, but culturally central relationship.

With this context in mind, Steinbeck and Baird's simultaneous choice to examine the male couple and to employ the small/large opposition seems a little less surprising. Both writers drew on culturally available depictions of the male couple, and both muted the conflicts articulated in contemporaneous leftist rhetoric by transferring the class opposition to a personal, morally charged relationship within a single class. For Baird and Steinbeck, the anxiety produced by the male couple figures the instability of social relations as a whole. Because both had reservations about the counter-cultural status of Communism, both preferred the language of "poverty" and moral responsibility to the language of class and struggle.

Unfortunately, this moral critique of economic relationships is at least as flawed and self-contradictory as a language of class struggle; it certainly does not provide a secure referential base for either novel. As the difficulty both novelists have in justifying the relationship between their two main characters reveals, the moral element conflicts with their conviction that the social world must be figured as a force field of aggression. *Of Mice and Men*, for instance, displays a social world organized around fist fights. From the moment Lenny and George enter the bunkhouse, they engage in contests with their peers. As a social microcosm, the farm is organized into a clear pecking order with women and African Americans at the bottom and layers of hormone-driven white men above them. At the local pinnacle of this pyramid is Curley, the boss's super-aggressive son, but Curley's testiness is simply a more open expression of the aggressivity contained by the others. As long as he keeps it relatively controlled, it supports him in this social Darwinist set-up. That Steinbeck is depicting a type of Darwinism is confirmed by the shooting of Candy's sickly dog. This incident can be read as a barely masked act of aggression against the equally unfit and aged Candy. Furthermore, it functions as a reminder of what is regularly sacrificed to fitness: the excessive, affective relations described above.

Similarly, in *Waste Heritage*, Baird stresses the military discipline at work in the unemployed camps; most of her dialogue reports the endless squabbling among the men and many of Matt's adventures document townspeople's hostility towards the trekkers. Several times in the novel, Baird describes gratuitous harassment of the unemployed, and, as in the following incident, we are repeatedly asked to sympathize with the men's ego-driven resistance to being organized, even when organization would counter such harassment. In this scene, Hep, the Red organizer, asks Matt to tone down his aggressive behavior:

> "You two go on back to the hall so there's two less to account for."
> "Can't I come along? I don't want to miss anything."
> "I said to go along."
> "Yeah? Well, suppose I don't go."
> Hep glared at him. He hissed like an angry snake, "What th'hell do you think you are anyway? One little squib or the whole damn revolution?"
> Matt's chin shot out resentfully. He got set to blow off then caught Hep's eye. "Okay," he muttered sulkily, "I'll go along."
> "You bet you'll go along. An' check right in as soon as you get there." . . .
> Matt looked after [Hep] resentfully. He said, "I didn't like that guy first time I met him an' I don't like him any better now."
> Eddy stared at him shocked. "Him?" he said, "Hep?"
> "Yeah, sure, Hep. Who d'you think I meant? The king of Spain?"
> "I don't know nothin' about no king of Spain," Eddy said gravely, "all I know is Hep ain't like other guys, he's a prince. I heard him called a prince often."
> Matt laughed, feeling small and angry. He began to walk on fast. "I guess I'm just too democratic to appreciate him, then," he said. (*WH*, 68–69)

The climax of this rambling scene is Matt's declaration that he is "too democratic" and feisty to do as Hep asks; this "democratic" impulse contrasts to an amalgamated view of Hep as snake, "king of Spain," and spokesman for "the whole damn revolution." That is, we find Baird implicitly criticizing leftist organizations for their similarity to a monarchical hierarchy. Although it would probably be a mistake to read this scene as expressing an entirely anti-Tory sentiment, Baird does suggest that Hep is a "snake" pretending to be a prince, that he too is motivated by a natural, even Biblical, aggressivity falsely recoded as cooperation. In this schema, Matt's macho individualism reads as the more honest expression of their common condition.

In these novels, then, aggressivity is being used both as a figure for economic competition and as a critique of political alternatives to competition. Both Baird and Steinbeck imagine a pitiless social world in which people coded as "poor" (rather than working class, for instance) are sacrificed to hostile forces beyond their control. In these novels, through no particular fault of their own, the poor cannot compete, a fact that is supposed to demonstrate the essential immorality of making competition the basis of a social or economic system. At the same time, both Baird and Steinbeck naturalize aggressivity by making it the motivating characteristic of the victims as well as the victors of competition.

This strategy is significant in part because it illustrates the kinds of revisions that could be made to the dominant liberal discourse about reform during the 1930s, a discourse that emphasized the weakness of the poor. The pathetic note struck by reformers is evident for instance in Roosevelt's famous "forgotten man" speech. Of course, this pathetic appeal was an improvement on nineteenth-century concepts of reform that stressed the immorality and shamefulness of the poor, but the New Deal emphasis on weakness and the morality of helping the weak had problems that emerged quite clearly during the 1930s. As letters written by recipients of the dole to FDR indicate, while New Deal relief funds helped people survive physically, they also produced a less tangible sense of "emasculation," isolation, guilt, dependence, and resentment of relief workers' maternalism.[16] Many of these problems (which are so much a part of contemporary rhetoric on welfare reform) were widely in evidence by the late 1930s, and it is partly in response to these psychic structures that Steinbeck and Baird wrote. Their emphasis on the aggressivity of transient men might well be taken as a challenge to the moral responsibility of the fit to care for the weak unfit; their novels might be read as demonstrations of their heroes' actual fitness for economic survival. By emphasizing the aggressive independence of the poor, Baird and Steinbeck shifted the metaphorical ground underlying the discourse on relief.

Nonetheless, while there is an activist or empowering element to Baird and Steinbeck's emphasis on aggressivity, we should still note that theirs is a discourse that "saves" the "poor" transients by normalizing them, by insisting on the identity of their interests and desires with those of the dominant group. Predictably, certain tensions arise when such a strategy is deployed, particularly in the representations of non-dominant or less normalizable persons, such as working-class women. At these sites, certain limits to the envisioned community become apparent. When we look closely, we find that both novels create worlds in which only one kind of woman is significant—the pretty, young tart. Although Baird's character Hazel is a more sympathetic one than Curley's flirtatious wife, in both novels the young single woman is a prize over which aggressive males fight. In *Of Mice and Men*, Curley's unnamed wife precipitates the climax of the novel by teasing slow-witted Lenny with her beauty, and, in *Waste Heritage*, Hazel's desires conflict with those of Hep, the organizer, causing several crises of conscience for Matt. The unifying theme here, as Matt reflects when Hazel comes to visit him, is that women's "presence made war, intruded the natural into the disciplined unnatural, brought with it forces at once savage and dividing" (*WH* 209). In these novels, women endanger social relations because they force men into a narrative of "natural" and competitive desire.

As numerous commentators on Steinbeck's work have observed, this is a very limiting and regressive ideology of gender; both novels clearly imagine worlds in which women are witless as well as dangerous. Furthermore, the limited roles available to women are not the topic of the novels' social critique. Neither Steinbeck nor Baird suggests that in a less aggressive world women would play any other roles. On the contrary, in both novels, we are asked to sympathize with the men's entirely natural desire for a family romance that marginalizes and objectifies women.

Of course, neither Baird nor Steinbeck is uniquely malicious in resorting to this domestic ideal. In fact, even today few protests against homelessness manage to avoid making reference to the sanctity of the home, the family, and associated gender roles. As Americans did during the New Deal, we still tend to ignore or downplay the effect of homelessness on women.[17] Often we do not remember that we forget women, even while we produce a pathos-ridden discourse about the specific exile of homeless men. . . .

One result of this scenario is that the domestic utopia at the heart of both novels is all-male. Lenny and George repeatedly invoke their dream of living together "off the fatta the land" on a little farm, and Matt wavers between two versions of domesticity: one unlikely possibility with Hazel, who wants a white-picket fence, and another, more promising one in the union, which promises a home for all the men together. As in many 1930s novels, the union is a source of security and unusual calm for Matt, and it figures in Baird's novel much the same inaccessible happiness that the farm does in *Of Mice and Men*. It gives Matt direction and hope briefly, although he does lose faith towards the end of the novel, just as George loses his chance for the farm (*WH* 316–17).

These domestic utopias, then, belong more to the characters than to the narrative, since the plots ensure their impossibility. Yet there is some narrative investment in them, since both novels pit their domestic utopias against the false consciousness of the mass media. Those "Western magazines" in *Of Mice and Men* that "ranch men love to read and scoff at and secretly believe" (*OMM* 17) are paralleled in *Waste Heritage* by the thrillers and pornography that the trekkers regularly recommend to one another. In neither novel are the secret beliefs which these materials encourage spelled out, but in both we are asked to see mass culture as continuous with the forces of aggression which the narrators criticize. The ideology of the Westerns conforms to the aggressive individualism that divides Steinbeck's bunkhouse, and the cagey marketing of pornographic pictures in Baird's novel is consistently associated with divisive and destructively individualistic characters. By contrast, the legitimate but impossible all-male domestic utopias are relatively shielded from implication in the world of the novel; their deferral outside the bounds of the novel guarantees their utopian potential.

To summarize the argument so far, then, Steinbeck and Baird's novels both depict affective relations among men as an ideal—though a strained, conflicted and repressed one; in so doing, both present a political alternative to discourses on masculinity, class and reform that were prevalent during the 1930s. Although reformulating Communist and genteel characterizations, neither novel's depiction of transient men strays too far from a version of liberalism that is still familiar today; in fact, these depictions of the male couple simply push contemporaneous cultural productions a little further. They are excessive extensions rather than utopian spaces outside the culture. Thus, it is my contention that, when we read these relations among men back into the dominant metaphorics of the nation, they present an interesting, relatively unexplored, possibility for rethinking North American international relations. Consequently, it is to the national context and reception of these novels that I now wish to turn.

Genre and National Culture

The depictions of transient men that John Steinbeck and Irene Baird confronted in their fictions existed in their cultures in particular genres. Thus, revising these depictions involved not only stating a difference in political theory, but also modifying the genres associated with particular political stances. Furthermore, since the trajectories of national cultures had granted different genres different places in the United States and Canada, Steinbeck and Baird were led to experiment with different generic hybridizations to express similar political positions. That is, variations in national culture influenced their depictions of a potentially trans- or international ideal. Most prominent among the genres having different political significance in the United States and Canada during the 1930s is the sentimental novel.

In Steinbeck criticism, sentimentalism has been a controversial topic. Because twentieth-century critical fashion has favored realism, allusive allegory and tragedy over sentimentalism, critics defending Steinbeck have usually emphasized these elements of his writing. Only occasionally has someone such as Desmond McCarthy claimed that Steinbeck's tough guy heroes present a sentimental view of human nature that is typically and importantly American.[18] For most, such an approach veers too close to likening Steinbeck to mass cultural traditions; and, if such linkages were to be made, critics have preferred to point to the slightly more respectable (because less feminized) genre of hard-boiled detective fiction as a point of comparison. For Steinbeck defenders, the main concern seems to have been to isolate Steinbeck's form of sentimental populism from versions of reform based on mothering; . . .

In recent years, however, a growing body of scholarship on sentimentalism has challenged the assumption that led Steinbeck's defenders to this strategy. Following the work of Cathy Davidson, Jane Tompkins, Susan Harris, Ann Douglas, and others, we can understand the sentimental

171

novel as a genre which afforded marginalized writers and readers room to recognize and educate one another.[19] Its achievements and values were decidedly popular, often in conscious rejection or recoding of high cultural standards, and at times these populist formulas lent themselves to the open expression of non-dominant ideologies, as in the case of Harriet Beecher Stowe's *Uncle Tom's Cabin*. Of course, Stowe's abolitionism came packaged with paternalistic concepts of race, but it was in part her recognition of contradictions between the ideologemes of Southern society as a collection of families and Southern society as racial hierarchy that made her novel a significant voice for reform.[20] In short, it was precisely the formulaic nature of the sentimental novel that allowed it to perform important cultural work.

With this thesis in mind, we may find Steinbeck's occasionally Manichean moral vision, his provocation of pathos, his invocation of the family and so on less of a liability than has previously been thought. These elements of his writing link Steinbeck to a tradition of sentimental protest writing and, although they conflict with other elements of his philosophy (such as his naturalist philosophizing), they suggest that, like sentimental novelists, Steinbeck might be recoding contemporary standards into an admittedly nostalgic but politically workable literary vocabulary. Since one of the most controversial and notably modern literary genres of the period in which Steinbeck wrote his trademark texts was the proletarian novel, it may well be that Steinbeck conceived of *Of Mice and Men* as a variation on this form. Certainly this was what a number of contemporary commentators took him to be doing.[21]

An interesting body of recent scholarship has argued that the proletarian novel was not the single coherent genre that its Depression-era proponents desired; instead, it took several variant forms—the collective novel, the strike novel, the proletarian *bildungsroman*, the intellectual *roman à clef* and so on.[22] What all these variants had in common, though, was a dialectic between their quasi-realist description of a particular community and quasi-utopian projection of future struggle and solidarity. Very often, as Paula Rabinowitz argues, the problems involved in resolving this dialectic led writers to revert to nostalgic gender stereotypes. For instance, although often undercut and rewritten, the figure of the good mother was a common feature in writings in this genre.[23] In other words, in their efforts to politicize popular discourses, the proletarian novelists often found themselves entangled in some of the dated stereotypes also employed by sentimental novelists of the mid-nineteenth century. These sentimental tropes have been noticed by many readers of the proletarian novel, but I mean to suggest that they may be read as performing certain kinds of cultural work, much like that performed by the sentimental novel proper.

Certainly, in this context, Steinbeck's sentimentalism looks a little less compromising. In *Of Mice and Men* we find him drawing explicitly on a part of the sentimental formula usually downplayed by the proletarian novelists—the marginal figure of the weak man, the sensitive man, the domestic man, the kind of man described in Douglas's *The Feminization of American Culture*.[24] Douglas argues that a major source of the sentimental novel was the institutionally disestablished clergy's desire to solidify their power by claiming the "heart" as their domain; hence, sentimental fiction approved by the clergy often valorized the sensitive man. By declassing the so-called feminized men of the sentimental tradition and placing them in social realist settings, Steinbeck fused modern elements of the proletarian novel with a politically viable side of the sentimental novel. In the process, he disrupts some of the oppositions (male/female, private family/public work) that organized each genre. Furthermore, this choice of disruptive strategy carries over into other features of Steinbeck's novel, and we might say that its most characteristic technique is a sort of symbolic displacement.[25] The central symbol of the novel shifts from the mice of the title, to rabbits, to women, to beauty generally, to utopia, to the "best laid plans" of which the Burns's quotation referred to in the title reminds us. The novel slides the reader along this chain of displacements, breaking up the initial opposition between mice and men, just as it slides us out of a strictly dualistic gender ideology and into a nebulous territory where men might somehow care for one another.

By contrast, Irene Baird wrote in a context about which one contemporary commentator could proclaim "there is no proletarian fiction . . . in Canada."[26] During the 1930s, Canadian writers seeking a revolutionary literature were poets more often than they were novelists, and much of their work involved variations on English modernist verse in the tradition of Auden and Spender. The dominant mode of fiction in Canada at the time was strongly sentimental and usually written by women. Occasionally this writing took on a political agenda (as in the work of suffragette

Nellie McClung), but on the whole the Canadian literary climate during the 1930s was considerably less left-wing and more middlebrow than in the U.S. It was, as one observer has asserted, "emphatically middling."[27] Middling here does not indicate the slippery disruptiveness of Steinbeck's text so much as an emphasis on reconciliation, on softening discrepancy and lessening controversy.

In this environment, Baird's efforts at documentary were an important and original experiment, and these efforts are most visible in her rendering of dialogue. Like the author figure in *Waste Heritage*, Baird seems to have taken great pains to note the slang of the men she observed, and she takes pleasure in reproducing it. In fact, sometimes her enthusiasm for certain phrases, such as referring to a spell in jail as years in "college," leads to overuse of slang, as if the interest in language overtook the responsibility to document social conditions. However, the overall impulse of the novel is to substitute the focus on feeling and character typical of sentimentalism with an emphasis on observation; although incompletely realized, Baird's documentary project authorizes her in the "man's world" which, as I shall explain further below, reviewers assumed she would not be able to reproduce through imagination.[28]

While noting the documentary effort, though, it is important to recognize how closely *Waste Heritage* adheres to the sentimental genre. The novel continues a Biblical allegory from Baird's first work, transparently referring to Vancouver as Aschelon and Victoria as Gath. Similarly, Baird names her characters allegorically; the labor activist hero, for instance, is Matt Striker. Also, the novel peripatetically follows the events of the strike; it borrows its structure from events, rather than progressing by a logic produced by characterization or thematic development. Although straining at certain points against sentimental structures, Baird ultimately does not replace them. At one point, she even has her main character reflect on the possible plotlessness of the novel, wondering whether his relationship with Eddy is the only fragile thread holding his experiences together. Such a fear points, I believe, to a desire to remain within recognizable generic patterns.

From this reading, I conclude that Baird's novel is a hybrid of sentimental and documentary impulses. Just as Steinbeck wrote against the masculinist assumptions of certain versions of the proletarian novel, Baird tried to supplement the gendered genre of the sentimental novel with documentary observation. Each writer confronted a dyadic notion of gendered genre and reworked it for his or her own purposes. Thus, the particular history of gendered writing in each nation influenced each writer's version of the story of the transient male couple, but not completely. These texts indicate national differences in gender/genre associations but also disrupt that difference by pushing towards a common generic hybridization.

Unfortunately, this common project has been largely obscured by the reception of these two novels. Although there is no evidence that Baird was familiar with Steinbeck's work, when *Waste Heritage* appeared in 1939, reviewers immediately noticed the "impregnable, obscurely sentimental relationship between two dispossessed men, one strong, the other weak" at the heart of Baird and Steinbeck's work. The major factor troubling analogies between the two texts resulted from Baird's gender; "I know of no woman writer," the Canadian reviewer continued, "who can write of men alone and in a man's world with any sustained credibility. Miss Baird has tried harder than most but with very little more success."[29] Reviewers in the United States agreed; they found the novel to be "strongly under the influence of Steinbeck" and called it "a Canadian *Grapes of Wrath*." The common conclusion was that, within a difference attributed to gender, *Waste Heritage* did "for the migratory workers of British Columbia what the stories of John Steinbeck have done for the migratory workers of the Pacific Coast."[30] Clearly, the terms of our discussion were laid out early; in the 1930s, Baird's novel was read as typically feminine and typically Canadian in its efforts to portray life among transient men with borrowed tropes.

This tendency to read the texts allegorically has if anything increased with time. In an essay originally written in the 1950s, Robert MacDougall saw Baird's novel as evidence that Canadian writers as a group could exhibit class consciousness, while literary histories written during the 1960s stressed Baird's "imitativeness" and extrapolated from that point to generalizations about a Canadian resistance to realist fiction during the interwar period. After Baird's novel was reprinted by the Laurentian library in 1973, historian Michiel Horn found the novel's style less significant than its politics, which he took to be illustrative of the debates over Canadian relief camps during the 1930s. The well-known Canadian cultural nationalist, Robin Mathews read Baird's novel as an allegory for class struggle and compares it to what he sees as the relatively class-bound orientation of Steinbeck's fictions and American fiction generally. Similarly, Roger Hyman also compares Baird's novel favorably to Steinbeck's, finding its didactic elements "representative of a peculiar particularity in the Canadian experience." Some years later, Anthony Hopkins found the novel's aimlessness an effect of the "attack of mass society upon the characters' essential humanity." In short, although the allegorical referents varied, the desire to read Baird's novel as a microcosm of the national literary condition was a common one; comparisons to Steinbeck's work provided opportunities for differentiating between national cultures—generally on the grounds of opposition.

This tendency for reviewers to recast the male-male relationships described in Baird and Steinbeck's fictions into a dyadic model of differences between genders and nations reintroduces the larger dynamics that are our overarching concern. Most commentators on these texts have attempted to recode the homo-social relationships into the gendered vocabulary used to describe relations between national cultures. As a result, these texts have become not only representations of their cultures but also emblems of those cultures. It is as emblems of U.S.-Canadian relations, however, that Baird and Steinbeck's texts can also serve to dislocate the gender-nation metaphor. From their novels, I have suggested, we can discern features of U.S.-Canadian relations other than opposition. First of all, the relationship is clearly asymmetrical. Discussion of *Waste Heritage* and *Of Mice and Men* as paired texts is a feature only of Baird criticism, not of Steinbeck criticism. The Steinbeck text is a reference point for discussions of Baird, much as the United States is a reference point for discussions of Canadian culture, but the situation is not reversible. Discussions of U.S. culture or multiculturalism call on comparisons to Canada just as rarely as discussions of Steinbeck call on Baird's text. Secondly, it is not simply the case that the United States habitually ignores Canada; it is also important that U.S. disinterest leads to a certain over-investment on the part of Canadian intellectuals in the problem of differentiating Canada from the U.S. Much as Baird critics work overtime in defense of Baird's singular achievements, Canadian cultural commentators, it has been argued, tend to overemphasize the "special relationship" between the United States and Canada—a relationship that is, arguably, not much different from that the United States holds with other so-called middle powers. The asymmetry of power in U.S.-Canadian relations results in the relationship being eclipsed or polarized, depending on your national point of view, and eclipsing and polarization are two sides of the same coin.

The point here has not been to urge the adoption of one strategy or national viewpoint over another; instead, my goal has been to reflect upon the relationship as a psychodynamic structure. This relationship—between a dominant culture which recognizes no boundaries or differences outside Itself and a marginal one which insists defensively on its own non-absorption into the dominant orbit—is structurally similar to the relationships described in the novels we have been considering and, more generally, to relationships examined in queer theory. In the next section, I will briefly sketch the theses of recent queer theory in hopes that the vocabulary provided there will be of use in our efforts to shift the terms of discussion from the difference-based gendered metaphor for U.S.-Canadian relations to one that focuses more clearly on power or, at least, one that can account for asymmetry and doubled strategies.

Theorizing Queer Borders

The central feature of both Baird and Steinbeck's texts, I have argued, is a male couple that represents possibilities for social organization other than those commonly recognized since the 1930s. The texts pair men of disparate sizes and capacities, and the denouements of both novels show that neither partner entirely controls the relationship. In both cases, the strength of the larger partner is something of a threat to the smaller one, while the intelligence of the smaller partner is not sufficient to save his larger friend from death at the hands of his fellow citizens. The relationship is asymmetrical in that one partner takes the leading role in most stations, but power does not flow entirely in one direction. It is possible to underestimate this bipolar aspect to the central relationship because in both cases the narratives report the thoughts of the dominant partner most closely, but nonetheless the sheer physical presence of the larger, slower partner remains a crucial factor in each story.

Naming and asserting the cultural centrality of just this kind of unequal, bipolar relationship has, in recent years, become the business of queer theory. Following Foucault's work on the history of sexuality, a number of scholars have concerned themselves with tracing the path by which a homosexual identity emerged in the nineteenth century out of an array of less fixed relations characteristic of earlier periods. After that emergence, subsequent shifts led to the articulation of gay and queer positions as well. An important feature of queer theory has been the insistence that the significance of homosexuality was not generated entirely from within the same-sex community, but rather was continuously produced in relation to an array of political and policing strategies. The result of this thesis is a recognition that questions of sexuality are always already in contact and, often, in conflict with hegemonic discourses about identity, subjectivity, normality and nationality. Fueled by the aggressive publicity of the campaigns for AIDS awareness and funding, 1990s queers like 1930s transients have challenged the whole matter of the privacy of suffering. Drawing attention to the influence that actions of the state and medical professions have on sexual practices, queers have also attempted to reverse the terms and make public assertions of queerness politically potent. The street chant "We're here, we're queer, and we don't like the government" might exemplify this dynamic; in such statements, publicly asserting a collective queer identity becomes continuous with asserting a critique of standing relations of power. The very fact of standing in the streets and asserting the presence of an identity that official powers seek to ignore becomes coterminous with demanding a rearrangement of power. As a political strategy, this assertion of presence is not unlike the sit-down strike described in Baird's novel. Queers, like the unemployed, have made the assertion of our/their physical presence the first step in wresting power from a hegemonic power structure that does not recognize us/them. Like Baird and Steinbeck, then, queer theorists describe relations between two disproportionately empowered but intimately linked entities.

At the same time that theorists and activists understand queerness as commonly and inherently critical of the homogeneous powers that be, a complementary emphasis has fallen on the plurality and proliferation of forms of sexuality. Understanding queerness as a negation of extant categories of sexuality, activists and theorists such as Judith Butler have stressed the non-categorical nature of queerness itself.[33] It is often asserted that there is no single identity, no single style, position, mode of address or behavior which counts as queer; in theory, no generic norm is being referenced via queerness. Like unemployment or transience then, queerness is supposedly ironic, marginal, and non-normative.

However, as organizers among the unemployed as well as Canadianists have often found, consolidating political power around an ironic position presents certain difficulties. Normative identities and narratives have so much power that figures on the margin who define themselves in negation to the normative are rarely free from partial integration into the normative. And, sometimes, it is sometimes difficult to distinguish parody from reinvention of the norm from which one seeks liberation. This has especially been the case with the category of M. nation. In the early 1990s, ACT UP! spawned a brief-lived but dramatically confrontational spin-off movement called Queer Nation. In a series of image-smart gestures and performances, Queer Nation sought to recapture the conceptual space of the nation for its own Utopian counter-cultural purposes, and ironic recreations of the festivities and representations of the nation were its primary tools.

As a result, among other questions raised about the viability of a politics based in irony is the provoctive theory that some forms of queer activism may be structurally similar to nationalism. Although critical of the separatist elements of gay and lesbian projects that focused on the nurturing of an isolated community within the nation, and although ironic vis-à-vis the nation in projects such as Queer Nation, certain tendencies associated with the queer community do remind some observers of a nation. The queer community is an imagined community that generates a narrative of rebellion and strength, and, despite protestations to the obverse, it does have insides and outsides, as the controversy over straight queers demonstrates. Also, within the bounds of queer nationalism, a commitment unto death applies, as does a kind of "militancy"—although it is certainly a stretch to analogize the tactics of ACT UP! and, say, the United States military's antics during the Persian Gulf War. Nonetheless, we might ask whether queer positions run the risk of collapsing polyvocal asymmetry into one-directional homogeneity, as the category of the nation seems to do. Whichever answer we give, this question suggests that the structure of queer and national identities are potentially isomorphic and will likely seem more so when a specific history of their emergence is considered.

With these caveats in mind, then, I want to stress the ways in which elements of queer theory can help us to think about the problem, not of national identity, but of international relations. It seems to me that the stress in queer theory on the performative aspects of gendered and sexual relations—such that any situation of gender-specific behavior implicitly cites a retroactive norm, even when it is disrupting that norm—also describes the logic of U.S.-Canadian relations. Much as Baird's Matt/Eddy relationship seems to cite Steinbeck's George/Lenny relationship, articulations of U.S.-Canadian relations in any particular moment in time cite some history, some prior moment of the relationship which is being continued or changed. This, in fact, is why metaphors are used to describe international relations. The introduction of metaphors, such as courtship, for relations between nations places these relations into normative narratives that suggest certain origins and outcomes.

What I hope is that, by locating a possible metaphor for U.S.-Canadian relations articulated in a period at odds in many respects with the present, we have shifted this narrative about the past and future from the limited options of a heterosexual union and revealed a wider array of narrative components. By recalling the proto-queer relationships described in and figured by Baird and Steinbeck's texts, we might at least have provided ourselves with an alternate set of citable norms. Certainly today in light of NAFTA and the emergence of transnational corporations and global migrations associated with such trading practices, it seems important to develop descriptions that can admit of triangulation, variation, and open-endedness—options that exceed the dyadic "special relationship" so often cited by North American politicians. I hope that the shift I have proposed from a masculine-feminine to a queer metaphor for understanding U.S.-Canadian relations might contribute to our ability to describe the polymorphous, trans-national culture into which we currently find ourselves backstepping.

Notes

Portions of this paper were presented at the Modern Language Association in December 1994 and the American Studies Association in October 1995. I would like to thank Jeffrey Nealon, Susan Harris, and the anonymous reviewers for their helpful suggestions.

1. Margaret Atwood, "On Being Canadian," in *The Facts on Free Trade*, ed. Ed Finn (Ottawa: Lorimer, 1988), 13–14.

2. William G. Watson, "The Draft Agreement: Cohabitation Worth a Try," in *Canadian-American Free Trade (The Sequel): Historical, Political and Economic Dimensions*, ed. A. R. Riggs and Tom Velk, 57–67 (South Halifax, NS: Institute for Research on Public Policy, 1988); Richard Lipsey, *Canada at the U.S.-Mexico Free Trade Dance: Wallflower or Partner?* (Toronto: C. D. Howe Institute, 1990). Watson mentions "intercourse."

3. Susanne Lotbinière-Harwood, "The Body Bilingual," in *canadas*, ed. Jordan Zinovich, 279–85 (New York: Autonomedia, 1994); Marie Ann Hart Baker, "Gotta Be on Top: Why the Missionary Position Fails to Excite Me," in Zinovich, *canadas*, 303–5.

4. Thomas Haig, "Not Just Some Sexless Queen: A Note on 'Kids in the Hall' and the Queerness of Canada," in Zinovich, *canadas*, 229.

5. On periodization of U.S.-Canadian relations, see John Herd Thompson and Stephen Randall, *United States and Canada: Ambivalent Allies* (Athens: University of Georgia Press, 1994), 77. On cultural imperialism, see Isaiah Litvak and Christopher Maule, *Cultural Sovereignty: The* Time *and* Reader's Digest *Case in Canada* (New York: Praeger, 1974), and Maria Tippett, *Making Culture: English-Canadian Institutions and the Arts before the Massey Commission* (Toronoto: University of Toronto, 1990).

6. Robert S. McElvaine, *The Great Depression, America 1929–1941* (New York: Crown, 1993), 179–84.

7. So argue interviewees in Studs Terkel's *Hard Times: An Oral History of the Great Depression* (New York: Pantheon, 1970), 213–35. See also Robin D. G. Kelley, *Hammer and Hoe: Alabama Communists during the Great Depression* (Chapel Hill: University of North Carolina Press, 1990), 1–10.

8. Morley Callaghan, editorial, *New Frontier: A Monthly Magazine of Literature and Social Criticism* (April 1936), n.p.

9. John Steinbeck, *Of Mice and Man* (1937; New York: Penguin Modern Classics, 1993); Irene Baird, *Waste Heritage* (1939; Toronto: Macmillan, 1974). Further references to these texts will be cited as *OMM* and *WH*, respectively, in the text.

10. This is Fredric Jameson's thesis in *Fables of Aggression: Wyndham Lewis, Modernist as Fascist* (Berkeley: University of California Press, 1979). Jameson's thesis is adapted by Tony Pinkney in *D. H. Lawrence and Modernism* (Iowa City: University of Iowa Press, 1990), and modified and greatly expanded by Eve Sedgwick in *Between Men* (New York: Columbia, 1985) and *The Epistemology of the Closet* (Berkeley: University of California Press, 1991); for a particularly insightful reading of Horatio Alger, see also Michael Moon's "'The Gentle Boy from the Dangerous Classes': Pederasty, Domesticity, and Capitalism in Horatio Alger," *Representations* 19 (Summer 1987): 87–110.

11. Leslie Fiedler, *Love and Death in the American Novel* (New York: Criterion, 1960).

12. For an influential discussion of the male couple as site of critique and reinscription, see Sedgwick, *Between Men*, 201–18.

13. Barbara Melosh, *Engendering Culture: Manhood and Womanhood in New Deal Public Art and Theatre* (Washington, D.C.: Smithsonian Institution Press, 1991).

14. For example, see Mike Gold, *Jews without Money* (1930; New York: Avon, 1965) and "Wilder: Prophet of the Genteel Christ," in *Years of Protest: A Collection of American Writings of the 1930's*, ed. Jack Salzman, 233–38 (New York: Pegasus, 1967). See also Paula Rabinowitz's discussion of homophobia in *Labor and Desire* (Chapel Hill: University of North Carolina Press, 1991), 22. We might also recall scenes from the Joe Williams narrative in Dos Passos' *U.S.A.* (1930; Boston: Houghton Mifflin, 1991), which contrast working-class male virility to the behavior of decadent queens.

15. In Fielding Burke's *Call Home the Heart* (1932; New Brunswick, NJ: Feminist Press, 1983) a similar climax occurs when a black and white woman embrace at the end of the novel; in Nathanael West's *A Cool Million* (1934; New York: Farrar, Strauss Giroux, 1988), the hero's experiences as a male prostitute serve as reminders of both the commodification of the body and of the pleasures of that commodification.

16. See McElvaine, *Great Depression*, 170–95. On nineteenth-century discourses of reform, see Dennis Guest, *The Emergence of the Social Security in Canada* (Vancouver: UBC, 1985), chap. 1.

17. Contemporary discussions of homeless women usually focus on their role as mothers; see Barry Jay Seltser and Donald E. Miller, *Homeless Families: The Struggle for Dignity* (Urbana: University of Illinois Press, 1993) and H. Peter Oberlander and Arthur L. Fallick, *Homelessness and the Homeless: Responses and Innovations, A Canadian Contribution to IYSH 1987* (Vancouver: UBC, 1988). Joan M. Crouse points out that it is difficult to estimate the actual number of homeless women during the Depression, since the policy in U.S. relief camps was to return transient women to their home state; not surprisingly, women avoided these camps and were under-counted. See *The Homeless Transient in the Great Depression: New York State, 1929–1941* (Albany: State University of New York Press, 1986), 191.

18. Desmond McCarthy, "The American View of Human Nature," *The New Statesman and Nation* 17 (22 April 1939): 605–6.

19. Cathy N. Davidson, *Revolution and the Word* (New York: Oxford University Press, 1986); Jane Tompkins, *Sensational Designs* (New York: Oxford, 1985); Susan Harris, *Nineteenth-Century American Women's Novels: Interpretive Strate-*

gies (New York: Cambridge, 1990); Ann Douglas, *The Feminization of American Culture* (New York: Knopf, 1977).

20. Arthur Riss argues in "Racial Essentialism and Family Values in *Uncle Tom's Cabin*," *American Quarterly* 46 (December 1994): 513–44.

21. This was Mike Gold's view. In *The Hollow Men* (New York: International Publishers, 1941), he names Steinbeck and Richard Wright as the two major proletarian novelists of the 1930s.

22. See Barbara Foley, *Radical Representations* (Durham, NC: Duke University Press, 1993); Rabinowitz, *Labor and Desire*; James Murphy, *The Proletarian Moment* (Urbana: University of Illinois Press, 1991).

23. See Rabinowitz's discussion of the "Great Mother" in *Labor and Desire*, 97–136.

24. Although Douglas' thesis has been criticized by many feminist scholars of sentimentalism, I consider her discussion of the utility of sentimentalism for men an important contribution. See Douglas, *Feminization of American Culture*, 17–49.

25. Peter Lisca describes the action of the novel as a process of displacement in "Motif and Pattern in *Of Mice and Men*," *Modern Fiction Studies* 2 (Winter 1956–1957): 228–34.

26. Ruth McKenzie, "Proletarian Literature in Canada," *Dalhousie Review* 19 (April 1939): 39–64.

27. For instance, one of the most popular Canadien romance novelists of the period was Mazo de la Roche, whose Jalna series is a family romance. We should not underestimate the liberating possibilities of this kind of middlebrow fiction, however; as Roche's biographer Joan Givner demonstrates in her *Mazo de la Roche: The Hidden Life* (Toronto: Oxford University Press, 1989). Roche's particular blend of sentimental and gothic fiction allowed her to give literary expression to her lesbian desires in a period and culture which, to understate, were not friendly to gay people. The phrase "emphatically middling" is Lee Briscoe Thompson's in "Emphatically Middling: A Critical Examination of Canadian Poetry in the Great Depression" (Ph.D. diss., Queen's University, 1975).

28. Margaret Wallace, "Labor on the March," *New Republic* (20 December 1939): 121.

29. Eleanor Godfrey, Review of *Waste Heritage* by Irene Baird, *Canadian Forum* (February 1940): 364.

30. Harold Strauss, "'Waste Heritage' and Other New Works of Fiction," review of *Waste Heritage* by Irene Baird, *New York Times Book Review*, 10 December 1939, 7; review of *Waste Heritage* by Irene Baird, *New Yorker*, 16 December 1939, 101–2; Margaret Wallace, "Labor on the March," review of *Waste Heritage* by Irene Baird, *Saturday Review of Literature*, 16 December 1939, 7.

31. Robert L. McDougall, "The Dodo and the Cruising Auk: Class in Canadian Literature," in *Contexts in Canadian Criticism*, ed. Eli Mandel, 216–31 (Chicago: University of Chicago Press, 1971). Literary historical accounts include W. H. New, *Literary History of Canada* (Toronto: University of Toronto Press, 1990), 155. In the influential *Literary History of Canada: Canadian Literature in English* (Toronto: University of Toronto Press, 1965), ed. Carl F. Klinck, we find F. W. Watt noting in passing (in "Literature of Protest," 457–73) that the "direct and savagely indignant protests of Irene Baird's *Waste Heritage* (1939) have no doubt permanently given way to the subtler and more profound probings and ironies of works like Gabrielle Roy's *The Tin Flute* and Hugh MacLennan's *The Watch That Ends the Night*" (472). In the same volume, Desmond Pacey (in "Fiction 1920–1940," 658–93) says *Waste Heritage* "succeeds very well in evoking the mass fury which resulted from long years of unemployment and frustration" but charges that it "suffers somewhat, however, from its imitativeness" (688). Robin Mathews, "*Waste Heritage*: The Effects of Class on Literary Structure," *Studies in Canadian Literature* 6 (Spring 1981): 65–81; Roger Leslie Hyman, "Wasted Heritage and *Waste Heritage*," *Journal of Canadian Studies* 17 (Winter 1982): 74–87; Anthony Hopkins, "Structure and Thematic Vision in *Waste Heritage*," *Studies in Canadian Literature* 11 (Spring 1986): 77–85.

32. This is Thompson and Randall's thesis in the epilogue to *United States and Canada.*

33. Judith Butler, *Bodies That Matter* (New York: Routledge, 1993).

34. Lauren Berlant and Elizabeth Freeman, "Queer Nationality: The Political Logic of Queer Nation and Gay Activism," *Boundary* 2, no. 19 (Spring 1992): 149–80.

35. See Biddy Martin, "Sexualities without Genders and Other Queer Utopias," *Diacritics* 24 (Summer–Fall 1994): 104–21; Simon Watney, "Queer Epistemology—Activism, Outing, and the Politics of Sexual Identities," *Critical Quarterly* 36 (Spring 1994): 13–27.

36. Lisa Duggan, "Making It Perfectly Queer," *Socialist Review* 22 (January–March 1992): 11–31.

Part Six
SINCE 2000

While the 1990s saw an interest in analyzing the novel mainly on the basis of gender and feminist points of view, the twenty-first-century critics not only revisited earlier contentions about the novel (see Marilyn Chandler McEntyre's expansion of William Goldhurst's 1971 study of Cain and Abel imagery in the novel and Mimi Reisel Gladstein's analysis of the different portrayals of the feminine in the three movie versions of the novel), but also attempted approaches to *Of Mice and Men* that heretofore had not been explored. For example, fiction writer Charles Johnson (*The Middle Passage*, *Oxherding Tale*) became one of the first critics to look at the racial issues at play in Steinbeck's portrayal of Crooks, the Negro stable buck. Johnson's keynote address at the Steinbeck Congress held at Sun Valley, Idaho, in 2006, addresses how Steinbeck saw racial division despite an apparent class equality (Crooks's family at one time owned a small homestead in the area). Johnson also foregrounds the threat of physical violence to African Americans and the frequency of lynching threats as a way to keep the black man "in his place." By noting the speech of Curley's wife, Johnson's unique perspective stresses the fact that white dominance and privilege was widely accepted during the late 1930s.

A similar original approach is found in the last essay written by Louis Owens before his untimely suicide in 2002. In his study, Owens places the issue of eugenics in the spotlight as a central concern of Steinbeck in *Of Mice and Men* and posits that the author's use of the German gun image (Carlson's Lugar) indicates that Steinbeck was keenly aware of the tenets of Adolph Hitler and his Third Reich government regarding the development of a master race. Owens suggests that Steinbeck addresses the fascist advocacy of the extermination of the weak, incompetent, and the racially impure individuals in several episodes of the novel including the drowning of the puppies by Slim, the execution of Candy's old sheep dog by Carlson, and the closing murder of Lennie by George. The latter event is especially portrayed as acceptable in George's recognition that, due to Curley's need for revenge. Lennie's future fate could only be death at the end of the rope. The question of eugenics as a valid concern of Steinbeck has also been raised in the criticism of Kevin Hearle, whose article "These Are American People: The Spectre of Eugenics in *Their Blood Is Strong* and *The Grapes of Wrath*," appeared in 2002 in *Beyond Boundaries: Re-Reading John Steinbeck*, edited by Hearle and Susan Shillinglaw, pages 243–54 (Tuscaloosa: University of Alabama Press).

Other Significant Studies Published since 2000

Cantor, Gary. "Crooks: Steinbeck's Illuminizing Victim." *Steinbeck Studies of Japan* 31 (May 2008): 33–41.

Cardullo, Bert. "On the Road to Tragedy: Mice, Candy, and Land in *Of Mice and Men*." *American Drama* 16.1 (Winter 2007): 19–29.

Cedarstrom, Lorelei. "Beyond the Boundaries of Sexism: The Archetypal Feminine versus Anima Women in Steinbeck's Novels." In *Beyond Boundaries: Re-Reading John Steinbeck.* ed. Susan Shillinglaw and Kevin Hearle, 189–204. Tuscaloosa: University of Alabama Press, 2002.

Doyle, Brian L. "Tragedy and the Non-Teleological in *Of Mice and Men*." *Steinbeck Review* and *Steinbeck Studies* 3(2) (Fall 2006): 79–86.

Fahy, Thomas. "Worn Damaged Bodies in the Literature and Photography of the 1930's." *Journal of American Culture* 26(1) (March 2003): 2–16.

Hart, Richard. "Moral Experience in *Of Mice and Men*: Challenges and Reflection." In *The Moral Philosophy of John Steinbeck*, ed. Stephen K. George, 61–71. Lanham, MD: Scarecrow, 2005.

Meyer, Michael J. *Cain Sign: The Betrayal of Brotherhood in the Work of John Steinbeck.* Troy, NY: Edwin Mellen, 2002.
    Contains Marilyn McEntyre, "*Of Mice and Men*: A Story of Innocence Retained," 202–22.

Simmonds, Roy. "*Of Mice and Men* and (Perhaps) Other Things." In *John Steinbeck: A Centennial Tribute*, ed. Stephen K. George. Westport, CT: Praeger, 2002.

Takahira, Yuki. "Movie Adaptations of *Of Mice and Men*: 1939 and 1992." *Steinbeck Studies of Japan* 31 (May 2008): 42–51.

CHAPTER FOURTEEN

OF MICE AND MEN:
A STORY OF INNOCENCE RETAINED

Marilyn Chandler McEntyre

Though not derived as directly from the story of Cain and Abel as *East of Eden*, and certainly not as ambitious as that novel in its attempts to explore the ramifications of the ancient tale, *Of Mice and Men* is still, in its way, a compelling invitation to revisit the biblical myth and recast its significance in new terms. The bevy of critics who have dismissed this small "play-novelette" as one of Steinbeck's lesser works if not failures, calling it exaggerated, mechanical, woodenly allegorical, and melodramatically parabolic, may have failed fully to appreciate the lasting power of allegory and parable even for the presumed audience of post-Freudian, post-Joycean readers.[1]

The apparent simplicity of this stark little tragedy (a term some think carries more weight than the tale can bear) belies the magnitude and complexity of the moral questions it raises. Roughly speaking, those questions are riddles of discernment: when is "evil" not really evil and "good" not really good? When do those "conditions which look alike" deceive us into false judgment? How do we know the good when it can look so like evil? Like the theologians and folklorists who transfer the logic of "*felix culpa*" to Eve's disobedience and proclaim it the first act of self-liberation, Steinbeck, along with a number of other modern writers, offers a revisionist perspective on Cain's story, attempting to understand this dark "hero" in terms of

Previously published in *Cain Sign: The Betrayal of Brotherhood in The Work of John Steinbeck*, ed. Michael J. Meyer, 202–22. Lewiston, NY: Edwin Mellen, 2000. Used by permission.

his willingness to accept the burden of consciousness, and ultimately the responsibility for murder in the effort to be his brother's keeper.

The situation of George, the "Cain" figure in this novel, is that of anyone limited by the dependencies of a weaker partner and wondering why the "virtue" of innocence seems so often to thrust moral and practical responsibility upon the one who consents to the fall into experience. Surely one of the questions the story raises is how much responsibility one can take for another human being. Getting the right relationship between independence, dependence, and interdependence has been a particularly vexing matter in American culture where the social contracts of family and friendship have been so variously and loosely construed, especially in marginal subcultures like that of the itinerant farm workers in this novel.

To recast Cain and Abel as George and Lennie, dispossessed survivors of an inequitable economic system, bound by a common vision of family life and shared labor, protector and protected and, humanly speaking, each other's *raison d'être*, is to clothe the old tale not only with poignancy and pathos but also with an audacious and uncomfortable immediacy. It is also to reframe our most basic hypotheses about that tale: What if Abel's gentleness were in fact weakness of mind or body? What if Cain's question to God could be read not as a rhetorical gesture of defiance, but as a cry of anguish wrung from a frustrated elder brother whose patience with the younger has been worn to the last thread? What if there are legitimate alternative readings to this moral tale? How shall we travel the forked path it maps?

In its framework of moral paradox, the story teaches us to reckon with the shadow. To empathize with Cain is to reevaluate what we call evil. To see the consequences of Lennie's "innocence" is to reconsider "things done ill, or done to others' harm / which once you took for exercise of virtue."[2] It is to complicate the idea of childlike innocence with a certain informed skepticism that says neither children nor those we call "innocents" are free of guile. Thus in the opening scene, when George catches Lennie with a dead mouse in his hand, Lennie makes "an elaborate pantomime of innocence," protesting transparently, "What mouse, George? I ain't got no mouse." George replies coldly, "You gonna give me that mouse or do I have to sock you?"(8)[3] The themes of innocence and violence are introduced and complicated here at one stroke. Lennie is indeed an "innocent," and also, like a child, manipulative and scheming in his own limited way. George's violence already has to be seen in the context of his taking responsibility, being the one to see the larger picture, to foresee consequences and to control Lennie's behavior for their mutual welfare.

Critics have attacked Steinbeck's relegation of the Abel role to a character who, being feeble-minded, cannot be assigned moral responsibility and so cannot bear the moral weight of his role in this drama of justice and mercy. This particular twist on the figure of the "innocent man," however, compels the reader to identify closely with the slayer of the innocent, to participate in his predicament, and to raise a troubling question about the economy of guilt: one man's innocence may require another man's guilt. To preserve innocence is costly, and finally undesirable. The fall requires humans to come into consciousness, and therefore into conscience, to experience guilt, and thereby be pointed toward redemption. Those who are willing to assume the moral responsibility of full participation in the muddy and ambiguous human condition, to be soiled and sinful, and to wrestle with intolerable ambiguities, emerge into a moral maturity unattainable by the "pure." The difference between becoming like a little child and remaining like one is vast. The first is an apotheosis of wisdom; the second either an infirmity or an abdication.

Purity is an old American theme, hardly peculiar to American culture, but certainly an abiding theme in literature and an axis of the moral reasoning that characterizes collective self-definition and public debate.[4] Every generation has needed its literary and political prophets to remind them that the pure in spirit may be blessed, but purists are dangerous, and a simplistic pursuit or valorization of purity is a kind of moral retardation, if not willful ignorance. When not willful—when it is, as in Lennie's case, an infirmity—it still exacts a cost; someone has to take on the burden of practical decision-making and planning that is required to carve out a place on earth to call home. And to do that, one must enter into compromising negotiation with world, flesh, and devil.

This was Cain's enterprise. A farmer and tiller of soil, whose name means "possession," he is indicted, among other things, for reducing the gifts of God to the terms of human economy, for presuming to own the land, and later for founding and investing his hope in the earthly city. The builders of the Tower of Babel are referred to as Cain's descendants—those who sought to secure and solidify their own base of power, literally to monumentalize it and fix it for all time, and by imperializing the territory between earth and heaven, to stake a final claim to the things of this earth and seek salvation in them rather than in the promises of their God.

This theme of presumption, brought into the twentieth century and placed in the framework of American capitalism, where private property is an index of success and independence, becomes both more personal and more problematic for modern readers. The Cain and Abel story is about a zero-sum economy, in which the success of one implies the diminishment or failure of the other. Thus the first murder is predicated not only on an illegitimate seizure of power over life and death, but also on a radical reduction of divine economy to human terms. Rather than returning to God to understand the terms of acceptable sacrifice, and being willing to seek what would please Him, Cain seeks instead to eliminate the offense of comparison by eliminating the foil that defines him as a failure. For George to dream of "making a stake" so he and Lennie can have their "little place" hardly seems culpable, based though it is on the very notions of private property, possession, ownership, and exclusion that relate capitalism to the sin of Cain. But for Steinbeck to make explicit that relationship between capitalistic pursuit of self-interest and the original crime of murder is to hack at one of the thickest roots of American culture.

Post-industrial capitalism as a framework of social and therefore moral life has forced society to reassess the terms in which it thinks about sin, guilt, and goodness. The erosion of family ties and therefore of the old tribal ethics of filial piety and fraternal loyalty has made the social contract more ambiguous. It is less clear now than it once was in what way we are our brothers' keepers, who, indeed, are our "brothers," what we may expect to give and receive, what are the terms of communal life, and how to do good in a system whose evils continue to implicate us all in erosion of intimate life, secularization of social life, and loss of moral direction.

One of the deepest motives in great literature of all ages, and, in a particular way, in modern literature since Faust's Mephistopheles and Byron's brooding heroes, has been to seek ways to reframe moral questions that move us beyond simplistic application of the categories of good and evil into a larger awareness of how, in human life and the human psyche, good and evil are deeply and interdependently entangled—how we live in a realm where blacks and whites turn grey.

The Cain and Abel story provides a useful vehicle for this kind of moral reassessment, precisely because it is predicated on strong dualities and polarities. Polarities, carefully considered, lead us to paradox. Extremes of any human attribute tend to point to and often generate their opposites. So Steinbeck, among numerous other nineteenth- and twentieth-century novelists and playwrights, returned to that story as an appropriate paradigm for examining the moral complexities of the time. His experiments with the Cain-Abel motif invite readers to consider how opposites may be related, and how "conditions that look alike" may contradict themselves. In Lennie, the half-wit, we have to consider the relationship between innocence and vacuity; in George, his protector and murderer, between cruelty and kindness. In the obvious and extreme oppositions between them we are finally led to contemplate what is the bond that unites them and, indeed, in what sense they are not simply opposites but also doubles, whose deep similarities belie their differences. Superficially, the differences are archetypal:

> The first man was small and quick, dark of face, with restless eyes and sharp, strong features. Every part of him was defined: small, strong hands, slender arms, a thin and bony nose. Behind him walked his opposite, a huge man, shapeless of face, with large, pale eyes, with wide, sloping shoulders; and he walked heavily, dragging his feet a little, the way a bear drags his paws. His arms did not swing at his sides, but hung loosely. (2)

The sharp physical differences: small and dark, big and fair, sharp human intelligence posed against animal-like dumbness—suggest larger contrasts: dark and light, aggression and submission, movement and stasis, and finally life and death.

Indeed, Lennie costs George a great deal in life energy. George experiences his caretaking of Lennie as a sysyphean task: "I ain't got nothing to do. Might jus' as well spen' al my time tellin' you things and then you forget 'em, and I tell you again" (4). He is controller, instructor, protector. He carries Lennie's work card and bus ticket for him, undertakes to foresee the trouble he might cause and prevent it, commits himself to second-guessing Lennie's purposes and behavior as watchful parents do recalcitrant children. George talks; Lennie acts. George has to engage in careful manipulation to secure the field of action in which he can act—to get them hired so the boss can see Lennie work. Once that is done, Lennie may be proven to be the better worker. "You jus' stand there and don't say nothing," George tells his charge. "If he finds out what a crazy bastard you are, we won't get no job, but if he sees ya work before he hears ya talk, we're set. Ya got that?" (6)

Thus the theme of the "acceptable sacrifice" is refocused in such a way as to lead us to consider the sacrifice or contribution required of one partner to enable the work of the other to receive due regard. George's reiteration to the boss that Lennie is the better worker, weak of mind, but exceptionally capable of performing the work he's being hired to do, directs the boss's attention to the goodness of the offering and prevents Lennie from being judged in the wrong terms. Consequently, the weaker brother has the means to please the "father" even though the gifts of the stronger, which ultimately seem to count for little, are necessary to the welfare of the weaker.

George, as itinerant ranch hand and caretaker of a retarded adult dependent, is caught in a fate that has little to do with the ideals of independence and self-determination that so deeply inform national mythology. He raises an old, old question that precedes and transcends our endless declarations of independence: how to be good in a bad world where violence begets violence and innocence itself is both dangerous and destructive, and where no human action may be fully undertaken or understood outside the context of community life. The moral categories that can so conveniently be appropriated to allow us to pass judgment on an individual's sins are challenged in this story which forces us to regard "sin" in systemic terms and individual acts of "evil" as mitigated by the constraints of economic and social oppression. Thus, though George must in some way be regarded as responsible for Lennie's murder, that responsibility is so modified by circumstances as clearly to warrant complete mercy.

Even the minor characters challenge simple moral categories. Crooks, the old black stable hand, is both victim and aggressor, one who, having found no mercy, has little to dispense. Old Candy, whose useless and suffering dog must be shot, an event which adumbrates both Lennie's fate and his own fears, finds himself unable to perform the act of violent mercy that will end the dog's suffering and so suffers from his own cowardly passivity. Similarly, Curley and his wife hopelessly mistake lust for love and vengeance for justice.

Slim, veteran ranchhand, natural leader, and "prince of the ranch," is the only character who seems not to be caught in the web of social and psychological tensions, whose moral vision is wide enough to comprehend the injustices of the system in which all are implicated, and who is able to hold a delicate balance between pragmatism and compassion, law and grace. He is a heroic figure in the American vein, descended from characters like Natty Bumppo and Captain Vere—solitary, seasoned, self-contained, a natural leader whose power derives not from institutional authority, but from the compelling force of personal integrity and wisdom born of reflection upon hard experience. Such characters serve as both critics and mediators in their social worlds. If the story were to be reduced to its allegorical schema, one might see Slim as the "Christ figure" and merciful counterpart to the ranch owner, who represents the absent but threatening "God-figure." Seen in this way, the two "bosses" represent two orders of authority and recourse between which George and Lennie and the rag-tag community of itinerant workers like them have to negotiate the terms and ethics of their own survival. Slim is not the focal character in this story. This is a story about life among the rank and file, life for those who cannot finally either accede to power or "light out for the territory," but have to work out their salvation from within the enmeshing nets of economic necessity and social immobility.

Beyond the social criticism so characteristic of Steinbeck's work is a certain bold playfulness in adapting this biblical material, grown large and weighty over time, to the very local and in some ways burlesque setting of the American West. The same spirit seems to inform this appropriation as that which allowed the Puritan settlers to regard themselves and their work in the world in unabashedly allegorical terms, thus dignifying with the largeness of historical precedent and theological significance the grubby business of survival. Various elements in the original biblical tale show up here in recognizable but changed and sometimes comic forms.

Cain, whose name may be taken to be a pun on "I have gotten a manchild,"[5] figures in several early biblical legends. The most noteworthy of these recounts how his sacrifice of crops to God is refused while the animal sacrifice of Abel, his brother, is accepted. Cain kills Abel out of envy (or anger, or frustration, or fear; the motive here offers a rich quarry for psycho-theological interpretation) and is banished by God to live the life of a nomad. The Lord, however, in an act of mercy which is in its own way inexplicable, puts a sign on his forehead, protecting him, since nomads were subject to no protective laws but those of vengeance. In another story, Cain is credited with building the first city and with inventing metalwork, achievements which mark him, the first murderer, as a founder of civilization with its crafts and industries as opposed to agrarian and nomadic culture. Thus he represents first the peasant farmer who revolts against the herdsman and later the city-dweller whose relationship to God has been complicated and vexed by power politics and commerce.

This connection of a "foundation murder" to the founding of a community is one René Girard has explored at length in two works that detail on a vast canvas the deep linkage between violence and the sacred. Murder as a symbolic act is one of differentiation, necessary to separate the fate of one from the other and to define and declare individuality in order, paradoxically, to provide a more conscious basis for community life. Another paradoxical consequence of "foundation murder" is the giving of law against murder: God responds to Cain's fear (that whoever finds him will kill him) by putting a mark on him and, further, by enunciating the law against murder. Girard comments that this divine intervention

> makes it clear . . . that the decisive murder, here as elsewhere, has a founding character. And to talk in terms of "founding" is also to talk in terms of "differentiating." . . . I see in this the establishment of a differential system, which serves, as always, to discourage mimetic rivalry and generalized conflict.[6]

This theory has significant implications for recognizing that the privately owned and settled West with its rough vigilante "justice" was a primitive culture that emerged into law, as other cultures have, by enacting vengeance and suffering its consequences. Characters like Curley abound in the literature of the far West—men who not only take justice and judgment into their own hands, but who actively seek occasions to exercise those illegitimately seized functions to establish their personal power as a basis for or in lieu of orderly political process. And men like Curley are finally defeated by men like Slim, who temper justice with mercy and the roots of whose authority lie in experience, empathy, and compassion. Steinbeck's story leaves us to speculate about what ensues after George kills Lennie, but the fact that the murder was performed as a ritual act of mercy instead of being left to the self-serving rage of Curley's jealousy must surely change the consequences for the community; the power of the owner and his son are modified in George's taking into his own hands the power to execute the law even in the act of submitting to it. Like Cain, George confronts punishment in such a way as to throw it into question rather than to confirm the terms of the law.

Abel, whose name may be derived from a Mesopotamian word meaning "son," was the second child of Adam, a herdsman, and thus a pastoral culture hero.[7] He was the first to offer animal sacrifice to God, and his sacrifice was accepted, thus establishing a tradition of animal sacrifice. In Christian history he is viewed as one of many forerunners or "types" of Christ whose stories adumbrate the ultimate story of sacrifice and salvation. He is the original innocent victim whose murder justifies succeeding generations of herdsmen in their feud against their enemies, the peasant farmers.

But the differences between the brothers' gifts, like the differences between those groups with their respective ways of living on earth, may not be as profound as their similarities. If murder is, as Girard suggests, an act of self-differentiation, it is impelled by a deep recognition of fear and similarity.[8] The fear that one's self or one's group might be subsumed and therefore obliterated is the root of rivalry, and rivalry is the first stage in individuation. Individuation produces both growth in consciousness and a threat to community life.

Literature has provided numerous reiterations of this story of envy and fratricide. Ricardo Quinones' useful study of the large body of "Cain and Abel" stories distinguishes three lines of development of that tradition, which he calls "Citizen Cain," "Monstrous Cain," and "Cain as Sacred Executioner." A fourth, a post-Byronic portrait, he calls "Regenerate Cain." If he is in any sense to be considered a "Cain" figure, George clearly belongs to the third or fourth type. In those readings, Cain is Abel's protector, the one who is able and willing to take on confrontation with the father and other powers, who is the more courageous and the more conscious of the two brothers, and who kills Abel out of benevolent rather than base motives. This describes George's relationship to Lennie. George is also a farmer; his work is slinging barley. He understands crops, finds jobs for himself and Lennie at harvest time, and bends his energies toward the dream of owning a farm. He understands when that dream is finally destroyed by Lennie's innocent but disastrous mistake, that he is condemned to wander from one ranch to another, nomadic, homeless, spending his pay in cities. He kills Lennie with a stolen gun, a Luger (the pun on "lie" may have some relevance here) which associates him also with "metalwork" and weaponry. He is dark as Lennie is fair, older than his companion, more canny, more alert to danger, more suspicious, less trusting, someone who has known temptation, has struck bargains, bent the truth, and devised strategies of subterfuge to survive and pursue happiness as he imagines it. That pursuit is not merely a selfish one, but neither is it transcendent. The very humble character of his ambitions may be a kind of tragic flaw—that he sought nothing higher.

But even George's limited ambitions are fraught with ambivalence. There are moments when having and loving come into conflict, and the pursuit of happiness as personal desire cannot coexist with commitment to care for another. One writer's speculative recreation of Cain's conflict might serve as an entrée to George's predicament as Lennie's caretaker: "Cain felt a shadow, cast by his brother Abel, falling across his life. How could he have his place in the sun with his brother's shadow in the way?"[9] This empathetic representation of Cain's state of mind before the murder of his brother locates the root of violence in desire, ambition, and envy. But possibly a deeper mystery of motive in fratricide lies not in these impulses, but in ambivalence born of the interdependency and love-hate paradox that characterize blood relationships, especially that of siblings who are in a certain sense equals and therefore inevitably rivals. That rivalry is, of course, exacerbated by the fact that in another sense siblings are specifically not equals. In both the original story and in Steinbeck's tale, the two men hold quite different places in the scheme of things. One (so the post-Byronic "Cain" tradition would suggest) has the greater responsibility, the larger imagination, and the greater possibility of both success and failure.

Throughout Judaeo-Christian history the presumed privilege of the firstborn son has been cited as the source of subterfuge, insubordination, and murder. The second, or "lesser," son resents the privilege of the firstborn and challenges it. When, in the story of Cain and Abel and later in that of Jacob and Esau, the younger son receives the blessing despite the legitimate expectations and efforts of the first, the firstborn rises in anger to avenge himself on his brother. The theme reappears in slightly different form in the parable of the prodigal son in the resentment of the elder brother who has been faithful and feels as if he is forfeiting something that belongs to him in witnessing his father's merciful compassion toward the younger.

It is this quality of resentment born of the frustrations of genuine commitment and recognized obligation that Steinbeck foregrounds in George and Lennie. Throughout the story George alternates between two visions: one of life with Lennie, one without him. The former is the binding force in their relationship: a shared vision of a little farm where they would live "off the fatta the lan'" with livestock and fruit trees, much abundance and little work, equally invested and equally rewarded. The other, darker vision George recites in his moments of frustration at shouldering the burden of being "his brother's keeper" in such a literal way:

> God a'mighty, if I was alone I could live so easy. I could go get a job an' work, an' no trouble. No mess at all, and when the end of the month come I could take my fifty bucks and go into town and get whatever I want. Why, I could stay in a cat house all night. I could eat any place I want, hotel or any place, and order any damn thing I could think of. An' I could do all that every damn month. Get a gallon of whisky, or set in a pool room and play cards or shoot pool. (11)

This is a vision of freedom from responsibility. It is also a vision of city life, a life free of physical toil, full of sensual indulgence that once again symbolically links George to Cain, mythological founder of cities. George periodically considers the meager fruits of his labors and finds them unsatisfying, recognizes himself as condemned first to work that yields no personal reward or approbation, and second to nomadic wandering. The city seems a refuge from this monotonous fate for one whose labors have not seemed to produce their just reward.

George also knows that this is a diminished vision. What he really wants is a little farm with Lennie. He wants family, companionship, shared responsibility, community. In a moment of generosity, he even enlarges the plan to include two other outcasts, men excluded by the infirmities of age and the social barrier of race from full participation in whatever community life the ranch offers. Almost, in that moment, we may see something Christlike in him—something that is willing to say, "Come unto me all ye that labor and are heavy laden and I will give you rest." He would like to be able to dispense such bounty. He would like to be as a god. And so the paradoxes continue, because even as he consents to widen the vision to include others, he fears some loss of control over the little kingdom he has planned for himself. He asks old Candy, who wants to cast his lot with theirs, "Say, what's it to you? You got nothing to do with us." And even after the offer of money that will make the vision possible says reluctantly, "I gotta think about that. We was always gonna do it by ourselves" (59).

Lennie, though he works the crops with George, is almost wholly identified by his love of animals and "soft things." He literally kills creatures out of love, stroking them and playing with them, unaware of the lethal force of his own large hands. Innocent victim himself, he is also a murderer; in a very literal way he kills what he loves, making them sacrifices to his innocence. He deals his final death blow to George himself in that his own death means the end of George's hope and lease on life. The "brother's" life consigned to his keeping is impossible to separate entirely from his own. Their shared fate is shared lifeblood, and both are vulnerable to what the weaker suffers.

The relationship between George and Lennie, partly because it is not a relationship of equals, has a ritual character that underscores the mystery of the bonds of fate and love that transcend or bypass rationality. Their conversations fall into repeated patterns, confined to recitations by the severe limitations of Lennie's mind. Those recitations, however, have a kind of power that rational conversation lacks; like incantation or prayer, they invoke a vision and a promise and bring both speaker and listener back to a place of fundamental faith and well-being. The two friends are comforted as one is comforted by liturgical formulae; the words they recite to one another are their heaven here and now—their place on earth to return to—the shared promise that stands in lieu of the thing promised, the hope of things to come that sustains in the absence of those things.

In both the opening and closing scenes of the novel, the same conversation occurs, both times after a breach of conduct on Lennie's part, an apology, and a forgiveness. The story of their private heaven is like an absolution and a resealing of the bond that keeps them in community and on their chosen path, and reminds them that they are "a peculiar people," different from others, and chosen for a special fate. As George begins the story, he takes on a priestly persona: "George's voice became deeper. He repeated his words rhythmically as though he had said them many times before." Then the words come, trance-like, separated from the preceding conversation in style, substance, and scope. The opening reference to "guys like us" hypothesizes the larger "mystical body" of the lonely, the outcast, the dispossessed, who wait, alike, for deliverance:

> Guys like us, that work on ranches, are the loneliest guys in the world. They got no family. They don't belong no place. They come to a ranch an' work up a stake and then they go inta town and blow their stake, and the first thing you know they're poundin' their tail on some other ranch. They ain't got nothing to look ahead to. (13–14)

But the next part of the ritual sets these two initiates apart even from that larger community and asserts their special status. "Now tell how it is with us," Lennie demands, playing acolyte to George's priestly ritual. And George continues his recitation of their "sacred story":

> With us it ain't like that. We got a future. We got somebody to talk to that gives a damn about us. We don't have to sit in no bar room blowin' our jack jus' because we got no place else to go. If them other guys gets in jail they can rot for all anybody gives a damn. But not us. (14)

Lennie, with the passion of a true believer, breaks into a triumphant recitation of his catechism: "*But not us! An' why? Because. . . . because I got you to look after me, and you got me to look after you, and that's why*" (14). Then he demands that George continue. When George points out that he could do it himself by heart, Lennie refuses the responsibility. He is unfit: "I forget some a' the things."

George's priestly responsibility is to remember and utter the sacred words. So he goes on: "Someday—we're gonna get the jack together and we're gonna have a little house and a couple of acres an' a cow and some pigs and—" (Lennie shouts the finish line) "An' live off the fatta the lan' . . ." (14). Overcome with the vision, he breaks into his own rendition of it, complete with rabbits, rain in winter, and thick cream on the milk. The ritual becomes a kind of revival meeting, a dialogue of call and response that brings both into a deep place of comfort and hope that obliterates for a time the bleakness of the present.

When, at the end of the story, this ritual is reenacted, for the third time in the text, it is to provide a context for Lennie's murder. Here again

Girard may help articulate the special nature of the act presented in his recognition that ritual is often the deliberate breaking of a prohibition—that in ritual that which is prohibited may be required.[10] The concept of the necessary evil is one of the most problematic of moral conundrums, and it is to this that the story of George and Lennie leads. The killing of an innocent victim is justified by the argument that in some way it will prevent greater harm. The immediate act is culpable. Its consequences are a presumed benefit to the community. In that way this murder comes under the large rubric of ritual sacrifice and is as offensive to the modern mind. But to confront that offense is to enter a specifically religious realm of reasoning where truth is ultimately paradoxical. Our challenge is to abide within it, recognizing that moral vision, like the sight of our eyes, must be binary to give us depth perception.

Thus the answer to the question, "Am I my brother's keeper?" is "yes" and "no." So often read as a rhetorical dodge to which Cain resorts when God calls upon him to confess the murder of Abel, the question might rather be taken as a real question, which as such leads to others: by what ordination? Why? Where are the boundaries between *my* desires, *my* needs, *my* destiny, and his? It is a question that underlies all community life: in what sense and in what ways are we responsible to and for each other? What obligations do our interdependencies impose upon us? And on what, when conflict comes to a choice between individual and communal welfare, as it so often does, are we to base our judgments about what is the greater good?

Three visions of community come into play in this short tale: first is the intimate partnership of George and Lennie which in both fact and fantasy is one of protection, affection, and sharing of labor; second is the larger community of the ranch, stratified into the owner and his son and daughter-in-law—the makers of law in this little world—foreman, skinners, swampers, and stable-bucks. The third is the larger world, that comes into play only as backdrop, and largely in terms of the corruptions of the city with its brothels and gambling places. None of the three will remain unchanged by the event of Lennie's innocent violence and the violent end to his innocent life. Murder is never an individual act; its consequence, if it is not simply a step in an unending cycle of revenge, is to lead the living to reflection and reconfiguration of community which never simply closes over the gap the victim leaves, but arranges itself around that absence in fear and commemoration and reinforced protection.

We are each other's fate. To turn the question around is to lead directly to Jesus' own rhetorical and endlessly resonant question, "Who is my . . . brother?" implying that the bond of blood is secondary to the bond of what Martin Luther King called "beloved community," created by shared vision.

In this story, then, Steinbeck puts a new spin on the old, mysterious and open-ended theological questions of guilt and innocence, sacrifice and reward, and right relation between the natural economy of the fruits of the earth and the labor of men's hands, so easily exploited and corrupted in human enterprise. He also recasts the question of how rightly to live in community, how to take care of one another, and how to understand our interdependencies in a way that generates mercy rather than blame. Surely that way has to do with assuming responsibility for "the least among us," for our "younger brothers," for the "innocents," like George, and with discerning, like Slim, what is needful in the moment to maintain balance between individual desire and collective peace.

It is pertinent to note that in the end, it is Cain who becomes the protected. The mark of Cain is a sign meant for his protection from random attack. He goes alone into exile, but goes under the hand of God. Steinbeck, here and elsewhere, takes on the romantic mythology of the lone hero by harkening back to a deeper and longer tradition. To go alone will not be, for George, a liberation so much as a condemnation. Nevertheless, it is an opportunity. It is a tragic fate now to be met. (Though few consent to call this limited story a tragedy, few would dispute the tragic character of this moment of loss and release into a terrible freedom.) What we read is Lennie's story. What is to come hereafter is George's. In a very real sense, his own story starts after the climactic event that seems to be his defeat. And, as Eliot puts it, "the end is where we start from."[11]

Notes

1. See, for instance, Howard Levant, *The Novels of John Steinbeck: A Critical Study* (Columbia: University of Missouri Press, 1974), 133–44.

2. T. S. Eliot, "Little Gidding" in *Four Quartets*, included in *T.S. Eliot: The Complete Poems and Plays 1909–1950* (New York: Harcourt, Brace & World, Inc.), 142.

3. John Steinbeck, *Of Mice and Men*, 1937 (New York: Penguin Modern Classic, 1993), 8. All further references to this work will be found in the text.

4. For a useful discussion of the idea of "purity" in American politics and public discourse, see Garry Wills' *Under God* (New York: Touchstone Press, 1990), relevant here to an understanding of the particularly "American" character of Steinbeck's moral universe.

5. John L. McKenzie, *Dictionary of the Bible* (Milwaukee: The Bruce Publishing Company, 1965), 113–14.

6. René Girard, *Things Hidden Since the Foundation of the World* (London: The Athlone Press, 1978), 146. For other aspects of this argument see also Girard, *Violence and the Sacred*, trans. Patrick Gregory (Baltimore: Johns Hopkins Press, 1977).

7. McKenzie, *Dictionary*, 113–14.

8. See Girard, *Things Hidden*, 38, for an elaboration of the idea of "enemy twins"—victim and aggressor as doubles.

9. Dale Aukerman, *The Darkening Valley: A Biblical Perspective on Nuclear War* (New York: The Seabury Press, 1981), 2.

10. See Girard, *Things Hidden*, 20–21.

11. T. S. Eliot, "Little Gidding," 144.

CHAPTER FIFTEEN

OF MICE AND MEN:
CREATING AND RE-CREATING
CURLEY'S WIFE
Mimi Reisel Gladstein

Curley's wife in Steinbeck's poignant tale *Of Mice and Men* has been a source of question and query, almost from her conception. George S. Kaufman, the play's Broadway director was the first to suggest that more was needed for her dramatic realization. He encouraged Steinbeck to enlarge her part: "The girl, I think, should be drawn more fully: she is the motivating force of the whole thing and should loom larger" (Steinbeck and Wallsten 136).

Steinbeck did just that for the play version, giving her a troubled background of battling parents and an alcoholic and lost father. Obviously, Clare Luce, who played the role on Broadway, still needed more and Steinbeck was moved, halfway into the play's run, to provide a fuller exposition, explaining her predatory behavior as defensive. She is, he explains "a nice, kind girl and not a floozy" (Steinbeck and Wallsten 154). We do not have a record of Luce's performance, so we cannot see for ourselves how she resolved the contradictions in this woman who was called a "tart" and "jail-bait" by the men in the play, but "not a floozy" by her creator.

In the ensuing half-century since "something happened" to Curley's wife, Steinbeck's poignant tale has continued to inspire interpretation in a variety of media. It has motivated four major film productions, two for the big screen, 1939 and 1992, and two television productions, one in 1968 and another in 1981, plus a stage-musical (1958) and an opera (1976).

From *Beyond Boundaries: Rereading John Steinbeck*, edited by Susan Shillinglaw and Kevin Hearle, copyright 2002 by the University of Alabama Press. Used by permission.

Luckily, there are readily available copies of three of the film productions and so we can study how different manifestations of Steinbeck's timeless fable have dealt with the apparent contradictions between the outer and inner being of the only woman in this male domain.

Judith Crist once commented that when Hollywood makes an historical movie, it tells us more about Hollywood at the time of the making of the film than it does about the time period the film portrays.[1] The same might be said about the portrayal of Curley's wife. A cursory exploration of the multiple possibilities that comparisons of the three film versions suggest to us are instructive, not only for what they demonstrate about this problematic character, but also about the times in which each text was produced. To illustrate, I have chosen three significant components of the characterization of Curley's wife as she is presented in the 1939, 1980, and 1992 film productions. They provide a beginning (how we are introduced to the character); a middle (some justification for her behavior); and, of course, her end or death. [The reader is directed to the three illustrative plates that coincide with these three significant junctures in her presentation: Introduction, Justification, and Death.][2]

The earliest film version followed shortly after the Broadway run. Lewis Milestone's 1939 cinema rendition starred Lon Chaney Jr. and Burgess Meredith. Betty Field played the role of Curley's wife. The audience introduction to her is spotlighted by Candy's cue line: "Just wait'll you see Curley's wife."

And our first sight is a revealing one. Her sexuality is foregrounded; her legs are what we see first, encased in dark silk stockings. She is wearing high heels, lifting and lowering a puppy, precariously clasped between her ankles.

The setting is in the barn, where she is lying on her back in the straw, blond hair, tightly curled. This provocative introduction is softened emblematically by showing her in conjunction with a cute, fuzzy puppy, a connection that also foreshadows her demise. Milestone's semiotic choices, first silk stockings, then puppy, convey the ambiguity of this pivotal character. On the one hand, she is dressed in sexually provocative clothing, like a thirties screen vamp. On the other hand, her universality is highlighted by her delight in the cute puppy, an emotion the audience can share. Her petting the puppy in the barn creates motivation for her final visit to the barn to get it before she leaves (see figure 15.1).

Figure 15.1. Curley's wife 1939, 1981, and 1992: The introduction to the character.

Robert Blake's 1980s television version was produced some two generations later. However, except for the change from large screen to the small one and the addition of color, it does not often stray far from its predecessor.[3] In fact, it is consciously modeled on the 1939 production, even dedicated to Lewis Milestone. For many scenes, the same script was used. This complicates my thesis somewhat, because sometimes, rather than being a reflection of its times, it is an homage to its inspiration and therefore highly derivative. The Blake script replicates not only scenes added in the Milestone production, such as the farmhouse eating scene, but exact shots, such as the close-up of the pie, Mae's fingers breaking off a piece of crust. There is also a marked similarity between Betty Field's and Cassie Yates' initial scenes with the puppy, a scene that is not in the novel.

Blake retains the barn setting for our introduction to the character, but, perhaps in response to some consciousness raising about the sexual objectification of women, we see Mae's hands first, not her legs. On the other hand, the reason for this change could also be cultural. The sight of a woman's legs, in silk stockings, did not carry the same sexual impact in the eighties that it did in the thirties. The thirties is the decade when Claudette Colbert, in *It Happened One Night* stops traffic by lifting her skirt to show her stockinged leg. By the 1980s the sight of a woman's legs, either in or out of silk stocking, did not have the same erotic punch. Instead, her provocative character is communicated by the camera's focus on her cleavage in a tight-bodiced, low-cut cotton dress. Her blond hair is still tightly curled, but she is not on her back, at least, at first. The suggestiveness of a woman on her back in the hay is another of the time-coded sexual signs of an era when even married couples could not be shown lying in bed together. Like her predecessor, she is playing with the puppies, appealing to the audience's sense that someone who loves dogs and children can't be all bad (see figure 15.1).

In both of these film versions, the contradictions inherent in this character are telegraphed in this opening scene, a scene not from Steinbeck's text, which changes the way Curley's wife is introduced to the audience. Rather than having her intrude into masculine space, the bunkhouse, as Steinbeck does, in the Milestone and Blake versions she is shown first alone in the barn. In these films, her loneliness, and its connection to her being the only woman in this male domain, is further underlined by another scene Milestone includes from the additional matter in the Eugene Solow screenplay. In both of these early productions, a scene just outside the barn follows this introductory scene. The camera pans from Mae, lying in the straw, to the open barn door which frames an interaction between Curley and his father. Curley is looking for his wife; the boss, his father, suggests that Curley needs to get his mind on his work and leave his wife alone. In the 1939 version, the boss speaks his understanding of her loneliness, noting that it would be better for her if she had some women to talk to. She is even named—Mae. Much has been made in the critical literature of the fact that Steinbeck never named this woman, identifying her only by her relationship to a man, as Curley's wife. Both Milestone and Blake remedy this situation. By giving her a name, she is humanized, achieving the same status as the men in the story. She becomes subject of her own story with an identity other than the one given her by marriage to Curley.

By adding the scene in the barn, Milestone can show the audience that Curley's wife is alone and innocently engaged in playing with a puppy. Therefore, her husband's suspicions are probably unfounded and the audience is moved to sympathy. The boss, Curley's father, also voices his disapproval of his son's obsession with his wife's activities. However, this sympathy is balanced by her looks, and emphasized by Candy's preparatory line, "Just wait'll you *see* Curley's wife." How she looks helps explain his disparaging attitude toward her and is accentuated by the voyeuristic camera focus on legs in the first film, cleavage in the second.

These additional introductory scenes are nowhere in the 1992 production. Gary Sinise's film owes its inspiration, not to either previous film version, but to Sinise's early affection for Steinbeck's work. He played Tom Joad in the successful translation of *The Grapes of Wrath* from text to stage. Sinise and John Malkovich had performed Steinbeck's *Of Mice and Men* onstage in Chicago (1980) while part of the Steppenwolf Company. With Elaine Steinbeck's approval, Horton Foote wrote his own adaptation for the screen, a screenplay which is, in some ways, more and, in other ways, less faithful to Steinbeck's texts. Like Steinbeck, Foote does not name Curley's wife.

As in the play and novel, we first meet Curley's wife, as do Lennie and George, at the bunkhouse. In the novel, she plays her first scene in the doorway, using the doorframe to pose for the new men, leaning against it to arch her body forward. Foote's script brings her into the bunkhouse. However, there is a marked contradiction in the visual message of her costuming and actions. Unlike her prototype in the novel, she is not "tarted" up in the little red ostrich feather mules nor is her hair tightly curled into little sausages. Sherilynn Fenn, as Curley's wife, definitely shows the effects of a nineties production. Her sexuality is less dependent on costume and make-up, better conveyed by her manner than her looks. She bursts into the bunkhouse with a breathy little girl quality. To add to her youthful mannerisms, she is toying with her skirt, pulling it up and playing with the hem (see figure 15.1). Her breathy, girlish voice resonates with a quality reminiscent of Marilyn Monroe.[4] This change in the nature of allure plays into a contemporary infantilization of sexuality, epitomized by such things as pre-pubescent high-fashion models hawking tight jeans and/or Calvin Klein's perfume ads featuring awkward young boys and girls, photographed in their underwear.[5] Her girlish behavior and voice qualities are a counterpart of what Susan Bordo, in a recent article for the *Chronicle of Higher Education*, calls the "eroticization of children."[6] Myra

Macdonald writes of the creation in the 1990s of the "little girl lost look," a reconstruction of feminine sexuality from that of power into a "waif-like innocence and insecurity" (112). Fenn's portrayal partakes of those characteristics. The concurrent qualities of innocence and sexuality are emphasized by the parting thrust of her breast and her form-fitting dress.

Once the audience is introduced to Curley's wife, made aware of her ambiguous nature, both predatory and needy, the script must furnish motivation for her behavior. Why is she so needy? In the novel, the reader first learns about the situation from the men's perspective. There are few early clues to provide understanding of the problems between her and Curley from her perspective. Curley's threatening behavior is explained by Candy to George and Lennie. After their initial unpleasant encounter, Candy notes that Curley is "worse lately" (27). This change Candy attributes to the fact that he "got married a couple of weeks ago . . . [and is] cockier'n ever since he got married" (27). He also calls attention to Curley's gloved left hand. Candy tells George that the glove is full of vaseline, which Curley says is to keep the hand soft for his new wife. George judges that as "a dirty thing to tell around" (28). However, it is not until three-fourths of the way through the novel that the reader gets the wife's viewpoint, her explanation of the problems in the marriage, what has created the situation that puts her in such need of company and consequently such jeopardy. Her words to Lennie, Candy, and Crooks tell of her frustration with being left at home while Curley goes off with the boys, "Think I like to stick in that house alla time?" (76). She speaks of Curley's one note conversations about how he is going to "lead with his left twict, and then bring in the ol'right cross" (76). But the men do not acknowledge her perspective. They view her as a danger and want her out of their living space.

When her dead body is discovered, Candy reproaches her for "messing" everything up. His final epitaph, over her dead body, is: "You Goddamn tramp . . . You lousy tart" (95). Is she to blame for her own demise as Candy's eulogy suggests? Are we to believe Whit's diagnosis that "she can't keep away from guys"? Or is it that she has "the eye" as Candy explains? Curley is always looking for her, but then always leaving her alone, in a situation of such isolation that she is content, in her own words to be talking to "a bunch of bindlestiffs." Even on Saturday night. "Ever'body out doin' som'pin'. Ever'body! An what am I doin?" (78) In her final scene, she corroborates what we already know from Curley's behavior throughout the novel, "He ain't a nice fella" (89).

In the play and the novel, we can only speculate about what life with Curley is like. This is not true in all three films. Each provides scenes that counterbalance Candy's condemnation of her. The Milestone version takes us into the ranch house to provide justification for the woman's need for congenial company. In a scene created for the Milestone film we encounter Mae, the boss, and Curley at the dinner table. The camera focuses on a pie, as Curley and the boss cut off huge pieces, while Mae's fingers nip off a small piece of the crust. The men then drench their portions in cream. Noisily, they devour the pie and slurp coffee. There is no conversation; Mae is so overwhelmed by the eating noises, that she puts her hands over her ears. Obviously, we are meant to sympathize with "Mae's" disgust. The men are uncouth and animalistic. They "wolf" down huge pieces of pie, while she barely eats. Still, her looks convey another message, one not so sympathetic. She is bejeweled and made up, wearing a low-cut dress (see figure 15.2).

Blake's fidelity to Milestone goes far in proving that imitation is the sincerest form of flattery. The dinner scenes are almost a carbon copy, the major difference being the addition of color. The camera eye first focuses on the pie; the men pack away pie and guzzle coffee. Once again, "Mae" is revolted by the gross and slurping dinner noises. If anything, either as a result of better sound equipment or by a conscious choice of the film editor, the noises are louder. The men are even more unmannered, going at their food with an added two-handed boorishness, fork in one hand, coffee cups in the other. We are ready to join her, putting our hands over our ears. During this entire scene, the audience is put in the position of empathizing with Mae. After the meal, our sympathy is evoked again when Curley leaves her at home to go out with the boys, although she expresses her desire to go out. Since both the men's bad table manners and Curley's lack of consideration for her feelings are material that is not in the novel, the added text for the 1939 and 1980 film scripts provides opportunity for audience commiseration with Mae's plight. The scenes inside the ranch house make her more sympathetic, justifying her dubious quest for company, even to her detriment.

There is no analogous scene in Horton Foote's screenplay. True to the novel, we are kept outside of the ranch house. But, if a 1992 conception

Figure 15.2. Curley's wife, 1939, 1981, and 1992: The middle, or some justification for her behavior.

doesn't turn our stomachs against Curley, his brutal nature is transmitted in another way. Annoying noise making, but of a more violent kind, is used to telegraph Curley's failures as a human being and husband. In an added scene that shows the men coming in from the fields, we encounter Curley pounding a punching bag. The scene is mid-way through the film and relevant in that it continues the motif of Curley's penchant for fighting, his violent nature. His wife's loneliness, even when they are together, is transmitted in their separation, the lack of interaction. She is sitting on the porch, some distance from him, uninvolved and eating something out of a white bowl. She has no lines. Her dress is pale and nondescript. It is not provocative in any way (see figure 15.2). Curley's father, the boss, is the one who expresses irritation at the noise, wanting a stop to the racket. The scene ends, punctuated with a last blow to the punching bag. Though brief, the scene is not in the play or either of the earlier film versions. It does not advance the plot in any way. It serves to establish Curley as a boxer and its purpose may be to sensitize the audience to his brutality and his wife's isolation, foreshadowing Curley's pummeling of Lennie. Curley's wife is in the scene, but not part of it.

Further indication of the impact of the time of production on how Curley's wife is portrayed in the 1992 film is Foote's importation of the contemporary issue of wife-abuse. This is accomplished in another of the few instances where Foote does tamper with Steinbeck's plot by adding a scene that clearly conveys an image of this woman as victim, more sinned against than sinner. First Foote omits her most unappealing scene from the novel, the one where Curley's wife goes into Crooks' room and throws cold water on the men's dream of owning a place of their own. Left out is her threat of lynching. Gone is her derogatory depiction of the man as "a nigger, a dum-dum and a lousy ol' sheep" (78). Instead, Lennie and George come out of Crooks' room and encounter her in the yard, almost crying. Curley has gone to town after breaking all her records. Contemporary audiences, sensitive to wife-abuse, respond all too readily to her plaintive lament about her broken records. She had only four. Not only does Curley leave her alone, but also he destroys her means of entertaining herself. What else can she do but seek the company of others? And even those pitiful outcasts reject her. She runs crying from the yard. The addition of scenes like this and an earlier one where she and George have a quiet exchange in the barn, an exchange that is almost suggestive of a possible romantic connection, elicit our sympathy for her and soften the femme fatale nature of her character. An added heart-tugging touch is her naming of the records Curley broke. One is "Am I Blue?" A telling title.

How, then, if all three films add scenes to provoke our sympathy for Curley's wife, is the negative or dangerous side of her nature communicated? The ambiguous nature of the characterization is communicated in essentially time-coded ways, ways that play on recognized signals of the time of production. The semiotics of costume and make-up choices is particularly revealing.[7] In other words, the way the character is dressed is a sign or code by which we evaluate her in her specific cultural context.

The 1939 film's visual presentation of "Mae" falls clearly in the trampy category. When we first see her, she is in high-heeled sandal shoes and dark-toned hose. This speaks of her alienation from her setting. It is difficult to negotiate a barnyard in open-toed shoes and easily torn hosiery. In the farmhouse dinner scene, she is heavily made-up, with a big ring on her finger, wearing a low-cut dress, all signs of her attempts at appearing alluring. Her décolletage is emphasized when she pulls a movie flyer out of the bodice of her dress. In the visual codes of 1930s movie-making, nice women did not use their bras for storage purposes. Later, in another added farmhouse scene, she confronts Curley in a ruffled house robe, the slatternly presentation emphasized by an even wider décolletage and an inappropriate combination of jewelry and negligee. For her final departure and death scenes, the outfit is quintessential thirties tart: see-through net blouse, tight skirt, and high heels. A close-up shows penciled eyebrows, polished nails, and lots of cheap jewelry (see figure 15.3). She fits the cultural commonplace of her times that if a woman dressed a certain way, she was "asking for trouble." Hers is clearly the least sympathetic portrayal,

Figure 15.3. Curley's wife, 1939, 1981, 1992: The character's end or death.

but then, in the 1930s, society had more rigid standards by which women were judged. Mae's dress and make-up mark her. They are not appropriate for a good woman living on a farm.

The 1980s costuming of Cassie Yates is more ambivalent. Little in her costuming or actions communicates the sign of a "floozy." Only in her introductory scene is there some question of décolletage. At the dinner table, Mae is wearing a simple plaid cotton dress, with a few pieces of plastic jewelry. When she reaches into her bodice for the movie flyer, the action is not highlighted. Her costume for her least sympathetic scene, the one where she goes to Crooks' room to dash the men's dreams, is markedly contrary to any depiction of her as a tart or jail bait. Her outfit is almost school-marmish. She is wearing a blouse with a white-eyelet collar and a blue sweater, clothing appropriate for a farm wife (see figure 15.2). In the farmhouse confrontation with Curley, a little-girl hair ribbon offsets her ruffled house-robe. In the death scene, her departure dress is not provocative; it is plain, black, full-skirted, and except for the bare arms, appropriate for a funeral, ironically her own (see figure 15.3). No heavy make-up highlights her close-ups; her face is wistful and tender in the final moments of her presentation. She does, however, wear bright red nail polish. Since the scripts for the Milestone and Blake versions are almost identical, the marked changes in the way the character is made up and costumed lend credence to the impact of cultural changes in attitudes toward women. Her verbal and visual signs are sometimes incompatible, but in a postmodern age audiences are more comfortable with contradictory and conflicting images. She can look like a sweet farm wife and act like a harpy. It contributes to the complexity of the character.

The costuming in the 1992 production is also sometimes contradictory. After her initial bodice-enhancing dress, there is little that suggests either tart or tramp in the shape or color of the costume or the actions of the character. The dresses are mostly frumpy and formless. We encounter Curley's wife, in a barn scene, carrying a book, hardly the emblem of a floozy. This emphasizes the fact that there is more to her than just body. Her postures are often casual, careless. Her hair is long and natural looking; she is not "heavily made up" nor does she have red fingernails. She is a brunette, not a blonde; her voice is not "nasal and brittle," but soft and girlish. Barelegged rather than in black silk stocking, she carries a non-threatening coke bottle for her final encounter with Lennie. The color of her dress in her final scene is white, communicating her innocence. This is in keeping with the earlier added scenes that portray her more as victim than seductress. There is about her a strong evocation of a "little girl lost" (see figure 15.3). She is in flat shoes instead of high heels. The flat shoes connote girlishness. The first thing little girls do when they want to play grown up is don high heels. It is significant that the costuming and camera in the earlier versions focus on those high heels. The fact that she has wandered into the barn purposelessly highlights her "lost" quality. Mae, in the earlier versions, comes to the barn for a purpose—to get her puppy before she leaves.

Finally, contemporary sensibilities and audience expectations have significantly altered the portrayal of Lennie's killing of Curley's wife. Lennie barely gets to stroke her hair once before Betty Field's character is worrying that he will mess it up, telling him to stop. The camera eye is averted from the actual struggle; we see only his hand in her hair and then her feet in the air, the dropping of one of her high-heeled black shoes emblematic of her death. When he drops her in the straw, the camera withdraws from the scene, revealing only a partial view of her hip protruding through the hay. This is in marked contrast to the novel, where the narrative focus is on her dead face. Steinbeck's final narrative retrospective on her character presents Curley's wife in a more sympathetic light than elsewhere in the novel. Although he does use the adjective "meanness," the other words he uses to describe her have more to do with her unhappiness and desire for communication. She is also characterized as sweet and simple (90). None of this is conveyed in the 1939 film. The protruding hip maintains the sexualized view of the camera.

Blake's replication of the scene differs little from the Milestone version. The camera does hesitate a little longer on the action. We see Lennie's rough petting of the back of her head as she asks him not to mess it up. Again, we are shifted to her feet, this time in red high-heeled shoes. Television at the time of this filming still showed less graphic violence and overt sexuality than did the movies. In both versions, a hip is all we see of the dead body Lennie drops in the hay. Her sweetness is conveyed only in the close-up of her live face, earlier in the scene, prior to her allowing Lennie to stroke her hair. Our last image is still partial and not inspiring of further thought about her aborted dreams.

Contemporary audiences, on the other hand, have become increasingly desensitized to violence and brutality, especially in the movies. Sex and mayhem, which were only suggested or symbolized in earlier films, are all too graphically depicted on today's big and little screens. Sinise's 1992 version lingers on the death scene, amplifying not only the violence, but also the sexual tension of the interaction. If she has been presented in a more sympathetic method earlier in this film, in this scene, the camera eye objectifies her in a near-prurient manner. She and Lennie are presented as much more intimately involved. Rather than beginning side by side as in the earlier films, they are face to face. The scene is played slowly. She responds to his petting, there is a sensual quality to their interaction as she assures him "I like it too. It feels nice." This addition implicates her more in what follows. When the scene suddenly turns violent, the camera does not avert its eye. We see her full body struggle, her bare kicking legs, her dress hiked up to her thighs. When Lennie drops her inert body, it is her feet we don't see. Instead the focus is her backside, dress pulled up, slip showing, the camera moving directly into her.

In her most recent materialization, Curley's wife is, in Vincent Canby's words, "sort of sweet and none too bright, which is politically correct." She is less blameworthy and more a victim. Jack Garner also registers the change in her characterization, crediting Sinise and Foote with making her "a more complex and sympathetic character, a lonely, warm-hearted woman whose goal is more friendship than seduction." But, if she is a more sympathetic character, in terms of plot, she is made less relevant to the main themes of loneliness and brotherhood, less an actor in the theme of aborted dreams. Since she is not leaving Curley and the farm, carrying a coke bottle to the barn rather than a suitcase, she does not achieve the same tragic status as the men. She is not fleeing to pursue her dream. She is less actor than acted upon. She does not confront Curley as her predecessors did. She is just there, going nowhere, to blame only because she is soft and appealing.

What are we to deduce, then, from the examples of these time-bound presentations of Curley's wife? There is no single answer. The actresses who play the role look progressively younger and their clothing and makeup are less suggestive of the conventional film vamp. Also, as the actresses become younger, the hardness inherent in the earlier portrayals is lost. But, even the words "floozy" and "tart" are now culturally anachronistic. The progressively less provocative costuming can also be the result of changing societal mores about dress. In the courts, the rationale that women invite trouble by the way they dress is no longer acceptable. Sherilynn Fenn does not need costuming or make-up to transmit sexual tension. In this post-Lolita era, her very childlike demeanor and voice project their own sexual message. The contradictions and ambiguity in the character inherent since her conception continue.

Some of these contradictions derive from the conflict between what is still a male-centered and male-driven cinema, what B. Ruby Rich calls "Cinema of the Fathers," and a less homogeneous audience.[8] The audience, both male and female, for the 1939 version could be expected to share the cultural codes of the time, whereas the audiences for the most recent versions are less likely to view the film from a unified perspective. Today's audiences must wrest meaning out of the struggle and negotiation between competing frames of reference.[9] Nevertheless, male gaze continues to dominate the camera in the 1990s as it did in the original film and Steinbeck's text.[10] Curley's wife, named or not, is still circumscribed by her position in relation to the men—a wife to Curley, a danger to the men. Though she struggles to define herself as subject, she remains object. If there is anything subversive in the text, as some commentators on her character have argued, it is still struggling to reveal itself. Oddly enough, in the most recent version, the one which should have been most influenced by contemporary cultural critique of woman as object, Curley's wife has even less subjectivity than her earlier manifestations. In the two earliest versions, she is at least shown as challenging Curley's authority, taking a step toward being the subject of her own text. This challenge, plus giving her a name and the added farmhouse scene provide the character some depth and more presence in the story of the earlier versions. Trapped within the patriarchal structure, she asserts herself, struggling to escape. Paradoxically, in the 1990s version, when the women in the audience have enlarged their personal and professional spheres, Curley's wife is more circumscribed than ever. Nameless, unassertive, and purposeless, she is, with a contemporary nod to her victimhood, considerably reduced. Myra Macdonald has noted that in Hollywood movies, woman is usually "put in her due place in the patriarchal order by the end of the film" (27). In the novel, as in the film versions, the threat woman presents is nullified by destroying her. Having done this, the 1990s script allows the camera a final violation as it moves phallically into her backside.

216

Of Mice and Men has become a classic in our culture and one characteristic of dramatic classics is that they contain characters who invite endless new portrayals, characters who present challenges for each new generation of actors. What else accounts for the numerous film versions of *Hamlet*, just in our generation? And while I don't mean to suggest any analogy between Curley's wife and Hamlet, they both embody puzzles for their interpreters. Steinbeck understood the sexual objectification of this character, her limitations in a masculine society. He explained to Claire Luce that "No man has ever considered her as anything except a girl to try to make" (Steinbeck and Wallsten 154). "It's a devil of a hard part," he concluded, and time has validated his description. In his final view of her, lying dead in a half-covering of yellow hay, the narrator of Steinbeck's novel observes: "the plannings and the discontent and the ache for attention were all gone from her face. She was very pretty and simple, and her face was sweet and young" (90). In death, Steinbeck acknowledges her aborted agency, focusing the narrative eye on her positive characteristics. The camera eye has not been that respectful. In the first two versions, once dead, she is gone, her only function to move the plot to it inexorable conclusion. In the most recent version, while the meanness and the planning are both gone from her character, so is any sense of agency. The problem of Curley's wife, present since her inception, has not been solved. In the medium of film as on stage and in text, she remains an interpretative puzzle and challenge.

Notes

1. Judith Crist was a guest for a film festival at the University of Texas at El Paso in the early eighties. We were discussing Boorman's *Excalibur* when she made this observation to me. Since that time, whenever I am watching a period piece, I am struck by the perspicacity of her remark. It seems particularly apt in terms of this text.

2. My thanks to Albert Wong for making the illustrative drawings, taken from relevant scenes in the videos of these three productions. Though I would have liked to reproduce stills from the films, permission costs are prohibitive.

3. One marked difference is the addition of the character of Aunt Clara who is only spoken about in the Milestone original and in Steinbeck's text. In the Blake version, a scene where George and Lennie visit with Aunt Clara comes early in the script. The scene illustrates the close bond between the dissimilar men.

George tries to leave Lennie with Aunt Clara, but cannot. E. Nick Alexander is given credit for the teleplay.

4. Marilyn Monroe was the prototype for a new kind of sex-goddess. Unlike her femme fatale predecessors, Marilyn projected a wraithlike image. She looked seductive and voluptuous, even hard, but the minute she opened her mouth, she communicated helplessness and vulnerability. One of her signature songs was her sensuous rendition of "My Heart Belongs to Daddy." Gloria Steinem comments on the critical praise Monroe elicited for acting "babyishly seductive." *Marilyn* (New York: Henry Holt, 1986), 119.

5. Ruth P. Rubinstein, *Dress Codes* (Boulder: Westview Press, 1995), 119. In her chapter on seductive imagery, Rubinstein notes that in the 1800s and 1900s sexual liaisons between older men and young females were satirized and discouraged, but that in the 1950s "the vulnerable look" as an alluring image initiated by men was legitimized. (118–19). Audrey Hepburn, whose body was adolescent and boyish, was seen as a seductive ideal. The baby doll look was the accompanying fashion. Rubinstein also notes that since the 1950s our society has "sexualized the 'childlike' look" (121). The globalization of this infantilization of sexuality is further evidenced by a story from Japan: "A Plain School Uniform Is the Latest Aphrodisiac," *New York Times*, 2 April 1997: A4. This story reports that schoolgirl uniforms is the latest turn-on for Japanese businessmen who frequent the brothels in Tokyo.

6. "True Obsessions: Being Unfaithful to 'Lolita'," *Chronicle of Higher Education*, 24 July 1998: B 7–8.

7. Rubinstein defines clothing semiotics as a "language" of clothing derived from "the storehouse of images," in our Western history and "significant only when used in a specific social context" (7).

8. B. Ruby Rich, "In the Name of Feminist Film Criticism," in *Multiple Voices in Feminist Film Criticism*, ed. Diane Carson, Linda Dittmar, Janice R. Welsch (Minneapolis: University of Minneapolis Press, 1994), 28.

9. Christine Gledhill, "Image and Voice: Approaches to Marxist-Feminist Film Criticism," in Carson, Dittmar, and Welsch, *Multiple Voices in Feminist Film Criticism*. Gledhill also argues that films present us with a version of woman that we, as female spectators must reject because of the "ideology privileged as the film's 'message'" (115).

10. Laura Mulvey, "Visual Pleasure and Narrative Cinema," *Screen* 16 (Autumn 1975): 6–18. Mulvey's influential article established the priority that classic American film gives to the male perspective, both narratively and visually. She shifted the questions of gender in film from the representations on the screen to the psychodynamic between spectator and screen.

Works Cited

Canby, Vincent. "New Facets Highlighted in a Classic," *New York Times*, 2 October 1992, Weekend: C5.

Garner, Jack. "'Of Mice and Men' Touches the Heart," *Gannett News Service*, 15 October 1992.

Gledhill, Christine. "Image and Voice: Approaches to Marxist-Feminist Film Criticism." In *Multiple Voices in Feminist Film Criticism*, ed. Diane Carson, Linda Dittmar, Janice R. Welsch, 109–23. Minneapolis: University of Minneapolis Press, 1994.

Macdonald, Myra. *Representing Women: Myths of Femininity in the Popular Media*. London: Edward Arnold, 1995.

Mulvey, Laura. "Visual Pleasure and Narrative Cinema." *Screen* 16 (Autumn 1975): 6–18.

"A Plain School Uniform is the Latest Aphrodisiac." *New York Times*, 2 April 1997, A4.

Rich, B. Ruby. "In the Name of Feminist Film Criticism." In *Multiple Voices in Feminist Film Criticism*, ed. Diane Carson, Linda Dittmar, Janice R. Welsch, 27–47. Minneapolis: University of Minneapolis Press, 1994.

Rubinstein, Ruth P. *Dress Codes*. Boulder: Westview Press, 1995.

Steinbeck, Elaine and Robert Wallsten, eds. *Steinbeck: A Life in Letters*. New York: The Viking Press, 1975.

Steinbeck, John. *Of Mice and Men*. 1937. New York: Penguin Books, 1993.

Steinem, Gloria. *Marilyn*. New York: Henry Holt, 1986.

"True Obsessions: Being Unfaithful to 'Lolita.'" *Chronicle of Higher Education*, 24 July 1998: B 7–8.

CHAPTER SIXTEEN

DEADLY KIDS, STINKING DOGS, AND HEROES: THE BEST LAID PLANS IN STEINBECK'S *OF MICE AND MEN*

Louis Owens

I n 1950, the eminent American man of letters Edmund Wilson dismissed Steinbeck's *The Grapes of Wrath* by writing, "it is as if human sentiments and speeches had been assigned to a flock of lemmings on their way to throw themselves into the sea" (42). Thirty years later, in a *New York Times* hatchet job on Steinbeck that masqueraded as a review of two new Steinbeck biographies by Jackson Benson and Thomas Kiernan, Roger Sale launched what the reviewer must have considered a definitive strike against Steinbeck's literary reputation, declaring that Steinbeck "seems a writer without a source of strength," and sneering, "there is a story to be told here, which would stress how hollow Steinbeck's dreams were, and how much he did with the little gift he had" (10). There have been a few champions of Steinbeck's writing among academic and popular critics, such as Malcolm Cowley, who wrote of *The Grapes of Wrath*, "A whole literature is summarized in this book and much of it is carried to a new level of excellence" (qtd. in Owens *Re-vision* 128), but voices such as Cowley's have been in the minority to say the least, and seldom found in the better universities.[1]

And the overriding damnation has been one of sentimentality. Alfred Kazin, in 1956, indicated Steinbeck for "moral serenity" and "calculated sentimentality" (qtd. in Hadella 19). Edwin Berry Burgum accused Steinbeck's values of being "paralyzed in the apathy of the sentimental" (qtd. in Hadella 20).

Previously published in *Steinbeck Studies*, Fall 2002, 1–8. Used by permission of the Martha Heasley Cox Center for Steinbeck Studies.

A writer with such indestructible international popularity as Steinbeck deserves, perhaps, a closer scrutiny to see if such criticism is valid. Is Steinbeck guilty of "moral serenity and calculated sentimentality"? If so, then his popularity is perhaps easily explained by the mass of reader's collective appetite for the simple and sentimental, a reality of lowbrow literary consumerism academic critics like to infer if not quite pronounce in the more egalitarian late twentieth and early twenty-first centuries. If not, then is there more to his craft than Kazin and Wilson and company, along with the academy, have been inclined to notice?

Of Mice and Men is an ideal subject for such scrutiny, for despite being a Book of the Month Club selection and best seller still read in virtually every high school in America, and, with minimal adaptation by Steinbeck, winner of the New York Drama Critics' Circle Award as the best stage production of 1937, this novella has been a particular target for critics who decry sentimentality in literature. Typical is Freeman Champney, who, in the *Antioch Review*, declared that "*Of Mice and Men* is little else besides a variation on the theme 'every man kills the thing he loves'" (qtd. in Hadella 20).

Of Mice and Men was written to be simultaneously a readable play and a stageable novel, an experiment that Steinbeck himself described as "a tricky little thing designed to teach me to write for the theater" (Steinbeck and Wallsten 132). The tricky little novel was first performed directly from the text, with no playscript, by the Theatre Union in San Francisco in the spring and summer of 1937 and then, after being adapted for stage by Steinbeck and George S. Kaufman, opened on Broadway in November 1937, with 80 percent of the novel's lines going into the playscript unchanged. The novel's protagonists, George and Lennie, are itinerant farm workers who travel around together. George is small, wiry, rough, and smart, while Lennie is a powerful giant with the intellectual and social development of a toddler. George takes care of Lennie, Lennie works hard for the two of them, and together they share a dream that creates a deep bond, the dream of owning their own farm and no longer being alienated from the product of their work or from themselves.

The cast of the novel, in addition to the dual protagonists, is simple. At the top of the ranch hierarchy is "the boss," who makes only a marginal appearance. In the novel, this character is referred to only as "the boss," with no further explanation, but in the playscript Steinbeck underscores the boss's position by having George ask, "Boss the owner?" to which the old swamper, Candy, replies, "Naw! Superintendent. Big land company" (Hadella 65). Next in line is the boss's bad son, Curley, who suffers from a clichéd little-man's complex and wants to beat up big guys. Also living in the ranch's big house is Curley's wife, who yearns pathetically for meaningful recognition as a human being and therefore drives Curley mad with fear he will lose his most valued possession. The ranch foreman, Slim, is an omnipotent and omniscient sort of Nietzschean superman, who, as Steinbeck writes,

> . . . moved with a majesty only achieved by royalty and master craftsmen. He was a jerkline skinner, the prince of the ranch. . . . There was a gravity in his manner and a quiet so profound that all talk stopped when he spoke. His authority was so great that his word was taken on any subject, be it politics or love . . . His hatchet face was ageless. He might have been thirty-five or fifty. His ear heard more than was said to him, and his slow speech had overtones not of thought, but of understanding beyond thought. His hands, large and lean, were as delicate in their action as those of a temple dancer. (33–34)

At one point, George looks at Slim and sees "the calm, Godlike eyes fastened on him" (40). Slim, as Steinbeck writes him, calls to mind Nietzche's description of ubermensch Goethe, a man who has "disciplined himself into wholeness, [who] created himself" and became "the man of tolerance, not from weakness but from strength . . . a spirit who has *become free*" (Kaufman[2]). Throughout the novel, Slim is depicted in near priestly terms. He appears to represent infinite justice and wisdom and is an ascetic, beyond sex, beyond temptation by Curley's wife, Curley's violence, or the ordinary weaknesses of life. Unlike all of the other characters, he seems unaffected by loneliness or the transcendent homesickness that haunts the novel. Slim is also the familiar American cowboy hero: solitary, stoic, above common needs and desires, serving out justice from his godlike, intuitive sense of right and wrong.

Next in the apparent hierarchy of the ranch is Carlson, a powerfully built and surly subordinate to Slim. Then comes Candy, an aging and crippled farmhand on the verge of being utterly useless, and Crooks, the Black stable hand with a twisted back and properly bitter perspective on the white world surrounding him. On this California farm George and

Lennie's dream takes a cropper when Lennie kills Curley's wife and in a final, intensely lachrymose scene, George shoots his best friend while intoning the words of their shared dream. We all cry. It's a heart-breaking, sentimental story.

In this reading of *Of Mice and Men*, George and Lennie share an impossible dream, on the one hand a version of the Jeffersonian agrarian dream of a piece of land—the American Dream—but more significantly a dream of brotherhood in a fallen world where we are all the children of Cain marked for our sins and set against one another in this last place to the east of the lost Eden. In a fallen Garden where men and women drift past one another alone and infinitely lonely, George and Lennie at least have each other, and together they symbolize humanity's inescapable need to be connected, to touch another human being profoundly in some inarticulate way. George and Lennie have what Curley's wife, Candy, and Crooks all long for: meaningful human contact, something like love. When George shoots Lennie, George is not only killing his dream, but more importantly he is acting as his brother's keeper, making the ultimate, and ultimately heroic, gesture of sacrifice and responsibility. As I wrote in my 1985 book, *John Steinbeck's Re-Vision of America*, "Cain's question is the question again at the heart of this novel: 'Am I my brother's keeper?' And the answer . . . is an unmistakable confirmation" (101). Slim, the God-like foreman of the ranch, validates George's heroic action when he sits down close to George and says, "You hadda, George, I swear you hadda" (107).

In this reading of the novel, Lennie may be read as something like a primal innocent, as Slim suggests when he tells George, "He's jes' like a kid, ain't he," and George answers, "Sure he's jes' like a kid. There ain't no more harm in him than a kid neither, except he's so strong" (43). Curley's wife tells Lennie, "You're nuts. . . . But you're a kinda nice fella. Jus' like a big baby" (90), and half a page later we read, "And then she was still, for Lennie had broken her neck" (91). Candy sums it up when they find her body: "He's such a nice fella. I didn't think he'd do nothing like this" (95). Lennie dies because he can't function in society. All he seeks is the same thing everyone seeks: human connection, warmth. This is what drives every character in the book, including poor Curley's wife. Pathos results from the novella's illumination of our human inability to transcend aloneness and loneliness.

In this reading, George is the modernist hero, the little man who makes the only gesture of control possible by sacrificing what he will lose anyway. . . . Readers love a good heart-rending in fiction. Thus read, this novel might well strike many of us as what Alfred Kazin called "calculated sentimentality" designed to leave its readers emotionally moved but certainly not intellectually or morally challenged (309). If this were the only story here, we would be forced to surrender Steinbeck to the anti-sentimental mob storming the literary castle. But there are other more interesting novels to be found in *Of Mice and Men*.

A non-teleological reading of *Of Mice and Men* can evoke a quite different kind of story, not a sentimental one at all. In *The Log from the Sea of Cortez* (published originally in 1941 as *Sea of Cortez*), Steinbeck and his friend Edward F. Ricketts define what they called non-teleological thinking as a non-causal and non-blaming viewpoint (110). Steinbeck had begun to investigate this kind of viewpoint as early as his second novel, *To a God Unknown* (1933), and he had developed it further in *The Pastures of Heaven* (1932) and *In Dubious Battle* (1936). His method of incorporating non-teleological thinking into his fiction in the first two of these works was to construct surface plots that lead the reader to draw erroneous teleological conclusions: in *To a God Unknown*, Joseph Wayne sacrifices himself and brings rain to a parched land; in *Pastures*, there is a curse that destroys lives in an Eden-like valley.

Steinbeck's working title for *Of Mice and Men* was "Something That Happened." Reading the novel through this title, in a non-blaming or non-causal way, Lennie's murder of Curley's wife and his death at George's hands are part of something that just happens. No one is to blame. The brutal facts are that Lennie Small was born too small in mental and emotional range and too large in physical dimension and that he is dangerous. It is not Lennie's fault that he kills mice, puppies, and vulnerable young women. He is incapable of the kind of control that would prevent such awful things from happening because he was born that way. He is indeed a "baby" or a "kid," and he ain't mean. But he's dangerous. In this reading, Lennie is an accident of nature, born with something missing. No one is to blame for the fact that Lennie kills things, and no one is to blame for Lennie's inability to survive within society. Society is not to blame when it rids itself of that which endangers it. It's a simple thing, not a tragedy. There's nothing more terrifying to contemplate than a giant toddler set loose upon the world. If they'd gotten the dream farm, Lennie would have killed the rabbits. He would have killed the neighbors.

The opening and closing scenes of *Of Mice and Men* are nearly identical. Each scene takes place beside a pool in the Salinas River, as evening is coming on. In the opening scene, two men—George and Lennie—walk down a trail to the pool. In the final scene, two men—George and Slim—walk up the same trail away from the pool. In both scenes, a little snake with a periscope head swims across the still pool. There seems to be perfect balance between beginning and end; nothing has really changed. However, in the novel's final scene, a heron stands motionless in the pool, and "A silent head and beak lanced down and plucked the water snake out by the head, and the beak swallowed the little snake while its tail waved frantically" (99). We cannot read tragedy into the little snake's frantic death, just as we should not read tragedy into Lennie's death. That's just the way life is. A paragraph after the demise of the water snake, we find that "Another little water snake swam up the pool, turning its periscope head from side to side" (100). Just as one little snake replaces another, Slim has replaced Lennie as George's friend, and surely Slim will be a more practical friend than the lumbering, deadly Lennie. Nothing has really changed. Something happened, that's all. Steinbeck has carefully neutralized the lachrymose sentimental-ism of the previous reading.

Critics have offered other readings of this novel, including quite persuasive Jungian analyses. Steinbeck was acquainted with Joseph Campbell, who had hung out at Ricketts's laboratory on Cannery Row and even read and commented upon a draft of *To a God Unknown*—undoubtedly affecting revision of that wasteland novel—and Steinbeck read Jung and even wrote a cleverly Jungian story called "The Snake." It is not difficult at all to read Lennie as George's "shadow-self" and Curley's wife his "anima" in Jungian terms, as critics have done (Hadella 52–55). At the same time, it is hard to avoid a socio-political reading of this novel that falls between Steinbeck's exploration of Communist Party organized labor strife in *In Dubious Battle* and the great call for social change that would be *The Grapes of Wrath*. In such a reading, the ranch is a microcosm of capitalist America. The boss is not the owner but a superintendent. The novel's characters are nothing more than capital used to generate profit. Slim is a version of Owen Wister's famous Virginian, a factotum who implements the will of the corporate owners. The ranch hands are used up, and when they are no longer useful, like Candy's dog, they are disposed of.

Crooks, the Black "stable buck" as he's called, is an animated reminder of America's slave-holding economy, his twisted back evidence of the human cost of that economy. The fact that Crooks's family once possessed a farm identical to the dream-farm George and Lennie yearn for underscores his commonality with these men who are fodder for the machine, but the volume of the California civil code for 1905 that sits on Crooks's shelf testifies to his awareness of difference. Just as Candy expects to be fired soon because of his age and lost hand—a significant liability for someone who is a "hired hand"—Crooks will soon be disposed of because of his age and damaged back. Crooks links his fate to that of Candy's dog when he says, "They say I stink. Well, I tell you, you all of you stink to me" (68), and he does the same for Lennie when he tells him that if George doesn't come back, "They'll tie ya up with a collar, like a dog" (72). Should we miss this message of bondage, Steinbeck fills the novel with the rattling of halter chains from offstage.

Curley's nameless wife, with her "sausage" curls and red "mules," (31) is defined as property, nameless except as property. "Well, ain't she a looloo?" (51) one of the ranch hands says, and we should not be surprised to find that the foreman's puppy-producing dog is called Lulu. Curley's wife is equated with the other chattel of the ranch, including the most powerless of the workers. It is Curley's wife who unconsciously clarifies Lennie's value in this world when she calls him a "Machine." Lennie is a profit-making machine, valuable until it malfunctions, when it must be gotten rid of. In this reading, George "uses" Lennie, and there is a hierarchy of those who use and are used.

Thus far, we can legitimately find not only the sentimental novel critics have decried, but also a Jungian novel critics have delighted in probing, and a very political novel befitting Steinbeck's reputation as social critic or author of what has been erroneously called social realism. There is, however, yet a still more interesting reading of this little novel, a reading that begins to open up when we consider the various deaths that punctuate the story.

The first victims we became aware of are the puppies that Slim drowns. In Slim's first scene, we learn that his bitch, Lulu has "slung" nine pups the night before, as he puts it. "I drowned four of 'em, right off," he tells George. "She couldn't feed that many. . . . I kept the biggest" (*OMM* 35). Immediately, Carlson begins agitating for Slim to give Candy one of the pups so that they can shoot Candy's old dog. "That dog of Candy's is so God damn old," Carlson says, "he can't hardly walk. Stinks like hell, too" (36). It becomes quickly apparent that Candy's dog's major sin is stinking. "I can smell that dog a mile away" (36), Carlson complains, adding later, "He don't have no fun. . . . And he stinks to beat hell" (45). To give his argument the kind of humanitarian bent euthanasia proponents prefer, he says, "Well, you ain't bein' kind to him keepin' him alive" (45). Despite Carlson's argument, there is no evidence that the old dog is unhappy or suffering terribly as he lies faithfully by Candy's bed. The truth is he's simply an annoyance—he stinks—and he's too old to be useful, though we're told that he was a great sheep dog in his prime.

Carlson turns to the God-like Slim for the final judgment, and Steinbeck writes, "The skinner had been studying the old dog with his calm eyes. 'Yeah,' he said. 'You can have a pup if you want to. . . . Carl's right, Candy. That dog ain't no good to himself. I wisht somebody'd shoot me if I got old an' a cripple'" (45). It isn't difficult to imagine how Candy, who is old and crippled himself, might be wondering if Slim will shoot him next. To make sure the reader places ultimate responsibility for the dog's fate with Slim, Steinbeck adds, "Candy looked helplessly at him, for Slim's opinions were law" (45). Then again, just before the dog is led away for execution, Steinbeck writes, "Candy looked a long time at Slim to try to find some reversal. And Slim gave him none" (47).

We don't have to accept Slim's rationale for drowning four puppies. Of course, the mother could have fed all nine, since dogs have been doing such things for millennia. However, had Slim allowed nine to live, the biggest and most valuable of the litter might not have become even bigger and more valuable. Slim was simply practicing a kind of Social Darwinism, assisting natural selection. And, of course, we don't have to accept either Carlson's or Slim's rationale for the execution of Candy's dog. The old dog was simply unproductive and unpleasant, an impediment to the smooth functioning of the bunkhouse and ranch society. There are other unproductive and therefore relatively valueless inhabitants of the ranch, of course, as Curley's wife suggests when she enters Crooks's room after Curley and George and the others have gone to town. Looking at Lennie and Candy and Crooks, she says, "They left all the weak ones here" (77). The fact that she, too, has been left behind and is drawn to the light of Crooks's room implicates her profoundly in this company of the doomed.

No one who reads *Of Mice and Men* can possibly miss the parallels between the shooting of Candy's dog and Lennie's execution by George. Steinbeck first makes sure that Carlson describes exactly how he will shoot the old dog and then shows George shooting Lennie in exactly the same way with the same gun. The unmistakable message is that dog and man are both annoyances and impediments to the smooth working of the ranch. One stinks and one kills too many things. But why shoot Lennie, with precisely the same weapon in precisely the same way? One reading would have us believe that Lennie's death is inevitable or that George is saving Lennie from a fate worse than death. When the body of Curley's wife is discovered, Slim tells George, "I guess we gotta get 'im" (97). George pleads with body language against what is implicit in Slim's words. Steinbeck writes, "George stepped close. 'Couldn' we maybe bring him in an' they'll lock him up?'" (97). But just as he would give Candy's dog no reprieve, Slim denies George this hope, replying, "An' s'pose they lock him up an' strap him down and put him in a cage. That ain't no good, George" (97). Clearly, Slim is telling George that Lennie has to die. He is making the decision that Lennie is better off dead, just as he did with Candy's dog. Siim is playing God.

Of Mice and Men is an extraordinarily efficient and carefully crafted little book in which every word, every sound, every nuance matters from the off-stated clanging of horseshoes to the slant of light across the bunkhouse doorway. However, one glaring bit of questionable writing stands out. Why, one wonders, does Steinbeck feel it necessary to repeat the name of Carlson's gun so many times? When Carlson offers to shoot the old dog, Candy says hopefully, "You ain't got no gun." Carlson replies, "The hell I ain't. Got a Luger" (47). Later, after they find Curley's wife's body, Carlson says, "I'll get my Luger." Then on the same page, Steinbeck writes, "Carlson came running in. 'The bastard's stole my Luger,' he shouted" (97). Fourteen lines later, Curley says, "He got Carlson's Luger" (98). Six pages later, when George shoots Lennie, we read, "He reached in his side pocket and brought out Carlson's Luger . . ." (105). Why repeat the name of the gun five times in such rapid succession that the repetition stands out glaringly?

To refresh my memory about the dangers and uses of repetition, I consulted James A. Hefferman and John E. Lincoln's *Writing: A College*

Handbook, a text I used in a classroom at UC Davis in 1982 and for some unfathomable reason still have on my shelves. Looking up "repetition" in the index, I found this:

> How do you emphasize your main point? . . . the two most important ways of emphasizing a point are repetition and arrangement. . . . You may have been told that you should never repeat a word or phrase when you write, that you should scour your brain or your thesaurus for syn- onyms to avoid using a word or phrase again. This is nonsense. If rep- etition gets out of control, it will soon become monotonous and boring. But selective repetition can be highly useful. . . . This selective repetition keeps the eye of the reader on the writer's main point. (108–9)

Why would Steinbeck want to keep the reader's eye on not just a gun but specifically a Luger pistol? The Luger has an interesting history. As a gun-collector's note puts it, "Without a doubt, the Luger semiautomatic pistol is one of the most famous firearms of the twentieth century." And, of course, it is famous for its association with the German military in both World War I and World War II. The Luger pistol was named for its designer, George Luger, in Karlsruhe, Germany, at the end of the nineteenth century. Following modification, the 1904 Luger became the weapon of choice for the German Navy and Army; and after 1904 "German military sales accounted for the vast majority of Lugers ever produced" ("History" n.p.). "The Luger was the standard German side arm throughout World War I. Luger production continued sporadically during the post-war period, in part due to restrictions on German arms manufacture imposed by the Treaty of Versailles. The allies permitted official production to begin [again] in 1925 at Simson and Company. Simson, however, was owned by Jews, and the company was liquidated when the Nazis came into power. The Luger manufacturing machinery was purchased by Krieghoff. Mauser purchased . . . Luger manufacturing machinery in 1929, and produced Lugers until the later part of World War II" (Chapman n.p.).

Here is a professional description of this famous gun:

> The Luger is a fairly complicated pistol, requiring quite a bit of precision hand-fitting to manufacture, and tight tolerances between parts. These things contribute to its accuracy, but detract from reliability. Even for its

time, the Luger was considered complex, expensive, large, and powerful. The factors limited civilian sales' especially given the ubiquity of small, cheap Browning-style pistols. Ultimately, even for military applications, more reliable and cheaper pistols replaced it. Even a little dirt on the exposed parts of the firing mechanism on the left side can cause failure to function. (Chapman n.p.)

Why would a ranch hand own such a delicate and expensive gun and keep it under his bunk? It would very likely have been a trophy from World War I, though there's nothing to indicate that Carlson is a veteran, and the novel contains no allusions to that war. It seems likely that Steinbeck wanted to associate Carlson and the gun that kills both dog and man with Germany. If we pursue that line of thought, it is interesting to note that the name "Carl" not only echoes the name of the town in which the Luger was created, Karlsruhe, but also derives from the Old High German word "karal," a peasant or bondman ranking below a thane who carries out the will of "the boss" and Carlson the bondman, the churlish muscle of the ranch. Steinbeck, a student of old and middle English and translator of Malory's *Morte d'Arthur* to American English, and, as his biographer Jack Benson called him, a polymath, would very likely have known this. Steinbeck loved this kind of play in his fiction, as can be seen even in such a light book as the 1954 novella, *The Short Reign of Pippin IV*, where he places his protagonist in a house on Avenue de Marigny to subtly remind those of us who may happen to know the history of the name of Enguerrand de Marigny, the royal chamberlain and principal minister of finance to Phillip IV of France, the destruction of the Templars, all of which history plays a significant role in the deep structure of that novel (Owens "Deep Dissembler" 252). Steinbeck was a voracious reader, student of history, and sharp political observer.

It's probably obvious by now that I'm attempting to lead you toward the theme of eugenics and its association with fascism in this novel, a reading that may admittedly seem to stretch the fabric of the text a bit. But consider these questions and the pattern they suggest: Did Slim really have to drown those puppies? Did they really have to shoot Candy's dog? Did George really have to shoot Lennie? Slim's dog could have raised nine puppies, though they might have all been less impressive specimens. Candy's dog could have been given a bath and allowed to sleep in the bunkhouse, or Candy could have kept the old dog in the barn where only poor Crooks would have smelled him. Finally, as George suggests, there is no reason at all that Lennie could not have been locked up where he wouldn't be able to accidentally kill things. None of these deaths had the inevitability the novel pretends to imply.

In 1936, when Steinbeck was writing his experimental novella, most Americans did not know much about circumstances in Germany, even though the concentration camp at Dachau had opened as early as 1933, followed a few months later by Buchenwald. In July of 1933 the Nazis had passed a law allowing for the forced sterilization of those found by a Heredity Court to have genetic defects. In November of that same year, they passed a "Law against Habitual and Dangerous Criminals" allowing beggars, homeless, alcoholics, and the chronically unemployed to be interned in concentration camps. In June of 1935, laws were passed allowing for forced abortions to prevent hereditary diseases from being passed on. Meanwhile, outside of Germany, the Euthanasia Legalization Society, later to be called the Euthanasia Society, was founded in England in 1935, and the Euthanasia Society of America in 1938. Eugenics was very much in the air on both sides of the Atlantic at this time. According to Steinbeck biographer Jackson J. Benson, Steinbeck's fascination with the idea of what he called the "phalanx," or group-man, came partly "out of discussions with Ed [Ricketts] about the theories of W.C. Allee, the University of Chicago biologist" and that Steinbeck was also reading John Elof Boodin at the same time in the early thirties (267).[3] In the summer of 1933, Steinbeck showed a short essay entitled "Argument of Phalanx" to his friend Dick Albee, an essay articulating Steinbeck's concept of what he called "group-man." In his biography, Benson writes:

> In recalling the background for "Argument of Phalanx," Albee noted the importance of the fact that the early thirties was a time when mass movements were much discussed. . . . Many watched and discussed the progress of the Soviet Union and thought of it as a possible model, and at the same time, of course, Hitler was leading another mass socialist movement in Germany. There, strikes, veterans' marches, protest rallies, and other mass demonstrations were commonplace news. That Steinbeck was now keenly aware of all of this activity, at home and abroad, is clear from his many references to such movements in his letters of the

period. The transformation of Germany was perhaps one of the most dramatic contemporary examples available to Steinbeck, and he wrote Dook [Sheffield in 1933]: "Think of the impulse which has suddenly made Germany overlook the natures of its individuals and become what is has. Hitler didn't do it. He merely speaks about it." (269–70)

Nine days later, on June 30, 1933, Steinbeck would write to Sheffield to say,

The investigations have so far been gratifying. I find that in Anthropology, Doctor Ellsworth Huntington, in History and cultural aspects, Spengler and Ouspenski, in folk lore and in unconscious psychology, Jung, in economic phases of anthropology, Briffault, in biology, Allee, and in physics, Shondringer, Planck, Bohr, Einstein, Heisenberg have all started heading in the same direction. None has gone far, and none apparently is aware of the work of the others, but each one is headed in the same direction and the direction is toward my thesis. (Benson 270)

Obviously drawn to the subject by his growing obsession with his "phalanx" theory, Steinbeck was paying close attention to events in Europe in the early thirties, at a time when most Americans weren't aware of the darkest realities of Nazi Germany. We also know that Steinbeck had been reading not merely Darwin exhaustively but such writers as Boodin, W. C. Allee, Mark Braubard, William Emerson Ritter, and Ellsworth Huntington, all of whom deal with eugenics in their writings, even if only to repudiate it. Ritter, in his 1919 book *The Unity of the Organism*, goes so far as to blame German social Darwinists for World War I, while Huntington, in *Civilization and Climate* (1924), makes claims for racial superiority and, according to one critic, "issues a call to eugenic action" (Hearle 251). One critic, Kevin Hearle, finds the direct influence of the "racialized discourse" of these authors in Steinbeck's writings on the displaced migrants in California in the thirties, particularly in his 1938 essays collected as *Their Blood Is Strong*, which would lay the groundwork for *The Grapes of Wrath*.

Based on the reading we know he did, Steinbeck was clearly aware of the widespread eugenics movement, which as early as 1873 had seen a call in England for the "gifted class" to consider those of "inferior moral, intellectual, and physical qualities" as "enemies of the state" if these inferior classes continue to breed (Galton 89). And based on his awkward repetition of the word "Luger," in *Of Mice and Men*, it would seem that he wanted his reader to associate the supposed "mercy killings" of the novel with the rise of Fascism in Germany.

In the end, this reading takes us far afield from the sentimentalism of our first reading. This version of the novel is neither heart-breaking nor a coldly objective rendering of non-teleological reality, nor is it a call for social action to better the lives of American workers. Rather, in this version of the novel, Steinbeck is laying out a cautionary tale deeply engaged with the profound human crisis of his times. In *Of Mice and Men*'s final scene, George sits despondently beside his friend's body, and Steinbeck writes, "Slim came directly to George and sat down beside him, sat very close to him. 'Never you mind,' said Slim. 'A guy got to sometimes'" (104). Slim is clearly displacing Lennie who in the novel's opening scene sat "close to George." But more interestingly here, in Slim's words, Steinbeck removes the killing of Lennie from the status of an isolated event and places it in a pattern of behavior, something that a guy has to do sometimes, like the drowning of puppies or shooting of old dogs. After Slim once again validates George's action by saying, "You hadda, George. I swear you hadda," Slim adds, "Come on with me" (107), and the two walk up the same trail that George and Lennie had walked down in the novel's first scene.

I believe that when he says, "Come on with me," Slim is inviting George into a new belief system, an altered way of viewing the world. Aiming up the trail toward the highway, symbolically George and Slim are moving out into the world, a kind of prophet and apostle of a new order, as if George has come into Slim's world to be purged of what Lennie represents, changed, and sent forth to do God's work, as Slim defines it. There's not much sentimental about that particular story.

Notes

1. Louis Owens read this essay at UC Davis in the fall of 2001 and was scheduled to read it at the Steinbeck Centennial Conference at Hofstra University but poor health prevented him from attending. This essay was to be part of a larger work, a revision of his 1985 book on John Steinbeck. Before his death, he agreed to have this essay published in *Steinbeck Studies*. *Western American Literature* is publishing the essay jointly with *Steinbeck Studies*.

2. Louis Owens did not complete his notes before his death. We have been unable to locate the source of the Walter Kaufman references because he wrote numerous books about and translations of Nietzsche.

3. Benson points out that Steinbeck read reprints of Boodin lectures on such subjects as "The Existence of Social Minds" and "Functional Realism," as well as Boodin's books, *A Realistic Universe* and *Cosmic Evolution* and others later (268). Steinbeck would later ask Boodin for permission "to use some of his philosophy in his own work" (269). [Owens note]

Works Cited

Benson, Jackson J. *The True Adventures of John Steinbeck, Writer*. New York: Viking, 1984.

Chapman, Richard. "Firearm by Type." www.recguns.com/Sources/IIIC2ka.1.html

Galton, Francis. *Frazer's Magazine* 7 (1873); quoted in Peter Medawar and Jean Medawar. *Aristotle to Zoos: A Philosophical Dictionary of Biology*. New York: Oxford University Press, 1983.

Hadella, Charlotte Cook. *Of Mice and Men: A Kinship of Powerlessness*. New York: Twayne, 1995.

Hearle, Kevin. "There Are American People: The Spectre of Eugenics in *Their Blond Is Strong* and *The Grapes of Wrath*." In *Beyond Boundaries: Rereading John Steinbeck*, ed. Susan Shillinglaw and Kevin Hearle, 243–54. Tuscaloosa: University of Alabama Press, 2002.

Hefferman, James A., and John E. Lincoln. *Writing: A College Handbook*. New York: Norton, 1982.

"The History of the Pistole Parabellum." Luger Forum. Founded by John Chapman. 1988. www.lugerforum.com/history.html.

Kazin, Alfred. *On Native Grounds*. 1942. New York: Doubleday Anchor Books, 1956.

Owens, Louis. *John Steinbeck's Re-Vision of America*. Athens: University of Georgia Press, 1985.

———. "Steinbeck's 'Deep Dissembler': *The Short Reign of Pippin IV*." In *The Short Novels of John Steinbeck*, ed. Jackson J. Benson, 249–57. Durham: Duke University Press, 1990.

Sale, Roger. "Stubborn Steinbeck." *New York Times Book Review* 20 (March 1980): 10.

Steinbeck, Elaine and Robert Wallsten, eds. *Steinbeck: A Life in Letters*. New York: Viking, 1975.

Steinbeck, John. *The Log from the Sea of Cortez*. 1951. New York: Penguin, 1995.

———. *Of Mice and Men*. 1937. New York: Penguin, 1993.

Wilson, Edmund. *Classics and Commercials*. New York: Farrar, Straus & Company, 1950.

CHAPTER SEVENTEEN

READING THE CHARACTER OF CROOKS IN *OF MICE AND MEN*: A BLACK WRITER'S PERSPECTIVE

Charles Johnson

Got one face
For white folks to see,
Got another one
That's really me.

—Old Black American Folk Verse

Three generations of readers world-wide have recognized John Steinbeck to be a powerful storyteller, and I believe it can be argued that his short, haunting novel, *Of Mice and Men*, contributed to shaping our twentieth-century definitions for a modern, literary classic. During the Great Depression, it also presented a strong and influential indictment of racial segregation, for which Steinbeck is still praised today, and rightly so. I first encountered this story when I was a young, African-American reader, someone who was not armed in his teens with aesthetic theories or various critical methodologies for dissecting and interpreting fiction; and, at that time, I was not yet, of course, a novelist or a teacher of the craft of literary fiction for three decades. For the most part, the characters in *Of Mice and Men* are white males, with two very important exceptions: Curley's wife, who is central to the story's conflict, and a marginalized "stable buck" (*OMM* 20) who is referred to only as Crooks. It is this latter character I wish to reflect upon today, deeply and in detail.

I want to examine him in ways I was not equipped to do forty years ago, because his presence in this novel adds a great deal to its thematic power (Chapter Four is entirely framed around Crooks), yet his portrait presents something of a challenge for African-American readers, especially for young ones. This is not just a literary question. Rather, it is one of the most important cultural problems facing any multi-racial society. We recently saw just how vexing a problem it can be when Muslims world-wide reacted so violently to twelve cartoons depicting the prophet Muhammad first in the Danish press, then in newspapers throughout Europe and America. The issue is this: How do we—as artists and thinkers—portray the racial and cultural Other? Black Americans have by necessity always been acutely sensitive to the fictional portraits of themselves created by white Americans in the early twentieth century, even when those portraits are as historically important and sympathetically drawn as the one Steinbeck offers us in *Of Mice and Men.* Let me see if I can clarify what I mean by that statement.

All black Americans, and all people belonging to a racial and ethnic minority in a predominantly white society, must learn at a very early age to "read" all manner of phenomenon from the nuanced and polyvalent standpoint of a bi-fold consciousness. Lately, I have been calling this an "Aleph consciousness." I borrowed this term from Jorge Luis Borges' short story "The Aleph," where he describes the *aleph* as "the place where . . . all the places of the world, seen from every angle, coexist."[1] It is the first letter of the Hebrew alphabet, and of its shape Borges says that it "is that of a man pointing to the sky and the earth, to indicate that the lower world is the map and mirror of the higher."[2] From its vantage point, Borges says, one can see "simultaneous night and day."[3] Historically, black Americans, Asians, and Hispanics had to develop this epistemic skill, and doing so required a lot of work, because it was incumbent upon them to know the white curriculum and its assumptions as well—and as thoroughly—as the white students sitting beside them, approaching with openness and humility (and sometimes clenched teeth) all those works composed *by* whites *for* whites with people of color never really part of the author-audience equation. They learned momentarily to identify with (though not necessarily internalize) the themes, figures, and tropes of the racial Other, to absorb the products of the Greek and the Judaic, the Roman, French, and British, to emotionally empathize and project themselves *behind* the eyes of whites as diverse as Homer and the Beowulf poet, Goethe and Dostoyevsky, Virginia Wolfe and Sylvia Plath. For children of color, this has always been a matter of survival. They had to know how to "read" American society in at least two ways. First, in terms of what they knew about the enormous contributions African Americans have made to this country since the time of the seventeenth-century colonies, a knowledge received from other black people and from unrecorded stories transmitted by family members and friends, which until only recently were marginalized in our history books and in "mainstream" media. Secondly, they had to understand, as any social (or racial) outsider must, the cultural formations of a WASP society, because such intimate knowledge of the white Other was necessary for navigating successfully through America's institutions—schools, jobs, social situations, etc.

So forty years ago when I first read *Of Mice and Men*, I found endearing the relationship between the story's two main characters, George Milton and Lennie Small. I found myself identifying with and caring about them when George and Lennie imagine the American dream of owning their own farm, a place where they will be safe and happy, and no longer lost like other itinerant American workers during the Great Depression. "Guys like us, that work on ranches," George tells Lennie,

> are the loneliest guys in the world. They got no family. They don't belong no place. They come to a ranch an' work up a stake and then they go inta town and blow their stake, and the first thing you know they're poundin' their tail on some other ranch. They ain't got nothing to look ahead to. (*OMM* 13–14)

That statement by George, delivered so early in the novel, and echoed by other characters, is the existential premise or conflict—one of homelessness and loneliness—that shapes and directs the speech and actions of *every* character and situation that Steinbeck presents. As a conflict, this premise is universal and timeless, deriving its power from the fundamental human desire to escape the aloneness and apparent separateness we experience throughout life, replacing it with an idealized place or Promised Land one calls "home," where there is peace, love, and community. It was that premise that enchanted me so when I was a teenager, just as it does now, but because I identified with George and Lennie—as the author encouraged me to do—I did not forty years ago reflect deeply on how this universal theme of loneliness and homelessness appears differently, and reveals its most radical dimensions, when it is incarnated in the life of a black fictional character like Crooks.

Now, scores of writers have written about the themes of loneliness and homelessness. But what distinguishes Steinbeck, and is a sign of his genius, is that at the center of this story about the desire to find a home, he places the most famous and iconic portrait we have in American literature of a friendship between two men, who could not be more opposite, physically and mentally. As a teacher, I tell my apprentice writing students to take a close look at George and Lennie as perfect examples of the dramatic principle that states how "character is the engine of plot." However, as a philosopher, looking at the book four decades after I first experienced it, I would add that Steinbeck's rendition of the friendship between these two men dramatizes nicely Aristotle's description of *philia* in Books 8 and 9 of *Nicomachean Ethics*.

For Aristotle, "man is a political creature and one whose nature is to live with others."[4] Thus, the Greek term *philia* specifically refers not just to friendship but also to loyalty to family, the *polis* (one's political community), and one's discipline. When speaking of friendship between two people, Aristotle distinguishes three forms that this bond might take. The first is based on utility, in which case people "do not love each other for themselves but in virtue of some good which they get from each other."[5] The second form of friendship is based on pleasure and, like utility, Aristotle says, "it is not for their character that men love ready-witted people, but because they find them pleasant. Therefore those who love for the sake of pleasure do so for the sake of what is pleasant to *themselves*."[6] It is only the third form of friendship that is truest for Aristotle, and this is based on the good, on two people recognizing the virtue and character of each other. It is a partnership founded on equality, says Aristotle, and it is fulfilled when two friends live together.

Based on all we learn about George and Lennie, their friendship is clearly not founded on utility or pleasure, certainly not for George Milton, who in a moment of frustration, rages at Lennie:

> God a'mighty, if I was alone I could live so easy. I could go get a job an'
> work, an' no trouble. No mess at all, and when the end of the month

come I could take my fifty bucks and go into town and get whatever I want. Why, I could stay in a cat house all night. I could eat any place I want, hotel or any place, and order any damn thing I could think of. An' I could do all that every damn month. Get a gallon of whiskey, or set in a pool room and play cards or shoot pool. . . . An' whatta I got? I got you! You can't keep a job and you lose me ever' job I get. Just keep me shovin' all over the country all the time. An' that ain't the worst. You get in trouble. You do bad things and I got to get you out. . . . You crazy son-of-a-bitch. You keep me in hot water all the time. (*OMM* 11)

Rather than pleasure or utility, George's friendship with Lennie has brought him only suffering and self-sacrifice. Then why, one asks, does he travel with Lennie if his friend is that much trouble? The friendship between these two men is so curious and atypical for the time and place in which they live that two other characters in the story feel the need to address it, perhaps because they feel there may be a little bit of *eros*—or homosexual attraction—intermingled with *philia*. The boss on the ranch where they find employment says, "Well, I never seen one guy take so much trouble for another guy" (*OMM* 22). And a short time later, a jerk-line skinner named Slim remarks that,

Funny how you an' him string along together. . . . Hardly none of the guys ever travel together. I hardly never seen two guys travel together. You know how the hands are, they just come in and get their bunk and work a month, and then they quit and go out alone. Never seem to give a damn about nobody. It jus' seems kinda funny a cuckoo like him and a smart little guy like you travelin' together. (*OMM* 39)

But throughout *Of Mice and Men*, we are given evidence that the bond between George and Lennie is based entirely on character and virtue. For example, George will not allow Slim to call Lennie a "cuckoo": "He ain't no cuckoo,'" said George. "He's dumb as hell, but he ain't crazy. An' I ain't so bright neither, or I wouldn't be buckin' barley for my fifty and found'" (*OMM* 39). Slim agrees that Lennie is a "nice fellah" (*OMM* 40), and that he isn't "mean" (*OMM* 41). Earlier in the story, George pleads Lennie's case with the boss, insisting his friend is strong and a good worker. In other words, he is constantly vouching for Lennie's character. Yet a reader will find it difficult to believe this is a friendship between two equals. Rather, it more resembles the unequal friendship Aristotle describes when he speaks of the relationship between a father and a son, or an elder to someone younger, for in this case, "Each party, then, neither gets the same from the other, nor ought to seek it."[7] Steinbeck's narrative lets us know that there is a sense of unselfish duty involved in George's devotion to Lennie, primarily because he knew Lennie's Aunt Clara, who raised him, and, after Clara's death, he gradually took her place as Lennie's protector.

Steinbeck brings his odd couple to work at a ranch where social life is destabilized by two somewhat thinly drawn characters, the boss's son Curley, about whom we only are told that he likes to pick fights with men bigger than himself (like Lennie), and Curley's unhappy, flirtatious wife. This is a place best described by Slim when he says, "Maybe ever'body in the whole damn world is scared of each other" (*OMM* 35). His observation is reiterated later by Curley's wife, who says, "You're all scared of each other, that's what. Ever' one of you's scared the rest is goin' to get something on you" (*OMM* 77). At this ranch, everyone seems to live in fear of Others, and that makes friendships—and especially inter-racial ones—impossible. As characters, they lack ethnic definition or background; they are simply "white," not White Anglo Saxon Protestant or Italian or Irish or Polish or Jewish or Welsh or Slav—they are just generically "white," which is a decision by the author that obliterates the historical and religious antagonisms among different kinds of "white" people. Among them we see relationships only of utility. And the character most segregated from relationships with others is the curious man named Crooks.

If you look even glancingly at the literal plot in *Of Mice and Men*, you realize that Crooks is in no way instrumental to the causal sequence of events and actions that lead to George's tragic killing of Lennie at the novel's end. In fact, as far as storytelling is concerned, Crooks—as a performer—can be eliminated. But if Crooks is not essential to the story's plot, he *is* crucial for elaborating the story's theme. Given the details Steinbeck provides for Crooks throughout the novel, and especially in Chapter Four, it would seem that the stable buck would be the perfect candidate for an Aristotelian friendship with others based on his character, more ideal for such a partnership than even Slim, whom Steinbeck calls a majestic "prince of the ranch" (*OMM* 33) in the longest and most fantastic character sketch the novel contains.

I say this because one of the first things we learn about Crooks is that even though he has a crooked back (as his name implies) due to his having been kicked by a horse, he is a good fighter, and defeated a skinner named Smitty. He can throw horseshoes better than anyone else at the ranch, where he has the longest tenure, which Steinbeck says is due to his disability. When we first see him stick his head into the bunkhouse, where he is not permitted to sleep with the others, but where even dogs are allowed, his "lean Negro head" is "lined with pain," but in his eyes there is "patience" (*OMM* 50). Since he cannot go into town to visit Susy's cathouse, praised highly by the character Whit, we assume that Crooks is celibate, which is also a sign of his emasculation, or at least of a de-sexualization common among "positive" black characters created by white authors in the early twentieth century. (Think of the asexual roles played by Sidney Poitier in films of the 1950s and early '60s. In other words, a de-sexualized black male is no longer a threat.) Like Slim and Candy, he can read. In the harness room, where his bunk is located, he "had books . . . a tattered dictionary and a mauled copy of the California civil code for 1905" (*OMM* 67), but significantly there is no Bible, the one text we might expect to find in the home of a black person in the 1930s. The absence of a Bible in Crooks' room suddenly makes this reader aware of the absence in the novel of details that might point to a religious or spiritual life for *any* of the characters portrayed; and *that* reminds us, of course, that *Of Mice and Men* truly is a work of the modernist period in American literature, a period when many authors either downplayed, dismissed or omitted entirely the significance of religious faith in the lives of characters portrayed in fiction.

Only the ranch's boss and Slim, "the prince," have visited his lodgings until Chapter Four when he hesitantly invites Lennie and Candy inside to talk, which suggests that Slim, whose primary characteristic in the novel is kindness and empathy, is above the system of segregation on the ranch and perhaps recognizes something of value in Crooks. Naturally, we wonder, what did they talk *about*? Steinbeck does not tell us that. He describes Crooks as "a proud, aloof man" (*OMM* 67). As a boy, he played with white children on his father's ten-acre ranch, and he found "some of them was pretty nice" (*OMM* 70). On that California farm, says Crooks, there was no other black family for miles around, a situation similar to his life in Soledad, where he tells Lennie there is only one black family in the area. He says that "now there ain't a colored man on this ranch" (*OMM* 70), implying perhaps that during his long employment there were others in the past.

But those African Americans are gone, and Crooks generally has no one to talk to, black or white. More than all the other characters in *Of Mice and Men*, Crooks has thought philosophically about the epistemological meaning of loneliness, and about how inter-subjectivity is crucial for confirming the truth of our perceptions. In what I feel is one of the most important passages in the novel, Crooks says,

> A guy sets alone out here at night, maybe readin' books or thinkin' or stuff like that. Sometimes he gets thinkin', an' he got nothin' to tell him what's so an' what ain't so. Maybe if he sees somethin', he don't know whether it's right or not. He can't turn to some other guy and ast him if he sees it too. He can't tell. He got nothing to measure by. I seen things out here. I wasn't drunk. I don't know if I was asleep. If some guy was with me, he could tell me I was asleep, an' then it would be all right. But I jus' don't know. (*OMM* 73)

Now, compare this speech by Crooks to one made by phenomenologist Maurice Merleau-Ponty in his book, *Adventures of the Dialectic*:

> My own field of thought and action is made up of imperfect meanings, badly defined and interrupted. They are completed over there, in the others who hold the key to them because they see sides of things that I do not see, as well as, one might say, my social back. Likewise, I am the only one capable of tallying the balance sheets of their lives, for their meanings are also incomplete and are openings onto something that I alone am able to see. I do not have to search very far for the others; I find them in my experience, lodged in the hollows that show what they see and what I fail to see. Our experiences thus have lateral relationships of truth: all together, each possessing clearly what is secret to the other, in our combined functionings we form a totality which moves toward enlightenment and completion. . . . We are never locked in ourselves.[8]

Sadly, and because of racial segregation, Crooks *is* locked inside himself. Experientially, the Other is our mirror, our means for checking the validity of our perspective. This is true in social relations as well as in the method of science, which always begins with a first-person seeing of some phenomenon that must be confirmed by the perception of others. If lone-liness and homelessness are the central themes in *Of Mice and Men*, then Crooks, despite the minor role Steinbeck gives him in the novel, epito-mizes these experiences more completely than all the other characters, for as the descendent of slaves kidnapped in Africa, then brought against their will to America, his original home lies across the Atlantic ocean, and, in America during the 1930s, he is a second-class citizen denied a true home among whites.

Yet when Crooks mentions fondly his two brothers (*OMM* 73), a reader wonders why he apparently has no contact with them now. Or with his parents, if they are still alive. If he can read, one assumes he can write. Does he not correspond with his brothers, using *them*—as any black person would—as mirrors to check his perceptions of the dangerous racial world of the Great Depression? And what of the other black family in Soledad? Where do *they* socialize and worship? If they have such places for community, why can't Crooks find fraternity there? By remaining on this ranch, where he is treated so badly, Crooks *chooses* his own racial vic-timization each and every day.

The novel makes one intriguing reference to a Jap cook, who feeds the ranch hands and, we suppose, also provides meals for Crooks. Although this cook is never on stage in *Of Mice and Men*, a reader wonders if he, too, experiences the same loneliness and racial segregation as the stable buck. In two of the film adaptations, he does appear for a second or two and is like a prop in the background of dinner conversations between the white workers, serving them and then quickly disappearing. A reader naturally wonders if Crooks feels some comradeship with this unnamed Asian cook, who does not sleep in the bunkhouse or visit Susy's cathouse either. On payday, when the ranch hands go into town, is it possible that the Japanese cook and Crooks—both racial Outsiders left behind—might play cards, share a bottle, or get to known each other? The author pro-vides no evidence for that possibility, and perhaps is unable to imagine a friendship between two people of color. Like many novels published be-tween World War I and the 1960s, the text simply presupposes that white people are the most important thing in the lives of black Americans.

The great American philosopher W. E. B. Du Bois, a contemporary of Crooks, also understood this loneliness. We are told that Crooks reads a great deal, but Steinbeck tells us very little about *what* he reads or even where he acquires these books. I cannot help but wonder if sometimes Crooks is reading books by black Americans of his time during the Great Depression—works by such Harlem Renaissance writers as Langston Hughes, Jean Toomer, Countee Cullen, and Zora Neal Hurston, books by Richard Wright, and Du Bois, who graduated from Harvard and says in a taped interview that during his college days not *one* of his white class-mates spoke to him.[9] Sadly, his years at America's most esteemed college were even more segregated than the life of Crooks. In *Of Mice and Men*, Steinbeck has Crooks "whine"—that is the word he uses, "whine"—about his voracious book reading (*OMM* 72). He says to Lennie,

> S'pose you didn't have nobody. S'pose you couldn't go back into the bunk house and play rummy 'cause you was black. How'd you like that? S'pose you had to sit out here an' read books. Sure you could play horse-shoes till it got dark, but then you got to read books. Books ain't no good. A guy needs somebody—to be near him. (*OMM* 72)

However, if Crooks has anywhere among his books a copy of Du Bois' *The Souls of Black Folks*, published in 1903, he would see a black man de-scribing a very different experience with books. "I sit with Shakespeare," writes Du Bois,

> and he winces not. Across the color line I move arm in arm with Balzac and Dumas, where smiling men and welcoming women glide in gilded halls. From out the caves of evening that swing between the strong-limbed earth and the tracery of stars, I summon Aristotle and Aurelius and what soul I will, and they come all graciously with no scorn nor condescension. So, wed with Truth, I dwell above the Veil.[10]

Clearly, Du Bois possessed what I call an Aleph consciousness. He can read white philosophers and novelists for the gems of color-blind truth their works contain, and leave any bigotry they might have off to one side. Through books, he can also find the human mirrors he needs to qualify and correct his own perceptions. This skill of being bi-focal is possessed by *any*one who is a minority in a predominantly white society—by people who are Jews in a gentile culture, by Muslims in America and Europe to-day, and by women in a patriarchal society. But this is a timeless survival skill that Crooks does not possess, nor does he seem to have the basic understanding of the racial world learned in childhood by people of color. The historic black American solution to racially imposed loneliness and homelessness was to embrace family. We can accept the novel's statement that the white characters are without families, for whatever reason. But black Americans were compelled to come together as a people despised by others, to shelter and protect family members and kin even to the point of creating "extended families," much as George assumes a protective role for Lennie, and then extends his dream for his own farm to include Candy, who is willing to put up most of the money for it. (Significantly, Crooks is not invited to join them, although he does broach that idea.) Every racial and ethnic minority in America in the 1930s—whether we are talking about Asians, the Irish, Italians, Poles, Hispanics, or Jews—understood the imperative of this strategy for survival, as African and Caribbean immigrants do today, because otherwise they would *not* have survived.

One other person comes to the place where Crooks is forced to live. That person is Curley's wife, and when she sees who is inside— Crooks, Lennie and Candy—she says, "They left all the weak ones here. . . . [*OMM* 77] Ever'body out doin' som'pin. Ever'body! An' what am I doing? Standin' here talking to a bunch of bindlestiffs—a nigger an' a dum-dum and a lousy ol' sheep" (*OMM* 78). Candy is an old man who is missing one hand. Lennie is mentally challenged. And Crooks? Well, Curley's wife describes him as being among the "weak" because he is crippled and a Negro, two conditions which Steinbeck conflates into being synonymous in the novel.

Among the three "weak" characters in *Of Mice and Men*, Steinbeck creates Crooks as what I would call a victim-savant. He is an insightful thinker who clarifies the meaning of loneliness for us, but he is an "outsider," someone for whom the reader feels more pity than respect. Contrast this with Steinbeck's astonishingly divine portrait of Slim, a white character he urges us to respect and admire based on such details as his being "tall," "ageless," with "God-like eyes," "gravity in his manner and a quiet so profound that all talk stopped when he spoke," and he also possesses an "understanding beyond thought" (*OMM* 33–34). (Does this description of Slim sound familiar? It should, because it occurs as a cliché throughout novels about the West, and was immortalized by John Wayne's portraits of cowboys who are soft-spoken, tall, strong, and deferred to by others.) Often in fiction published during the modernist period, the racial Outsider is given the role of being a vehicle for truth, a truth that "insiders" and people who are privileged or conform to society cannot know. White writers of novels and screenplays in the twentieth century have often assigned the problematic position of victim-savant to the American Negro—as they also did with native Americans. This is not the most pleasant vehicle for the imagination of a person of color to inhabit during the reading experience. And it was for this reason that when I read Steinbeck's classic in my teens, I was simply unable to identify or sympathize very much with the way he presented Crooks, whose character raises more questions than it answers. We can say he functions in the novel as a "symbol." But that is just another way of saying he is more of an idea—Steinbeck's idea of blacks—than he is a well-rounded, realistic character.

Earlier, I said that Crooks seems to have virtues of character that would make him a candidate for friendship. But while Steinbeck details those virtues, he also includes serious defects in the personality of the stable buck. Crooks is an extremely bitter man, who at first does not want Lennie, and then Candy and Curley's wife to enter his segregated space, despite his intense hunger for friendship. Of the white men in the bunkhouse, he says, "They play cards in there, but I can't play because I'm black. They say I stink. Well, I tell you, you all of you stink to me" (*OMM* 68). That statement seems to contradict his being "patient," which we were told earlier. In Chapter Four, when Crooks asks Curley's abrasive wife to leave his room, she emasculates him when she replies, "Listen, Nigger. . . . You know what I can do to you if you open your trap? . . . [*OMM* 80] Well, you keep your place, Nigger. I could get you strung up on a tree so easy it ain't even funny" (*OMM* 81). Three film and television adaptations of the novel made in the '30s, '80s, and '90s omit this bristling speech that Curley's wife delivers to Crooks, as does the 1937 stage adaptation (the actor's edition) written by Steinbeck. The most recent film version, starring Gary Sinise and John Malkovich, and adapted by Horton Foote, removes Curley's wife *entirely* from the scene in Crooks' place in Chapter Four. Why Steinbeck, and such screenwriters as Eugene Solow, E. Nick Anderson, and Horton Foote, took out this speech, I do not know, because the fact that she does say this in the novel has great implications for the portrayal of Crooks. Steinbeck says Crooks' response to this threat is "to grow smaller, and he pressed himself against the wall.

. . . [*OMM* 80] [He] reduced himself to nothing. There was no personality, no ego—nothing to arouse either like or dislike" (*OMM* 81). He sits "perfectly still, his eyes averted, everything that might be hurt drawn in" (*OMM* 81) as he retreats into what Steinbeck calls "the terrible protective dignity of the Negro" (*OMM* 79).

What shall we make of this passage repeatedly and deliberately deleted from the film and theater versions? As critic Jim McWilliams recently pointed out to me after reviewing a draft of this paper, what Curley's wife does with this threat is *re*-sexualize Crooks in order to bring about his *second* emasculation in the novel. Furthermore, this putting of Crooks back "in his place" is probably the psychological motive for his taking back his earlier desire to join Lennie and Candy on the farm they hope to buy. On the surface, the author is saying that the threat of death—the danger of a lie told by a flirtatious white woman during the era of Jim Crow—makes Crooks cowardly, and that this is the condition of the Negro who hopes to survive in 1930s America. The truth of this situation is undeniable, and for it there is enough documentation in the historical record for it to assume the status of a cliché. But I would venture to say that for a young (or old) black reader, and certainly for a black writer, something here rings false. Crooks' reaction and childlike repeating of the phrase, "Yes, ma'am" as if he were an eighteenth-century slave, is hardly "dignified." I don't believe Steinbeck would have directed a character like Slim to behave as Crooks does. One wonders if Crooks—or Steinbeck—is acquainted with stories about twentieth-century black heroes like pugilist Jack Johnson or Paul Robeson, or the black folk hero Stagolee; and I wonder if he considered that for blacks during and after the era of slavery, identification with Christianity's sense of an eternal soul that could not be violated was the most common source of maintaining one's dignity and ego in the face of threats presented by people like Curley's wife.

In addition to being cowardly, Crooks' character is further discredited because he is depicted as being mean-spirited (as Lennie is not), and he torments the simple, bear-like Lennie with the possibility that George might one day abandon him, or become unable to protect him. Steinbeck says he takes pleasure in this tormenting of Lennie. He explains that without George around, "They'll take ya to the booby hatch. They'll tie ya up with a collar, like a dog" (*OMM* 72). This sadistic delight in causing fear and suffering in someone who is not his mental equal is yet another reason Crooks can never become a "prince of the ranch," and why I felt distanced from and uncomfortable with him when I was a young man insofar as he is the *only* black character in the story, a figure through whom we are asked to understand something about the lived-experience of black America.

But in Crooks that lived-experience is truncated. He is a culturally and spiritually impoverished man. Perhaps this explains why Crooks is the only black character Steinbeck attempts to create in his body of work, for it is extremely difficult to free ourselves from the racial and cultural presuppositions we have been conditioned to accept uncritically, and to achieve accurate and compelling portraits of racial, gender and cultural Others. Yet the attempt to do so is socially and artistically necessary if an American writer hopes to present a fictional world that reflects the diversity and complexity of America in the twentieth and twenty-first centuries. The fact that Steinbeck was one of the pioneers in such a risky but essential project is yet another reason why we honor his contribution to our literature.

Notes

1. Jorge Luis Borges, *Collected Fictions*, ed. Andrew Hurley (New York: Viking, 1998), 281.

2. Borges, *Collected Fictions*, 285.

3. Borges, *Collected Fictions*, 283.

4. Alan Soble, *Eros, Agape and Philia: Readings in the Philosophy of Love* (New York: Paragon House, 1989), 68.

5. Soble, *Eros, Agape and Philia*, 59.

6. Soble, *Eros, Agape and Philia*, 59.

7. Soble, *Eros, Agape and Philia*, 64.

8. Maurice Merleau-Ponty, *Adventures of the Dialectic*, trans. Joseph Bien (Evanston, IL: Northwestern University Press, 1973), 138–39.

9. Harvard Black Studies scholar Werner Sollors played a copy of this tape for me.

10. James Weldon Johnson, Booker T. Washington, and W. E. B. Dubois *Three Negro Classics: "Up from Slavery," "The Souls of Black Folks," "The Autobiography of an Ex-Colored Man"* (New York: Avon Books, 1965), 284.

Works Cited

Borges, Jorge Luis. *Collected Fictions*. Ed. Andrew Hurley. New York: Viking, 1998.

Johnson, James Weldon, Booker T. Washington, and W. E. B. Dubois. *Three Negro Classics: "Up from Slavery," "The Souls of Black Folks," "The Autobiography of an Ex-Colored Man."* New York: Avon Books, 1965.

Merleau-Ponty, Maurice. *Adventures of the Dialectic*. Trans. Joseph Bien. Evanston, IL: Northwestern University Press, 1973. [Originally published in French under the title *Les Aventures de Dialectique*. Paris: Editiones Gallimard, 1955.]

Soble. Alan. *Eros, Agape and Philia: Readings in the Philosophy of Love*. New York: Paragon House, 1989.

Steinbeck, John. *Of Mice and Men*. 1937. New York: Penguin Modern Classics, 1993.

Part Seven
NEW ESSAYS

The new critical studies included in this volume approach *Of Mice and Men* from a number of unique angles. Daniel Griesbach's assessment of the changes Steinbeck made in adapting his novel into a Broadway play suggests that several of the more controversial episodes have been excised or radically changed and that some of the original characters have been modified, perhaps in an attempt to temper the harshness of the play's message, and as a result, to attract theater-goers who might prefer to see sympathetic heroes on stage rather than to be accosted by blunt social critique. More importantly, perhaps, this chapter suggests that the major disadvantage of Steinbeck's theater revision is that the character of Crooks loses significance, a pattern that continues in the film versions; as a consequence of this, Steinbeck's commentary on race in America is diminished. Michael J. Meyer speculates that Steinbeck's interest in loneliness was well grounded in his own experiences with isolation/solitude and that, in typical Steinbeck ambiguity, several characters demonstrate that being alone has its pluses and minuses. His essay also argues that Steinbeck's assessment of his own life experiences as recorded in his correspondence indicates that he was aware of this paradox and wished to record the combative status between the two views of this human emotion in *Of Mice and Men*.

Barbara A. Heavilin's essay considers all the literary labels that have been applied to the novella and queries whether either Realism or Naturalism is a correct category for *Of Mice and Men*. Is the novel's emphasis really on mechanistic determinism and fate or might readers more fruitfully concentrate on its Romantic elements, including compassion, the multiple voices of the dispossessed, and empathy for the lower class. Finally, Chris Goering, the creator of the LitTunes website on the Internet, suggests that any present-day attempt to teach a classic novel such as this should be accompanied by yoking the text to the language of music, a media so valued by today's twitch-speed kids. Using input from five of his students, who are potential high school teachers, Goering links *Of Mice and Men* to a number of musical performances and to several widely divergent artists and artistic styles.

In each new analysis, readers will find creative ideas for approaching a novel that is over seventy years old and yet still holds appeal to a wide group of readers and is studied in classrooms across the world for its masterly style and it non-teleological presentation of events.

The following essays were developed exclusively for this volume and appear here for the first time.

Griesbach, Daniel. "Reduced to Nothing: Race, Lynching, and Erasure in the Theater Revision of Steinbeck's *Of Mice and Men.*"

Heavilin, Barbara. "Emotion Recollected in Tranquility": A Context for Romanticism in *Of Mice and Men.*"

Meyer, Michael J. "'One Is the Loneliest Number': Steinbeck's Paradoxical Attraction and Repulsion To Isolation / Solitude."

Goering, Christian Z. et al. "Musical Intertextuality in Action: A Directed Reading of *Of Mice and Men.*"

CHAPTER EIGHTEEN

REDUCED TO NOTHING: RACE, LYNCHING, AND ERASURE IN THE THEATER REVISION OF STEINBECK'S *OF MICE AND MEN*

Daniel Griesbach

The theater is the political art par excellence; only there is the political sphere of human life transposed to art. By the same token, it is the only art whose sole subject is man in his relationship to others.—Hannah Arendt, *The Human Condition*

I am interested in having a vehicle exactly adequate to the theme.—John Steinbeck, on the "new set of techniques" used in writing *Of Mice and Men*

Returning from his travels in northern Europe and the Soviet Union, John Steinbeck arrived in New York in August of 1937 to find unfinished work obligations waiting for him.[1] Annie Laurie Williams, a literary agent who was facilitating a Broadway stage production of Steinbeck's most recent novel, *Of Mice and Men*, encouraged him immediately to finish converting the short novel into a script, since the play was to begin rehearsals within a matter of weeks. The stage production was in the hands of George S. Kaufman, the accomplished Broadway playwright, director, and producer. Even before Steinbeck's European trip, Kaufman had written with suggestions for the dramatic adaptation. Williams convinced Steinbeck on his return to spend time at her country house in Connecticut to complete the script. Then, when they were finished, Kaufman invited Steinbeck to his Pennsylvania farm for what biographer Jackson Benson describes as "a week of intensive work" in which Steinbeck "molded the final script under Kaufman's guidance."[2]

The resulting collaboration produced the script for a play that would open at the Music Box Theatre in New York in November 1937, and would run for 207 performances.

Why did these people have to apply so much pressure to persuade the author to convert his story into a play? Likely because in Steinbeck's mind it was already a play. *Of Mice and Men* was his first of three attempts at a hybrid "play-novelette" form, which he described as "a play that can be read or a novel that can be played."[3] In fact, the first theatrical production of *Of Mice and Men*, by a workers' theater group called the San Francisco Theatre Union, undertook the challenge of "playing" the novel in the way Steinbeck intended. In May through July of 1937, the Theatre Union staged sixteen performances working directly from the novel, which had been published in March. Both parties had been enthusiastic at the start: Steinbeck personally read his manuscript aloud to the Theatre Union and the group chose *Of Mice and Men* as the opening production in their new location at the Green Street Theatre in San Francisco's North Beach district.[4] But something was amiss: one reviewer noticed that because "Steinbeck was writing primarily for readers" the Theatre Union's production was "a play that seems slightly ill at ease in the theatre."[5] Although he would go on to use his play-novelette form in *The Moon Is Down* (1942) and *Burning Bright* (1950), Steinbeck himself had doubts about this first attempt at fusing a novel and play, telling a *New York Times* reviewer that "the experiment flopped" and that when he "came up against a practical man of the theatre like Kaufman," he felt compelled to "do a lot of extensive rewriting."[6] In contrast to the Theatre Union's attempt to put *Of Mice and Men* on stage, Kaufman's Broadway play was a clear success, receiving praise from reviewers and eventually winning the New York Drama Critics Circle award for the best American play of that year. It seems, therefore, that the conventional play script succeeded where the experimental play-novelette failed, that the Broadway production eventually triumphed over the Theatre Union's effort to make good on Steinbeck's vision of a novel that could be played. Nevertheless, those interested in the story should imagine what the Theatre Union's performance might have looked like. This performance was truer to Steinbeck's original artistic vision, lacking the emendations encouraged by the major Broadway producer.

This chapter explores the changes that occurred to Steinbeck's novel as it was transformed into Kaufman's play. Most critics comparing the two versions have noted that the theater version gives an expanded role of the unnamed character of Curley's wife, a lonely woman trapped by her marriage to the ranch boss's tyrannical son.[7] However, there are reasons to believe that the most significant transformation involves Crooks, the black "stable buck" (as he is referred to) who lives in his own room separated from the other workers on the ranch. The most evident changes are those made to the scene in Crooks's room (the fourth chapter in the novel and act 2, scene 2 of the play), where one can find striking divergences in *Of Mice and Men*'s novel and stage versions. While Curley's wife's role is expanded, the character of Crooks is reduced, possessing considerably fewer lines than he is given in the short novel. Furthermore, the play removes the conflict between Curley's wife and Crooks, which culminates in a dramatic scene in which Curley's wife threatens to have Crooks lynched. My argument makes two main points. First, while some have noted the removal of the lynch scene as one of the revisions,[8] commentary has mostly focused on the expanded role of Curley's wife. I contend that the removal of Crooks's conflict with Curley's wife is an equally important change in the story. The two revisions are connected in the restructuring of characters that enhances the portrait of Curley's wife and diminishes that of Crooks. Second, the perspective offered in this chapter insists on the centrality of Crooks's story to the novel's plot, both in the optimistic moment of his willingness to join George, Lennie, and Candy in their hopes to gain their own farm and in the devastating refusal to join the men that follows from the threat of racial lynching. Far from being a secondary "subplot," Crooks's story plays an important part in one of this literary work's main topics: whether it is possible for the dispossessed characters to gain a better life through the overcoming of pessimism and isolation. Crooks's shattered hopes are consistent with the novel's premise that our best plans, according to the Burns poem from which the novel takes its title, often go awry.

As Steinbeck revised his work on Kaufman's ranch, he no doubt considered many aspects of how it would appear on the Broadway stage. He also had the benefit of having seen the Theatre Union play that relied solely on the novel. But while the Drama Critics award would suggest that the Broadway changes were an improvement to the work, I believe that what comes out is less complex and less powerful. The Broadway version weakens the story's response to the racial segregation and antiblack violence of

Steinbeck's America. *Of Mice and Men* was written in an era when many writers and artists responded to the legacy of lynching.[9] According to Jacqueline Goldsby, writers were particularly alert to how lynching, while still present, also seemed to be transforming into other forms of regularized violence.[10] Such transformations are perhaps typified by what many saw as a "legal lynching" in the highly publicized Scottsboro case during the 1930s, in which a group of nine black teenagers accused of raping two white women received death sentences from all-white juries despite numerous problems with the evidence and the trials.

The Kaufman version has proved an enduring piece of American drama, influencing the movie versions from directors Lewis Milestone (1939), Reza Badiyi (1981), and Gary Sinise (1992) as well as adaptations for musical theater and opera. Since these different adaptations often follow the play, the changes Steinbeck made at Kaufman's behest, especially in the story's climactic middle section, can greatly affect how readers understand the story—hence the importance of comparing and contrasting the different versions. In the novel, the scene in Crooks's room can be understood as the first of two tragic endings and consequently as an integral part of the plot. The men's hope for their own farm starts tumbling with the ruinous energies unleashed during the lynch threat scene and finally collapses with Lennie's killing of Curley's wife. One might even think of two kinds of tragedy in *Of Mice and Men*: one is written in the stars, the other written in script of American history.

Childhoods Added and Subtracted

The revision of the story starts with an alteration of the characters, a process of enhancing the portrait of Curley's wife while simultaneously erasing aspects of Crooks. According to the correspondence between Kaufman and Steinbeck, Kaufman suggested a need for "fresh invention" in the second act, specifically that Steinbeck should enlarge the part of Curley's wife, stating that "the girl . . . should be drawn more fully: she is the motivating force of the whole thing and should loom larger."[11] In the play version, significantly, we see Curley's wife protest being called a "tart" by the farmhands, drawing out the tension in her character between how she is represented by others and how she represents herself.[12] The additions to her role place more emphasis on the question of her sexual "purity" and marital fidelity, a topic that is present in the novel but less pronounced.[13] She states, for example, that Curley is "sure" that "nobody never got to me before I was married"; she insists that her husband "wouldn't stay with me if he wasn't sure" (*Play* 47). This obsession with sexual purity is a reflection of the characterization of Curley's wife Steinbeck would later reinforce in his letter to Claire Luce, the actress in the Music Box Theatre cast who played Curley's wife. He informs Luce that Curley's wife was "told over and over that she must remain a virgin. . . . This was harped on so often that it became a fixation."[14]

Details of Curley's wife's childhood and parents are also added. Even though she claims earlier in the play that she was raised in "a nice home" and that she "was brung up by nice people," we soon learn that this assertion is merely a defense against being called a tart by George (*Play* 45). Other statements reveal that "nice people" is just a façade for her family and that her mother's pretenses to decency are only hypocritical. "My ol' man was a drunk. They put him away," Curley's wife confides to Lennie in her final scene (*Play* 61). It is clear that Curley's wife finds relief in speaking honestly about her family, as she adds, "There! I told" (*Play* 61). She gains our sympathy when she tells Lennie about the way her father would often "get drunk an' paint crazy pitchers an' waste paint" and how her mother and father were "always fightin'" (*Play* 61). In the compact forms of the play and play-novelette, these revelations convey how Curley's wife has known mostly unhappiness. At the same time, her ability to speak freely to Lennie breaks the code of silence with which the characters conduct themselves: suspicious of each other, none of the ranch workers except Candy share their personal pasts or hopes for the future in this way.

In this expanded role, Curley's wife shares a strange story of how her father once took her away in the night, perhaps stealing the child from her mother, promising "No arguin' and fightin' . . . because you're my little daughter" (*Play* 61). As the father promises to escape conflict and live peacefully together "because you're my own little girl, an' not no stranger," the story of Curley's wife and her father seems to mirror the theme of companionship in George and Lennie's story. The father's words, as Curley's wife relates them, even take on some of the dreamy patterns of George and Lennie's dialogue: "Why, you'll bake little cakes for me, an' I'll paint pretty pitchers all over the wall" (*Play* 61). All this dreaming is brought down to reality, however, when she states bluntly, "In the morning they caught us . . . an' they put him away. (*Pause.*) I wish we'd 'a' went" (*Play* 62, ellipses in original). Curley's wife's last words on this subject would suggest she approved of her father's actions. Perhaps she prefers him only as an alternative to her mother, who Curley's wife thinks stifles her wish to pursue a career in the movies. But despite the rosy picture Curley's wife paints of leaving with her father, the reader is left to doubt whether Curley's wife as a young girl is even safe with an alcoholic father who has a proclivity to fighting. Furthermore, the father's wish for her to "bake little cakes for me" oddly seems to fit his daughter into the role of woman-as-domestic-servant, or in other words the unfortunate role Curley's wife's mother previously occupied. Rather inexplicably, Curley's wife criticizes her mother while pardoning her father for his obvious mistakes. This pattern recurs in her relationship with Curley, where she has clearly withstood his destructive behavior for too long. While she will criticize Curley's actions and eventually decide to leave him, this attitude has been extremely difficult to achieve. Her words imply that she is not the best judge of her own past and that possibly some of the main reasons for her feelings and actions are not transparent to her. They also function to suggest that Curley's wife's words and behavior, far from being the natural behaviors of a tart and troublemaker that the ranch hands label them, are the outcomes of specific patterns of human relationships Curley's wife has been exposed to.

The connection between a character's childhood experience and their current predicaments is equally evident in Crooks. In contrast to the extension of Curley's wife, however, the stage version and movie adaptations reduce Crooks's childhood biography. In both the novel and the play, Crooks remembers spending nights with his brothers in the idyllic setting of his father's chicken ranch. The details he remembers in this passage—alfalfa, chickens, and strawberries—are significant in their resemblance to the alfalfa, rabbits, and garden George and Lennie dream of. But above all, Crooks remembers the constant companionship of his brothers, how "they was always near me, always there."[15] This, of course, is the kind of companionship George and Lennie share, wish to maintain, and even expand.

A key omission from the play, however, is the other half of Crooks's childhood history. In the novel, this passage comes as soon as Crooks claims that Lennie "don't know what the hell it's all about" when someone talks to him (*OMM* 70). Confiding in Lennie, Crooks locates his experience regionally, declaring he "ain't a southern negro . . . I was born right here in California" (*OMM* 70). He proceeds to tell of his experiences playing with the white children who lived nearby. "My ol' man didn't like that," says Crooks, "I never knew till long later why he didn't like that. But I know now" (*OMM* 70). As a child, Crooks's desire to connect with the other children is hampered by the society's code of racial segregation. That code is manifested in Crooks's father's suspicion of the white children and his (not unsubstantiated) fears about the negative reactions the racial mixing among the children might incite. Crooks "know[s] now" the social codes he could not have fully understood as a child. Crooks recounts how "there wasn't another colored family for miles around," so he did not have the option of playing with the other children free of adult-world troubles. Finally, Crooks reveals how "now there ain't a colored man on this ranch an' there's jus' one family in Soledad," meaning that his isolation as an adult is a repetition of his childhood experience (*OMM* 70). As is the case with Curley's wife, formative experiences bear down on—compound and complicate—Crooks's adult experience.

The omission of this portion of Crooks's history from the play not only lessens the amount an audience will know about Crooks, but also changes how one understands his claim that Lennie "don't know what the hell it's all about." In the novel, the recognition of Lennie's lack of comprehension means that Crooks feels he can speak freely and openly about his past. In the play, by contrast, Crooks immediately transitions from the idea that Lennie will not "go blabbin'" to what the stage directions call "his torture" and words uttered "cruelly" (*Play* 51). Crooks torments Lennie with the suggestion that "s'pose George went into town tonight and you never heard from him no more"—a thought that enrages Lennie (*Play* 50–51). But the intervening information the novel provides—the passage in which Crooks reveals he was separated from his childhood companions—makes a difference. In the novel, Crooks's experiment to get Lennie to imagine or acknowledge his experience of loneliness follows the telling of the stable buck's own childhood loneliness.

The play alters the novel's careful sequence in Crooks's monologue. Instead of Crooks's cruel experiment with Lennie being interwoven with his eagerness to recall his experience of racial segregation as a child, the cruel or malicious side of Crooks emerges spontaneously, seemingly naturally. Eventually, the play resolves Crooks's "torture" of Lennie into "very gently" delivered lines in which Crooks explains to Lennie, "Maybe you can see now. . . . A guy needs somebody" (*Play* 51). Even in this passage, the play removes some of the more philosophical implications Crooks draws in the novel, specifically the idea that one needs the presence of others to "measure" perceptions of the exterior world. The result is a less developed character and a much less sympathetic one.

The changes in Crooks's role that make him appear committed to verbally torturing Lennie stand in direct opposition to Steinbeck's other revisions, which generally seek to soften the relationships between characters by adding friendlier dialogue. These changes are most perceptible at the ends of scenes, as in the end of act 1, scene 1, when George and Lennie are going to sleep along the river bank. This scene ends with George being directed to "amiably" say, "Aw, shut up" in response to Lennie's threat that he can "jus' as well go away . . . and live in a cave" (*Play* 16). Lennie closes the scene with an endearing line in which he bothers George one last time to remind him, "I'm shutting up, George" (*Play* 16).[16] Contrast this ending with the novel chapter, which ends on George's rather abrasive response, "You can jus' as well go to hell. . . . Shut up now" (*OMM* 16). In keeping with this softening of characters' relationships, even the Boss, who behaves as a rigid authoritarian in the novel, is directed to "relax" and "allow a little warmth into his manner" (*Play* 21). After interrogating George and Lennie about arriving late, traveling as companions, and their reasons for leaving Weed, the Boss tries to joke with them about nightclubs in San Francisco. The Boss's brief change of manner in the play leads George and Lennie to question whether a "boss" can also be a "nice guy"—a thought they do not seriously entertain in the novel (*Play* 21).

The revisions amount to a general expanding and softening of characters, and yet Crooks's role is smaller and harder by comparison. As if there were a zero-sum of character development, the more Curley's wife "looms," the less Crooks's presence and substance is allowed to shine through. If the idea that to build up one character means to dismantle another sounds improbable, consider how the different versions have played out. While Crooks's character has been portrayed vividly and dynamically in the movies by some excellent actors (Leigh Whipper in 1939, Whitman Mayo in 1981, and Joe Morton in 1992), his lines in the film versions have been reduced even beyond those of the play version. In Carlisle Floyd's opera version, the character of Crooks is removed entirely. Admittedly, this is only one of many changes Floyd makes to transform the story into an operatic work in three acts, and he was likely using a different decision making process than either that which Steinbeck and Kaufman used in their collaboration or that the movie directors have used. But the trend has been persistent in diminishing Crooks's role in the writing and rewriting for different venues (drama, film, and musical drama). While the seeds of this trend can be seen in the absence of some of Crooks's significant biographical details, its roots gain hold when the conflict in Crooks's room is shifted from one that takes place between Crooks and Curley's wife to one that occurs between Curley's wife and George.

In contrast to Kaufman's perception that Curley's wife is "the motivating force," I would contend that forces in the story arise from the characters' intense social relationships. Even though the story is about loneliness, Steinbeck's characters are mutually defining: one finds George's identity revealed in his interaction with Lennie and vice-versa. It would be a mistake to see George and Lennie as the main characters and Crooks, Candy, and Curley's wife the "secondary" characters whom the protagonists encounter. Such a simple division would obscure the interaction among the characters, which is primary. Kaufman's designation of Curley's wife as a "motivating force" could be extended to Candy, who contributes his savings to join Lennie and George. In some respects, the way Candy unites with the protagonists is reminiscent of the Wilsons joining the Joads in Steinbeck's next novel, *The Grapes of Wrath* (1939). Looked at this way, Crooks's momentary willingness to join the expanding group of protagonists reveals his role to be significant and integral to the story, just as Candy's is. In the details of Crooks's room that Steinbeck was motivated to alter, one finds the dramatic contrast between the energy building around the characters' dream of gaining their own farm and the counteracting, destructive force that can lead to the threat of death by the cruelest of interracial hostilities.

Effacing Crooks

In his rich and detailed analysis of Crooks, Charles Johnson notes that the repeated removal of Curley's wife's threat in the stage and film versions has "great implications for the portrayal of Crooks."[17] Johnson sees these changes more or less in concert with Steinbeck's overall problematic characterization of Crooks as conforming to the stereotype of the emasculated black male character. In addition to this point, I would like to add that by comparing these different versions we can see even more clearly how the novel emphasizes the importance of Crooks's character and the scene that takes place in his room: the threat of racial lynching is the point at which the bindlestiffs' dream is revealed as an impossibility. This aspect of the novel could not survive Steinbeck and Kaufman's changes to make the story a Broadway play. In the novel, the central, climactic conflict of the fourth chapter takes place between Crooks and Curley's wife, where Crooks joins the other men in their effort to expel Curley's wife from their presence, an action that leads her to threaten to have him lynched. In revising the novel for the stage, this conflict is shifted to one between George and Curley's wife, where George almost assaults her for interacting with Lennie. To get a sense of this contrast, one can look carefully at the sequence of events portrayed in the novel and then in the Broadway script.

At the apex of the novel's version of this scene, Curley's wife has interrupted Crooks, Lennie, and Candy, as the three were discussing future plans for a farm. The men, harboring misogynist suspicions of Curley's wife and fearing trouble from Curley, implore her to leave. Crooks says, "Maybe you better go along to your own house now. We don't want no trouble" (*OMM* 77). Following Crooks's example, Candy says, "You got a husban'. You got no call foolin' aroun' with other guys, causin' trouble" (*OMM* 77). Curley's wife, however, sees through their fear. She notes frankly that "you're all scared of each other" and challenges their entrenched assumptions about a "woman's place" by asking, "Think I like to stick in that house alla time?" (*OMM* 77).

All these tensions reach their breaking point when Crooks tells Curley's wife, "You got no rights comin' in a colored man's room. You got no rights messing around in here at all. Now you jus' get out, an' get out quick. If you don't, I'm gonna ast the boss not to ever let you come in the barn no more" (*OMM* 80). One should immediately hear the repetition of "rights" in Crooks's statement, which first occurred at the beginning of the scene when he warns that Lennie had no "right" to enter his room. Curley's wife responds with the assumption that Crooks has no rights, stating, "Listen, Nigger, . . . You know what I can do to you if you open your trap?" (*OMM* 80). The implication is that a mere accusation that a black man has tried to violate her, a white woman, is enough to raise a lynch mob against the accused. In this social context, such an accusation has a destructive potential that can neither be matched nor adequately defended against. The power dynamic is represented spatially: working in the opposite direction of Crooks's attempt to remove Curley's wife's presence from his room, this threat opens up Crooks's personal space to Curley's wife's total domination. We are told that Curley's wife "closed on him" as she repeats, "You know what I could do?" (*OMM* 80). This "closing on" has the effect of erasing Crooks's presence, as he "drew into himself . . . seemed to grow smaller" (*OMM* 80).

Curley's wife's threat is a concentrated expression of white society's pathological myth of the black rapist, which, according to Anne P. Rice, "allowed white men to violently police a status quo aimed at the social and economic subjugation of both black men and white women."[18] In a society under the spell of this myth, the accusation carries a force that Crooks can hardly counter. In this racist narrative, white women were constructed as taboo to black men. Lynching was justified as the protection of white women's "purity" from what were imagined to be the monstrous sexual advances of the black man. Trudier Harris describes this imagination in the following passage, which can be thought of as the background assumptions behind Curley's wife's words:

> She is beauty; he is beast. She is to be protected; he is what she needs protection from. Her existence must be continued; he is expendable. She is the bearer of the best of her race's traditions; he bears nothing worthy of respect. She inspires confidence; he inspires fear. She is pedestalized; he is trampled beneath the feet of those who have created her pedestal. She can control his life by mere whim. He has little control over his life as far as she is concerned. She is innocence; he is guilt.[19]

Upon hearing his own subjectivity being written into this script, Crooks "reduced himself to nothing. There was no personality, no ego—nothing to arouse either like or dislike. He said, 'Yes, ma'am,' and his voice was toneless" (*OMM* 80). Presented at once with the possibility of personal harm and the reminder that racially motivated mob violence always lurks in the background to enforce his own second-class status, Crooks is quite literally *effaced* by Curley's wife, even after having "stood up from his bunk and *faced* her" (*OMM* 80), my emphasis). We are reminded of the face he has built up in the scene, the face that expresses his profound sense of loneliness both in his cruel pestering of Lennie ("Crooks' face lighted with pleasure in his torture") and in his elaboration of how one can be isolated to the point that he or she has "got nothing to measure by" (*OMM* 73).

Through a careful juxtaposition of characters, furthermore, Steinbeck implies how powerful this myth is. None of the men on the ranch trust Curley's wife and all see her as a threatening "tart." By contrast, even though Crooks is treated poorly, no one on the ranch expresses any mistrust of his sincerity or motives. And yet Curley's wife is confident that the mere allegation a black man has violated her will be convincing enough to drive these same white men to murder. Furthermore, Steinbeck's novel suggests the travelling power the myth possesses: whatever the meanings of Crooks's statement "I ain't a Southern negro," it is clear his regional identity offers little protection from the racial paradigms that extend throughout the United States.

Steinbeck's repeated use of the word *nigger* in this section is a troubling part of the novel, as the word carries the history of being used precisely in the way Curley's wife uses it: as a threat and as a tool to enforce racial hierarchy and terror. One thing to notice is that characters using the word use it frequently, as when Candy says it five times in the ten or so sentences relating the story of the Christmas whisky and fighting (*OMM* 20). One of his last published works, *Travels with Charley* (1962),[20] provides some of Steinbeck's ideas about this racial epithet. In *Travels with Charley*, Steinbeck notes that while traveling through Texas and Louisiana he heard "many repetitions" of the word; "at least twenty times" strangers approached him to call his dog Charley a "nigger" (*Travels* 249). Steinbeck, in a tone of sarcasm, notes that "it was an unusual joke—always fresh and never Negro or even Nigra, always Nigger or rather Niggah" (*Travels* 249). He concludes with a thought about whites' use of the word through which one might understand its appearance in *Of Mice and Men*: "That word seemed terribly important, a kind of safety word to cling to less some structure collapse" (*Travels* 249). The compulsive repetition of the word, Steinbeck suggests, signifies the shaky foundations it rests on. When used to dehumanize other humans, its use is always a misuse. Since the word cannot adequately refer to Crooks any more than he can embody it, Curley's wife and, at an earlier point in the story, Candy are forced to repeat it compulsively. This repetition, in Curley's wife's mouth and in the mouths of the whites Steinbeck met traveling through the United States, is a symptom of the problematic nature of the word and the ideology behind it.

The threat of Crooks's lynching calls up the related issue of the mob-violence that constitutes a significant undercurrent in *Of Mice and Men*. All three films begin with chase scenes of mobs following George and Lennie after Lennie has frightened a woman in Weed by grabbing her dress, scenes that recreate the background story that George relates to Slim in the third chapter in the novel. The story ends with George killing his best friend as the mob raised by Curley is in pursuit. On a simple level, Crooks is vulnerable to the same mob violence that threatens Lennie. But as a black man, he is specifically vulnerable to antiblack lynching that inundated American culture after the Civil War and on into the twentieth century. In the context of the story, the threat of lynching produces palpable damage in the characters' interpersonal relationships. While Lennie's death at George's hands at the end the story represents the *final* collapse of the characters' hopes, the lynch threat that forces Crooks to give up a hope of joining his three fellow workers in their pursuit of a different and better life signifies the beginning of the end. And this sudden change is more than a mere "foreshadowing" of the threat and failure to come. If the failure of one's dreams gives the story its tragic quality, as if the characters' misfortune were an inescapable law of the universe, the story of Crooks provides a sociological counterpoint, where the failure is a result of social practices and institutions as well as individual decisions and agency.

This last point becomes especially evident when we contrast the lynch theme in *Of Mice and Men* with Steinbeck's other portrayals of lynching and mob violence. The most obvious point of comparison is the story "The Vigilante" (1936) in which Steinbeck writes of a racial lynching and the hours after, focusing on the banality and nihilistic attitudes of a white man who participates. Expanding further, Steinbeck was interested in mob violence as an expression of his "group man" or "phalanx" ideas for human behavior, ideas that can be seen taking shape in Steinbeck's letters, short stories, and novels of the 1930s. *Of Mice and Men*, in which George and Lennie have been pursued by a mob in Weed and will be pursued by Curley's mob at the end, fits squarely within these stories. But

DANIEL GRIESBACH

what separates *Of Mice and Men*, however, is its sympathy with, and focus on, the *victims* of mob violence. Our sympathies are fully with George and Lennie as they are pursued by the group. The outbursts of collective violence are portrayed as posing a serious moral or ethical dilemma. Similarly, Crooks can be seen as the human face of the potential victim of racial lynching, a face that is hauntingly obscured in "The Vigilante." If *Of Mice and Men* relates thematically to Steinbeck's interest in the workings of mobs, vigilantism, and lynching, it also importantly links this interest to a consciousness of the history of lynching in America. In *Of Mice and Men*, Steinbeck is treating mob violence not just as a dimension of human behavior to be explored intellectually, but as an authentic tragedy of his society, a sure sign of social failure to be felt, acknowledged, and comprehended.

The deep sense of this failure emerges in the contrast between the lines Crooks delivers when he decides he wants to join the farm and those in which he retracts his proposal before the scene's end. His skepticism is first displayed in his response to Lennie's idea that he and George will get their own farm. "You're nuts," says Crooks, "I seen hundreds of men come by on the road an' on the ranches, with their bindles on their back an' that same damn thing in their heads. Hundreds of them" (*OMM* 74). When Candy arrives and conveys the same wish, Crooks's response is the same: "you guys is just kiddin' yourself" (*OMM* 75). Crooks's initial attitude conveys a stark difference between the ideal and the real when he states that, "I seen too many guys with land in their head. They never get none under their hand" (*OMM* 76). It also reflects a deep pessimism, a spiritual pessimism, as he declares with finality that "nobody never gets to heaven, and nobody gets no land" (*OMM* 74).

But eventually Crooks's ideas take a different direction. In a surprising change of heart, he hesitantly states, ". . . If you . . . guys would want a hand to work for nothing—just his keep, why I'd come an' lend a hand" (*OMM* 76, ellipses in original). In a matter of a few lines, upon gaining the information that Candy, George, and Lennie have a "stake," Crooks realizes there is something new, some substance, in Lennie's and Candy's words. These are not just more empty dreams, but the intentions of a group of people really committed to their plan. It is definitely significant that Crooks's attitude changes from pessimistic to optimistic. Crooks's about-face reflects a major theme in this novel, which is the power to overcome pessimism and cultivate a hopeful outlook through ideas and ideals shared with others, not to let uncertainty become paralyzing despite the fact that one's plans often go astray. Of course, this theme is most evident in George and Lennie's story. At times, even their dream can be seen as a myth that merely exists to keep Lennie at ease, something George patronizingly repeats to him so that the two can get along. Such a view will be reinforced when George retroactively judges that there was no hope for a farm, that he "knowed from the very first . . . we'd never do her" (*OMM* 94). But it is also important to note that George's skepticism falls away when Candy offers his savings so that he might join George and Lennie. Noting that Candy's contribution would enable the three to place a down payment within a month, George is filled with hope. With his "eyes . . . full of wonder," he says, "Jesus Christ! I bet we could swing her. . . . I bet we could swing her" (*OMM* 60). As is the case with Crooks, George becomes optimistic when he realizes they can put their money where their mouths are. But besides this purely material basis, Steinbeck is suggesting that some energy is created with the simple fact of the group growing. That Candy would sign on adds legitimacy, potential, and, to borrow Crooks's words, "something to measure by" (*OMM* 73). In the best aspect of the group-man theory, people attain new abilities through their cooperation. The joining of intentions toward the same end makes people feel they "could swing her" (*OMM* 60) in almost any context.

But the verbal threat Curley's wife launches against Crooks deflates all hope for Crooks to join the men in swinging their dream farm. In the novel, the scene ends with Crooks telling Candy, "Member what I said about hoein' and doin' odd jobs? . . . Well, jus' forget it. . . . I didn' mean it. Jus' foolin'. I wouldn' want to go no place like that" (*OMM* 83). The lynch threat reintroduces in place of the dream farm the mutual suspicion and divisiveness between people who remain subject to the traditional system of racism and patriarchy. The momentary hope that Crooks, who has lived his life being segregated from the others on the ranch, will "lend a hand" to the others on the farm is a hope for integration. One must imagine that Crooks's brief enthusiasm is for a social arrangement different from that which he experiences, that the farm the men imagine is one where the color line is not an ever-present division. On the one hand, the group can seemingly accommodate all those marginalized because of mental or physical disability, in the cases of Lennie and Candy; because of skin color, in the case of Crooks. The group functions as an antidote to the ranch's reproduction of social division and inequalities. On the other hand, this spirit of inclusion stops at Curley's wife. Would they or could they ever overcome the misogyny that compels them to exclude Curley's wife? This would be the next logical step. But we never find out: in a complex story, Steinbeck allows the dream farm (and the politics it stands for) to dissolve when it is exposed to the social inequalities constructed around gender and race.

The cluster of American social problems erupting in Crooks's room is almost completely missing in the version Steinbeck and Kaufman created for the Broadway stage. In this version and in the movie versions that follow, George returns from town and enters Crooks's room *before* Curley's wife arrives. This changes the scene entirely. Now, the main conflict takes place between George and Curley's wife, rather than Crooks and Curley's wife. George, instead of Crooks, demands that Curley's wife "get out of here" and repeats again, "Get the hell out of here" (*Play* 56). Curley's wife refuses and demands, "I got a right to talk to anybody I want to" (notice how it is Curley's wife who now takes up the language of "rights," which originally was Crooks's). George loses his temper and, according to the stage directions, "furious, steps close," saying only, "Why, you—" (*Play* 56).

In place of Curley's wife's physical imposition on Crooks ("She turned on him in scorn. . . . She closed on him"), Steinbeck's revision gives stage directions for George to "leap" at Curley's wife (*Play* 57). George is directed to "ferociously" grasp her shoulder, whirl her around (away from Lennie, whose shoulder she is directed to be "stroking"), and then finally "step close" with his "hand . . . raised to strike her" (*Play* 57). Reacting to George's raised hand, Curley's wife, now taking on the gestures Crooks had in the novel, "cowers a little" (*Play* 57). George "stiffens, seeing BOSS, frozen in position" (*Play* 56–57). In place of the piercing words that accompany these movements—"Listen, Nigger," "You know what I could do?" and "You keep your place then, Nigger"—Steinbeck first inserts George's threatening "Listen . . . you! I tried to give you a break. Don't walk into nothing!" (*Play* 56, ellipsis in original), then Curley's wife's response "I got a right to talk to anybody I want to," and, finally, George's truncated, "Why, you—" (*Play* 56). The language and gestures clearly demonstrate what has happened in the revision: the roles of aggressor and victimized have switched. Where Curley's wife and Crooks were victims in the novel, Curley's wife absorbs all the victimization in the play.

The different film versions vary in their treatment of this interchange between George and Curley's wife. Milestone's movie shows George lifting his hand, while the Badiyi has George grab her arms in an attempt to shove her outside. The Sinise version avoids the conflict altogether, opting instead to have Curley's wife's interaction with the men completely nonconfrontational: she approaches George and Lennie outside, telling them that "Curley got mad at me after supper, broke all my records." When Curley's wife says, "I know how you got them bruises on your face, how Curley got his hand busted," all traces of hostility or contention are gone. She merely seeks truth and sincere dialogue. Sensing that Lennie and George are sticking to their story, she merely says, "Alright, if you say so." She is crying as she runs back to the house, telling of how someday she will go to town, not to be seen again by the men she lives among so unhappily. Sinise's version, therefore, continues the process of making Curley's wife a more sympathetic character, placing a larger emphasis on a real person under duress while also removing more traces of her previous role as a femme fatale. In doing so, however, Sinise's interpretation goes furthest in dissociating what in the original story are dramatically integrated parts. He decides to isolate Lennie and Crooks's interaction from Curley's wife's appearance and to depict Candy as completely absent, therefore eliminating Candy's "figuring" for the farm as a factor in this scene. These revisions eliminate the group dynamic that is a mainstay in earlier versions of the scene.

The other movie versions continue to downplay Crooks's role as the story unfolds. They start well: in Milestone's and Badiyi's films, Crooks appears to have fully joined the enthusiasm built up around the dream farm. Milestone heightens this feeling by beginning the scene focused on Crooks's arms raised in the air and his voice intoning, "There's a meeting here tonight," the chorus lines from the African American spiritual by that title. But in both of these films, Crooks visibly fades, first into his seat when George enters the room and then into the background when Curley's wife arrives. He is only drawn out of that background momentarily when George suggests that Curley's wife "ask Crooks what she come to ask an' then get the hell home." By fading into the background seemingly naturally (without a specific cause), Crooks is again "reduced . . . to nothing." But now he is reduced not by Curley's wife's words, but by the film script itself.

In Sinise's version, Candy never enters Crooks's room, and therefore Crooks never entertains the thought of joining the other men. The dialogue about the farm stops at Crooks telling Lennie, "You're nuts." George does not turn Crooks down, but simply says "goodnight" after reprimanding Lennie for wandering into Crooks's room. By removing from Crooks's room the optimism brought by Candy and the pessimism brought by Curley's wife, Sinise's version avoids the question of Crooks's fate, as well as his connection to whatever the other men will make of their immediate situation and their future.

In the novel, Crooks's words "Jus' forget it. . . . Jus' foolin'" (*OMM* 83) follow directly on the heels of his encounter with Curley's wife, indicating the threat of lynching changes Crooks's mind about joining the dream farm. In the movie scripts, by contrast, Crooks's ability to join the farm is foreclosed before Curley's wife even arrives. Milestone's and Badiyi's films have George grow angry that Candy and Lennie have broken the vow of secrecy and have told their plans to Crooks. When George, in a patronizing manner, tells Crooks that it "'taint nothin' against you," it is unclear whether the broken secrecy or whether Crooks's race (that is, the same reason he is segregated from the bunkhouse) is ultimately why George denies Crooks's inclusion. But Crooks seems to accept his exclusion as a fait accompli, responding with, "I know. Them guys comin' in an' settin' made me forget."

We have to look once again at the textual history to see what has really happened here. Crooks's line "You guys comin' in an' settin' made me forget" comes from the concluding lines in the fourth chapter of the novel, but it gains a different meaning in the films, as its context is changed (*OMM* 82). In the movie script (Milestone's and Badiyi's), George returns from town and enters Crooks's room before Curley's wife appears there (and hence can be the one to fight with Curley's wife). In the novel, George enters the scene after Curley's wife has threatened Crooks and left the barn. These words were not originally delivered to George as a response to George rejecting the idea that Crooks can join in their plans for a farm, but rather to Candy. In the novel, Crooks's admission that the men sitting in his bedroom made him "forget" is a response to Candy's complaint that "that bitch didn't ought to of said that to you," an assertion that Crooks does not deserve the cruelty Curley's wife has shown in threatening to raise a lynch mob against him. That is, Crooks's "forgetting" was at first a forgetting that his skin color always marks him as different, subject to different rules and a lack of guaranteed rights. To hear these lines when they are delivered to George in Milestone's and Badiyi's films is to hear an echo of the novel's original criticism of socially instituted racism, but now fashioned in a weaker, veiled form.

And yet this is one area where the movies are closer to the novel than the play. In the Broadway script, Crooks's lines about "forgetting" do not appear. When George says to Crooks, "It ain't nothing against you, Crooks. We just wasn't gonna tell nobody," the stage directions note that Candy "tries to change the subject," asking, "Didn't you have no fun in town?" (*Play* 54). In the play, therefore, Crooks's inclusion in the dream farm is less obviously denied than in the movie versions (Milestone's and Badiyi's, the films in which Crooks's inclusion remains a question). As the play's scene ends with the Boss entering the room just as George's hand is menacingly raised above Curley's wife, the topic of Crooks joining the farm is simply not brought up for the rest of the scene. On the one hand, this version holds out the possibility of Crooks joining the dream farm (with the implication of racial integration). On the other hand, since the lynch threat is removed, the scene also diminishes the importance of the very question by removing the commentary on race, and in particular interracial violence, in America.

It has often been noted that a fatalist worldview resides at the core of Steinbeck's *Of Mice and Men*. This worldview is reflected in its original title, "Something That Happened," and is apparent in the inexplicable force that makes Lennie lose control over his strength when he pets soft things, or in George's naiveté in judging that Lennie could make it through another bout of working without getting them in trouble. In contrast to this level of tragic meaning is the scene in Crooks's room, which is the key moment of what one might call the social tragedy in *Of Mice and Men*. This part of the tragedy reflects how the structure of this society blocks the realization of people's individual and collective dreams and ideals. Richard Hart has explored the depth with which *Of Mice and Men*, through its characters of Curley's wife and Crooks, treats sexism and racism as moral questions, concluding that "by portraying the lived realities of racism and sexism—in dramatically ugly but honest terms—Steinbeck wants us to go inside the skins of all those affected by the shaping conditions of social existence and to feel their bitter loneliness and desperation."[21] What I would hope to add is just how this goal is integrated into the work of art itself and how, since this is so, even small changes to the story greatly affect its meaning. The stage and film adaptations have their virtues. But the most evident changes made in revising the story for Broadway and the big screen unfortunately lose something of the force with which Steinbeck, by addressing the social and psychological effects of the all-too-prevalent racial violence, was writing against the racism and sexism that were entrenched in his society—an aim that necessitated a particular balance of characters and the inclusion of a complex and troubling scene.

Notes

1. For biographical accounts, see Jackson Benson, *The True Adventures of John Steinbeck, Writer: A Biography* (New York: Viking, 1984), 351–58, and Jay Parini, *John Steinbeck: A Biography* (New York: Henry Holt, 1995), 185–92.

2. Benson, *True Adventures*, 358. Also see Don Swaim, "Steinbeck and Kaufman at Cherchez La Farm," *Steinbeck Studies* 13, no. 1 (Winter 2001): 8–14.

3. Elaine Steinbeck and Robert Wallsten, eds., *Steinbeck: A Life in Letters* (New York: Viking, 1975), 138.

4. For information on the Theatre Union's production of *Of Mice and Men*, see especially Warren French, "The First Theatrical Production of Steinbeck's *Of Mice and Men*," *American Literature* 36 (January 1965): 525–27; Robert Morsberger, "Steinbeck and the Stage," in *The Short Novels of John Steinbeck*, ed. Jackson J. Benson. (Durham, NC: Duke University Press, 1990), 272–73, and Margaret Shedd, "Of Mice and Men," *Theatre Arts Monthly* 21 (October 1937): 774–80.

5. Qtd. in French, "First Theatrical Production," 526.

6. "Mice, Men and Mr. Steinbeck." *New York Times*, 5 December 1937, sec. 12: 7.

7. Morsberger, "Steinbeck and the Stage," 273–75; Mimi R. Gladstein, "*Of Mice and Men*: Creating and Re-creating Curley's Wife," in *Beyond Boundaries: Rereading John Steinbeck*, ed. Susan Shillinglaw and Kevin Hearle (Tuscaloosa: University of Alabama Press, 2002), 205.

8. Morsberger, "Steinbeck and the Stage," 275; Charles Johnson, "Reading the Character of Crooks in *Of Mice and Men*: A Black Writer's Perspective," in

John Steinbeck and His Contemporaries, ed. Stephen K. George and Barbara A. Heavilin (Lanham, MD: Scarecrow, 2007), 119–20.

9. See, for example, Marlene Park, "Lynching and Anti-Lynching: Art and Politics in the 1930s," in *The Social and the Real: Political Art of the 1930s in the Western Hemisphere*, ed. Alejandro Anreus, Diana L. Linden, and Jonathan Weinberg, 155–77 (University Park, PA: Pennsylvania State University Press, 2006).

10. Jacqueline Goldsby, *A Spectacular Secret: Lynching in American Life and Literature* (Chicago: University of Chicago Press, 2006), ch. 6.

11. Steinbeck and Wallsten, *Life in Letters*, 136.

12. John Steinbeck, *Of Mice and Men: Play in Three Acts*, acting edition, 1937 (New York: Dramatists Play Service, 1964), 45. Subsequent quotations are cited parenthetically in the text as *Play* followed by the page number.

13. For an examination of Curley's wife as she is portrayed in the film adaptations, see Gladstein's "*Of Mice and Men*: Creating and Re-creating Curley's Wife."

14. Steinbeck and Wallsten, *Life in Letters*, 154.

15. John Steinbeck, *Of Mice and Men* (New York: Penguin Classics, 1993), 73. Subsequent quotations are cited parenthetically in the text as *OMM* followed by the page number.

16. Kaufman also counseled Steinbeck to "include a *little* more humor . . . both for its lightening effect and the heightening of the subsequent tragedy by comparison" (Steinbeck and Wallsten 136).

17. Johnson, "Reading the Character of Crooks," 115. Johnson also makes the point that "if Crooks is not essential to the story's plot, he *is* crucial for elaborating the story's theme," which Johnson identifies as the theme of friendship. Crooks qualifies for the Aristotelian friendship at the heart of the story, but his character is denied its fullest implications because Steinbeck ultimately makes him conform to stereotypes of the romanticized racial outsider, what Johnson also calls the "victim savant," and the emasculated black male. I am indebted to Johnson's essay, which clearly establishes the need to pay attention to this character and how much one can find in the details of the story. (Essay also included in this volume.)

18. Anne P. Rice, "Introduction," in *Witnessing Lynching: American Writers Respond*, ed. Anne P. Rice (New Brunswick, NJ: University of Rutgers Press, 2003), 12.

19. Trudier Harris, *Exorcising Blackness: Historical and Literary Lynching and Burning Rituals* (Bloomington: Indiana University Press, 1984), 26.

20. John Steinbeck, *Travels with Charley in Search of America*. 1962. New York: Penguin, 1980. Subsequent quotations are cited parenthetically in the text as *Travels* followed by the page number.

21. Richard Hart, "Moral Experience in *Of Mice and Men*: Challenges and Reflection." In *The Moral Philosophy of John Steinbeck*, ed. Stephen K. George (Lanham, MD: Scarecrow, 2005), 70.

Works Cited

Arendt, Hannah. *The Human Condition*. Chicago: University of Chicago Press, 1958.

Benson, Jackson J. *The True Adventures of John Steinbeck, Writer: A Biography*. New York: Viking, 1984.

French, Warren G. "The First Theatrical Production of Steinbeck's *Of Mice and Men*." *American Literature* 36 (January 1965): 525–27.

Floyd, Carlisle. *Of Mice and Men: A Musical Drama in Three Acts Based on the Novel and Play by John Steinbeck, Libretto*. New York: Belwin-Mills, 1971.

Gladstein, Mimi R. "*Of Mice and Men*: Creating and Re-creating Curley's Wife." In *Beyond Boundaries: Rereading John Steinbeck*, ed. Susan Shillinglaw and Kevin Hearle, 205–20. Tuscaloosa: University of Alabama Press, 2002.

Goldsby, Jacqueline. *A Spectacular Secret: Lynching in American Life and Literature*. Chicago: University of Chicago Press, 2006.

Harris, Trudier. *Exorcising Blackness: Historical and Literary Lynching and Burning Rituals*. Bloomington: Indiana University Press, 1984.

Hart, Richard E. "Moral Experience in *Of Mice and Men*: Challenges and Reflection." In *The Moral Philosophy of John Steinbeck*, ed. Stephen K. George, 61–71. Lanham, MD: Scarecrow, 2005.

Johnson, Charles. "Reading the Character of Crooks in *Of Mice and Men*: A Black Writer's Perspective." In *John Steinbeck and His Contemporaries*, ed. Stephen K. George and Barbara A. Heavilin, 111–21. Lanham, MD: Scarecrow, 2007.

"Mice, Men and Mr. Steinbeck." *New York Times*, 5 December 1937, sec. 12: 7. *ProQuest Historical Newspapers: The New York Times (1851–2004)*. ProQuest, University of Washington Libraries, Seattle, WA. www.proquest.com .offcampus.lib.washington.edu/ (accessed 8 July 2008).

Morsberger, Robert. "Steinbeck and the Stage." In *The Short Novels of John Steinbeck*, ed. Jackson J. Benson, 271–93. Durham, NC: Duke University Press, 1990.

Parini, Jay. *John Steinbeck: A Biography*. New York: Henry Holt, 1995.

Park, Marlene. "Lynching and Anti-Lynching: Art and Politics in the 1930s." In *The Social and the Real: Political Art of the 1930s in the Western Hemisphere*, ed. Alejandro Anreus, Diana L. Linden, and Jonathan Weinberg, 155–77. University Park: Pennsylvania State University Press, 2006.

Rice, Anne P. "Introduction." In *Witnessing Lynching: American Writers Respond*, ed. Anne P. Rice, 1–24. New Brunswick, NJ: University of Rutgers Press, 2003.

Shedd, Margaret. "Of Mice and Men." *Theatre Arts Monthly* 21 (October 1937): 774–80.

Steinbeck, John. *Of Mice and Men*. 1937. New York: Penguin Modern Classics, 1993.

———. *Of Mice and Men: Play in Three Acts*. Acting edition. New York: Dramatists Play Service, 1937.

———. *Travels with Charley in Search of America*. 1962. New York: Penguin, 1980.

———. "The Vigilante." In *The Long Valley*, 93–100. 1986. New York: Penguin, 1995.

Steinbeck, Elaine and Robert Wallsten, eds. *Steinbeck: A Life in Letters*. New York: Viking, 1975.

Swaim, Don. "Steinbeck and Kaufman at Cherchez La Farm." *Steinbeck Studies* 13, no. 1 (Winter 2001): 8–14.

CHAPTER NINETEEN

EMOTION RECOLLECTED IN TRANQUILITY: A CONTEXT FOR ROMANTICISM IN *OF MICE AND MEN*

Barbara A. Heavilin

To the administration they were an eyesore and a humiliation, and its determination to exorcise them reflected a general hardening throughout the land of the attitude of the well-fed toward the ill-fed.—William Manchester, *The Glory and the Dream: A Narrative History of America*

In *The Glory and the Dream: A Narrative History of America, 1932–1972*, William Manchester describes the summer of 1932, five years before the publication of Steinbeck's *Of Mice and Men*, when thousands of destitute World War I veterans and their families camped out in Washington, D.C., seeking "relief from the Great Depression":

The men drilled, sang war songs, and once, led by a Medal of Honor winner and watched by a hundred thousand Washingtonians, they marched up Pennsylvania Avenue bearing American flags of faded cotton. Most of the time, however, they waited and brooded. . . . They wanted immediate payment of the soldiers' "bonus" authorized by the Adjusted Compensation Act of 1924 but not due until 1945. If they could get cash now, the men would receive about $500 each. Headline writers had christened them "the Bonus Army," "the bonus marchers." They called themselves the Bonus Expeditionary Force.[1]

Parts of this essay were previously published in *John Steinbeck's "Of Mice and Men": A Reference Guide*. Westport, CT: Greenwood Press, 19. It is used by permission.

In response, President Herbert Hoover barricaded himself in the White House, isolating himself and setting up guards so that no one could pass. When some veterans resisted attempts to evacuate them from the city, the White House accused them of being Communist agitators. Although they were unarmed, a short time later General Douglas McArthur drew out all of his forces against men, women, and children:

> Troopers of the 3rd Cavalry, led by Major Patton, pranced along brandishing naked sabers. Behind the horses marched a machine gun detachment and men from the 12th Infantry, the 13th Engineers, and the 34th Infantry, the sun glinting on their bayonets. Behind these units rolled the six tanks, the caterpillar treads methodically chewing up the soft asphalt.[2]

The veterans could not believe that the government they had served would send out the armed forces against them. Nor could they believe that those whom they viewed as fellow soldiers would attack them. They were wrong. Routed out and herded out of the state, they found no welcome anywhere: "One railroad," Manchester writes, "put together a special train to carry those bound for the plains states; Kansas City civic leaders raised $1,500 to keep it from stopping there, and the boxcars hurtled onward. . . . By autumn, most of the BEF had merged into the enormous transient population which roamed the land in 1932."[3]

As well-fed Americans closed their hearts against these ill-fed and homeless veterans in their midst, so they closed their minds and hearts to the ominous signs of the beginning Holocaust in Nazi Germany and the plight of the Jews there—with the State Department's issuing a news release that Jews were no longer being mistreated, a report based on cables received from Berlin. To belie these claims, by 1935 some 80,000 German Jews had fled to the United States for refuge.

Such was the general tenor of the times worldwide—human suffering, horror, and a general indifference or denial. Such is the national and worldwide backdrop when John Steinbeck was writing *Of Mice and Men*. In this novel, sympathy for a world that often goes sorrowfully wrong—as in Robert Burns's "To a Mouse" that is reflected in the novel's final title—is submerged beneath a seemingly existential depiction of "something that happened," as Steinbeck first titled the book. Even though this title may suggest an empirical, coolly objective recording of an event, Steinbeck has much in common with Burns's empathy for the mouse upturned by his plow and with St. Francis of Assisi's mystic insight into the nature of things that calls for us to walk softly upon the earth, for the rocks are also our brothers. Clearly, Steinbeck does not share the fatalistic outlook of the existentialists and naturalists of his time. In the beauty of the novel's opening and closing scenes, the delicacy of character delineation (including a faithful old dog), the authenticity of voices, and the poetic quality of the language there is pathos in the truest sense, a speaking to the heart and the human condition that is indicative of all great literature.

Steinbeck saw around him firsthand a world of suffering and indifference; and his personal experiences inform his writing of *Of Mice and Men* and later of *The Grapes of Wrath*. Jackson J. Benson's *The True Adventures of John Steinbeck, Writer* finds the genesis of character and setting in *Of Mice and Men* in Steinbeck's observations of bindlestiffs and hobos while he was working on the Spreckels sugar ranches during harvest. There he met bindlestiffs and hobos who started at the southernmost ranch and worked their way north until harvest was ended. The novel's characters Lennie and George are like these bindlestiffs, who go from place to place in search of work, carrying their few belongings on their back. Benson pinpoints the location of the novel as "Spreckels ranch number 2, just south of Soledad on the west side of the Salinas River."[4] Japanese, Mexicans, and Filipinos likewise worked on these ranches; and there is a brief, if peripheral, reference to the Japanese presence in *Of Mice and Men* in George's complaint about having to move around the country, being fed "by a Jap cook."[5]

Claudia Durst Johnson's 1997 *Understanding "Of Mice and Men," "The Red Pony," and "The Pearl": A Student Casebook of Issues, Sources, and Historical Documents* records the life of "the vagrant farm worker," and classifies Lennie and George as "non-Depression . . . migratory laborers" who, nonetheless, endure a hand-to-mouth existence. While their life at the ranch is relatively decent—with shelter, adequate if unpalatable food, a place to sleep and store a few possessions—it reveals "the inevitable psychological effects of homelessness and hopelessness."[6] She documents the life of such men by selections from diaries, documentaries such as Carey McWilliams's *Factories in the Fields*, and histories of the times. In one entry, Johnson cites Josiah Royce's early history of California that was as well "a study of the American character."[7] Specifically, Johnson points out the similarities between Royce's description of the 1849 pioneers who became irresponsible and miserable as a result of their "homelessness, vagrancy, and lack of family life" and the social structure in *Of Mice and Men*

> that contributes not only to the riotous drinking and whoring of the men, but to their failure to grow beyond boyhood, and because they have no lasting connections with one another, to a cold and mean streak. This is especially true in their treatment of Candy, whose beloved old dog is shot and who knows that he will soon be thrown out with no means of supporting himself. It can also be seen in their treatment of Crooks, who is ostracized and used as a whipping boy and who, in turn, has developed a bitter, suspicious attitude toward the rest of the men.[8]

Steinbeck's *Of Mice and Men*, then, not only reflects its own times, but it is a universally applicable portrait of the psychological impact of dispossession, homelessness, and loneliness.

Critics have variously viewed *Of Mice and Men*, and attempts have been made to categorize it variously as Realism, Naturalism, or Romanticism. The details of Steinbeck's description of setting, character, and circumstance in *Of Mice and Men* are certainly realistic—as he intended them to be—having set out to write about "something that happened," a seemingly nonjudgmental story focused around a central incident. And this novel does have much in common with realism, which *The Harper Handbook to Literature* defines as literature that is a "faithful representation of life."[9] Holding to the "materialistic belief that truth is a commodity accessible on the surface of things, perceptible to the senses," the realists' aim was to take Nature rather than art as a model, choosing subject matter from "ordinary life closest to the experience of the writer."[10]

Unlike the eighteenth-century British satirists, whose purpose is to hold the mirror so that society may see itself as it is and set things right, the realists' nonjudgmental purpose is merely to reflect things as they are, or how the writer perceives them to be. *Harper* delineates the techniques by which realists seek to achieve this aim of "rigid selectivity," with the mirror positioned to capture representative scenes that place emphasis on the ordinary. In setting, character, and plot, there is verisimilitude in abundant and accurate detail that describes everything from houses and furniture, to clothes, seasons, patterns of speech, and societal behavior.

The language tends toward a "plain style" that places emphasis on plot rather than on the narrator, whose carefully chosen perspective presents a "window on truth." Although the story is often told in third person, this perspective strives to avoid subjectivity and omniscience in order to enhance a sense of reality. In realistic novels, events often seem inevitable because the reader cannot envision any other result of the characters' choices.[11]

This depiction of realism is *almost* a formula for *Of Mice and Men*. Steinbeck's subject matter is from close, personal experience. Events are selective and representative, details abound—from the slant of sunlight that marks the passing of time, to the ranch hands' personal items stored in apple boxes above their bunks, to the sharpness of George's features and the vagueness of Lennie's. The story's objectivity also conceals the narrator, and the plot has a seemingly inevitable outcome (given these particular characters in their circumstances).

But Steinbeck, unlike the realists, does not depict truth as "a commodity accessible on the surface of things, perceptible to the senses." There is another, higher definition of truth, one not dependent upon empirical verification and surfaces. Aristotle, for example, finds poetry to be a higher thing than history because the first deals with what is true to the human condition whereas the latter deals with facts. And *Webster's Seventh New Collegiate Dictionary*'s third definition of "truth" as "a transcendent fundamental or spiritual reality" goes beyond the factual and the superficial, revealing a higher level of reality than that available on "the surface of things."[12] In the character of the feebleminded Lennie, for example, Steinbeck has created a person who is more than the sum of his parts. Slow-witted, childlike, and innocently dangerous to himself and others, Lennie depends on George for survival in a world he cannot fully comprehend. But after the reader has found the measure of Lennie's intelligence quotient, his height, his weight, his girth, his extreme limitations, his childish manipulation of George, his inability to function on his own, and his innocent and unwitting propensity to hurt small animals, there is more to him than that, something that defies measurement.

Lennie emerges as a fully realized human being—one who is capable of dreams, aspirations, love, abiding friendship, commitment. He is a highly sympathetic character, in other words, one with whom the insightful reader can identify and empathize. The reader has been made to care when Lennie's dream dies along with him. Read in this light, *Of Mice and Men* has more in common with the Romantics' idealization of the ordinary and the commonplace than with the realists' accurate portrayal of surface things.

Steinbeck critic Warren French's 1975 revised edition of *John Steinbeck* goes a step beyond realism when he classifies *Of Mice and Men* with the Naturalists, maintaining that the 1930s works are "the most remarkable and consistent body of Naturalistic writing in American literature." In these novels, French asserts, Steinbeck "presents the pathetic defeats of naturalistic characters."[13] Yale critic Harold Bloom also places this novel with the Naturalists, asserting that Steinbeck's "heavy naturalism is very close to fatalism" and comparing *Of Mice and Men* (unfavorably, of course, considering his general disregard for Steinbeck) with Dreiser's naturalistic and fatalistic *Sister Carrie* and *An American Tragedy*.[14]

According to *The Harper Handbook to Literature*, naturalism is a derivative of scientific determinism, especially Darwinism, because it perceives

> a person's fate as the product of blind external or biological forces, chiefly heredity and environment, but in the typical Naturalistic novel chance played a large part as well, suggesting a formula something like H + E + C = F (Heredity plus Environment plus Chance equals Fate).[15]

Viewed in this light, *Of Mice and Men* might *almost* be considered naturalistic—but not quite, although there is certainly a strong sense of inevitability in the novel. Given Lennie's peculiar abnormalities, the environment into which he has been thrust, and the unhappy consequences of an ill-fated meeting with Curley's wife in the barn, the novel's outcome *may* seem fated. As in Sophocles' *Oedipus Rex*, however, opportunities for choice occur throughout the novel. George *chooses*, for example, to ignore both his and Lennie's forebodings about the ranch. He *chooses* to go into town, leaving Lennie unsupervised even though he knows that Lennie is not a responsible adult. Urged on by Slim's approval of the action, he finally *chooses* to pull the trigger that kills his friend even though he is most hesitant and reluctant to do so.

Steinbeck does, however, share some of the Naturalists' techniques, which—as *Harper* points out—Naturalists share with the realists but extend and apply differently. Naturalists do not choose a mirror that reflects life but a lens that focuses where they please. More experimenter and scientist than observer, they manipulate both "characters and plot."[16] As tightly controlled as a poem and sharply focused on the events surrounding a single incident—something that happened—*Of Mice and Men* serves like the lens of a microscope that zeroes in on the object in question rather than like the more encompassing and nonselective view of a mirror that simply reflects everything before it equally.

Steinbeck's interest in non-teleological thinking in the novel fits with the lens image of the Naturalists as well, for he closely examines characters and contains events within narrow confines, without providing a broader context or explaining how things came to be the way they are or why they turn out as they do. French finds connections between a non-teleological point of view and naturalism, leading him to declare (as noted above) Steinbeck's 1930s writings to be remarkably and consistently Naturalistic.[17] But there is more to Steinbeck's 1937 *Of Mice and Men* (and his other 1930s writings as well) than is evident in his use of a seemingly non-teleological perspective. The presence of love (in the sense of *caritas*, or caring) in George and Lennie's friendship that contrasts with the absence of love in the lives of the ranch hands and even in the relationship between the newly married Curley and his girl wife takes the novel beyond a mechanistic, non-teleological world in which things just happen into a world of what ought to be.

Non-teleological Thinking versus What Ought to Be

Benson discusses the influence of the Darwinian philosophy of evolution and the survival of the fittest and of non-teleological thinking on Steinbeck's writings of the thirties. He defines non-teleological thinking and Steinbeck's use of it in his writing:

> Non-teleological thinking is mechanistic. One event leads to another, and what happens is dictated by physical laws. There is no possibility of free will—all events are determined—and there is no way of knowing whether or not there is a divine Providence, an overall design. . . . Steinbeck presented almost from the beginning of his published work a world that was mechanistic and independent of the desires of man and the presence of God. . . . There is a pervasive sense that things just

happen. People who act by their dreams are defeated; people who try to change things are unsuccessful.[18]

Here Benson's definition *almost* provides an outline for *Of Mice and Men*. The very title, taken from Robert Burns's poem, seems mechanistic and fatalistic; the original title, "Something That Happened," even more so. Both negative and positive criticism has noted the novel's Sophoclean sense of things that happen of necessity, given these particular characters, in this particular place and circumstances, at this particular time. But "almost" is a key word here; there is more to be noted about this novel than its surface fatalism. For Steinbeck provides another measure for human beings and their affairs: a strongly implied sense of what ought to be.

Side by side with *Of Mice and Men*'s seemingly mechanistic, haphazard universe is another world that is ruled not by a scientific determinism that looks hard at what *is* (non-teleological thinking) but is ruled rather by a strongly implied and inescapable metaphysical and ethical sense of *what ought to be*, or a way of measuring life's events—possibly even of finding some meaning. The black stable buck, Crooks, confides to Lennie that the most difficult thing about his life of separateness and aloneness is that he has "nothing to measure by."[19] "Measure" is a rich word; for Crooks it means some way of determining what is real and what is not, including himself and his experiences—a criterion by which he can judge, measure, appraise, regulate, and govern his life. Reality, or what *is*, then, needs to be measured in some way, and, according to Crooks, that measurement is not to be determined by oneself, but is dependent upon community.

In the world of *Of Mice and Men*, Slim with his "Godlike eyes" is the surface measure of all things in the ranch community—from love, to politics, to the desirability (or not) of killing dogs and men. His decisions are accepted without question. Hence, when he agrees with Carlson that Candy's smelly old sheepdog must be killed and prods George into killing Lennie, no one questions his assessment. But there is another dimension alongside in *Of Mice and Men* that implies a moral universe in which the strong are not to be praised for their oppression of the weak (as in the case of Lennie and Candy) or different (as in the case of Crooks). In this alongside, moral world, there is another measure, a something higher than a human being, however godlike his eyes and demeanor.

Such a world goes beyond a tale of the mechanistic and determined—something that merely happened—into a story that Steinbeck will later, in *East of Eden*, declare to be the only story in the world:

> I believe that there is one story in the world, and only one, that has frightened and inspired us, so that we live in a Pearl White serial of continuing thought and wonder. Humans are caught—in their lives, in their thoughts, in their hungers and ambitions, in their avarice and cruelty, and in their kindness and generosity too—in a net of good and evil. I think this is the only story we have and that it occurs on all levels of feeling and intelligence. Virtue and vice were warp and woof of our first consciousness, and they will be the fabric of our last, and this despite any changes we may impose on field and river and mountain, on economy and manners. There is no other story. A man, after he has brushed off the dust and chips of his life, will have left only the hard, clean questions: Was it good or was it evil? Have I done well—or ill?[20]

This question of good and evil extends beyond the world of science into the realm of ethics and theology. It extends beyond the empirical verification of telescopes, microscopes, scales, and weights into a world of measurement based on a criterion and a standard of behavior that recognizes that human beings should be their brother's or sister's keeper—a responsibility that George accepts, even if at times grudgingly. Such behavior is a mark of *caritas*, charity, and love for a fellow human being.

In *East of Eden*, such a love is the final criterion by which a dying Adam is enabled to reach out to his son Cal and leave him with the enabling assurance that it will be his own choices that determine his character and his future, not an inherited wickedness from his prostitute mother. In *Of Mice and Men*, an acute absence of this love (in the sense of *caritas*, or charity)—other than that between the friends George and Lennie—governs the novel's tragic outcome. Although on the surface *Of Mice and Men* enacts a Darwinian philosophy of evolution and the survival of the fittest, a strong undercurrent persistently questions, "Am I my brother's keeper?" and invites speculation on a higher, more ethical way: "Who is to take care of the Lennies of this world?" Such questions provide something "to measure by."

Compassion as the Hallmark of Steinbeck's Art

Unlike those critics who classify *Of Mice and Men* with the mechanistic universe of the Naturalists, the early reviewer Lewis Gannett centers on "compassion" as the hallmark of Steinbeck's art and the criterion by which it may be measured:

> Compassion, even more than the perfect sense of form, . . . marks off John Steinbeck, artist, so sharply from all the little verbal photographers who record tough talk and snarl in books which have power without pity. The most significant things John Steinbeck has to say about his characters are never put into words; they are the overtones of which the reader is never wholly conscious—and that is art.[21]

These "overtones" that draw readers into the story are not only significant in Steinbeck's art, they are also, unfortunately, why he is wrongfully accused of sentimentality. As Gannett insightfully observes, Steinbeck is a most evocative writer who not only explores thematically the age-old question, "Am I my brother's keeper?" he involves his readers in a participatory role in a story of dispossession and isolation that seems to have no end. Steinbeck, then, seems to have as much or more in common with St. Francis of Assisi's "Tread softly, the rocks, too, are thy brothers" as he does with scientific determinism.

Although *Of Mice and Men* shares some commonalities with the Realists and Naturalists of Steinbeck's time, it nevertheless has much in common with British Romanticism. While the objectivity of its telling and the authenticity of its characters lends an aura of realism, in style and tone this novel shares with the British Romantics a concern with casting the aura of imagination over the commonplace, with speaking in the real language of the people, and with reflecting strong emotion recollected in tranquility. It further has in common with the Romantic poets a poetic style and tone that speak to the heart—belying the mechanistic universe envisioned by the Naturalists and Realists.

The major points of *Harper*'s discussion of Romanticism reveal Steinbeck's affinity for the Romantics both in demeanor and practice. Like the Romantics, Steinbeck experiments and expresses his own individuality both in subject matter and in writing technique, while celebrating the individual by turning to "common humanity as a proper subject for art."[22] Steinbeck's experiment, *Of Mice and Men*, elevates "common humanity"—those on the lowest rungs of the social ladder—to the status of art. His experiment in combining elements of novel and drama results in a story told with such simplicity that the text itself almost serves as a script for a play (as he intended), with lighting, scenes, and entrances and exits of characters.

With the Romantics, Steinbeck shared a faith in the basic goodness of people and their capacity to transcend their faults, hardships, and difficulties. Like the Romantics, he eschewed the dark Calvinistic and Puritanical belief that human beings are born in a state of total depravity and sin but seemed, rather, to share with Wordsworth a belief that they are born in innocence and may strive toward transcendence. An "imperfect society would be perfected through individual good released, encouraged, and made all-encompassing."[23] Despite its seeming fatalism, the friendship of *Of Mice and Men*'s George and Lennie in the midst of deprivation and hardship bears witness to the possibility of the fulfillment of an ideal of brotherhood. That their example does not extend to their society at large does not diminish its light.

The Romantics idealized the natural and primitive, such as Jean Jacques Rousseau's "noble savage . . . freed from the limiting restraints of civilization."[24] With a grotesque twist on Rousseau's "noble savage," Steinbeck creates the character of Lennie, who is innocently free of civilization's "limiting restraints," but also free of those inner restraints that hold violent behavior in check. He is nevertheless a sympathetic character, totally devoted to George and capable of affection for the small animals he inadvertently kills. His heart is gentle, although his hands, unfortunately, are not. Like Wordsworth's Idiot Boy and Mad Mother, he is portrayed as a human being who has worth.

Like the Romantics, then, Steinbeck is egalitarian, viewing each person as equal from birth in the eyes of God and, therefore, to be valued as an individual. Steinbeck's meticulous treatment of characters—even the most minor ones—demonstrates this egalitarian bent. Each is treated with the utmost care: from William Tenner, a former worker on the ranch whose love of reading is revealed in a published letter to a magazine; to Candy's faithful old sheepdog; to Whitey, the former occupant of George's bunk, who probably had once been faithful in attending church because he dressed up every Sunday, put on a necktie, and sat in the bunkhouse. Other characters are similarly sketched and brought to life as persons of value and worth as human beings.

In accord with their emphasis on the value and worth of each person, the Romantics valued literature that speaks to the heart and has empathic appeal:

> Emotional, intuitional, and sensual elements of artistic, religious, and intellectual expression were counted in some ways more valid than the products of education and reason. The heart versus the head became one of the great conflicts of the nineteenth century, with Romanticism raising the issue and pointing the way.[25]

Such a Romantic, empathic appeal is one of the hallmarks of the Steinbeck aesthetic, so that how the reader *feels* becomes as important as what the reader *thinks*. There is never a dichotomy between the head and the heart: the human capacity to know and understand depend on both. Like the Romantics, Steinbeck speaks to the heart, with an empathic understanding as the desired end result.

In the preface to the 1969 edition of *Steinbeck and His Critics*, E. W. Tedlock Jr. describes his own empathic experience in reading Steinbeck, showing how it *feels* to enter into an "atmosphere of marvelously fresh, non-conceptual awareness":

> As for the insight, there is at times in Steinbeck an experience that I think of as purely existential and native or basic to him, beyond cavil. It can be seen in a note of his on an early morning encounter with some farm laborers camped by the road. The note is of great objective purity and is also most humanly attractive.[26]

Here Tedlock describes a moment of "non-conceptual," pre-linguistic awareness: an insight and a feeling—a quintessentially Romantic experience and way of knowing. Steinbeck purposefully creates just such an awareness. He originally intended *Of Mice and Men* to be a children's book and wrote in a letter to Ben Abramson that he wanted to capture the world of a child in which colors are clearer, tastes sharper, and feelings more intense than they are to adults. He writes that he wanted to capture the feeling of an afternoon and of evening bird song.[27] This intention to capture what Wordsworth called "emotion recollected in tranquility" is the essence of Romantic literature—and the essence of Steinbeck's *Of Mice and Men* as well. Persistently and intentionally, Steinbeck calls for an empathic response and a heightened awareness from his readers. What these readers take from the text, however, will depend on whether or not their own inner resources are deep or hollow, as he stated in a 1939 letter to Pascal Covici concerning the manuscript of *The Grapes of Wrath*.[28] His stories, then, have no end. The last word depends on the response of the reader.

Notes

1. William Manchester, *The Glory and the Dream: A Narrative History of America*. 2 vols. [reprinted in paperback in 1984]. (New York: Little Brown, 1974), 1.

2. Manchester, *Glory*, 13–14.

3. Manchester, *Glory*, 20.

4. Jackson J. Benson, *The True Adventures of John Steinbeck, Writer* (New York: Viking Press, 1984), 39.

5. Benson, *True Adventures*, 54.

6. Claudia Durst Johnson, *Understanding "Of Mice and Men," "The Red Pony,"* and *"The Pearl": A Student Casebook of Issues, Sources, and Historical Documents* (Westport, CT: Greenwood Press, 1997), 101.

7. Johnson, *Understanding "Of Mice and Men,"* 118.

8. Johnson, *Understanding "Of Mice and Men,"* 118.

9. Northrop Frye, Sheridan Baker, and George Perkins. *The Harper Handbook to Literature* (New York: Harper and Row, 1985), 389.

10. Frye, Baker, and Perkins, *Harper Handbook*, 386–87.

11. Frye, Baker, and Perkins, *Harper Handbook*, 387.

12. *Webster's Seventh New Collegiate Dictionary* (New York: Merrian Webster, 1965).

13. Warren French, *John Steinbeck*, 2nd ed., rev. (Boston: Twayne, 1975), 87, 173.

14. Harold Bloom, ed. *John Steinbeck's "Of Mice and Men": Bloom's Notes* (Broomall, PA: Chelsea House Publishers, 1996), 6–7.

15. Frye, Baker, and Perkins, *Harper Handbook*, 307.

16. Frye, Baker, and Perkins, *Harper Handbook*, 307.

17. French, *John Steinbeck*, 87.

18. Benson, *True Adventures*, 242–43.

19. John Steinbeck, *Of Mice and Men* (New York: Penguin 1993), 69. Subsequent quotations are cited parenthetically in the text as *OMM* followed by the page number.

20. John Steinbeck, *East of Eden* (New York: Penguin, 1986), 543.

21. Lewis Gannett, "Books and Things," *New York Herald Tribune*, 25 February 1937: 17.

22. Frye, Baker, and Perkins, *Harper Handbook*, 403.

23. Frye, Baker, and Perkins, *Harper Handbook*, 403–4.

24. Frye, Baker, and Perkins, *Harper Handbook*, 404.

25. Frye, Baker, and Perkins, *Harper Handbook*, 404.

26. E. W. Tedlock Jr. and C. V. Wicker, *Steinbeck and His Critics: A Record of Twenty-five Years* (Albuquerque: University of New Mexico Press, 1969), v.

27. Benson, *True Adventures*, 325–26.

28. Elaine Steinbeck and Robert Wallsten, eds. *Steinbeck: A Life in Letters* (New York: Viking, 1975), 178.

Works Cited

Benson, Jackson J. *The True Adventures of John Steinbeck, Writer.* New York: Viking Press, 1984.

Bloom, Harold, ed. *John Steinbeck's "Of Mice and Men": Bloom's Notes.* Broomall, PA: Chelsea House Publishers, 1996.

French, William. *John Steinbeck.* 2nd ed., rev. Boston: Twayne, 1975.

Frye, Northrop, Sheridan Baker, and George Perkins. *The Harper Handbook to Literature.* New York: Harper and Row, 1985.

Gannett, Lewis. "Books and Things." New York *Herald Tribune*, 25 February 1937: 17.

Johnson, Claudia Durst. *Understanding "Of Mice and Men," "The Red Pony," and "The Pearl": A Student Casebook of Issues, Sources, and Historical Documents.* Westport, CT: Greenwood Press, 1997.

Manchester, William. *The Glory and the Dream: A Narrative History of America* [2 vols.] New York: Little Brown, 1974.

Steinbeck, Elaine and Robert Wallsten, eds. *Steinbeck: A Life in Letters.* New York: Viking, 1975.

Steinbeck, John. *East of Eden.* New York: Penguin, 1986.

———. *Of Mice and Men* (modern critical edition). New York: Penguin, 1993.

Tedlock, E. W., Jr., and C. V. Wicker. *Steinbeck and His Critics: A Record of Twenty-five Years.* Albuquerque: University of New Mexico Press, 1969.

CHAPTER TWENTY

ONE IS THE LONELIEST NUMBER: STEINBECK'S PARADOXICAL ATTRACTION AND REPULSION TO ISOLATION/SOLITUDE

Michael J. Meyer

My books endeavor to include characters who resemble me physically and spiritually in all my gorgeous loneliness and splendid isolation.— Sherman Alexie in his acceptance speech for the 2007 National Book Award for Young People's Literature for *The Absolute True Diary of a Part-Time Indian*

It is easy in the world to live after the world's opinion; it is easy in solitude to live after our own, but the great man is he who in the midst of the crowds keeps with the perfect sweetness of the independence of solitude.—Henry David Thoreau, *Walden*

According to the words of the popular 1970s hit by Three Dog Night, "One is the loneliest, number one is the loneliest / Number one is the loneliest number that you'll ever do." While listeners might nod in assent at this obvious statement and wonder why anyone would need to repeat this phrase as if it were a rare insight, a closer look reveals that the lyric contains a very ambiguous statement, making a comment far beyond the common interpretation about loneliness. Perhaps the band understood that the varying positions occupied by the word *number* in the lyrics when accompanied by a shift in form class from adjective to noun would create potential variation in meaning for listeners. For in our success-oriented Western society, being number one is seldom thought of as isolating and/or negative. Instead, it generally is seen as an indicator of uniqueness, of popularity, of being on top of the world. Yet ironically, as many famous artists have discovered, such popularity and recognition are often accompanied by "dis-ease": indeed, attaining success in any field might not be a comfortable accomplishment, and there are many celebrities who long for a time when life was simpler, when their personal space was not invaded, and when their actions were not under intense scrutiny.

John Steinbeck also discovered the vagaries that accompanied his achievement as one of America's premier literary artists. As Steinbeck climbed the ladder toward becoming number one in the field of literature, he discovered that his rise in popularity and critical acclaim was accompanied by a growing sense of isolation and loneliness. As his books became best sellers, he found himself increasingly set apart from others, as if he didn't belong in any group. Whether this was a self-imposed emotional crisis or whether it was generated from the outside by friends and foes alike is ultimately immaterial. What is important is that, misunderstood and underappreciated, he became more and more reclusive, hesitant to interact with others, beset by intrusive admirers as well as by intractable critics of his literary production. Not surprisingly, the loneliness that accompanied his success, and indeed which was present in Steinbeck's formative years as a child and as an adolescent, soon began to infiltrate his fictional output and to find reiteration in many of his most memorable characters.

However, although the themes of isolation and loneliness have been accorded critical acknowledgement as a principal Steinbeckian fictional emphasis, to my knowledge no critic has yet traced the impact of these elements in his personal correspondence nor suggested that Steinbeck held an ambiguous paradoxical viewpoint about them in real life, a viewpoint that also extended into his fictional output. For Steinbeck, as for many artists, both literary and musical, the loneliness/isolation that they encountered as a result of their professions was bane as well as blessing. It brought a sense of rejection and alienation that resulted in depression and a disconsolate apprehension about the world around them, but it also offered positive refuge, a quiet space or down time when they could contemplate their message to the world in a time of silence and could create new works without interference by others.

Through close analysis of Steinbeck's nonfictional output, including letters and essays, and observation of the fictional characters who struggle with loneliness/isolation (especially those in *Of Mice and Men*), it will become evident that the author clearly recognized the duality of loneliness. Although "one is the loneliest number" in both senses of the phrase's meaning, there remains a positive element in "alone" time that the author found difficult to understand as an inherent character trait in a species that deliberately seeks out and values companionship and social interaction as healthy and positive aspects of human life.

Excerpts of correspondence recorded in *A Life in Letters* give evidence that, even as a young man, Steinbeck possessed a keen awareness of the human duality that existed in moments of isolation. He realized that such moments could be times of cruelty and insensitivity because individuals were cut off from others; conversely, they could prove regenerative hours when solitude allows uninterrupted contemplation. Yet as an immature writer, Steinbeck seems to have experienced more episodes of the former than the latter and to have gained an appreciation of the positive nature of isolation only as his age and experience advanced.

As early as 1930, Steinbeck wrote in a letter to Amasa (Ted) Miller that he felt a "lostness" when he was not engaged in writing, in sharing a story with others.[1] Later, despite his burgeoning success, he mentions his "sadness" and a "feeling of impending doom" (*LIL* 44), no doubt as a result of his fear of rejection or critical disapproval from a reading public who might misunderstand what he was trying to communicate. His early concerns about artistic recognition and renown indicate that he may have felt that his relative obscurity and its accompanying isolation were evidence of failure and defeat as a literary artist. Yet Steinbeck's need for interaction with others, especially a reading public, is sometimes mitigated by his realization of the simplicity of his own human necessities. In a 1934 letter to George Albee Jr. for example, he writes: "I don't want to possess anything, nor to be anything. I have no ambition because, on inspection, the aims of ambition achieved seem tiresome" (*LIL* 93).

Steinbeck also expressed his desire for anonymity and solitude when *Tortilla Flat* (1935) became a best seller. Despite his pride in the achievement and the positive reception his novel received, the author shares his fear of becoming a "trade mark" in a letter to critic Joseph Henry Jackson. In it, he expresses the problematic state of being a celebrity and wonders how he will cope with the loss he will experience as a result of becoming well-known. Expressing how uncomfortable he is with the increased social interaction that is required of him (*LIL* 119), Steinbeck seems to recognize that some "alone time" is essential to insure quality artistic expression. Similarly, when writing to his close friend, Dook Sheffield, Steinbeck shares the ironic result of his popularity: "I get more cut off all the time because people are like you, afraid of this thing that has been built up, and I don't see them often. Knowing I am watched, I don't go any place. Knowing I'll be quoted, I don't say anything" (*LIL* 198).

During the early 1940s, the negative qualities of loneliness seem to have occupied Steinbeck's personal as well as fictional focus to a greater degree. Another letter to Sheffield states:

> The loneliness and the discouragement are by no means a thing that has passed. In fact, they seem to crowd in more than ever . . . [even though] I now possess the things that the great majority of people think are the death of loneliness and discouragement only they aren't. (*LIL* 212)

Later, by the time the war years arrived, Steinbeck seems to have discovered once more the renewing rather than the destructive powers of solitude. Writing to his second wife, Gwyn, he mentions meeting several naval officers in Africa and muses on how they dealt with their "nerve strain" simply by being there "in that very quiet place and getting rest that can't be got anywhere else. They listen to music and sleep and it does them a great deal of good" (*LIL* 261).

Returning from the war and establishing a residence in New York City, Steinbeck similarly tried to establish a restricted working space for himself—a working cellar—"no window, no ability to look out and see the postman and the garbage wagon" (*LIL* 287). Nevertheless, the dark side of loneliness, rejection, and a lack of self-confidence often returned to plague him, especially when he tried to write. Just a page later, in a 1946 letter recorded in the *Letters*, he notes the following: "I have been feeling lousy in my mind today. It has been a period of blue despair such as I haven't had in quite a long time (*LIL* 288).

Perhaps it was the increasing marital tension between John and Gwyn and their ultimate separation and divorce that account for Steinbeck's return to an emphasis on the negative aspects of loneliness in the late 1940s. Describing the isolated feeling as similar to "little fingers of ice" that occasionally bring "blind panic" (*LIL* 330), Steinbeck seems to be searching for peace and satisfaction that some of his characters find only in death; in short, Steinbeck craves the forgetfulness and escape that isolation/solitude can provide. Yet the downside of being alone (both the divorce from Gwyn and the death of his close friend Ed Ricketts occurred in 1948) seems so predominant that he cannot see past it. The negatives outweigh the positives.

A careful critic senses that comments which suggest control ("I still get the panic aloneness but I can work [it] out by thinking of what it is" and "I realized more than any time in my life that there is nothing anyone can do. It's something that has to be done alone" [*LIL* 334–35]) are merely hollow sounds rather than a reality that Steinbeck believes in. He desperately needs to believe his dilemma can have an absolute solution rather than remain an interminable paradox. By late 1949, however, more of a balance returns as the author, having returned to his former home in Pacific Grove, California, writes to fellow novelist, John O'Hara: "I have had seven months of quiet out here to try to reduce the maelstrom to kettle size. Being alone here has allowed me to think out a lot of things. There is so much rapping in the world (*LIL* 359).

Steinbeck continues by stating, "I think I believe in one thing powerfully—that the only creative thing our species has is the individual lonely mind" (*LIL* 359). Yet while celebrating the mind's ability to foster and preserve the very best in mankind, Steinbeck now recognizes and stresses the duality he has observed. Describing his writing as a "cold and lonely profession," he identifies his beginning research on *East of Eden* as "the coldest and loneliest [of all], because this is all I can do" (*LIL* 360).

By the 1950s then, the stress produced by critics' high expectations for another *Grapes* or at least a return to creative skills which some felt were gradually waning, Steinbeck began to describe his existence as a "restless unhappy coma, just short of manic-depressive" (*LIL* 459). Finding it more and more difficult to keep in mind the dual nature of all things which he had delineated in *The Log from the Sea of Cortez* (1951), he was only occasionally able to break away from seeing his lonely self as an individual who was forced to endure depressing conditions of rejection and exclusion; isolation was no longer viewed as a positive opportunity to relax and to redesign his work nor as a time to seek regenerative self-confidence or peaceful contemplation. One indication of his infrequent looks at the positive side of isolation appears in a 1954 letter to Elizabeth Otis in which he observes: "I think it has been good to be out of touch with the news. Nothing gives you more of a sense of not being able to help than non-hearing" (*LIL* 478). Here isolation is almost equated with self-imposed ignorance.

Since Steinbeck felt a nagging need to connect and share his impressions with others, the author seems to have convinced himself that somehow aloneness was something undesirable for an artist, and his pessimistic attitude toward it grew rather than diminished. Perhaps his struggle for an empathetic understanding of the author's plight over isolation/solitude is best expressed in a letter to Peter Benchley in 1958. Emphasizing his own dilemma, Steinbeck writes:

> A writer out of loneliness is trying to communicate like a distant star sending signals. He isn't telling or teaching or ordering. Rather he seeks to establish a relationship of meaning, of feeling, of observing. We are lonesome animals. We spend all our life trying to be less lonesome. One of our ancient methods is to tell a story begging the listener to say—and to feel—
>
> "Yes, that's the way it is, or at least that's the way I feel it. You're not as alone as you thought." (*LIL* 523)

Happily, at the end of the decade, Steinbeck, by then well past fifty, demonstrates that with maturity comes a more complete understanding of the cyclical nature of loneliness and an individual's shifting perception of whether it is a positive or negative in life. As he grows older, a more introspective Steinbeck seems to establish some methods for coping with the dark side of loneliness. Although he cannot prevent its recurrence or the dark moods that descend on him, he does begin to understand how to deal with it. Advocating a contemplative walk in a cold wood as a restorative for the depression brought on by loneliness, Steinbeck attests to the "soothing and quieting" effect it has on his psyche (*LIL* 544). The sadness and gloom that once accompanied the dark side of isolation lifts as the author indulges in a type of animal-like hibernation that restores and reenergizes him.

A similar renewing sensation occurred during the time Steinbeck spent on his boat, sometimes when it was anchored in Sag Harbor and occasionally when it was taken out to sea. Always a writer who designated rooms or areas for composition and who withdrew for hours to engage in the writing process, Steinbeck saw the boat—like "Joyous Garde," his writing space on Long Island—as an island of solitude where the author could retreat. He writes: "I can't tell you what solace I get from the new boat. I can move out and anchor and have a little table and a yellow pad and some pencils. I can put myself in a position where nothing can intervene. Isn't that wonderful?" (*LIL* 575).

As he aged, Steinbeck sought this type of solitude more frequently, and he no longer seemed intent on dreading the dark side of this human emotion. For example, he describes Sag Harbor as "really heaven out here. There is only one drawback to it. If there are guests or children, I have absolutely no place to go to work or to be alone" (*LIL* 581).

Given this discovery, it is in no way surprising that when Steinbeck was in the process of a work he considered to be the definitive accomplishment of his career, *The Acts of King Arthur and His Noble Knights*, he decided to travel to England's Lake Country and establish residence at Discove Cottage in Somerset, which not only offered quiet, but also provided an enclosed atmosphere that absolutely exuded the Arthurian legend. Finding New York had "too many friends, relations, children, duties, requests, parties, too much drinking—telephones—play openings. No chance to establish the slow rhythm and keep it intact" (*LIL* 605), Steinbeck chose to ensconce himself in an Arthurian surrounding in an attempt not only to connect to the past but also, in the process, to recreate both Arthur and himself in a very restricted and enclosed environs.

As the decade drew to a close, Steinbeck seems to have completely understood the double nature of loneliness and its place as a vital part of his craft. In fact, the final letters indicate an increasing recognition, appreciation, and acceptance of its duality. To his editor, Pascal Covici, he writes:

> This is a lonely business. The difficulty comes when you try to think it isn't. It's not a social racket at all. It has nothing to do with conversation or criticism or even compliments. It is and should be the most alone thing in the world. I guess that is why writers are hard to live with, impossible as friends and ridiculous as associates. A writer and his work is and should be like a surly dog with a bone, suspicious of everyone, trusting no one, loving no one. It's hard to justify such a life, but that's the way it is if it is done well. (*LIL* 610)

Steinbeck also mentions that he values the contemplative alone time afforded by Discove Cottage, telling Elizabeth Otis that the retreat offers "a luxury of rest and peace, something I can only describe as in-ness" (*LIL* 623). In earlier letters to Mr. and Mrs. Graham Watson, to James Pope, and the Covicis, he further emphasizes the calmness, the relaxation and the dream-like state of such a retreat (see *LIL* 615–18). No longer does the writer seem to find an introspective time spent in solitude as something to be feared as if he has become a social isolate or rejected individual. Rather, he treasures the time, having perhaps come to terms with the fact that mutual inter-communication with readers and total understanding by the critics are all but impossible. His 1959 letter to director Elia Kazan echoes that sentiment, as Steinbeck writes of his seclusion: "This is the most wonderful time. . . . I am alone—the largest aloneness I have ever known, mystic and wonderful" (*LIL* 626). Finally, to his third wife, Elaine Scott Steinbeck, he writes: "And I can stand the loneliness as you can. There it is. It's an antidote for a poison that gets into very many men of my age and makes them emotional and spiritual cripples" (*LIL* 685).

As *Life in Letters* draws to a close, the hostile and frustrated young man evident in the earlier correspondence has grown sedate and perhaps even reclusive in his acceptance of solitude. Like Frost in "Stopping by Woods on a Snowy Evening" or Pope in "Solitude," he has broken through to an understanding of the paradox. He accepts the fact that the scary feeling brought about by aloneness does have a mirror image, an emotional trait that does not frighten but offers a reflective quiet time to assess the world that surrounds him. Like the silence of Plato's cave, such solitude cures mankind's restless longing for fame and fortune and makes him aware that such goals are not as indispensable as they appear to be. Self-introspection and discovery are far more valuable and can be attained by setting aside a still quiet alone time.

No doubt the Steinbeck work that has received the most attention regarding its portrayal of loneliness is *Of Mice and Men*. In this 1937 novel, the brotherhood cultivated by Lennie and George makes their relationship both unusual and special. Unfortunately, though numerous essays have centered on George's bond with Lennie, only a few have noted that George often wishes that bond could be broken.

Though he cares for Lennie, George often finds his companion to be more of a trial than a blessing since his mentally challenged friend impedes George from the pleasures in life he most desires: eating food, drinking whiskey, playing cards, shooting pool, and enjoying the sexual company of women. Such impositions anger George, and he is constantly contemplating how comfortable he would be if he did not have to worry about Lennie:

> I could get along so easy and so nice if I didn't have you on my tail. . . .
> If I was alone, I could live so easy. I could go and get a job an' work, an' no trouble. No mess at all, and when the end of the month came I could take my fifty bucks and go into town and get whatever I want. Why I could stay in a cat house all night. I could eat any place I want, hotl or any place, and order any damn thing I could think of. An' I could do all that every damn month. Get a gallon of whisley, or set in a pool room and play cards or shoot pool.[2]

Later he assaults Lennie verbally, stating: "I got you. You can't keep a job and you lose me ever' job I get. Jes' keep me shovin' all over the country all of the time. An' that ain't the worst. You get in trouble. You do bad things and I got to get you out. . . You crazy son-of-a-bitch. You keep me in hot water all the time" (*OMM* 11).

Here George realizes that having a relationship with another individual is frustrating and demanding as well as productive and pleasurable. While companionship can sometimes be rewarding and satisfying, it also has its drawbacks. Thus, being alone can often be seen as a more desirable option since then an individual is only responsible for his personal actions and is not obligated to defend or tolerate the whims of others. "When I think of the swell time I could have without you,' George tells Lennie. "I go nuts, never get no peace" (*OMM* 12).

Despite this antagonistic reaction, George is torn between desiring solitude and fearing isolation, frequently expressing two emotions he observes in being alone, valuing and condemning the emotional state almost simultaneously. For example, only a few pages later he says: "I seen the guys that go around on ranches alone. That ain't no good. They don't have no fun. After a long time, they get mean. They get wantin' to fight all the time" (*OMM* 47). Elsewhere George reiterates the ambiguity of loneliness, reassuring Lennie, "No look, I was jus' foolin', Lennie. 'Cause I want you to stay with me" (*OMM* 13). Barely a paragraph later, he repeats the idea and indicates that their camaraderie serves as a protective device that mitigates Lennie's limited intelligence and helps to keep him out of trouble. "Stay with me," he implores. "Jesus Christ, somebody'd shoot you for a coyote if you was by yourself. No, stay with me. Your Aunt Clara wouldn't like you running off by yourself, even if she is dead" (*OMM* 13). Clearly their camaraderie is depicted as beneficial for both individuals.

Yet most critics have persisted in emphasizing only the latter character trait, preferring to see the bond as what distinguishes the two men from the crowd. Given this penchant for a positive look at the brotherhood, the pair seems to celebrate their status as lifelong friends and companions. Surely the most quoted lines from the novel are George's comment, "We got someone to talk to that gives a damn about us. We don't have to sit in a bar room blowin' in our jack jus' because we got no place else to go. If them other guys get in jail they can rot for all anybody gives a damn but not us." and Lennie's reply, "But not us. Because . . . because I got you to look after me and you got me to look after you" (*OMM* 14). The conclusion seems to be that even though the bonds of friendship are demanding, the advantages of being a part of a community far outweigh the disadvantages. Since the two have grown accustomed to being isolated from others who treat them in a negative manner, they cling to each other as anchors that allow each man to weather the seas of lonely wandering and homelessness, all the while having a safe harbor of love and acceptance available in their alter egos.

Yet Steinbeck is not content with displaying this dualized pull only in George. Using parallel plots, he examines the feelings of other isolates on the ranch: Candy, the old swamper; Crooks, the black stable buck; and Curley's wife, the sole woman in the novel. While two of the remaining major characters seem to see no major difference between solitude and loneliness, it is clear that Steinbeck creates an echo of George's ambiguous reaction to this controversial human condition in at least one other individual.

Specifically, Crooks's speeches reveal a similar ambiguity about isolation. When Lennie appears in the harness room at the beginning of chapter 3, Crooks's physical appearance is described by Steinbeck as "raising his eye, stiffen[ing] and [allowing] a scowl [to] come on his face" (*OMM* 68). "You got no right to come into my room. This here's my room. No one's got a right in here but me," he says (*OMM* 68). His hostility at the thought of companionship reveals how comfortable he has become with isolation and how resigned he is to the lack of acceptance he experiences from his fellow farmhands. The barn has become a safe and secure environment, and he fears that the intrusion of others will cause more problems than it will solve. "You go on—get out of my room," he tells Lennie. "I ain't wanted in the bunk house, and you ain't wanted in my room" (*OMM* 68). Stressing the inappropriateness of Lennie's visit, Crooks make it clear that he values his own territory and is willing to protect his space from those who would encroach on its boundaries.

Nonetheless, Lennie persists, staying where he is unwelcome and eventually causing Crooks to modify his rejection of fellowship. "Long as you won't get out and leave me alone," he tells Lennie, "You might as well set down" (*OMM* 69). As they talk, Crooks becomes more comfortable with social interaction and even shares his past with this stranger, revealing how his existence has been immersed in isolation and rejection. His treatment of Lennie is based on his own lack of trust in others, an attitude that has developed as he discovers that most bonds of "friendship" are fake or "put on" and are mostly self-serving rather than considerate or kind. "George knows what he's about. Jus' talkin' and you don't understand anything—I seen it over and over—a guy talkin' to another guy and it don't make no difference if he don't hear or understand. It's just the talking. It's just being with another guy" (*OMM* 71).

Since Crooks feels that most human interaction is a sham, he begins to develop other ways of escaping loneliness, ways which may be attained without trusting the sincerity or honesty of other people. Specifically, he has found that books provide companionship that will enable him to ease his tensions about the lack of real relationships in his life. Initially, books seem to make up for his inability to play cards or throw horseshoes with the other ranch hands, but later Crooks senses this substitution has its flaws: "Books ain't no good," he says. "A guy needs *somebody* [emphasis mine] to be near him. A guy goes nuts if he ain't got nobody. Don't make a difference who the guy is, long's he's with you. I tell ya—I tell ya a guy gets too lonely an' he gets sick" (*OMM* 72–73).

The major reason Crooks gives for seeking some personal human contact is his need to acquire affirmation for his decision making.

> Sometimes he gets thinkin', and he's got nothing to tell him what so an' and what ain't so. Maybe if he sees somethin' and he don't know whether it's right or not. He can't tell. He got nothing to measure by.

If some guy was with me, he could tell me—an' then it would be all right—but I just don't know. (*OMM* 73)

Yet clearly this need for real human attachment has proved unattainable and impractical as far as Crooks is concerned. Therefore when Candy enters his space as well, Crooks expresses a similar ambiguity about interaction as that with which he greeted Lennie. As he invites the swamper in, his emotions are a mixture of pleasure and anger: "Come on in. If ever'body's comin' in, you might as just as well" (*OMM* 75).

Ironically, Candy's own comments as he enters the harness room also reveal Steinbeck's careful perception about the duality of loneliness. It is almost as if he is jealous of what Crooks has. "You got a nice cozy place here," he says. "Must be nice to have a room to yourself this way" (*OMM* 75). Crooks's reply to this is a sarcastic and bitter comment that denies the values of aloneness. "Sure—" he retorts. "And a manure pile underneath the window. Sure, it's swell" (*OMM* 75). The ambiguity of solitude is obvious in this passage, but Crooks also seems intent on puncturing the universal dream that it is possible for human relationships to offer happiness and contentment instead of contention and sadness.

When Curley's wife enters the scene, she too comments on how easy it is to deal with individuals when one is alone but how difficult it becomes to interact with others when she finds human beings in groups. "You're all scared of each other—that's what," she says. "Ever' one of you is scared that the rest is goin' to get somethin' on you" (*OMM* 77).

Several pages later Crooks thinks better of his previous wish for human companions, recognizing that more problems than solutions may result from interacting with white people. This realization has been motivated by the threat of Curley's wife as she reacts to Crooks's assertion that he has a right to be alone, to refuse to associate with individuals who might cause him to come to harm. "I had enough," he [Crooks] said coldly. "You got no right comin' in on a colored man's room. You got no rights messing around in here at all. Now you jus' get out, an' get out quick" (*OMM* 78). Perhaps he comprehends that the "white" status of the woman and the power behind that status makes isolation preferable to community, no matter how hurtful that "aloneness" might appear to be.

Curley's wife's response is fraught with racial tension, suggesting that she will cause more trouble if Crooks continues to reprove her. Readers can sense why Crooks feels that he will be better off alone; it is basically a perception based on his observation that human interaction is actually more trouble than it is worth. The threat of retribution is graphic and violent: "You just keep your trap shut, nigger. I could get you strung up on a tree so easy it ain't even funny" (*OMM* 81). After hearing this threat, readers may be justified in concluding that a lonely existence is preferable to a human interaction that is accompanied by a threat of death. Crooks is so taken aback by this potential violence that Steinbeck describes him as reduced "to nothing. There was no personality, no ego—nothing to arouse either like or dislike" (*OMM* 81). As he acquiesces to the demands of Curley's wife, Crooks sits "perfectly still, his eyes averted, everything that might be hurt drawn in" (*OMM* 81). Despite this negative description of his isolation, Crooks realizes that he is better off when he is separated from others. Yet it remains a paradox that confuses and irritates him.

Only a few moments later then, he breaks his silence and ends his robotic actions, acknowledging the presence of Candy and Lennie but urging them to leave and rejecting a potential alliance with a mutual dream of freedom and acceptance. "You guys better go," he says. "I ain't quite sure I want you in here no more. A colored man got to have some rights even if he don't like 'em" (*OMM* 82). While isolation does not always seem subject to the harassment of others or the imposition they might place on his life, Crooks decides he is better off without being in a community.

In conclusion, *Of Mice and Men*, rather than merely being a treatise on the values of community and acceptance, may be far more complex than readers have previously thought. Crooks ends the penultimate chapter by being resigned to a solitary existence.

As his uninvited guests leave, he momentarily glances toward the door (perhaps in regret) but then proceeds to concentrate on his physical ailments rather than his emotional ones, applying a soothing lineament to his sore back and resolving not to take the risk of interaction again. He has experienced the trauma that comes with community, a trauma that is perhaps indicative of the negatives an individual can encounter when opening one's life, establishing ties with others, and moving away from self-consideration to embrace a demanding whole.

As with George and Lennie, Steinbeck suggests that feelings of isolation or loneliness are often based on perceived differences and centers his portraits of the other "lonely" and isolated people in his novel primarily on an individual's physical or mental deformities, emphasizing how prejudices based on race and gender are mistakenly magnified until brotherhood is superseded by "Otherhood." These "minor" characters in *Of Mice and Men* suffer largely as a result of their nonacceptance, since that nonacceptance reinforces their singularity rather than suggesting that a unity can be obtained in the bond they form with others. Many times in the novel, one *is* truly the loneliest number as the characters strive in different ways to escape their isolation: for example, Candy uses his dog as a valued animal companion, Crooks relies on books to find respite from his rejection by the ranch hands, and Curley's wife seeks acceptance by hanging around the bunkhouse trying to find only a decent conversation, rather than looking for sex as some of the men assume. She also fantasizes about a Hollywood career where she will be the center of attention and have many fans.

While Candy and Curley's wife serve as depictions of the norm (desiring interaction and closeness with others be they human or otherwise), a brief look at Crooks confirms Steinbeck's intent to show both sides of the predicament and to emphasize the duality of perception the stable buck has about his situation. We can sense the struggle Crooks faces as he attempts to transform his relegation to the harness room from a negative to a positive. For example, when Lennie enters to talk, Crooks's immediate reaction is that his space has been invaded: "You got no right in my room," he says. "This here's my room. Nobody got any right in here but me" (*OMM* 68). By rationalizing in this manner, Crooks transforms the forced separation he has experienced due to his racial "Otherness" to an asset of not being bothered by others and having his own space. Yet later in the novel, Crooks admits that his isolation has caused him problems:

A guy needs somebody—to be near him. A guy goes nuts if he ain't got nobody [he tells Lennie] . . . Don't make no difference who the guy is as long's he's with you. . . . I tell ya a guy gets too lonely an' he gets sick. . . . A guy sets alone out here at night, maybe readin' books or thinkin' or stuff like that. Sometimes he gets thinkin', an' he got nothing to tell him what's so and what ain't so. . . . He can't turn to some other guy

and ast him if he sees it too. He can't tell. If some guy was with me . . .
then it would be all right (*OMM* 72–73).

At one point, Curley's wife also expresses her frustration with loneliness to Lennie: "Why can't I talk to you. I never get to talk to nobody. I get awful lonely . . . I get lonely, . . . but I can't talk to nobody but Curley. Else he gets mad. How'd you like not to talk to anybody" (*OMM* 86). In her attempt to overcome the isolation she find herself trapped in, she chooses a different solution than Crooks. Instead of becoming reclusive, she instead becomes assertive, an attribute that others interpret as sexual aggressivity. As a result, her loneliness is hidden beneath a façade of flirting, and she is mistaken for a tramp or floozy who leads men on without the intention of sexually satisfying them. In reality, of course, she is merely a woman who yearns for compassion and comradeship as well as for full acceptance of her gender.

In a 1961 letter to John Murphy, Steinbeck writes:

Once the words go down, you are alone and committed. It's as final as a plea in court from which there is no retracting. That's the lonely time. Nine tenths of a writer's life do not admit of any companionship nor friend nor associate. And until one makes peace with loneliness and accepts it as part of the profession, as celibacy is a part of the priesthood, until then there are times of dreadful dread. (*LIL* 859)

By refusing to admit that there are widely divergent truths about singularity, that one is not always the loneliest number, the community members fail to break through to an understanding that only "through a long consideration of the parts [can one] emerge with a sense of the whole."[3] It is this type of understanding, this "feeling of fullness, of warm wholeness," which Steinbeck sought on the journey of the Western Flyer to Baja California in 1940, that George seems to find in his decision to sever the bond with Lennie in order to rescue him from a painful retribution and death at Curley's hands. Readers ultimately conclude that the sacrifice of the relationship is in his partner's best interest. The collecting trip was a voyage on which Steinbeck discovered that somehow the Native Mexican people were much more likely to have "a wholeness of sense and emotion—the good and bad, beautiful, ugly and cruel all welded into one thing" (*Log* 124). Obviously, it is just such a balanced view of the world that makes reclusive characters so admirable and so respected by the author.

Although Steinbeck had previously considered duality as a human trait, his ultimate breakthrough and complete understanding did not occur until he began to accept its paradoxical nature, that both sides were true at the same time. In a letter written to Pascal Covici in 1941, he states: "It seems fairly obvious that two sides of a mirror are necessary before one has a mirror, that two forces are necessary in a man before he is a man" (*LIL* 221). As Steinbeck became increasingly conscious of this philosophical tenet, it is not surprising that his fictional work such as *Of Mice and Men* often demonstrates the ambiguity he saw in human attitudes, emotions, and attributes and that he expressed in his correspondence. In his dual-faceted fictional pictures, he asserts that while one may indeed be the loneliest number, there are times when that may not be all bad; it all depends on one's perspective and the balance the observer is able to maintain.

By "breaking through" and acknowledging man's role as a two-legged paradox (*Log* 98), Steinbeck discovered that although "everyone searches for absolutisms . . . and imagines continually that he finds them," it is more just to see everything "as a mere glimpse—a challenge to consider also the rest of the relations as they are available—to envision the whole picture as well as can be done with given abilities and data" (*Log* 145). Thus Steinbeck realized that it is only when one accepts duality, when one moves beyond the mysteries of existence, that one can attain a balanced view wherein loneliness, isolation, and alienation, on the one hand, and solitude, uniqueness, and singularity, on the other, are equal parts of the whole picture, rather than separate and opposite entities. Advocated by Eastern sages like Lao Tze in the *Tao Teh Ching*, it is a philosophy that is difficult for Western intelligence to comprehend, but it is also a belief system whose tenets fascinated Steinbeck in both his real life and his fictional constructs.

> Empty your mind of all thought.
> Let your heart be at peace
> . . .
> Returning to the source is serenity.
> Immersed in the wonder of the Tao
> You can deal with whatever life brings you
> And when death comes, you are ready.[4]

To his editor, Pascal Covici, Steinbeck wrote: "Paradoxes as verities? I think the best way is to set it (a story) down just as it happened and let the sense of paradox grow out of the material just as it has out of my seeing" (*LIL* 444). Clearly, his life and his work mirrored the dichotomy he observed; moreover, it affirms the fact that one of the most basic fears of mankind (being lonely) is not an absolute. As the novel's original title suggests, it is simply "something that happens," and it has the potential to be either positive or negative depending on the circumstances.

Notes

1. Elaine Steinbeck and Robert Wallsten, eds., *Steinbeck: A Life in Letters* (New York: Viking, 1975), 25. Subsequent quotations are cited parenthetically in the text as *LIL* followed by the page number.

2. John Steinbeck, *Of Mice and Men* (New York: Penguin Classics, 1993). Subsequent quotations are cited parenthetically in the text as *OMM* followed by the page number.

3. John Steinbeck, *The Log from the Sea of Cortez*, 1951 (New York: Penguin Books, 1976), 63. Subsequent quotations are cited parenthetically in the text as *Log* followed by the page number.

4. Lao Tze, *Tao Teh Ching*. Trans. Stephen Mitchell. (New York: Harper Perennial, 1991), stanza 16.

Works Cited

Steinbeck, Elaine and Robert Wallsten, eds. *Steinbeck: A Life in Letters*. New York: Viking, 1975.

Steinbeck, John. *The Log from the Sea of Cortez*. 1951. New York: Penguin Books, 1976.

Steinbeck, John. *Of Mice and Men*. New York: Penguin Books, 1993.

Tze, Lao. *Tao Teh Ching*. New York: Harper Perennial, 1991.

CHAPTER TWENTY-ONE

MUSICAL INTERTEXTUALITY IN ACTION: A DIRECTED READING OF *OF MICE AND MEN*

Christian Goering, Katherine Collier, Scott Koenig,
J. Olive O'Berski, Stephanie Pierce, and Kelly Riley

While much work exists on the musical influences on Steinbeck's work, a method of examining his (and any author's) relevance and relationship in the world today depends on the individual reader and her very personal response to his text. While the intent of any author is critical to understanding the purpose behind the writing of a text, the reader provides an essential part of any literary endeavor since, as Louise Rosenblatt related some seventy years ago, a reader's background and experiences establish a work's ultimate meaning and contribute to the depth of the reading event. Since the meaning of text relies so heavily on the individual, it, by definition, could not be exactly the same for every individual. Thus, for every individual reader who picks up Steinbeck's words, his living text will create different meanings for each. Rather, two readers will arrive at different understandings as they grapple with images, words, structure, and conflict. In much the same manner, no two individuals have the same knowledge of music, and when people listen to a song, they interpret it with a multitude of unique background knowledge and experience.

So I began to wonder what would happen when the two worlds combined and people were asked to make connections to songs after reading a piece of literature. These very connections, a musical intertextuality, or, by definition, connecting from the written page to the lyrics and/or music of a song, is fundamental to LitTunes, the name of my learning-centered literacy project established in November of 2007. LitTunes is a relatively new website that links popular music to canonical literature in ways designed to inspire and cause twitch-speed kids to pause just long enough to consider the value of classic fiction to their individual and personal lives. In this case, I asked five future secondary English teachers (included here as authors) to read *Of Mice and Men* with a distinct purpose: to find and connect popular tunes from their musical library—their musical canon—that elucidate the characters, plot, tone, setting, and themes they discovered in a directed reading of that novella.

Without a moment's hesitation, the five students began reading Steinbeck's most widely taught work with an ear to the California ground for connections to the music they knew. Their efforts netted ninety-eight unique connections to songs in the categories of themes, plot structures, characters, setting, and tone. Artists ranged from James Taylor to Rick James and from the Squirrel Nut Zippers to Rage against the Machine. Song titles ranged from "Hard Time Killing Floor Blues" to "Somewhere over the Rainbow" and from "Pinball Wizard" to "Superfreak." As each student brought his or her unique musical background to the new reading of *Of Mice and Men*, the diversity of their knowledge, experiences, and tastes bubbled to the surface in this project. These teachers in training not only created a new perspective on the novella but also developed a methodology that will impact their future students and will help readers to approach any piece of literature, not just *Of Mice and Men*.

Background

As an educator and advocate of literacy at any legitimate cost, I was ecstatic when this volume editor involved me to join the chase for fresh and compelling ways to win anew readers for *Of Mice and Men*. Though the novella is short in length and accessible in terms of readability and language, it is also true that nowadays students increasingly fight any reading experience longer than a text message. The focal point of this essay is how to strengthen the appeal of book-length literature and how to situate its increasingly tenuous place in the curriculum. Novels and even novellas at times confound the present generation of young readers, students coming into maturity fully wired to digital sound and digital text. Since they are twitch-speed kids who respond to quick-cut flashing images and who speak a coded language accessible in a seeming instant, it is no wonder that they are also the ones who ask, between the byted lines, "Why are we reading this? It's over seventy years old and has no relevance to the here and now."

In agreement with many theorists and critics writing in the ill-defined time beyond postmodernism, I believe that literacy is created through an inexhaustible flow of connections between personal experience and those ideas learned through fiction, poetry, film, journalism, song, and any other type of plastic narrative: If this is true, then why not lead a student to Steinbeck through their own tunes?

The LitTunes Approach

My website, LitTunes, sets aside unfettered space on the World Wide Web to help educators incorporate music into their classrooms. Specifically, the site aims to provide a collaborative online community to assist teachers who are motivated to reach disenfranchised students through their favored language—music. Geared as an open-access educational outreach, LitTunes features essays, research, and lesson plans in addition to a database with over six hundred song-to-literature connections. The *Lit* in LitTunes refers to both literature *and* literacy. Through artists such as Neil Young, Bruce Springsteen, and the Bastard Sons of Johnny Cash, and through authors such as Steinbeck, Harper Lee, George Orwell, William Shakespeare, and Kate Chopin, website visitors are provided the opportunity to enrich and enliven their classrooms and motivate students, and they are also encouraged to contribute additional connections and lesson plans, as well as relating their own classroom successes with this approach.

Specifically, LitTunes features connections to works of literature frequently taught in schools around the country. These connections can be classified in six different categories. The first type of connection relies on the scholarly work of Deborah Pardes, who created the Artists for Literacy website, featuring over three hundred songs inspired by literature (SIBL). A SIBL is an instance when an artist has, through liner notes or an interview, disclosed that her or his song was inspired by the reading of a work of literature. The LitTunes database reflects some of the songs featured on Artists for Literacy, and we credit Pardes for helping to light the way toward creation of LitTunes. The central difference is that we focus primarily on literature taught in the schools, while the SIBL site has a broader focus.

A second type of connection is a thematic link. For example, the song "Teenager" by 1990s rockers Better than Ezra demonstrates a thematic link to William Shakespeare's *Romeo and Juliet*. The angst-ridden teens depicted in the Better than Ezra song connect closely to that of the main characters of Shakespeare's tragedy. Similarly, "Man in Black" by Johnny Cash provides an example of a character link to Harper Lee's *To Kill a Mockingbird*, and more specifically, to the character of Atticus Finch. While Cash was writing about the country as a whole, his lyrics undeniably connect to Atticus in Lee's novel. Another example of a character connection is Neil Young's "Like a Hurricane" and its connection to Zora Neale Hurston's *Their Eyes Were Watching God*. Specifically, the line from Young's song "I saw your brown eyes turning once to fire" connect to Janie and depict how the emotions she experiences and embodies throughout the novel are reflected in her physical experience. Songs can also connect in terms of setting, tone, and plot structure, which provide teachers with other modes of intertextuality.

However, the most powerful use of the LitTunes concept is when students are provided opportunities to make literature-to-song connections on their own; indeed, such potential as demonstrated in this chapter. When students read a text and attempt to make connections to songs, movies, websites, poems, short stories, novels, or plays, they reinforce a central skill needed in order to become expert readers.

When I examine an artist's heritage and legacy, I immediately think back to how teachers either create or destroy the same elements depending on the creativity of their presentation of a work. How will today's teachers present Steinbeck's *Of Mice and Men* and stress its relevance to students across America, a country much different from the era when George and Lennie lived? How will they approach the kids with twitch-speed values and those without when they ask them to read the Steinbeck classics? You've seen this scene before. The teacher trots out the stacks of books, blows off the dust, records the numbers, and passes them down the rows of desks in classrooms from Oklahoma to California, from Florida to Maine. How many of these students, given this less-than-inspirational approach, will choose the saga from the stack? How many fewer will read it all the way to the end? While this is more of a concern with longer works, it remains one with all literature. Eventually, I came to the conclusion as a teacher that if I wanted every student to read a work, I would need to read it aloud.

As a literary form, the novel has become a suspect approach to reaching readers. Even as he was finishing *The Grapes of Wrath*, Steinbeck wrote to his close friend, Carlton "Dook" Sheffield:

> The point of this all is that I must make a new start. I've worked the novel—[as] I know it as far as I can take it. I never did think much of it—a clumsy vehicle at best. And I don't know the form of the new but I know there is a new which will be adequate and shaped by the new thinking.[1]

Have teachers over the past seventy years slain the novel once and for all by their refusal to espouse the new, and, as a consequence, have they also killed the great work that inspired this chapter?

Perhaps we have reached a point in American secondary education some have termed "the adolescent literacy crisis."[2] Not only are students not reading, but often students *cannot* read book-length literature when it is passed back to them in the language arts classroom, perhaps primarily because they don't have the reading stamina or attention spans of the students of the past. Yes, yes, I know, the students of today aren't the students of yesterday. But where does that kind of cynical analysis get the profession? Why do teachers insist upon teaching the senior class of 2009 with the methodology of yesteryear? It didn't work so well in 1969. It didn't even inspire student readers in 1989. Why should it be expected to work today?

As Teri Lesesne believes,

> Today's adolescents are connected beyond the walls of their bedrooms and their classrooms through e-mail, instant messaging, social networking, blogs, and personal web pages. They connect with other adolescents around the world via e-mail. They download music from other countries. . . . Adolescence is all about speed and convenience and immediacy.[3]

However, I refuse to believe that these differences mean that today's students are bad, wrong, incompetent, indifferent, or downright hopeless. In fact, the opposite is true. If they appear to be less than excited about delving into *Of Mice and Men*, then let's accept it and find alternative ways to excite them.

Enter LitTunes and the potential for social justice that is inherent in the development of individual literacy or even more audaciously, in the development of individual literary literacy. Enter Springsteen, Guthrie, Dylan, Waits. My plea is this: let's use the artists to help model an intertextual, reader response approach to the novella. High school students can be motivated and inspired to read John Steinbeck's *Of Mice and Men* and the other great works that populate the incredibly rich and vital literary canon. Come, teachers, and find the level shore of common ground on which all students may dance. Let the lyrics of pop tunes provide the enticement and the melody; then allow the works of the literary canon to provide the footing and the foundation. In this shared space devoted to literacy, the joy of reading can be rediscovered, and students can learn about the wonders of allusion, metaphor, and original imagery. In short, they can learn to read again.

Such approaches as the one detailed here may motivate today's students to try Steinbeck's novella and to discover the depth of narrative and character, the sustained richness of imagery and tone, and the profound insights into *life and life only* that a pop tune can never provide. It is with these goals in mind that I decided to ask my own college students to participate in this educational outreach and ultimately search out the songs on their iPods that they felt offered connections to Steinbeck's novella. The theoretical underpinnings of this work are entrenched with intertextuality and reader response.

Theoretical Background

The idea of connecting lyrics to works of literature in a classroom setting rests in part on the theory of intertextuality—the proposition that readers are constantly connecting past texts to current texts during the act of reading. *Intertexto*, the Latin word meaning "to intermingle while weaving," symbolizes the theoretical analysis of Julia Kristeva, a French semiotician who, in the 1960s, declared that "any text is constructed of a mosaic of quotations; any text is the absorption and transformation of another."[4] In such a landscape, where no text is an island, I believe that, during the sustained act of its creation, Steinbeck's novella fell under sway of the prevailing textual influences of the 1930s—all that came before him. Likewise, a significant (though indeterminate) number of literary works crafted in the seventy years following publication of *Of Mice and Men*—all the artistic endeavors that came after him—bear the influence of Steinbeck's characters, themes, style, and word choice. Clearly, once a work enters the canon, it has influence on other texts, an influence that plays out in myriad and unique ways.

Similarly, tunes play on a similar intertextual landscape of original performance. Listeners respond to lyrics in ways connected to their own personal experience. Sometimes this experience converges with that of other listeners and results in a pop hit, the proverbial gold record. Other times the individual's reaction in the multiple strands of subculture raise unique but stratified voices.

Yet do we remember text, and how do we relate that which we remember to that which we are experiencing, moment by moment, in the now? When do your words become mine? When do Steinbeck's words become those of Hemingway, for example? What changes in the act of transference? Does it make any difference? The point is that when anyone writes, the text cannot emerge free of influence. My words are *their* words, and *I am he as you are he as you are me and we are all together.*

This assertion of influence also aligns with theories of Roland Barthes, another mid-twentieth-century semiotician, who wrote:

> Any text is a new tissue of past citations. Bits of code, formulae, rhythmic models, fragments of social languages, etc., pass into the text and are redistributed within it, for there is always language before and around the text. Intertextuality, the condition of any text whatsoever, cannot, of course, be reduced to a problem of sources or influences; the intertext is a general field of anonymous formulae whose origin can scarcely ever be located; of unconscious or automatic quotations, given without quotations.[5]

Thus, my students performed purposeful intertextuality when they participated in this project. Furthermore, when they enter the teaching profession and have their own students carefully and purposefully read *Of Mice and Men* and think about it with a studied ear, they too will recognize countless musicians.

Of course one could claim that intertextuality is merely a reconstructed term for allusion, but that would miss a significant difference between the two. One is a dynamic theory of the relatedness of things, "overarching" in the jargon of the day, while the latter has become an outdated teaching term for the indirect reference to appropriate fragments of other works.

Relation of Intertextuality to Reader Response Theory

Around the original publication date of the Steinbeck novella, educational theorist Louise Rosenblatt developed the Reader Response Theory in her seminal 1938 work, *Literature as Exploration*. Considered the "inaugural text"[6] of the reader response movement, *Literature as Exploration* puts forth the idea that in making meaning when engaging a text, readers will rest heavily on their past experiences with literature and life. "The reader brings to the work personality traits, memories of past events, present needs and preoccupations, a particular mood of the moment, and particular physical condition . . . in a never-to-be-duplicated combination."[7]

Intertextuality, at least in the context of the classroom, is a byproduct, perhaps even a result of Reader Response Theory. It supports the assertion that the making of meaning in what we read is as much the function of us, the lonely reader or imbibing member of the audience, as it is the responsibility of the distant author. According to Graham Allen, "The act of reading . . . plunges us into a network of textual relations." He continues, "To interpret a text, to discover its meanings, is to trace those relationships." Similarly, Daniel Chandler contends that texts are framed by others, which ultimately "provide[s] contexts in which other texts can be created and interpreted."[8]

Earnest Morell and Jeffrey Duncan-Andrade lend further support for the use of music lyrics in a language arts setting. "Literary texts can be used to scaffold literary terms and concepts and ultimately foster literary interpretations. [These texts] are rich in imagery and metaphor and can be used to teach irony, tone, diction, point of view . . . theme, plot, motif, and character development." Certainly, state and national standards can be met with the use of music lyrics. In fact, the standards are likely to be exceeded when teachers have students "perform feminist, Marxist, structuralist, psychoanalytic, or postmodern critiques" of the lyrics.[9] While it isn't my goal to torch the literary canon in favor of a lyrics-based curriculum, it *is* my goal to direct all educators to look beyond traditional forms of textual reality and embrace alternative versions of the written word. In particular, I champion the value of pop-tune lyrics in their written form in order to enhance student literacy, and I advocate the utility of such lyrics because they inspire critical thinking skills as they open thoughtful connections to the "classic" novels, plays, poems, and essays that presently dominate the curriculum.

In addition to the activities and connections, musical lyrics can help teachers attempting to introduce great literature to their students and can also directly affect the climate and social context of a classroom, because normally, such lyrics are the student's domain outside of the halls and walls of today's schools. In a previous publication, I stated that music, if properly used, is a key way to engage the students in today's standards-based curriculum: "Rarely do teenagers go without music. Whether it is in their cars, at home, or even on a portable player, music serves as the universal backdrop to almost all adolescent lives."[10] However, when a student's musical connection is not properly acknowledged (for example, if a teacher asks students to make connections to something the class is reading and then rejects the music or the lyrics they provide), the social context of a classroom can be destroyed just as easily as it can be enlivened and enriched by including popular culture. Carol Lee agrees the potential for social benefits outweighs any inherent risk to the classroom or the instructor. "The interplay between structures of knowledge constructed through social activity outside classrooms and structures of knowledge embedded in school learning is potentially powerful because the resulting network of associations is richer in both its specificity and generalizability."[11] It follows that when students are able to effectively manipulate a medium such as song lyrics with skill and comfort they are likely to find greater motivation to tackle a text that might otherwise seem distant or irrelevant to them.

Consequently, the use of music is favorable because it ultimately builds in students the skills to tackle difficult canonical texts. Through discussions of music lyrics, students gain the critical eye with which they can view other works. And, as Steven Luebke advocates, teachers will want to "illuminate and make relevant what may appear to [their] students as the cryptic experiences of obscure humans in ancient times."[12] I advocate classrooms rich with intertextuality, classrooms where students' personal opinions of texts are valued and raised above the teachers and authors. When this occurs, students can be motivated and enticed to read the highest quality literature; today's educators need to accept that the days of simply assigning a book-length text and expecting it to be read are forever lost.

Methodology

For the purposes of this chapter, I asked a class of twenty-one pre-service English educators in a methods of English instruction course at the University of Arkansas if anyone self-identified as both interested in and knowledgeable about music. I also asked whether or not they would be willing to read another book in addition to the current exorbitant reading requirements for the course. Five students volunteered for just such a challenge; their task was to read *Of Mice and Men* and record all of the connections they made from the text with music. Next, I provided students with copies of the novella, a list of the various LitTunes connection types (theme, setting, character, tone, plot), a set of instructions regarding how to read the text and make connections, and a printed table to record musical connections during the process of reading with categories of page, type of connection, song title, and artist.

The next step in the process was for the students to read the book and bring in their results. A friendly conversation ensued as the students realized both how different their musical backgrounds were and how similar some of their connections were. Once the connections were compiled, I asked the students to select three to five of their connections to expound upon in greater detail. Selections were made based on three stated criteria: uniqueness of connection, clear association between song and text which could be described without the use of the song's lyrics, and a connection based on each person's individual taste in music. These connections, given here in the writing voices of the students, provide a glimpse into the reading minds at work as these individuals discovered the importance and relevance of musical intertextuality.

Participants

As mentioned, the five coauthors of this piece are currently students working towards a master of arts in teaching (MAT) degree, and as such, are part of the pre-service licensure program at the University of Arkansas. As we write, they are enrolled in nine hours of graduate studies, preparing to embark on a full-time internship as the fall semester begins in the local schools. The group brings diverse talents and insights of previous experiences to the methods course as well as to this writing effort. Kelly (age 36), a Texas native, has earned an MA in English and is working on a Reading Specialist Licensure in addition to her training as a secondary English teacher. J. Olive (age 36) came from the University of Michigan and has switched careers from landscaping to English education. Stephanie (age 25) was born in North Carolina, raised partially in California before moving to Arkansas with her family. She finished a degree in marketing before returning and taking the necessary coursework to be a high school English teacher. Scott (age 31) also hails from California and has worked as a counselor for youth since earning his English degree a few years ago. Finally, Katherine (age 25), another Texas native, dual majored in clarinet and English at the University of Arkansas and after her husband went through the MAT program, she exchanged a bank job for another year of school and the chance to affect the lives of students. Interestingly, out of a class of twenty-one future teachers, these five are all second career seekers, and though that is not the focus of the program, in this particular section the nontraditional students outrank the traditional students. The geographical and age diversity represented in this group and class in general is also remarkable. In contrast, last year's pre-service English teachers were all under twenty-seven and most were native to Arkansas.

Results

The musical intertextuality created during the reading experiences of these five students resulted in a database (see Appendix A) of nearly one hundred songs connected to *Of Mice and Men*. Many of these songs would connect for any reader, but it is the individuality of each reader as he or she meets the text that provides the unique nature of this list. I have elected to leave the text as it was when I received it from the students. Here, their words sing out the connections between classic text and their accessible musical knowledge. As each student describes three to five selections of their choice, an understanding of their unique musical intertextuality emerges.

From Kelly

Steinbeck's *Of Mice and Men* depicts, among other things, the conflicted relationship between George Milton and Lennie Small. Throughout the novella, George expresses and demonstrates his love for Lennie—"We got somebody to talk to that gives a damn about us."[13] Although George loves Lennie like a brother, his love is complicated by feelings of burden—"If I was alone I could live so easy" (*OMM* 7, 11); feelings of responsibility for Lennie's dangerous actions—"You ain't gonna do no bad things like you did in Weed, neither" (*OMM* 7); and feelings of guilt for being conflicted about Lennie—"He looked across the fire at Lennie's anguished face, and then he looked ashamedly at the flames" (*OMM* 11). Bruce Springsteen's song "Highway Patrolman" portrays a similarly conflicted relationship between two brothers. Both the lyrics and the tone of the song correlate to the novella.

Similarly, in Gillian Welch's "One Little Song," the persona expresses a longing to write a song that no one has ever sung before. This song artfully weaves together opposing moods of mournfulness and hopefulness in a way that parallels the tones in Steinbeck's *Of Mice and Men*. Like the persona in Welch's song, the characters in the novella find both hope and despair in their dream of having a little plot of land to call their own. Crooks describes these feelings of despair when he says, "Every damn one of 'em's got a little piece of land in his head. An' never a God damn one of 'em ever gets it. Just like heaven" (*OMM* 72); yet, shortly after making this comment he exposes his own desire for hope when he requests to be included in the dream: "If you guys would want a hand to work for nothing—just his keep, why I'd come an' lend a hand" (*OMM* 75). At the end of the novella, Steinbeck leaves readers on their own to sort out the tensions between despair and hope, for Lennie's death certainly invokes despair; however, George's sincerity and sacrifice inspires hope.

The characters in *Of Mice and Men* persistently long for connection with yet remain alienated from the people around them. Steinbeck fills the work with fleeting moments of intimacy that seem to open doors for connection between characters. Sadly, these doors always close just before any authentic connection can be forged. However, Steinbeck leaves one of these doors ajar at the end when he depicts, in the final scene, a moment of understanding between George and Slim—"You hadda, George.

I swear you hadda. Come with me" (*OMM* 104–5). This final moment seems to suggest the possibility for genuine connection between these two characters. Like the Steinbeck novella, Jamie Byrd and Steve Fisher's duet "String of Pearls" describes the divergent perspectives that inhibit connection between two people. The song ends with both characters standing in front of and looking through an open door, which implies that they will overcome the obstacles and reach a point of understanding.

Finally, Tracy Chapman's "Fast Car" is told from the perspective of someone who is attempting to escape a desperate situation. In the song, the persona is addressing someone who is also trying to escape. The persona expresses her fear that they will end up remaining in and dying in their current position. With urgency, she presses for a decision, fearing that if they don't decide quickly their chance for escape will be lost. Although the song has a moments of hope, the dark tone and bleak situation ends up overshadowing brightness. Chapman's song echoes the situation of many of the characters in *Of Mice and Men*. Lennie, George, Candy, and Crooks all face poverty, oppression, and alienation. However, Lennie and George's dream of owning their own land gives them hope for escape, and this hope spreads to both Candy and Crooks. Interestingly, by sharing this dream, these characters are able to briefly connect with one another; however, all is lost when Lennie accidently kills Curly's wife. Their chance for escape has passed.

From Scott

Male relationships are rarely explored in literature, let alone in music. Steinbeck takes a risk with *Of Mice and Men* by presenting a friendship rooted in a dangerous, unspoken notion—that of love. George and Lennie travel the country working toward the American dream, not alone and isolated like the other farmhands, but together, with the bond at the base of any true friendship. In Sufjan Stevens's song "The Predatory Wasp of the Palisades Is Out to Get Us!" he echoes Steinbeck by taking that same chance, singing about the love of another male, a best friend from his youth. Though the music doesn't stir up the dusty back roads of Salinas, Stevens's sentiment plays beautifully with Steinbeck's theme of brotherhood, and the profession—if never in words or lyrics such as Stevens's song—of love for your fellow man.

319

Another parallel can be seen in the reaction of Steinbeck's characters to the loss of home. When the dream is crushed—when the reality of the farm, with the rabbits, with the fat of the land, is cruelly taken from his hands—Candy spits out anger toward Curley's wife. And who could blame him? Surrounded by a society that devalues the working man, Candy—as well as Crooks, George, and Lennie—has been scraping for his small piece of nothing all of his life. Matthew Ryan's dark, brooding song "American Dirt" takes Steinbeck's anticapitalist rage and places it squarely in today's world. A man works, a man dreams, and all he's left with at the end of a long day of baling hay, or tacking horses, is the taste of the dirt in his mouth, and the angry rock sound of Ryan's bitter vocals.

Finally, Paul Westerberg's playful song "Mr. Rabbit" fits nicely in relation to Lennie's obsession with the farm and with the rabbits. Westerberg constructs a deceptively simple piece, with an almost nursery rhyme quality—just a wise, knowing voice and an electric guitar—that suits Lennie's naïve ideas and hopes for a better life. All things must have their place—"shine," according to Westerberg—and Steinbeck mirrors this in his writing. To Steinbeck, a human being, no matter the station, should have value. A man's work should have value. A man's life should have value. Even a rabbit and Lennie's childish dreams for a rabbit have their valued place.

From John

Pulsing red from lip to instep, Curley's wife seems to slink into the bunkhouse solely to tempt and torment, entangle and endanger the working stiffs in *Of Mice and Men* (*OMM* 31). She is described variously as "tart," "bitch," and "jailbait" throughout the book, but, when she later confides in Lennie in the barn (*OMM* 88), Steinbeck paints a subtler portrait of her as a small town girl yearning for recognition and a better life. Like Jezebel in the Sade song of that name, Curley's wife may be better understood as a poor, disempowered female who makes use of her beauty to free herself from limitations. Both women have been reviled for over-exercising the very qualities that draw attention and admiration to them; they are hated for wanting to be loved.

In the Squirrel Nut Zippers' "That Lowdown Man of Mine," the vocalist laments being not only mistreated but also misunderstood by her lover. Curley's wife also expresses this dual suffering, for her complaint is not just that Curley "ain't a nice fella" (*OMM* 86) but that he won't "let her talk to nobody" (*OMM* 84). In this book full of tough but lonely characters, only verbal communion lightens the heaviness of isolation.

Even in death, Curley's wife is not recognized as a human loss. Like the dead puppy that shares her fate, she is only another accident to Lennie—a problem insofar as it may bring possible punishment. Candy and George, too, mourn the dissolution of their dream more than her loss of life. In fact, Candy still calls her a "God damn tramp" (*OMM* 93) and blames her for *his* loss. Similarly, Nick Cave relates his own pain while waxing accusingly about some other bitch in the song "Your Funeral . . . My Trial."

From Stephanie

George and Lennie's relationship, with all of its unusual circumstances and acceptance of their individual characteristics, mirrors a marriage that is less than ideal and picturesque. On page 12, the pair are having an evening meal together, silently chewing their food and discussing how Lennie should behave on the ranch. This scene reveals that, much like the song "In Spite of Ourselves" by John Prine and Iris DeMent, George and Lennie act as a team and remain together despite their shortcomings and disagreements.

On page 84, Steinbeck opens the chapter by describing the quiet laziness of a Sunday morning. The tone of the passage is calm and fluid, much like the sound and feeling evoked by The Commodores in their song "Easy Like Sunday Morning."

On pages 87–88 (among others that seem to mark the loneliness and alienation that the hired hands suffer from), Steinbeck echoes the theme of isolation that Pink Floyd laments in "Is There Anybody Out There?" When the band begs if anyone can hear them or if anyone is around, they articulate the feeling of loneliness that pervades the bunkhouse and disillusions its occupants. The song also acts as a cry that many of the ranch hands fail to vocalize and, in so doing, fail to form bonding relationships with each other.

From Katherine

Ben Harper's "Glory and Consequence" represents the theme of the American Dream in *Of Mice and Men* for me. After the reader is initially introduced to Lennie and George's plan to "live offa the fatta the lan'," (*OMM* 14) the reader wants them to attain that goal. Although every individual in the story who is introduced to their idea of a farm is initially skeptical, they all want to join the quest for independence and happiness. They even raise a reasonable amount of money toward attaining a mutual goal. However, their dreams are overshadowed by Lennie's tragic flaw resulting in their potential success being overshadowed by tragic consequences.

While "Wouldn't It Be Nice" by the Beach Boys is slightly unconventional because the relationship in the song is between lovers, it still holds merit and connects with Lennie's character. Lennie is a simple thinker, and, if he knew this song, I am confident it would be playing in his head while he daydreamed of his farm and rabbits. The idea of their self-sustaining farm and his simple wish to tend the rabbits and bag alfalfa deserves a happy, dreamy song such as this one.

The main appeal that "Killing the Light" by Black Rebel Motorcycle Club has to the book is the sound in relation to a specific scene in the book, a scene where Lennie is in the barn with Curley's wife. Since the music has a dark tone and strong pulse, it helps mimic and intensify the death of Curley's wife. Also, the lyrics of this song mention that there is a wasted effort that perpetuates an unwelcome result, which, in turn, lends itself to foreshadow Lennie's fate.

Simply because of its title, "Don't Go into That Barn" by Tom Waits can also be easily paralleled to the book. Once the music starts and there is a gritty character singing the lyrics with the sounds of men in intense labor in the background, the listener can't help but imagine that scene and try to imagine what it must have felt like to have Lennie's simple mind as he attempts to understand what he has done. Eventually, he recognizes that Curley's wife is dead and that his dream of tending the rabbits is shattered; he has to run to escape from the consequences of the murdering strength of using his massive hands to caress animals and human beings.

The narrative of "Storm Coming" by Gnarles Barkley is particularly interesting when looking at the progression of death throughout *Of Mice and Men*. Since the song describes a storm coming from the distance, each death in the story becomes stronger and more meaningful: the mouse,

Candy's dog, Lennie's puppy, Curley's wife, and finally Lennie. There-fore, it is easy to compare this perpetual flow to that of a storm building on the horizon. Eventually even the American Dream will die as the ap-proaching storm escalates to its highest pitch.

List of Connections

Appendix A is the compilation of the connections all five participants made during the directed reading of the novella. As previously mentioned, there are ninety-eight original connections made. Of those ninety-eight connections, Woody Guthrie's song, "Blowin' Down the Old Dusty Road" was chosen three times as a connection, making it the most frequent song to appear. In terms of artists, Guthrie, Bruce Springsteen, Gillian Welch, and Tom Waits all received four connections, with Guthrie the only artist receiving multiple connections to a single song. Notably, Pink Floyd and Simon and Garfunkel each received three connections. While the number of connections is interesting, perhaps more intriguing is different types of connections made. If a song connects by theme, in other words, that is one connection, but if it connects to theme, character, and tone, that is three. The five readers classified 202 types of connections to the songs during their reading of *Of Mice and Men*. While examining the list in this way is insightful, the purpose of creating such a list is for these future teachers to use it as a tool for teaching this classic work.

Discussion

Clearly these five students have not only demonstrated an interest in music and reading but also indicated a clear desire to further professional knowledge by offering their insights here and subsequently on LitTunes. As the students brought their unique experiences as listeners to the table to create the list of connections and shared their descriptions of the con-nections, they entered into the professional dialogue on the teaching of literature, or more importantly, book-length literature. Their connec-tions and writing about their ideas provide an understanding of what kind of musical influences were at play as they read the novella, but more importantly perhaps, they also provide essential insight into their reading processes. The list they have compiled could be used to help others teach *Of Mice and Men* at a variety of scholastic levels and serves as a stellar example of musical intertextuality to their future students.

While these students have helped create a resource for anyone interested in using this approach to teaching, they have also helped uncover a promising research agenda. Since no limit exists in terms of books taught in schools or different groupings of people with whom a project such as this could be done, ideas for future projects have begun to spin out of this first attempt. For example, it would be interesting to repeat this same project with high school students reading the novella for the first time but even more interesting to complete this with students who represent diversity in race, gender, and culture. In much the same way, selecting a random multiage group from around the country would yield still other, different results. If five students can connect the novella to nearly one hundred different songs, it stands to reason the number of text-to-song connections that could be made from one book is nearly limitless, only restricted by the number of people who would read the book and make the connections. I suspect as more people engage in this activity, more songs would repeat, providing potential for deep textual analysis of the songs appearing with the most frequency. In a similar fashion, a teacher or researcher could ask participants to read a book and instead make connections to other media including film, television, or art.

Of course, *Of Mice and Men* was never intended to be discussed alongside the genres and styles of music as those represented here. Steinbeck wasn't eyeing Rage against the Machine or Gillian Welch or even Bruce Springsteen with his carefully woven tale. Nevertheless, the musical intertextuality on display provides long-studied Steinbeck aficionados with new material for discussion and consideration; it provides new readers of any age the potential to engage their own musical knowledge and apply it to reading. This explicit musical intertextuality demonstrates the wide variety of ways a student or scholar can look at any text through music. Whether or not this type of approach takes hold in the scholarly world is of little importance to me. It ultimately serves as a model, desperately needed for some less reader-friendly books, for teaching book-length literature in an innovative, creative, and engaging manner—in a LitTunes way.

Notes

1. Elaine Steinbeck and Robert Wallsten, eds. *Steinbeck: A Life in Letters* (New York: Viking Press, 1975), 193.

2. Jane Norwood (chair of the study group), *Reading at Risk: The State Response to the Crisis in Adolescent Literacy, the Report of the NASBE Study Group on Middle and High School Literacy*, rev. ed. (Alexandria, VA: National Association of State Boards of Education, 2006), 6; David Moore, Thomas Bean, Deanna Birdyshaw, and James Rickik, *Adolescent Literacy: A Position Statement* (a report for the Commission on Adolescent Literacy of the International Reading Association, Newark, DE: International Reading Association, 1999), 1.

3. Teri Lesesne, "Of Times, Teens, and Books," in *Adolescent Literacy: Turning Promise into Practice*, ed. Kylene Beers, Robert E. Probst, and Linda Rief (Portsmouth, NH: Heinemann, 2007), 62.

4. Julia Kristeva, "Word, Dialogue and Novel," trans. Alice Jardine, Thomas Gora, and Leon S. Roudiez. In *The Kristeva Reader*, ed. Toril Moi (New York: Columbia University Press, 1983), 56.

5. Roland Barthes, "Theory of the Text," in *Untying the Text: A Post-Structuralist Reader* (New York: Routledge, 1981), 39.

6. John Clifford, ed., *The Experience of Reading: Louise Rosenblatt and Reader-Response Theory* (Portsmouth, NH: Boynton/Cook, 1991), 1.

7. Louise Rosenblatt, *Literature as Exploration* (New York: Appleton-Century Crosts, 1938), 30–31.

8. Graham Allen, *Intertextuality: The New Critical Idiom* (New York: Routledge, 2000), 1; Daniel Chandler, "Semiotics for Beginners," www.aber.ac.uk/media/Documents/S4B/sem09.html (accessed 5 November 2003), 5.

9. Earnest Morell and Jeffrey Duncan-Andrade, "Promoting Academic Literacy with Urban Youth through Hip-Hop Culture," *English Journal* 91, no. 6 (July 2002): 89.

10. Christian Goering, "Music and the Personal Narrative: The Dual Track to Meaningful Writing." *Quarterly* 26, no. 4 (December 2004): 14.

11. Carol Lee, *Signifying as a Scaffold for Literary Interpretation: The Pedagogical Implications of an African American Discourse Genre* (Urbana, IL: National Council of Teachers of English, 2003), 8–9.

12. Steven Luebke, "In Defense of Popular Music" (paper presented at the joint meetings of the Popular Culture/American Culture Association, Philadelphia, PA, 12–15 April 1995), www.eric.ed.gov (accessed 10 June 2005), 11.

13. John Steinbeck, *Of Mice and Men*, 1937 (New York: Penguin Classics, 1993), 14. All subsequent quotations will be cited parenthetically in the text as *OMM* followed by the page number.

Works Cited

Allen, Graham. *Intertextuality: The New Critical Idiom.* New York: Routledge, 2000.

Artists for Literacy. "Songs Inspired by Literature." Deborah Pardes, founder. www.artistsforliteracy.org (accessed 3 April 2008).

Barthes, Roland. "Theory of the Text." In *Untying the Text: A Post-Structuralist Reader*, 31–47. New York: Routledge, 1981.

Chandler, Daniel. "Semiotics for Beginners." www.aber.ac.uk/media/Documents/S4B/sem09.html (accessed 5 November 2003).

Clifford, John, ed. *The Experience of Reading: Louise Rosenblatt and Reader-Response Theory.* Portsmouth, NH: Boynton/Cook, 1991.

Goering, Christian. "Music and the Personal Narrative: The Dual Track to Meaningful Writing." *Quarterly* 26, no. 4 (December 2004): 11–17.

Kristeva, Julia. "Word, Dialogue and Novel." Trans. Alice Jardine, Thomas Gora, and Leon S. Roudiez. In *The Kristeva Reader*, ed. Toril Moi, 34–61. New York: Columbia University Press, 1983.

Lee, Carol D. *Signifying as a Scaffold for Literary Interpretation: The Pedagogical Implications of an African American Discourse Genre.* Urbana, IL: National Council of Teachers of English, 2003.

Lesesne, Teri. "Of Times, Teens, and Books." In *Adolescent Literacy: Turning Promise into Practice*, ed. Kylene Beers, Robert E. Probst, and Linda Rief, 61–79. Portsmouth, NH: Heinemann, 2007.

Luebke, Steven. "In Defense of Popular Music." Paper presented at the joint meetings of the Popular Culture/American Culture Association (Philadelphia, PA, 12–15 April 1995). www.eric.ed.gov (10 June 2005).

Moore, David, Thomas Bean, Deanna Birdyshaw, and James Rickik. *Adolescent Literacy: A Position Statement.* A Report for the Commission on Adolescent Literacy of the International Reading Association. Newark, DE: International Reading Association, 1999.

Morrel, Earnest, and Jeffrey M. R. Duncan-Andrade. "Promoting Academic Literacy with Urban Youth through Hip-Hop Culture." *English Journal* 91, no. 6 (July 2002): 88–92.

Norwood, Jane. *Reading at Risk: The State Response to the Crisis in Adolescent Literacy, the Report of the NASBE Study Group on Middle and High School*

Literacy. Rev. ed. Alexandria, VA: National Association of State Boards of Education, 2006.

Rosenblatt, Louise. *Literature as Exploration*. New York: Appleton-Century Crosts, 1938.

Steinbeck, Elaine and Robert Wallsten, eds. *Steinbeck: A Life in Letters*. New York: Viking Press, 1975.

Steinbeck, John. *Of Mice and Men*. 1937. New York: Penguin Classics, 1993.

Appendix A—Musical Intertextuality Table

Key

Text used: Steinbeck, John. *Of Mice and Men*. New York: Penguin, 1993.

Types of Connections

1. A song is inspired by literature directly.
2. A song connects to a text thematically.
3. A song's setting connects to the setting of a literary work.
4. Characters in a song mirror the characters from the literary work.
5. The tone of a song is similar to the tone of a piece of literature.
6. A song's plot structure or narrative follows that of a literary work.

Author	Page	Type of Connection	Song Title	Artist
JO	3	3,4,5,6	"Blowin' Down This Old Dusty Road"	Woody Guthrie
JO	8	2, 3, 6	"Friend of the Devil"	The Grateful Dead
JO	15	2	"You've Got a Friend"	James Taylor
JO	31	4, 5, 6	"A Red Headed Woman"	Gershwin (Porgy & Bess)
JO	Whole	4	"Superfreak"	Rick James
JO	31/86	4,5,6	"Jezebel"	Sade
JO	49	4	"I am the Walrus (Dead Dog)"	The Beatles
JO	51	2	"Little Drop of Poison"	Tom Waits
JO	56	3, 6	"Peaches"	Presidents of the USA
JO	77	3, 5, 6	"Don't Fence Me In"	David Byrne (Bing Crosby)
JO	84	4, 5	"Red Shoes"	Tom Waits
JO	84	2, 4, 6	"(Angels wanna wear my) Red Shoes"	Elvis Costello
JO	89	3, (6)	"Murder in the Red Barn"	Tom Waits

(continued)

Author	Page	Type of Connection	Song Title	Artist
JO	89	4, 5, 6	"Your Funeral . . . My Trial"	Nick Cave and the Bad Seeds
JO	93	4 (ironic)	"All I Have to Do Is Dream"	The Everly Brothers
JO	103	3, 5, 6	"A Place in the Sun"	Stevie Wonder
JO	103	3, 4, 5, 6	"Blowin' Down This Old Dusty Road"	Woody Guthrie
JO	86	4, 5	"That Lowdown Man of Mine"	Squirrel Nut Zippers
SP	15	2	"Golden Girls Theme Song"	Cynthia Fee
SP	Whole	4	"In Spite of Ourselves"	John Prine and Iris DeMent
SP	31	6	"Roxanne"	The Police
SP	57	2	"When the World Ends"	DMB
SP	82	5	"Easy Like Sunday Morning"	The Commodores
SP	84	5	"Hello"	Pink Floyd
SP	86	4	"American Woman"	Pink Floyd
SP	5	4	"Don't Drink the Water"	DMB
SP	Whole	6	"Going to California"	Led Zeppelin
SP	102	4	"Wish You Were Here"	Pink Floyd
SP	22	4	"Pinball Wizard"	The Who
SK	103	5	"Underneath Weeping Willow"	Granddaddy
SK	61–62	5	"Flight Test"	Flaming Lips
SK	85–86	5	"Get the Wheel"	Greg Dulli
SK	14–15	2, 5	"Paradise City"	Guns 'N Roses
SK	4	3	"Waiting for the Sun"	The Jayhawks
SK	38	2, 5	"Nobody's Darlings"	Lucero
SK	93	2, 5	"American Dirt"	Matthew Ryan
SK	103	2, 5	"Mansion on the Hill"	Bruce Springsteen
SK	3	2, 5	"The World at Large"	Modest Mouse
SK	59	2, 5	"Heavenly Day"	Patty Griffin
SK	56	2, 5	"Mr. Rabbit"	Paul Westerberg
SK	81	2, 5	"Nothingman"	Pearl Jam
SK	69–70	2, 5	"High and Dry"	Radiohead
SK	72	2, 5	"Freedom"	Rage Against the Machine
SK	37	2, 5	"Gimmie Shelter"	The Rolling Stones
SK	39–40	2, 5	"The Predatory Wasp of the Palisades Is Out to Get Us"	Sufjan Stevens
SK	72	2, 5	"I Still Haven't Found What I Am Looking For"	U2
SK	59	2, 5	"Dreams"	The Cranberries
SK	15	2, 5	"Bastards of Young"	Replacements
SK	52	2, 5	"Here Comes a Regular"	Replacements
SK	12	2, 5	"Ball and Chain"	Social Distortion
KC	Whole	2	"Glory & Consequence"	Ben Harper

Author	Page	Type of Connection	Song Title	Artist
KC	103	2, 5	"Apres Moi"	Regina Spektor
KC	12–16, 55	2, 3, 5	"Wouldn't It Be Nice"	The Beach Boys
KC	7	2,3	"Mother Nature's Son"	The Beatles
KC	84	2, 4	"Killing the Light"	Black Rebel Motorcycle Club
KC	Whole	2, 4	"Never Let Each Other Down"	Brad
KC	89	2, 3, 4, 5	"Don't Go into That Barn"	Tom Waits
KC	45	2, 5	"Storm Coming"	Gnarles Barkley
KR	56	2, 4	"Vincent"	Don McClean
KR	103	2, 4, 5	"Pretty Bird"	Hazel Dickens
KR	34	4	"Kindle My Heart"	Patrick Doyle
KR	8–9	2, 4, 5	"Highway Patrolman"	Bruce Springsteen
KR	44–46	4, 5	"Old Dogs and Children and Watermelon Wine"	Tom T. Hall
KR	75	2, 4, 5	"Everything Is Free Now"	Gillian Welch
KR	31–32	4	"Barroom Girls"	Gillian Welch
KR	34	2, 4, 5	"Song to Woody"	Bob Dylan
KR	36–37	4	"Every Breath You Take"	The Police
KR	27–28	4	"Cecilia"	Simon and Garfunkel
KR	15–16	2, 4, 5	"One Little Song"	Gillian Welch
KR	Whole	2, 3, 4, 5	"Alone and Forsaken"	Hank Williams Sr.
KR	57–58	2, 4, 5	"Hope"	Twista
KR	89–90	2, 4, 5	"Broken Wings"	Cherish the Ladies
KR	Whole	2, 4, 5	"Star'n Through My Rearview"	2Pac
KR	Whole	2	"Somewhere Over the Rainbow"	Judy Garland
KR	Whole	2, 4, 5	"String of Pearls"	Jamie Byrd
KR	103	2, 4, 5	"My City of Ruins"	Bruce Springsteen
KR	57–58	2, 4, 5	"America"	Simon and Garfunkel
KR	15–16	2, 4, 5	"Innisfree"	Clandestine (Yeats's poem set to music)
KR	57–59	2, 4, 5	"Fast Car"	Tracy Chapman
KR	103	2, 4	"The Fields of Athenry"	Tom Donovan
KR	84–85	2, 4, 5	"Somebody"	Depeche Mode
KR	3	2, 3, 4, 5	"Blowing Down This Old Dusty Road"	Woody Guthrie
KR	15	2, 3, 4, 5	"I Ain't Got No Home"	Woody Guthrie
KR	15–16	2, 4, 5	"Castle on a Cloud"	Cosette from Les Miserables
KR	15–16	2	"Big Rock Candy Mountain"	Harry McClintock
KR	32–33	2, 4, 5	"One More Dollar"	Gillian Welch
KR	42–43	4	"I Love"	Tom T. Hall

(continued)

Author	Page	Type of Connection	Song Title	Artist
KR	48	2, 5	"Sounds of Silence"	Simon and Garfunkel
KR	56	2, 4	"Someday I'm Gunna Fly"	George Woodard
KR	72–73	2, 4, 5	"Hard Time Killing Floor Blues"	Chris Thomas King
KR	99	4	"White Rabbit"	Jefferson Airplane
KR	99	4, 5	"River"	Joni Mitchell
KR	98	4, 5	"Father and Son"	Cat Stevens
KR	98	4	"Puff the Magic Dragon"	Peter, Paul, and Mary
KR	103	2, 4, 5	"Reconciliation"	Nimah Parsons
KR	Whole	5	"Iree Seose"	Emma Chistian
KR	Whole	5, 6	"Nebraska"	Bruce Springsteen

APPENDIX

Online Sites for Teaching *Of Mice and Men*

Ausland, Brian. "*Of Mice and Men*: Cast the Roles." www .education-world.com/a_tsl/archives/00-1/lesson0039.shtml

BestNotes.com staff. "Monkey Notes: *Of Mice and Men* by John Steinbeck." www.pinkmonkey.com/booknotes/monkeynotes/pmOfMice Men01.asp

Bjork, Linda. "Teacher CyberGuide: *Of Mice and Men* by John Steinbeck." Revised by Mary Jewell. www.sdcoe.k12.ca.us/score/mice/ micetg.html

BookRags. "*Of Mice and Men* by John Steinbeck." www.bookrags.com/ Of_Mice_and_Men

Burleson, Carolyn and Daniel Brewer. "WebQuest: *Of Mice and Men*." Created 2002 and updated 7 September 2007. drb.lifestreamcenter .net/Lessons/mice-men/index.htm

edhelper.com "*Of Mice and Men* by John Steinbeck." www.edhelper .com/books/Of_Mice_and_Men.htm?gclid=CMurpZCTjo0CFQ9 EgQodzEzXng

    Mixed literature review unit containing chapter question, crossword puzzles, word searches, final review, word scramblers; designed for grades 9–12

enotes.com. "*Of Mice and Men* Summary/Study Guide." www.enotes .com/ofmice/

Grade Saver."*Of Mice and Men* Study Guide." www.gradesaver.com/classicnotes/titles/miceandmen/

The Martha Heasley Cox Center for Steinbeck Studies. "*Of Mice and Men* (1937)." www.steinbeck.sjsu.edu/works/Of Mice and Men.jsp

The New York Times. "*Of Mice and Men* (1939)." http://movies2.nytimes.com/gst/movies/movie.htm?v_id=35975

NovelGuide.com. "Novel Analysis: *Of Mice and Men.*" www.novelguide.com/ofmiceandmen/

"*Of Mice and Men*: John Steinbeck." www.bellmore-merrick.k12.ny.us/mice.html

Reifschneider, Suzanne. "Lesson Plans." http://homepage.wmich.edu/%7Es0reifsc/lesson_plans.htm

Rutherford, Nancy Louise. "*Of Mice and Men*: The Student Survival Guide." www.lausd.k12.ca.us/Belmont_HS/mice/

Stephan, Ed. "Steinbeck: *Of Mice and Men.*" www.ac.wwu.edu/~stephan/Steinbeck/mice.html

TeacherVision. "*Of Mice and Men.*" www.teachervision.fen.com/curriculum-planning/teaching-methods/3754.html

Web English Teacher. "John Steinbeck, *Of Mice and Men*: Lesson Plans and Teaching Resources." www.webenglishteacher.com/mice.html

INDEX

ABOUT THE EDITOR
AND CONTRIBUTORS

Michael J. Meyer is adjunct professor of English at DePaul University in Chicago. He is the present bibliographer for Steinbeck studies, having published *The Hayashi Steinbeck Bibliography: 1982–1996* (Scarecrow, 1998) and a follow-up volume in 2008. In addition to his bibliographic work, Meyer's essays have appeared in *The Steinbeck Quarterly*, *The Steinbeck Review*, and *The Steinbeck Newsletter*. He has contributed chapters to numerous monographs and books, including serving as editor for *Cain Sign: The Betrayal of Brotherhood in the Works of John Steinbeck* (2000). He is presently the poetry editor and bibliographer for *The Steinbeck Review* and serves on its editorial board. Meyer's other publications include *A John Steinbeck Encyclopedia* (2006), where he served as coeditor with Brian Railsback. Since 1994, Meyer has been the senior editor of Rodopi Press's new *Dialogues* series, which will feature a two-volume set entitled *The Grapes of Wrath: A Reconsideration* scheduled to appear in 2009, the 70th anniversary of the novel's publication.

***

Jean Emery was a freelance journalist and independent scholar when she wrote her analysis in 1992. At that time she was studying for an MFA at the University of Montana.

Mimi Reisel Gladstein is current president of the John Steinbeck Society of America. She has been awarded both the John J. and Angeline Pruis

Award for Outstanding Steinbeck Teaching and the Burkhardt Award for Steinbeck Research. At the University of Texas at El Paso where she teaches, Gladstein has been named Outstanding Faculty Member in the College of Liberal Arts and won the University Award for Service to Students. The author of three books and coeditor of two, Gladstein has numerous articles in scholarly journals and anthologies.

Daniel Griesbach earned his PhD from the University of Washington in 2007. His dissertation is a study of artists who depict migrant farm workers in the United States, including photographer Dorothea Lange and writers John Steinbeck, Raymond Barrio, and Helena María Viramontes. He has written articles on Steinbeck and an essay for *MELUS* on U.S. Hispanic folklore during the Great Depression. He lives and teaches in Seattle, Washington.

William Goldhurst was professor of the humanities at the University of Florida. He is author of *F. Scott Fitzgerald and His Contemporaries* (1983) and served as the editor of a journal entitled *Contours of Experience*.

Christian Z. Goering is assistant professor of secondary English and literacy education at the University of Arkansas where he coordinates the English education program and codirects the Northwest Arkansas Writing Project. He received a PhD in curriculum and instruction from Kansas State University in 2007. He currently serves on the executive board of the Arkansas Council of Teachers of English Language Arts and provides educational outreach through his website dedicated to literacy and teaching literature through the use of music (www.LitTunes.com).

Charlotte Cook Hadella is professor of English and writing in the Department of Language, Literature, and Philosophy at Southern Oregon University in Ashland. She teaches courses in American Literature and English Education, and is director of the Oregon Writing Project at Southern Oregon University. Her publications include a number of articles on the work of John Steinbeck, the Twayne Masterwork study, *Of Mice and Men: A Kinship of Powerlessness*, and *Warm Springs Millennium* (coauthored with Michael Baughman).

Barbara A. Heavilin is coeditor of *The Steinbeck Review* and has published several books and numerous articles on John Steinbeck. She teaches linguistics, grammar, and Restoration and Eighteenth-Century British Literature, among other subjects at Taylor University in Upland, Indiana.

Caren Irr teaches American literature at Brandeis University. She is the author of *The Suburb of Dissent: Cultural Politics in the United States and Canada during the 1930s* (1998), as well as a number of essays on U.S. and Canadian fiction. Her most recent research concerns the resurgence of the political novel in 21st-century fiction.

Howard Levant was one of the first critics to examine Steinbeck's work on a structural level. His work *The Novels of John Steinbeck: A Critical Study* (1974) drew attention to what Levant considered serious flaws in Steinbeck's organizational plan for several of his works.

Peter Lisca (1925–2001) was the author of the first major Steinbeck study, *The Wide World of John Steinbeck* (1958) and followed that with *John Steinbeck: Nature and Myth* (1974). He is considered the dean of early Steinbeck scholars along with Warren French. During his academic career, he taught at University of Florida where he was a full professor and dean. His articles on twentieth-century literature also included studies of Faulkner's *The Hamlet* and *Sanctuary*, Hemingway's *Across the River and Into the Trees*, and Fitzgerald's *The Great Gatsby*.

Anne Loftis is a historian and freelance writer based in California. Her work includes *Witnesses to the Struggle: Imagining the 1930s California Labor Movement* (1998) and, with Dick Meister, *A Long Time Coming: The Struggle to Unionize America's Farm Workers* (1977). She is also known for her study of Japanese internment camps, *The Great Betrayal: The Evacuation of Japanese–Americans During World War II* (1969), which was cowritten with Audrie Girdner.

Charles Johnson is author of several books, including *Faith and the Good Thing, Oxherding Tale, Middle Passage, Dreamer, The Sorcerer's Apprentice*, and *Soulcatcher and Other Stories*. In 2007, Johnson coauthored, with photographer Bob Adelman, *Mine Eyes Have Seen: Bearing Witness to the Struggle for Civil Rights*, and his comic art appeared in *The Writer's Brush: Paintings, Drawings and Sculpture by Writers*, edited by Donald Friedman. A professor at the University of Washington, Johnson is also a National Book Award winner and was the recent recipient of an Academy Award in Literature from the American Academy of Arts and Letters.

Marilyn Chandler McEntyre, having taught English for thirty years, is now a writer living and working in Northern California. She remains affiliated with Westmont College as a fellow of the Gaede Institute for the Liberal Arts. She has written widely on literature and spirituality, literature and medicine, and, in *Caring for Words* (forthcoming in 2009) the vocation to stewardship of language.

Louis Owens was professor of English at the University of California, Davis, and author of two major Steinbeck studies, *John Steinbeck's Re-Vision of America* (1985) and *The Grapes of Wrath: Trouble in The Promised Land* (1989). In addition, during his academic career, Owens served as coeditor of *American Literary Scholarship: An Annual* and was the recipient of Fulbright, NEH, and NEA Fellowships. His Native-American fiction, including the novels *Nightland*, *Dark River*, and *Wolf Song*, established him as a major American novelist as well as a stellar Steinbeck critic. He died suddenly in 2002 at the peak of his career.

Leland S. Person is professor of English and senior associate dean for academic affairs at the University of Cincinnati. He is the author of *Henry James and the Suspense of Masculinity* (2003), *Aesthetic Headaches: Women and a Masculine Poetics in Poe, Melville, and Hawthorne* (1988), and many articles on 19th-century American writers. His most recent books are *A Historical Guide to James Fenimore Cooper* (2007), *The Cambridge Introduction to Nathaniel Hawthorne* (2007), and a Norton Critical Edition of *The Scarlet Letter and Other Writings* (2005).

Michael W. Shurgot retired from South Puget Sound Community College in Olympia, Washington, where he received four Exceptional Faculty Awards. He is the author of *Stages of Play: Shakespeare's Theatrical Energies in Elizabethan Performance* (1998); editor of *North American Players of*

Shakespeare: A Book of Interviews (2007); and has published on James Joyce and Nadine Gordimer. He reviews Shakespeare productions in the Pacific Northwest for *Shakespeare Bulletin*, and the Oregon Shakespeare Festival and London's Globe Theatre for *The Upstart Crow*.

John F. Slater was assistant professor at the University of Wyoming when he produced his analysis in 1974.

Mark Spilka was professor of English at Brown University from 1963 to 1995 where he chaired the English department from 1968 to 1973. For many years, he also edited the journal, *Novel: A Forum on Fiction* (1967–1995). During his lengthy career in academe, Spilka published eight books, including *The Love Ethic of D. H. Lawrence* (1958); *Virginia Woolf's Quarrel with Grieving* (1980); and *Hemingway's Quarrel with Androgyny* (1990). A deep and ground-breaking thinker and an eloquent writer, he published numerous other articles and was active in academic debates at MLA conventions as well as through prolific correspondence with other scholars and writers. Spilka died in 2001 at the age of seventy-five.

John Timmerman is professor of English at Calvin College in Grand Rapids, Michigan, and is the author of twenty-two books, primarily on American literature, and more than fifty critical articles. Among them are two books on Steinbeck: *John Steinbeck's Fiction: The Aesthetics of the Road Taken* (1986) and *The Dramatic Landscape of Steinbeck's Short Stories* (1990).